Jews in Gotham

*New York Jews in a
Changing City, 1920–2010*

CITY OF PROMISES was made possible in part through the generosity of a number of individuals and foundations. Their thoughtful support will help ensure that this work is affordable to schools, libraries, and other not-for-profit institutions.

The Lucius N. Littauer Foundation made a leadership gift before a word of CITY OF PROMISES had been written, a gift that set this project on its way. Hugo Barreca, The Marian B. and Jacob K. Javits Foundation, Mr. and Mrs. Peter Malkin, David P. Solomon, and a donor who wishes to remain anonymous helped ensure that it never lost momentum. We are deeply grateful.

CITY OF PROMISES

A HISTORY OF THE JEWS OF NEW YORK

GENERAL EDITOR: DEBORAH DASH MOORE

VOLUME 1

Haven of Liberty

New York Jews in the
New World, 1654–1865

HOWARD B. ROCK

VOLUME 2

Emerging Metropolis

New York Jews in the
Age of Immigration, 1840–1920

ANNIE POLLAND AND

DANIEL SOYER

VOLUME 3

Jews in Gotham

New York Jews in a
Changing City, 1920–2010

JEFFREY S. GUROCK

Advisory Board:
Hasia Diner (New York University)
Leo Hershkowitz (Queens College)
Ira Katznelson (Columbia University)
Thomas Kessner (CUNY Graduate Center)
Tony Michels (University of Wisconsin,
    Madison)
Judith C. Siegel (Center for Jewish History)
Jenna Weissman-Joselit (Princeton University)
Beth Wenger (University of Pennsylvania)

CITY OF PROMISES

A HISTORY OF THE JEWS OF NEW YORK

JEWS IN
GOTHAM

NEW YORK JEWS IN A CHANGING CITY, 1920–2010

JEFFREY S. GUROCK

WITH A FOREWORD BY

DEBORAH DASH MOORE

AND WITH A VISUAL ESSAY BY

DIANA L. LINDEN

NEW YORK UNIVERSITY PRESS ■ NEW YORK AND LONDON

NEW YORK UNIVERSITY PRESS
New York and London
www.nyupress.org

References to Internet websites (URLs) were accurate at the time of writing.
Neither the author nor New York University Press is responsible for URLs that
may have expired or changed since the manuscript was prepared.

Library of Congress Cataloging-in-Publication Data
City of promises : a history of the Jews of New York / general editor, Deborah Dash Moore.
v. cm.
Includes bibliographical references and index.
Contents: v. 1. Haven of liberty: New York Jews in the New World, 1654–1865 / Howard B.
Rock — v. 2. Emerging metropolis: New York Jews in the age of immigration, 1840–1920 /
Annie Polland and Daniel Soyer — v. 3. Jews in Gotham: New York Jews in a changing city,
1920–2010.
ISBN 978-0-8147-7632-2 (cl : alk. paper) — ISBN 978-0-8147-4521-2 (ebook) —
ISBN 978-0-8147-7692-6 (ebook) — ISBN 978-0-8147-1731-8 (boxed set : alk. paper) —
ISBN 978-0-8147-2932-8 (e-set)
1. Jews—New York (State)—New York. 2. New York (N.Y.)—Ethnic relations.   I. Moore,
Deborah Dash, 1946– II. Rock, Howard B., 1944–
F128.9.J5C64 2012
305.892'40747—dc23   2012003246

New York University Press books are printed on acid-free paper,
and their binding materials are chosen for strength and durability.
We strive to use environmentally responsible suppliers and materials
to the greatest extent possible in publishing our books.

Manufactured in the United States of America

10   9   8   7   6   5   4   3   2   1

For Zev Jacob, Margot Harper, and Hannah Leah

CONTENTS

"[O]f all the big cities," Sergeant Milton Lehman of the *Stars and Stripes* affirmed in 1945, "New York is still the promised land."[1] As a returning Jewish GI, Lehman compared New York with European cities. Other Jews also knew what New York offered that made it so desirable, even if they had not served overseas. First and foremost, security: Jews could live without fear in New York. Yes, they faced discrimination, but in this city of almost eight million residents, many members of its ethnic and religious groups encountered prejudice. Jews contended with anti-Semitism in the twentieth century more than German Protestants or Irish Catholics dealt with bias, perhaps; but the Irish had endured a lot in the nineteenth century, and Jews suffered less than African Americans, Latinos, and Asian New Yorkers. And New York provided more than security: Jews could live freely as Jews. The presence of a diverse population of close to two million New York Jews contributed to their sense that "everyone was Jewish."[2] New York Jews understood that there were many ways to be Jewish. The city welcomed Jews in all their variety. New York Jews saw the city as a place where they, too, could flourish and express themselves. As a result, they came to identify with the city, absorbing its ethos even as they helped to shape its urban characteristics. When World War II ended in Europe with victory over Nazi Germany, New York's promises glowed more brightly still.

New York's multiethnic diversity, shaped in vital dimensions by its large Jewish population, shimmered as a showplace of American democratic distinctiveness, especially vis-à-vis Europe. In contrast to a continent that had become a vast slaughterhouse, where millions of European Jews had been ruthlessly murdered with industrial efficiency, New York glistened as a city Jews could and did call their home in America. The famous skyline had defined urban cosmopolitanism in the years after World War I. Now the city's thriving ethnic neighborhoods—Jewish and Catholic, African American and Puerto Rican, Italian and Irish—came to represent modern urban culture. New York's economy responded robustly to demands of war production. By the end of hostilities, its per capita income exceeded the national average by 14 percent.

But as a poster city for immigration, with a majority population composed of immigrants and their children, the city had to contend with negative perceptions. Considered undesirable by many Americans, Jews and other foreigners in the city contributed to impressions that New York seemed less American than other cities with large percentages of native-born residents.[3]

As the city flourished during and after the war, it maintained its political commitments to generous social welfare benefits to help its poorest residents. Jews advocated for these policies, supporting efforts to establish a liberal urban legacy. In modeling a progressive and prosperous multiethnic twentieth-century American city, New York demonstrated what its Jews valued. Versions of Jewish urbanism played not just on the political stage but also on the streets of the city's neighborhoods. Its expressions could be found as well in New York's centers of cultural production.

By the middle of the twentieth century, no city offered Jews more than New York. It nourished both celebration and critique. New York gave Jews visibility as individuals and as a group. It provided employment and education, inspiration and freedom, fellowship and community. Jews reciprocated by falling in love with the city, its buildings' hard angles and perspectives, its grimy streets and harried pace. But by the 1960s and '70s, Jews' love affair with the city soured. For many of the second generation who grew up on New York's sidewalks, immersed in its babel of languages and cultural syncretism, prosperity dimmed their affection for the working-class urban world of their youth. Many of them aspired to suburban pleasures of home ownership, grass and trees that did not have to be shared with others in public parks. Yet New York City remained the wellspring of Jewish American culture for much of the century, a resource of Jewishness even for those living thousands of miles west of the Hudson River.

Jews had not always felt free to imagine the city as their special place. Indeed, not until mass immigration from Europe piled up their numbers, from the tens of thousands to the hundreds of thousands, had Jews laid claim to New York and influenced its politics and culture. Its Jewish population soared from five hundred thousand at the turn of the twentieth century to 1.1 million before the start of World War I. On the eve of World War II, Jews, over a quarter of New York's residents, ranked as the largest ethnic group.[4] Demography both encouraged many outsiders to perceive New York as a Jewish city and underwrote local cultural productions, such as a thriving theater scene, a flourishing popular music business, and extensive publishing in several languages. Jews were used to living as a minority in Europe and the Middle East. New York offered life without a majority population—without one single ethnic group dominating urban society. Now Jews could go about their business, much of it taking place within ethnic niches, as if they were the city's predominant group.

When and in what sense did New York become a city of promises for Jews? Certainly not in the colonial era. During that period, seeds for future promises were planted, most importantly political, economic, and religious rights. While New York's few hundred Jews lived in the shadow of far more prosperous Jewish communities in London and Amsterdam, New York Jewish men enjoyed citizenship rights and responsibilities that their peers in London could only envy. These rights gradually led New York Jews to emerge from a closed synagogue society and to participate with enthusiasm in revolutionary currents sweeping the colonies. Jews in New York absorbed formative ideas regarding human rights; they tasted freedom and put their lives on the line for it during the Revolution. In the decades that followed, they incorporated ideals of the American Enlightenment into their Jewish lives.

Sometime during the nineteenth century, these changes attracted increasing attention from European Jews. New York began to acquire a reputation as a destination in itself. Arriving from Europe at Castle Garden, increasing numbers of Jewish immigrants decided to stay. New York's bustling streets enticed them, so they put off riding west or south to peddle or settle. Sometimes, older brothers made that choice, as did Jonas and Louis Strauss, who sent their younger brother Levi to the West Coast via steamship in 1853 to open a branch of their New York City dry-goods firm. Levi Strauss did better, perhaps, than they expected when he went into manufacturing copper-riveted denim work pants after the Civil War.[5] But such a move into garment manufacturing from selling dry goods and, especially, used clothing had already taken root in New York prior to the war. It formed the basis of an industry that became the city's largest, and more than any other, it made New York the city of promises.

In 1962, the historian Moses Rischin published his pioneering book, *The Promised City: New York's Jews, 1870–1914*. Rischin aimed to "identify those currents of human and institutional vitality central to the American urban experience that converged on the Lower East Side in the era of the great Jewish migration just as New York emerged as the nation's and the world's most dynamic metropolis."[6] The interlocking themes of Jewish immigration from eastern Europe and the rise of New York as a "city of ambition" led Rischin to cast his account as a "revolutionary transformation" not only in American urban history but also in Jewish history.[7] Rischin saw a universal paradigm of modernization unfolding in the very particularistic experiences of New York Jews. His vision of democratic urban community remains relevant to contemporary scholars.

What did the city promise? First, a job. Close to half of all immigrants sewed clothing in hundreds of small-scale sweatshops that disguised an ever-burgeoning industry that soon became one of the nation's most important. Second, a place to live. True, the overcrowded Lower East Side bulged with residents, even its modern tenements straining to accommodate a density of Jewish population that rivaled Bombay. Yet by the early twentieth century, bridges to Brooklyn and rapid transit to Harlem and the Bronx promised improvements: fresh air, hot and cold running water, even a private toilet and bathroom. Third, food. Jewish immigrants had not starved in Europe, but New York's abundance changed their diets and attitudes toward food and its simple pleasures. In New York, a center of the nation's baking industry, Jews could enjoy a fresh roll and coffee each morning for pennies. Fourth, clothing. It did not take long, especially laboring in the garment industry, for Jews to trade their old-world clothes for the latest ready-made styles. Thus properly attired, they looked and felt like modern men and women, able and willing to make their way.[8]

Such promises might be quotidian, but they opened Jews' eyes to other more important ones. Young Jewish immigrants embraced the city's promise of free public education, from elementary school to secondary school, all the way through college. Only a handful of Jewish immigrants in the nineteenth century and years before World War I ever managed to take advantage of such a magnificent offer. Although a family economy that privileged sons over daughters when decisions about post-elementary education had to be made and costs of forgoing income from teenaged children often required Jews to go to work and not attend school, increasingly Jews flocked to the city's free schools. Some immigrants, especially women, thought the city promised freedom to choose a spouse, though matchmakers also migrated across the ocean. Still others rejoiced in what they imagined was a promise of uncensored language: written and spoken, published and on stage, in Yiddish, Hebrew,

German, Ladino, and English. Some conceived of the city's rough democracy as holding a promise of solidarity among working men and women, while a significant number demanded extension of civil and voting rights to women.

Then there were more ambiguous promises. Did New York offer Jews a chance to live without a formal, legally constituted Jewish community? Did it suggest that Jews no longer needed to practice Jewish rituals or observe the Sabbath? Some Jewish immigrants thought they could leave behind old-world ways of thinking and acting; they secularized their Jewish lives, often starting the process in Europe even before they emigrated. Others fashioned ways of being Jewish, both secular and religious, in tune with New York's evolving cultures. Both groups identified their own visions of what it meant to be Jewish in America with New York itself.

That New York City bloomed with such promises would have been hard to anticipate in 1654. Then the ragged seaport only reluctantly welcomed its first contingent of miserable Jewish migrants. In fact, not receiving permission to settle, Jews had to petition to stay, to live and work in the outpost. They agreed to practice their religion in private even as they participated in civic culture. When the British turned New Amsterdam into New York, they accepted these arrangements, giving Jews unprecedented legal rights. Here lay hints of future promises. Gradually the British increased opportunities for public religious expression and extended to Jewish men civil rights, including citizenship, the right to vote, and the right to hold office. When Jews founded their first congregation, they called it Shearith Israel (Remnant of Israel), an apt name for the handful living in a colonial town far from European centers of Jewish life. Yet during the eighteenth century, Jews integrated into the fabric of New York life. They faced challenges of identifying as Jews within a free society. As the first to enjoy such political freedoms, they struggled to balance assimilation with Jewish distinctiveness. By the time of the Revolution, many New York Jews felt deeply connected to their city and fellow American patriots, enough to flee the British occupation for Philadelphia. The end of the war marked a new democratic consciousness among New York Jews who returned to rebuild their city and community.

A democratic ethos pervaded Jewish urban life in the new republic, opening possibilities for individual and collective ambition as well as cooperation. This republicanism changed how Jews organized themselves religiously and how they imagined their opportunities. Shearith Israel incorporated and drafted its own constitution, modeled on the federal example. Republicanism animated women, inspiring them to establish charities to help succor the poor. Once Jewish immigration brought sufficient ethnic and economic diversity to New York in the 1830s and 1840s, Jews started to build a different type of community. They forged bonds based on intimacy, gender, shared backgrounds, common aspirations, and urgent necessities. Jewish religious life became increasingly diverse, competitive, and strident. Democracy without an established religion fostered creativity and experimentation. Congregations multiplied in the city, but most Jews chose not to join one, despite variety ranging from Orthodox to Reform. The city saw a fierce battle between proponents of orthodoxy and advocates of reform. These debates engaged Jews deeply but did not lead the majority to affiliate. Still, increasingly synagogue buildings formed part of the cityscape, an indication of Jewish presence. Democratic freedoms permitted a new type of urban Jewish life to emerge. Lacking formal communal structures, Jews innovated and turned to other forms of organization as alternatives. They established fraternal orders and literary societies, seeking a means to craft connections in a rapidly growing and bewildering city. Yet soon they multiplied these activities as well. Pleas for charity and education, hospitals and libraries, mobilized Jewish New Yorkers.

With the extension of the franchise, more Jewish men acquired the right to vote, irrespective of their economic situation, encouraging them to enter political debates with enthusiasm. They paid attention to events overseas affecting fellow Jews, especially examples of anti-Semitism, and tried to convince the president to help. New York Jews mastered the arts of petition and protest. They took sides as individuals in election cycles, first between Federalists and Jeffersonians, later between Democrats and Whigs, and finally between Democrats and Republicans. Domestic issues divided Jews; even the question of slavery found supporters and opponents. Rabbis debated the subject in pulpit and press until the Civil War ended their polemics and both sides rallied to the Union cause. Politics necessarily pushed Jews into public consciousness; non-Jews noticed them. Prejudice began to appear in social life, and stereotypes started to circulate in the press. Yet Jewish New Yorkers were hardly the retiring sort, and many gave as good as they got.

Jewish immigrants readily found employment, entering the city's expanding economic marketplace as they carefully tested its promises of personal fulfillment. Although the Panics of 1857 and 1873 threw thousands out of work, during normal times, Jews coped with capitalist volatilities. Many gravitated to small-scale commerce and craft production. Men and women both worked and drew on family resources, especially the labor of their children, to help make ends meet. Jews saved regularly to withstand seasonal swings in employment. Within the city's diversifying economy, they located ethnic niches that became occupational ladders of advancement for many. Some of the merchants trading in old clothes around Chatham Street initiated manufacturing of cheap goods. A garment industry took shape; it received a big boost with demand for uniforms in the Civil War. As the industry grew, its need for workers increased steadily, employing an ever-greater proportion of Jewish immigrants to the city. Small shops and a competitive contracting system continued to dominate the industry. Despite miserable conditions, the system tempted many workers with a promise of self-employment. Taking a risk, some immigrants borrowed money, often from relatives and fellow immigrants from the same European town, to supplement meager savings. Then they plunged into contracting, trying with a new design idea to secure prosperity. As often as not, they failed, falling back into the laboring class. But success stories trumped failures; they stood as reminders that the city had fulfilled its promise.

Merchants and peddlers, who occupied another popular Jewish economic niche, viewed the rise of department stores as an urban achievement. These commercial emporiums proffered a magical array of goods under one roof and represented the pinnacle of success for local hardware-store owners or dry-goods shopkeepers. Retail establishments proliferated around the city as it grew; Jewish entrepreneurship flourished on local shopping streets in the Bronx and Brooklyn. Pitkin Avenue in Brownsville and Fordham Road in the Bronx could not rival Manhattan's Fifth Avenue or even Fourteenth Street. But they provided a measure of prosperity and independence to Jewish merchants, enough so that they could enjoy some of the perquisites of middle-class living, such as sending one's sons and even one's daughters to high school and college. Mobility came in many forms, and often immigrant Jews achieved economic and social mobility first through business and then through education.

New York's explosive growth at the turn of the twentieth century produced radical social movements based on class struggle and politics. For many Jewish immigrants, becoming a small manufacturer paled beside a larger vision of a just society, one without workers living in overcrowded, filthy tenements, exposed to disease, and wracked by despair. Hedging their bets, they dreamed of becoming capitalists even as they sought in socialism better living conditions, fair wages, and reasonable working hours. Socialism as a utopian ideal promised equality, an economic system that took from each according to his or her ability and returned to everybody whatever he or she needed. Even some Jewish capitalists subscribed to such an ideal. But on a pragmatic level, socialism appealed to Jewish workers for its alternatives to unrestrained capitalist exploitation. Paths to socialism led through union organizing, the polling booth, fraternalism, and even cooperative housing. Jewish immigrants embraced them all. They forged vibrant garment-workers unions, as well as unions of bakers and plumbers, teachers and pharmacists. They voted for Socialist candidates, sending Meyer London in 1914 to represent the Lower East Side in Congress. They organized the Workmen's Circle, initially in 1892 as a mutual-aid society and then in 1900 as a multibranch fraternal order in which they could socialize with fellow workers and receive health and social welfare benefits not provided by a wealthy but stingy city government. And after World War I ended, New York Jews pushed for legislation that would allow them to build cooperative housing projects, so that they could enjoy living in decent apartments together with other Jewish workers. These examples of democratic community radically reshaped the city and contributed to its progressive commitments even as Jewish struggles for social justice empowered them both individually and as a group.

For several centuries, until the beginning of the twentieth, most New York Jews lived in Lower Manhattan, with smaller numbers residing in Williamsburg and Bedford, in the city of Brooklyn. The consolidation of New York with Brooklyn and the creation of a city of five boroughs, including the Bronx, Queens, and Staten Island, stimulated construction of subways and bridges which expanded opportunities for Jewish immigrants to leave the constricted quarters of the Lower East Side. Once they started to move, only the Great Depression, discrimination, and wartime constraints made Jews pause. New neighborhoods held out hopes of fresh beginnings. Adjusting to the strangeness of a neighborhood invited ways to reimagine one's relationship to New York City. Jews adopted different perspectives on themselves and their city as they exchanged views out kitchen windows. Modern tenements, with steam heat, hot and cold running water in the kitchen sink, and an icebox, proclaimed a sense of accomplishment worth the pain of dislocation produced by immigration. Modern apartment buildings with parquet floors, windows in every room, and the latest conveniences announced a form of success. It did not matter that these apartments were rented; home ownership did not rank high on Jewish New Yorkers' requirements for either the good life or economic security—better to be able to catch the express train and in ten minutes travel two stops on the subway to reach the Midtown garment district than to own a house in the suburbs with a commute of an hour to work each day. And renting let Jews move as their finances fluctuated, freeing funds for other purposes.

New York Jews committed themselves to a wide array of neighborhoods, reflecting different desires. Did one wish for a neighborhood filled with modern synagogues and kosher butcher shops, bakeries, and delicatessens? There was a range of choices based on how much rent one was willing to pay. Did one seek a lively center of radicalism where socialism was considered "right wing" in comparison to "left wing" communism, an area filled with union activities, cultural events, and places to debate politics? A slightly narrower number of neighborhoods fit the bill. Did one yearn to speak Yiddish or German or Ladino or Russian, to find traces of the old home in familiar styles of shopping and praying? Neighborhoods, not just a block or two but a cluster of them, catered to those who yearned for what they had left behind in Europe or the Middle East. Did one seek a yeshiva for sons and eventually for daughters, as well as intimate congregations for daily study and prayer? New York made room for these as well. In all of them, Jews had neighbors who were not Jewish, but that mattered less than the neighbors who were Jewish. Jews lived next door to other white ethnics, as well as to African Americans, and, after World War II, Puerto Ricans. While most Jews tolerated their non-Jewish neighbors, economic competition, national and international politics, and religious prejudice ignited conflict. An uneasy coexistence among neighbors characterized many New York neighborhoods. Despite this diversity of residential neighborhoods, Jews stayed in an area usually only for a generation. New neighborhoods beckoned constantly; children moved away from parents; parents lost money or made money. Primarily renters, unlike other groups, Jews did not remain committed for long to a neighborhood. They were ready to move elsewhere in the city, to try something different. Such was New York's promise of community for Jews.

New York Jews began to leave their city in the 1960s, a process that continued for the rest of the century. The largest decline in Jewish population occurred in the 1970s when the city's fiscal crisis arrived, just in time to welcome

Abe Beame, New York's first Jewish mayor. As Jews departed, African Americans and Puerto Ricans moved into the city in ever-greater numbers. By the mid-1950s, a million African Americans lived in New York. After liberalization of immigration laws in 1965, an increasingly diverse array of immigrants from Asia, especially China, and also from the Caribbean, Latin America, and Africa arrived in New York. Jewish immigrants figured among them, most prominently from the Soviet Union; these new immigrants brought some of the same drive and energy that had made New York a city of promises a hundred years earlier.

At the start of the twenty-first century, New York still lacked a majority population. In contemporary ethnic calculus, Jews made up a significant percentage of white New Yorkers. But whites constituted a minority in the city, hence Jews' overall percentage of the population declined. Most Jews were college educated; many had advanced degrees. Having overcome occupational discrimination that endured into the 1960s, Jews held jobs in real estate, finance, publishing, education, law, and medicine in this postindustrial city. They still congregated in neighborhoods, but Queens attracted more Jews than the Bronx did. They still worked in commerce, usually as managers of large stores rather than as owners of small ones. New York Jews still debated how to observe Jewish rituals and holidays. Most declined to join a congregation, yet many retained a consciousness of being Jewish. Often awareness of Jewish differences grew out of family bonds; for some, their sense of Jewishness flowed from work or neighborhood or culture or politics. A visible minority rigorously observed the strictures of Judaism, and their presence gave other Jews a kind of yardstick by which to judge themselves. Despite Jews' greatly reduced numbers, the city still honored Jewish holy days by adjusting its mundane rhythms. New York Jews knew they lived in American Jews' capital city; the cluster of national Jewish organizations announced this fact. These organizations, able to mobilize effective protests or to advocate for a cause, focused on problems facing Jews throughout the world. Jewish cultural creativity also endured along with effervescent, experimental, multiethnic commitments to new forms of democratic urban community.

City of Promises portrays the history of Jews in New York City from 1654 to the present. Its three volumes articulate perspectives of four historians. In the first volume, Howard Rock argues that the first two centuries of Jewish presence in the city proved critical to the development of New York Jews. He sees an influential template in communal structures created by colonial Jews and elaborated in the nineteenth century by Jewish immigrants from central Europe. Rock emphasizes the political freedom and economic strength of colonial and republican Jews in New York. He shows that democratic religious and ethnic community represented an unusual experiment for Jews. Using American political models, Jews in New York innovated. They developed an expansive role for an English-language Jewish press as a vehicle for collective consciousness; they introduced fraternal societies that secularized religious fellowship; they crafted independent philanthropic organizations along gendered lines; they discussed the pros and cons of reforming Judaism; and they passionately debated politics. They were the first American Jews to demonstrate how political and economic freedoms were integral to Jewish communal life. Although many of them arrived as immigrants themselves, they also pointed a path for future migrants who confronted the city's intoxicating and bewildering modern world. In so doing, these eighteenth- and early nineteenth-century Jews laid the foundations for the development of a robust American Jewish community in New York.

In the second volume, Annie Polland and Daniel Soyer describe the process by which New York emerged as a Jewish city, produced by a century of mass migration of Jews from central and eastern Europe as well as from the Middle East. Focusing on the urban Jewish built environment—its tenements and banks, its communal buildings and synagogues, its department stores and settlement houses—the authors convey the extraordinary complexity of Jewish immigrant society in New York. The theme of urban community runs like a thread through a century of mass migration beginning in 1840. Polland and Soyer revise classic accounts of immigration, paying attention to Jewish interactions in economic, social, religious, and cultural activities. Jews repeatedly seek to repair fissures in their individual and collective lives caused by dislocation. Their efforts to build connections through family and neighborhood networks across barriers of class and gender generated a staggering array of ethnic organizations, philanthropic initiatives, and political and religious movements. Despite enormous hardship and repeated failures, Jewish immigrants in New York developed sufficient institutional resilience to articulate a political vision of social solidarity and reform. New York Jews also stepped forward into national leadership positions by establishing organizations that effectively rallied American Jews on behalf of those still suffering in Europe.

New York City became the capital of American Jews in these years and the largest Jewish city in history.

In telling the story of twentieth-century New York Jews in the third volume of the series, Jeffrey S. Gurock looks to the neighborhood, the locale of community and the place where most Jews lived their lives. Jews liked their local community and appreciated its familiar warmth. But New York Jews also faced demands for political action on behalf of a transnational Jewish world. During the crucial decade from 1938 to 1948, New York Jews debated what course of action they should take. How should they balance domestic needs with those of European Jews? World War II and the Holocaust demonstrated the contrasts between Jews in New York and Jews in Europe. Gurock shows how Jewish neighborhoods spread across the boroughs. He describes Jewish settlement in Queens after World War II, illuminating processes of urban change. Ethnic-group conflict and racial antagonism left deep scars despite efforts to overcome prejudice and discrimination. New York Jews were found on both sides of the barricades; each decade produced a fresh conflagration. Yet Jewish New Yorkers never ceased to lead movements for social change, supporting women's rights as well as freedom for Soviet Jewry. New York City retained its preeminence as the capital of American Jews because of deep roots in local worlds. These urban neighborhoods, Gurock argues, nourish creative and unselfconscious forms of Jewishness.

Each volume contains a visual essay by art historian Diana L. Linden. These essays interpret Jewish experiences. Linden examines diverse objects, images, and artifacts. She suggests alternative narratives drawn from a record of cultural production. Artists and craftspeople, ordinary citizens and commercial firms provide multiple perspectives on the history of Jews in New York. Her view runs as a counterpoint and complement to the historical accounts. Each visual presentation can be read separately or in conjunction with the history. The combination of historical analysis and visual representation enriches the story of Jews in New York City. In the first essay, Linden emphasizes the foreignness and loneliness of being Jewish in the colonial and republican periods, even as Jews integrated themselves into Christian society. They were the first to create a new identity as "American Jews." The second visual essay chronicles the challenges of navigating a rapidly expanding city. It explores contrasts of rich and poor. Jews in immigrant New York fashioned new charitable, educational, and cultural institutions as they established the city as the capital of the

American Jewish world. The third visual essay takes as its theme New York Jews in popular American imagination. It presents many meanings and identities of "New York Jew" over the course of the twentieth century and the beginning years of the twenty-first century.

These different viewpoints on Jews in New York City situate their history within intersecting themes of urban growth, international migration, political change, economic mobility, religious innovation, organizational complexity, cultural creativity, and democratic community. Jews participated in building the Empire City by casting their lot with urbanism, even as they struggled to make New York a better place to live, work, and raise a family. Their aspirations changed New York and helped to transform it into a city of promises, some fulfilled, some pending, some beckoning new generations.

DEBORAH DASH MOORE

GENERAL EDITOR'S ACKNOWLEDGMENTS

All books are collaborative projects, but perhaps none more than this three-volume history of Jews in New York City. The eminent historians directly involved in the project, Jeffrey S. Gurock, Annie Polland, Howard Rock, Daniel Soyer, and art historian Diana L. Linden, have devoted their considerable skills not only to their own volumes but also to evaluating and enhancing each other's work. Editorial board members helped to guide the project and served as crucial resources. City of Promises began during my term as Chair of the Academic Council of the American Jewish Historical Society, and I owe a debt of gratitude to David P. Solomon for making a match between Jennifer Hammer of New York University Press and the Academic Council.

Good ideas have legs, but they require the devotion and support of influential men and women. City of Promises fortunately found both in William Frost z"l of the Lucius N. Littauer Foundation and Jennifer Hammer of NYU Press. Bill Frost generously underwrote the project when it was just an idea, and I think that he would have treasured this history of a city he loved. Jennifer Hammer worked prodigiously to turn vision into reality, never faltering in her critically engaged commitment despite inevitable obstacles. I am indebted to both of them for staying the course, and I greatly appreciate the opportunity to work with Jennifer, an excellent, flexible, and insightful editor.

City of Promises received additional important financial support from individuals and foundations. I want to thank the Malkin Fund, The Marian B. and Jacob K. Javits Foundation, Hugo Barreca, David P. Solomon, and an anonymous foundation donor for significant support, as well as several other individuals including Judd and Karen Aronowitz, David and Phyllis Grossman, Irving and Phyllis Levitt, Irwin and Debi Ungar, and Rabbi Marc Strauss-Cohen of Temple Emanuel, Winston-Salem, North Carolina. All recognized the importance of this project through timely contributions. I appreciate their generosity.

Several students at the University of Michigan provided assistance that helped to keep the volumes on track. Alexandra Maron and Katherine Rosenblatt did valuable research, and I am grateful for their aid.

These volumes are dedicated to my family of New York Jews. Without their steadfast encouragement, and especially that of my husband, MacDonald Moore, City of Promises would not have appeared.

Dedicated to my grandchildren,
Elijah Axt, Zoe Bella Moore, and Rose Alexa Moore,
authors of future chapters

DEBORAH DASH MOORE

AUTHOR'S ACKNOWLEDGMENTS

It is a pleasure to thank the many people who encouraged and assisted me in the writing of this book. At the outset of my academic career, some thirty-five years ago, I was intrigued with the question of Jewish neighborhood persistence and migration within the great metropolis of New York. As these interests were refined in examining Jewish movement into and out of Harlem, I became keenly aware that there was a concomitant internal communal life worthy of detailed exploration. How did Jews of different economic and social classes and varying political and religious orientations define and live their lives, many miles and subway rides removed from the hub of the Lower East Side? In the decades that followed, I moved away from my Harlem story but took what I learned there to other projects, articles, and books. Innovative institutional activities in Harlem helped me understand how different religious Jewish movements throughout the United States worked to cope with disaffection from faith traditions. In retrospect, development of these strategies may have been Harlem Jews' greatest contributions to American Jewish life.

I now have received the opportunity to revisit these essential elements in New York neighborhood history: movement within and without localities, life on the streets, and institutional contributions that transcend time and place that made up Jewish city life. Three years ago, after writing a book-length study of Orthodox Jews in the United States, I began to pick up the metropolis's Jewish story where I had left off in the 1920s and have followed its saga into the new millennium. I am very grateful to Jennifer Hammer, editor at New York University Press, and to my colleague Professor Deborah Dash Moore for inviting me to walk with New York Jews through my home city's streets over the past ninety years as I joined the team of scholars who have worked assiduously on this multivolume history, City of Promises. Both Jennifer and Deborah challenged me in a firm but friendly way to broaden the scope of the book's dimensions. I also feel privileged to have shared my work and learned from the labors of Diana Linden, Anne Polland, Howard Rock, and Daniel Soyer, who are illuminating earlier and other dimensions of New York Jewish history. Likewise, my thanks to the several readers of the manuscript for the time and effort they devoted to refining and expanding my arguments. My friend Professor Benjamin R. Gampel of the Jewish Theological Seminary of America was, as always, of great help on technical, practical, and above all, scholarly issues. Dr. Jack Ukeles taught me much about the demographic resources available to quantify Jewish movements and persistence in New York over the past half century. As with all literary endeavors, all advice and criticisms were well taken, but any errors of fact or judgment that appear in this work are mine alone.

In my search for sources and materials, I was assisted, as in the past, by the outstanding library staff at Yeshiva University, including John Moryl, Zvi Erenyi, Zalman Alpert, and the indefatigable Mary Ann Linahan. At my home institution, I am always heartened by the encouragement of its president, Richard M. Joel; chancellor, Dr. Norman Lamm; and provost, my "rabbi," Dr. Morton Lowengrub. I am also grateful to the archivists at several distinguished New York institutions for their kind assistance, beginning with Yeshiva's own Shulamith Z. Berger and Deena Schwimmer and including Laura Tosi at the Bronx County Historical Society and Joel Rudnick at the Division of Archives and Special Collections at the City College of New York. I am extraordinarily appreciative of the efforts of my research assistant, Zev Eleff, a budding historian in his own right, who fulfilled the arduous job of digging up many of these resources. I am likewise thankful for the work of Audrey Nasar, another outstanding student, who uncovered many important primary sources. At the technical end, Peter Robertson of Yeshiva University's public affairs department was a great help in preparing photos for publication.

All of my family members are—or should be— avid readers of my books. At least that is the demand that I have imposed on my children, Eli and Sheri, Rosie and Dan and Michael. Two of my granddaughters, Audrey Sofia and Mira Abigail, may prefer to read Harry Potter, but they also like seeing their names in print. Our three newest additions, Zev Jacob, Margot Harper, and Hannah Leah, are not quite ready to check out this acknowledgment. But it is an immeasurable pleasure to dedicate this book to them. As always, Pamela shares with me the joy of another completed project and the boundless pride we have in our children and grandchildren whether or not they now, or ever, fulfill their filial obligation to read my work.

JEFFREY S. GUROCK

Jews in Gotham

New York Jews in a
Changing City, 1920–2010

The Borgenichts' brownstone and block in a gentrified Harlem, 2010. (Peter Robertson)

Prologue:
Neighborhood Dreams
and Urban Promises

Shoshana and Yoel Borgenicht believe deeply in the promises that New York City offers young Jews in the twenty-first century. They feel comfortable in their safe and secure neighborhood, where they are earning their livelihoods, raising their children, and living among Jews while sharing with others the best the metropolis has to offer. Their successful search for such a wholesome environment began in 2006 when they embarked on the quintessential Jewish New York journey, a common quest by families dating back generations, to find the right place to live in close proximity to the city's major financial, commercial, and cultural centers. Initially the couple resided in a cramped Midtown Manhattan apartment, but they desired a home with a backyard along streets where their youngsters might eventually play. As they contemplated their move, Shoshana was pregnant with their first child. They found their dream house, at 341 West 122nd Street, between Manhattan and Morningside Avenues in the western reaches of Harlem, just one block from Morningside Park, down the hill from Morningside Heights and Columbia University. They quickly closed the deal.

Their aging three-story brownstone, built in 1889 at the cost of $16,000, was originally an elegant single-family dwelling, a well-appointed abode with hand-carved wood-paneled walls, polished grained floors, beveled glass mirrors, ornate fireplaces and fancy crown molding, a receiving room and a formal dining room, and servants' quarters set aside for its live-in help. The house and its surroundings remained quite the stylish location during Harlem's pre–World War I heyday as a predominantly Jewish community. That section of uptown was especially attractive to upwardly mobile eastern Europeans. Rising out of the poverty of the Lower East Side, they melded with the well-established German American Christians and Jews who had migrated uptown in the early 1880s. After World War I, the building, like the larger neighborhood, declined. Harlem became the metropolis's first and most famous black slum. As of the 1960s, comparable buildings on that block were valued at $10,000, less even than the 1889 market value without adjustments for inflation. For close to sixty years, 341 West 122nd Street was a single-room-occupancy rooming house, home to the poor and transient. As late as the 1990s, some ten people shared the living space. The Borgenichts retained, for a while, one artifact of 341's prior history, a pair of lights outside of the brownstone house that when illuminated had told potential customers that rooms were available. When the Borgenichts moved in, they worked hard to make the residence livable according to twenty-first-century middle-class standards, including updating the hundred-year-old plumbing and constructing a modern kitchen. Still, this family of five—Rex came along in 2006, Theo in 2008, and Delia in 2009—would be happy on a street that has become increasingly gentrified.[1]

The Borgenichts did not seek out Jewish neighbors when they bought the building, but they were pleasantly surprised to find them. One Saturday morning, Yoel encountered what he described as two Orthodox Jews walking down Manhattan Avenue. A neighborhood street encounter is perhaps the most time-honored Jewish tradition in this city. After stopping to greet them, Yoel discovered that they were part of a newly created Chabad (Lubavitch) Hasidic outpost on Manhattan Avenue and 118th Street. This renowned Orthodox Jewish outreach movement had recently set up shop in the community. Jewish religious life was returning to Harlem after more than half a century. Like most other New York Jews, Shoshana and Yoel appreciated having a congregation near them, though they did not plan to attend the synagogue. As young parents, their prime issue was finding the right kind of Jewish-multicultural preschool program for their older boy.

While the Borgenichts enjoy their circle of Jewish friends, they get along well with their African American neighbors, including a couple they describe as "elderly, sweet," who have lived on the block for forty years. As Yoel and Shoshana relate their neighbors' story, "back then"—that is, in the 1960s— "if you got a good deal in the neighborhood, [you] never left, due to public transportation," coupled with the draw of "a strong [African American] social community." If the Borgenichts did not live in the most salubrious of personal settings, they still felt comfortable and relatively safe on essentially a dead-end block, even if Morningside Park, notorious during the 1960s–1970s as a crime-ridden, veritable no-man's-land, was a block away.

For Yoel Borgenicht, Harlem was much more than just a great place to raise a family; it was an open field for investment. He is the principal of Harlem Partners, a real estate development company. Yoel believes that "Harlem has a unique opportunity in terms of long-term real estate promise for two reasons: . . . [its] architecture is magnificent [and] access to public transportation." His company's website asserts that "Harlem today, with its beautiful tree lined streets and rich cultural heritage, is inhabited by a diverse mix of young professionals, growing families and longtime residents. All share in a sense of excitement and community that comes only when a neighborhood experiences an extraordinary renaissance." Yoel also relies on word of mouth to exude his enthusiasm. "On the weekends," he has related, "friends [from other parts of the city] come up and say, 'Wow, this is nice!' and one person brings two people and two people bring four people."[2]

The Borgenichts acknowledge that "there exists some resentment among people who do not own property in Harlem to this process" of gentrification, which Shoshana and Yoel attribute to some people's "bitterness or frustration at their economic situation." They recalled, "At first when we moved into the neighborhood, some of the old-time residents were a little suspicious of us as newcomers." "Whose Harlem is it?" asked *New York* magazine in July 2008. Its cover story spoke candidly about perceptions among "the average African-American in Harlem" that gentrification means "nonblack people are moving in and we're being forced out." However, the article did not name Yoel and his associates as the focus of communal ire. Rather, "the most successful and reviled real-estate broker in Harlem" was reportedly a black woman who over the past decade or so had "almost single-handedly pushed up sale prices on many Harlem homes to ten, twenty, even 40 times what they were previously worth."[3] Notwithstanding some floating animosities toward change makers, back home neighborliness prevailed on the Borgenichts' own block as folks "look out for each other." Often neighbors knock on their door to remind them to move their car across the street during alternate-side street-cleaning days, sparing them costly tickets from the sanitation department police. Amidst a bustling city, there is a mood of calm and serenity on 122nd Street.

Possessed of a strong sense of Harlem's Jewish history, the Borgenichts recognize that they are players in a remarkable reversal of fortune within a neighborhood whose Jewish heyday ended three quarters of a century ago.[4] In the

1930s, young, upwardly mobile Jews were leaving Harlem en masse. An anonymous Yiddish writer recounted in 1938 that "the removal is voluntary and the reason is not gloomy. Jews on the road to bettering themselves and making life more convenient . . . moved from Harlem up to the Bronx."[5] The young couple is also keenly aware that Yoel's entrepreneurial efforts are akin to turn-of-the-twentieth-century Jewish real estate endeavors that brought "all-rightniks," that is, eastern European Jewish immigrants on the make financially, to invest and to settle in Central Harlem. Then, as now, advertisements and word of mouth drew aspiring Jews in a chain migration to a region of Manhattan that was earning a reputation for its tree-lined, wide thoroughfare streets, situated close to Midtown and downtown work places. At the same time, severe overcrowding on the Lower East Side, exacerbated by downtown gentrification and urban renewal, pushed poor, working-class immigrant Jews to East Harlem. That region became "El Barrio," the Latino ghetto, in the 1930s.[6]

There is, however, even more historical resonance to the Borgenichts' settlement within their new neighborhood. The extensive trail that led this family to Harlem, notwithstanding some idiosyncratic twists and turns along the way, mirrors the life experiences of many New York Jews. Yoel's family saga extends back more than a hundred years.

Yoel is a fifth-generation New Yorker: his mother's family immigrated in the mid-nineteenth century from central Europe. His maternal grandparents owned a cigar shop on Lower Park Avenue. By the time Yoel's mother was born, in the mid-1930s, they had prospered and moved uptown to 116th Street between Morningside and Amsterdam Avenues, one of the regions of Manhattan that absorbed Jews from Harlem. Borgenicht's father's family hailed from German-speaking Poland and Austria. They settled on the Lower East Side in the late nineteenth century and peddled herring. In time, they too prospered enough to settle in the Crown Heights section of Brooklyn. Yoel's father, a women's dress manufacturer, subsequently moved to the Upper East Side, where he and his wife began raising a family. But in the 1970s, due to financial reverses, they "gave up on the city," as Yoel put it, and relocated to a farm in rural New Jersey. At age fifteen, Yoel, with his elders' consent, made a very unusual personal move. Feeling a lack of Jewish identity, as where he lived, he said, "was predominantly Christian," he migrated to Israel, where he served in the Israeli army before earning a law degree at the Hebrew University. Still, he said that as much as he "fell in love with Israel," he also "loved New York" and ultimately the city's "endless opportunity" enticed him to return to this city of promises.

Shoshana, by contrast, is a full-fledged immigrant. Her embrace of New York points to the metropolis's enduring character as a Jewish immigrant city. Her family, originally from Romania, lived in Montreal for four generations. But they left Quebec during the difficult times for Jews following separatist agitation. Her parents landed in Florida, where she attended college prior to exploring what New York's horizons offered. She settled in Midtown Manhattan, found employment, and met Yoel.

The Borgenichts' story highlights a central focus of this book, namely, the role of neighborhoods in the history of New York Jews in the twentieth century. This volume explores Jewish life on the streets of the city, seeking to explain how men and women, native born and immigrants, earned their livelihoods, raised their children, and related to those who shared their backgrounds in Jewish spaces that they called their own. It considers how Jews, as they sought comfort and stability, interacted and negotiated boundaries with other religious, ethnic, and racial groups who also occupied urban turf. In so doing, it details the complex dynamics that caused Jews to persist, to abandon, or to be left behind in their neighborhoods during critical moments in the city's history. And it focuses on the forces that convinced some Jews who gave up on Gotham during its most difficult times eventually to return. Throughout close to a century of transformations, declines, and revivals within New York City, there was never just one but many Jewish stories. Neighborhoods in every borough approached, each in their own differing ways, the opportunities and challenges that this city of promises presented and posed.

Beyond these accounts of daily Jewish life in New York over close to a century stands a complementary saga of men and women who believed and acted on the faith that their city could be the incubator of great ideas and the center for transformative movements. While for most Jews, in each generation, the neighborhood was solely the realm of ongoing life experiences, a minority imagined it as a place where they dreamed dreams of their blocks building new realities far and wide from their homes. Starting out in the streets of their birth, or attracted to energized enclaves, some of these activists believed that they and their comrades could fundamentally alter human destiny. Jewish radicals, for example, in a heyday of the 1920s–1930s, sought to galvanize masses to end injustices that stemmed from what they damned as an evil economic system. Other activists battled with no less vigor for specifically Jewish concerns, responding to crises on streets often thousands of miles away. Threats to the very survival of their people, whether in Warsaw during the tragic Holocaust period or in Moscow in the midst of the 1970s–1990s struggles for Soviet Jewry or in Jerusalem throughout the triumphant and threatened rise and history of Israel, became consummate neighborhood concerns. Within this city of multiple Jewish stories and possibilities, there were also those who resolved to challenge patriarchy, most notably, feminists who found their voices beginning in the 1970s. But at the same time, they influenced a cadre of their sisters to transform Jewish ways of life in New York and across the country and around the world. Such political activism ultimately elevated the New York Jewish story above the neighborhood nexus and centered it squarely within contemporary Jewish and American history.

Jews with transcendent objectives petitioned and protested against the backdrop of the massive metropolis itself, with its unparalleled communications, intellectual, and cultural hubs. Beginning with their friends and relatives living in the world's largest Diaspora Jewish city, they determined to harness the power of all New Yorkers. If properly roused, citizens of America's most populous city could also join as their causes' foot soldiers.

But for activists to fulfill their missions, they had to overcome the often frustrating apathy of those very people among whom they lived—mostly fellow Jews but Gentiles too—who strolled blithely past their neighborhood demonstrations concerned with mundane matters. On the streets, the daily and the dynamic competed constantly. Radicals were frequently disconcerted when potential comrades joined in solely when the cause of the day served their personal or family needs. The many that showed tepid allegiances riled them more than the minority who would stop to harangue the protestors for promoting ideas and projecting an image of their community perceived as out of step with American values and specific Jewish needs. As skilled debaters and dialecticians, activists relished intellectual combat, but they also understood that winning a verbal contest was one thing; convincing audiences to stay for the long struggle was another matter entirely. Feminists, for their parts, not only struggled to enlist their own committed followers to contest strident patrimonies. But, on occasion, they also had to deal with those around them who gave lip service to the cause but did not judge the liberation of women as a highest priority in creating a new society.

For street advocates of Jewish causes, beyond the constant challenge of raising hues and cries, there was their own dilemma of dealing with a collateral dynamic, as what happened in New York was so special within twentieth- and twenty-first-century Jewish history. Midtown Manhattan was, and continues to be, American Jewry's political capital. While a myriad of Jewish organizations were on the scene in the heart of the nation's media center and, for the past sixty years, close to the United Nations, Midtown acquired a reputation as a headquarters district for those who claimed—and frequently possessed—privileged access to powerful local, national, and international leaders. Outside activists seeking to lead "grass-roots" groups—to use their own self-designation—asserted that their strength stemmed from the power of Jewish neighborhood people and opposed organizations branded as a domineering Jewish "establishment." It was a loaded term full of opprobrium for those deemed to be circumspect in their response to crises and, perhaps, all too concerned with their reputations. On all Jewish issues, it was said, the rarified, comfortable in their wood-paneled suites, arrogated to themselves the right to speak as the representatives of the Jewish community to governments neither with the assent nor reflecting the views of the men and women in the streets. If local activists had a Manhattan address, it was usually little more than crowded office space strewn with reusable demonstration placards. Over the generations, disputes have recurred over whether the neighborhoods or the headquarters best understood how to prosecute the most weighty concerns. Memories of heated disagreements in one era fired up confrontations in later periods. Although the primary battles were over intense foreign matters, fundamentally different perspectives that often boiled down to how comfortable and trusting vying spokespeople were with the larger world, at some local flash-point moments also roiled controversies over how New York Jews themselves might live their own lives and share the city with others.

Meanwhile, back home in the neighborhoods, over the years and from among the masses that simply searched for calm and serene space in the city, another elite arose that harbored its own transformative dreams. These New York Jewish style setters were determined to move beyond the precincts of their streets and enclaves with the élan that the city embodied, in order to influence their nation, if not the world. They would be doyens and doyennes of the ways millions far and wide dressed, ate, entertained themselves, and even appreciated the finer things in life, partaking from a distance much of the best that this metropolis had to offer. It is to the delineation of these different visions of New York's promise—its multiple stories—and to the intersection of these varying dreams and realities that we now turn our attention.

Grand Concourse: view south from Mosholu Parkway, July 1932. (Courtesy of the Bronx County Historical Society, New York City)

CHAPTER 1

Building and Sustaining Common Ground

New York had always been a walker's city. Strollers loved passing friends on neighborhood avenues. Window shopping, a favored pastime, drew crowds during holiday seasons. Customers journeyed by foot in and out of stores across wide expanses of commercial districts in search of bargains. Residents and visitors enjoyed perambulating as they took in the sights and sounds of the metropolis's entertainments even if a bus, trolley, or in more recent decades, a subway had brought them close to their destinations. But, in 1919, a disgruntled New Yorker told state officials that "her shoes had been worn out" beating the pavement in a totally unsuccessful quest. She had marched all around town in search of decent housing for her family and was "unable to find better quarters." Her husband, children, and so many others were stuck together "crowded in dark, ill-smelling apartments."[1]

At the close of World War I, New York—so often renowned for its excitement, advantages and opportunities—teetered on the brink of failing to fulfill a most basic promise to its citizenry: to provide decent and safe places to live. Housing authorities reported dolefully that "over twenty thousand of the worst dwellings in the city that were not in use in 1916 were back on the market" because there were "practically no unoccupied apartments" that were "fit for human habitation." Even apartments in the better class of buildings were "unobtainable" as "rents . . . were rising and families were 'doubling up.'" War industries had attracted hundreds of thousands of workers, many of them African Americans from the South, and governmental restrictions during the European hostilities on all but essential construction had severely constricted new housing starts. Both new settlers and immigrants who arrived right under the restrictionists' wire as quotas became the law in the early 1920s struggled with Gotham's longtime residents for limited space. From 1915 to 1920, the population within the five boroughs rose by 600,000. Overcrowded Manhattan acquired an additional net growth of 146,000. Squeezed within tight residential quarters, the metropolis might have shared the fate of twenty-five other American cities during the so-called Red Summer of 1919 where tensions boiled over into race riots. Living cheek to jowl on heated streets and coming into close contact at crowded beaches and other public accommodations, whites and blacks violently confronted each other.[2]

Fortunately, New York legislators—with a discerning eye on what had happened elsewhere—spared their city calamitous outbreaks. In 1921, the Board of Estimate passed a tax-exemption ordinance that galvanized new safety-valve construction. The law, extended several times during the 1920s, basically freed "all new buildings planned for dwelling purposes" from ten years of real estate taxes. Attractive neighborhoods soon rose in Manhattan and the outer boroughs. This far-reaching solution to New York's most pressing dilemma profoundly affected how its Jews lived, worked, and in many cases prospered during the next two decades.[3]

Energized by this mandate, local builders and real estate operators, with Jews prominently among them, immediately sprang into action. In Brooklyn alone, during the first nine months of 1921, plans were filed for 6,303 new multiple dwellings with 22,338 apartments. Many of the buildings differed little from prewar construction of four- and five-story "walk-ups," even if promoters said that they were "up-to-date . . . with spacious interior courts for light and air." But in the Bronx in 1922, the first "million dollar apartment house" signaled a new era of housing. This nine-story edifice on Kingsbridge Road and the Grand Concourse boasted "modern, fire proof apartments arranged so that each living unit occup[ied] an entire wing of the structure, equipped with high speed elevators, intercommunication system, [and] a steam laundry in the building." Such construction set a pattern for new developments for the entire decade in the city until the Great Depression. The previously underpopulated borough of Queens sprouted new neighborhoods in Long Island City, Astoria, and Jackson Heights. While Manhattan, in the 1920s, lagged behind in the number of new housing starts, its relatively few new luxury apartment houses were usually more expensive than those built elsewhere in the city. Riverside Drive, Central Park West, Park Avenue below

Ninety-Sixth Street, and to a lesser degree, Washington Heights emerged as elegant communities.[4]

Prospective tenants—with Jews again heavily part of the mix—appreciated these houses' location within "subway suburbs." The mass movement of New Yorkers to suburbia beyond the city's legal limits was still a generation away. The notion that a merchant, a manufacturer, or even a worker could relocate the family to a wholesome setting and commute quickly and cheaply to Manhattan offices, factories, or stores represented a promise fulfilled—that is, if they possessed the economic wherewithal to make a move. And in the good-times decade of the 1920s, "labor was never as prosperous as it is today," reported one tenement-house official. He continued, "The American worker has always been desirous of bringing up his family in the best possible surroundings. He has tried to get away from the sordidness and the present prosperity has afforded him an opportunity of which he has taken full advantage." Sometimes, children convinced parents to seek these better neighborhoods. The impressionable would "go to school and visit the homes of their classmates and see how much better they are living in the Bronx, Brooklyn and Queens, with all modern improvements at a little more rent." They would then persuade their parents to move to apartments with "electric light, bath rooms, hot and cold water and clean rooms."[5] But the ability to commute every workday easily and inexpensively from home to job was critical. As "long as dwellings are within the 5 cent zone, such as new rapid transit routes afford," a real estate journal observed early in 1921, "tenants are willing to go to the [outer] boroughs."[6]

Whole new communities coalesced within walking distance of the rapid-transit lines. The South Bronx had elevated railroad links to downtown as early as the 1880s, and in 1906, the Lenox Avenue subway was extended under the Harlem River. However, after 1917, Bronx Park, White Plains Road, Jerome Avenue, and Pelham Bay Park lines made much larger regions readily accessible. In the late 1910s–early '20s, subway lines were constructed over and under the East River, bringing Brooklyn and Queens neighborhoods into close contact with Manhattan. By the same token, locales just beyond the subway's reach, such as Forest Hills, Queens, experienced much less growth. Only when the Independent Subway line (IND) was built in the 1930s, providing fifteen-minute service to Manhattan, was the neighborhood transformed.[7]

As backers, beneficiaries, and builders of a refashioned New York, Jews in the 1920s continued longstanding patterns of group economic, industrial, and

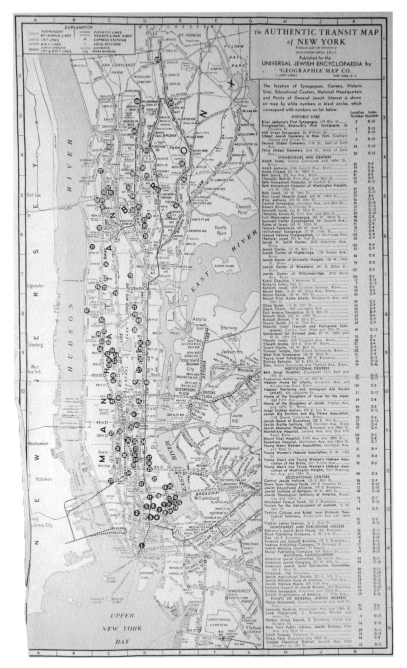

"The Authentic New York Transit Map." (Published for the *Universal Jewish Encyclopedia*, circa 1939)

social behavior in the city. In Abraham Cahan's famous novel *The Rise of David Levinsky*, the renowned Yiddish newspaper man and downtown man of letters described the real estate fever that had gripped the Lower East Side at the turn of the century, when ambitious immigrants hoped to make their fortunes in that neighborhood and on Harlem properties. He wrote about how a "boom" was "intoxicating a certain element of the population" of "Jewish carpenters, house-painters, bricklayers, or installment peddlers," emerging, in true rags-to-riches style, as "builders of tenements or frame dwellings." His central character, Levinsky, depicted as a real estate aspirant, spoke of "huge fortunes . . . growing like mushrooms": "I saw men who three years ago had not been worth a cent and who now were buying and selling blocks of property." Real-life success stories, such as those of Harry Fischel and David A. Cohen, emerged as major communal figures. In Cohen's case, this erstwhile housewares peddler from Suwalk, Russo-Poland, rose to the presidency of Gold and Cohen Realtors. As owner of several large parcels in Harlem, he even harbored the fantasy that the uptown neighborhood to which he and his family relocated in the early years of the twentieth century would replace downtown as the foremost center of Jewish religious life. When he died suddenly in 1911, he was battling to have his former home synagogue, Kehal Adath Jeshurun of Eldridge Street, shift from the Lower East Side of Manhattan to 113th Street to be part of a communal complex that would include elementary and secondary schools, a Talmud Torah, and a yeshiva.[8]

That same era of widespread construction also provided important employment opportunities for Jewish skilled laborers. To gain a foothold in those industries, painters, plasterers, paperhangers, and decorators worked as scabs, agreeing to salaries considerably less than those of other tradesmen. Predictably, these maneuvers earned Jews the enmity of the Irish-dominated construction-trades unions. But then again, the ethnically exclusive labor brotherhood denied membership to Jewish construction workers. Meanwhile, once upscale apartments were available, Harlem attracted "a great Jewish bourgeoisie made up entirely of East Siders who ha[d] outgrown their station." The quest for "greater privacy and larger quarters" had begun. Conventional wisdom claimed "the further uptown" the Jew moves, "the larger, one may be sure is his bank account."[9]

Now, in the 1920s, Jewish realtors and laborers capitalized on even greater opportunities. At the same time, their upwardly mobile coreligionists settled where fellow Jews built and worked. The ethnic connection that largely determined where those capable of moving to new neighborhoods would live was stronger than ever before. A historian of New York Jews in the 1920s has explained that "the bonds of ethnicity supported ethnically separate construction industries catering to an ethnically distinct housing market."[10] Once more, aggressive Jewish entrepreneurs "ran lustily when they heard the bell of opportunity tolling its promise." A contemporary observer of a new generation of real estate speculators further reported that "aflame with schemes, plans and ambitions for bigger things," they had "grown rich, prosperous, financially independent, . . . strutting in front of their skyscrapers and breathing freely with their chests out."[11]

To get the job done, through informal networking, Jewish builders typically turned to a Jewish architect to draw up plans and relied on a mix of Jews and other ethnic groups to perform the construction. Once the building was ready to rent, the entrepreneurs who owned and operated the apartment houses got the message out to fellow Jews—either through word of mouth or local advertising—that some of the most commodious housing going up in the city was available. For an advancing class of Jews who had risen out of factory work to owning a small business, an apartment on the Grand Concourse in the Bronx or on Eastern Parkway in Brooklyn or even on the Upper West Side of Manhattan signaled success in America. Economic and social calculi called for them to invest heavily in their shop or industry while setting aside enough money to rent an appropriate home. Buying a house appealed neither as a personal desideratum nor a measure of achievement. A spacious apartment would more than do. Once word got back to friends and relatives in older neighborhoods, a chain migration began.[12]

Very often, the children of Jewish immigrants led their parents on the exodus out of the old environment. A longtime downtown resident told a survey taker, "I lived on the east side all those years which was very uncomfortable because my earnings were too small to afford a higher rental." But then, fortunately, when "my children started to work," the family was able to seek out an "apartment with at least the toilet in the apartment and also steam heat and a bath tub."[13]

The resourceful flocked from densely populated Jewish enclaves, including not only from the Lower East Side. As late as 1917, that renowned neighborhood still housed approximately 300,000 Jews, but some 200,000 departed in less than a decade. Their destinations included the Bronx and newer parts of Brooklyn, such as Boro Park, Flatbush, and Bensonhurst; some even migrated across the Hudson to sections of northeastern New Jersey. But Jews also moved rapidly out of Central Harlem, once the home of the rising Jewish bourgeoisie. Tens of thousands, possessed of considerable means, escaped the uptown area's overcrowding for the Grand Concourse and for the Upper West Side of Manhattan, settling as far north as Washington Heights, as poor African Americans moved in. Left behind were aspiring African Americans, Harlemites too of long standing. The city extended its promises discriminately. They who once lived among Jews were trapped in this ever-deteriorating neighborhood either by their own lack of comparable economic mobility or by racist conventions and covenants. A federal study concluded in 1931 that while the children of immigrants possessed the "possibility of escape, with improvement of economic status to more desirable sections of the city," among "Negroes . . . certain definite racial attitudes favorable to segregation interpose difficulties to . . . breaking physical restrictions in residential areas." Such was the case in Washington Heights, where Jews could settle but a Neighborhood Protective Association pressured landlords, many of them Jews, to sign racially restrictive agreements. Meanwhile, as blacks, regardless of class, were "jammed together" in Harlem, many Jews from the Lower East Side who had spilled over into working-class areas of prewar Williamsburg in Brooklyn set their sights on new Brooklyn enclaves. By 1930, Brooklyn's 800,000 Jews constituted a full one-third of that borough's population. Less commanding, though certainly noticeable, was the new presence of Jews in sections of Queens, such as Jamaica, Astoria, Whitestone, Woodhaven, Laurelton, and Forest Hills. Its newly successful residents came from older sections of Brooklyn, such as the poorer areas of Brownsville and East New York. By the end of the 1920s, the Bronx housed some 585,000 Jews, up from the some 200,000 who lived there in 1917.[14]

During this decade of extensive relocations, working-class Jews moved to their own substantial, if less elegant, locales in the city. In the Bronx, particularly, Jewish labor unions and radical organizations built cooperative apartment complexes for their members. In the case of the Amalgamated housing development, home by 1931 to some seven hundred families in the Van Cortlandt section of the northwest Bronx, workers benefited from another important piece of state legislation. The Limited Dividend Housing Companies law of 1926 granted tax breaks to builders who limited dividends to 6 percent, established moderate rents, and opened their doors to tenants with low incomes. The Amalgamated Clothing Workers Union, among the largest predominantly Jewish labor groups in the 1920s, with a rank and file of some 175,000, secured mortgages from the Metropolitan Life Insurance Company, the Yiddish-Socialist newspaper the *Jewish Daily Forward*, and its own Amalgamated Bank. When the Amalgamated's cooperative doors opened around Thanksgiving of 1927, a family could occupy an apartment in a six-floor walk-up, for a modest $500 investment per room—$150 down payment with monthly installments spread out over the next ten years—and a carrying charge of $11 per month. By contrast, that same year, just to rent a three- to five-room apartment on the Grand Concourse near Tremont Avenue cost $55–$85 a month. The luckier co-op residents lived on the lower floors, with "a view of Van Cortlandt Park, the waters of the city reservoir, and the palisades of the Hudson," as well as access to the "tennis courts, ice skating and other outdoor recreation made available by the park facilities." Subsequent construction completed from 1928 to 1931 offered the added convenience of elevators. Everyone enjoyed the "landscaped gardens" around the buildings and took full advantage of the "new subway and elevated lines [that] provided a quick and easy commute to jobs in Manhattan's garment district."[15]

The 1920s also witnessed more ideologically committed Jewish laborers, such as the Jewish Communist garment workers, find homes together in the United Workers' Houses, a few miles east from the Amalgamated in the Bronx Park East section. This radical project found its financial footing not from government incentives but through loans extended by its party's Yiddish newspaper, the *Morgen Freiheit*. Still, through pooled resources, the cooperative offered deals to its residents comparable to the Amalgamated's. Concomitantly, and also in the Bronx, on Sedgwick Avenue, Yiddishists established their Cooperative Heim Geselschaft, which bore the popular name of the Sholom Aleichem Houses. Socialist Zionists gathered within the Farband Houses on Williamsbridge Road in the Bronx. In each project, developers did more than provide housing. They built libraries, auditoriums, day-care nurseries, classrooms, and gymnasia all aimed at creating and nurturing an ideological community.[16]

Elsewhere in the Bronx, other Jews of limited means relied not on union or political group initiatives but on pooled family incomes to pay rents that were only slightly higher than those charged by Manhattan tenement landlords. For example, Jews of East Harlem realized that while the Grand Concourse was economically beyond them, for just a bit more money than they presently were paying, they could relocate to the Morrisania or Hunts Point sections of the Bronx. There were eastern European synagogues in those less pricey sections as early as 1914. These Jewish immigrants and their children abandoned East Harlem in the 1920s, setting the stage for it soon to become "El Barrio," housing the first wave of Puerto Rican migrants to the city.[17]

Though the majority of Jews on the move were the children of eastern European Jews, parallel peregrinations occurred among Sephardic and Mizrachi families. In the period before World War I, some fifty to sixty thousand Jews from the Ottoman Empire entered the United States. Like their Russian, Polish, Romanian, and Hungarian counterparts, this variegated group, which included Ladino, Greek, and Judeo-Arabic speakers, settled primarily on the Lower East Side, largely on Christie, Forsyth, Eldridge, Allen, Orchard, and Essex Streets. The more affluent, but with some working-class Jews too, relocated to Harlem during the 1910s. Like so many other New Yorkers, their second generation took advantage of the building boom in the 1920s and moved to the Bronx and to Brooklyn. A substantial community of Syrians found homes in Brooklyn's Bensonhurst and Flatbush. New Lots too acquired Sephardic newcomers.[18]

When eastern Europeans and Sephardim arrived in their new neighborhoods, they caught up to central European Jews who had made the Bronx and Brooklyn their homes when these boroughs were still remote outlying districts. But cultural divides persisted. Although there was room in the Reform sanctuaries established by American Jews of long standing, those who may have prayed as youngsters in immigrant Orthodox synagogues hesitated to join. The Tremont Temple, for example, on the Grand Concourse and Tremont Avenue at 180th Street, boasted that it was the "Temple Emanu-el of the Bronx." A new member would have to be comfortable with the "dominant [synagogue] culture of the Germans," complete with its organ and mixed-gender choir but no cantor. The rabbi, in his "frock coat," led the devotions. As late as a generation after the 1920s, the synagogue still prided itself on its "dignity, stature and formality." It also contravened traditional Jewish practice, passing a charity basket at Friday-night services, admonishing male worshipers if they dared to cover their head by wearing a yarmulke, a basic traditional

Jewish custom. Second-generation synagogue-goers of eastern European Jewish background preferred the Concourse Center of Israel, a different commodious congregation directly across the Grand Concourse from Tremont Temple and three blocks north at 183rd Street, where they could find Orthodox rituals. After Sabbath services, as these Concourse Center members sauntered past the temple, they might comment derogatorily about those "*chazzer fressers*" (those who ate pork) who opted for Reform Judaism. One memoirist, who "lived next door to the Tremont Temple," recalled, "it was reform [*sic*] and the attendees were more elegantly dressed and more impressive than those at the Concourse Center." But then again, some of the Tremont Temple's members who were in the neighborhood when "the Grand Concourse was really grand, . . . [when] there were only private homes, no apartments," occasionally reciprocated, referring to the newcomers as "not our kind of Jews."[19]

While so many New York Jews of the 1920s associated with their own kind, some ventured into emerging Christian preserves and were frequently rebuffed. Particularly invidious were the actions of Edward McDougall, principal of the Queensboro Corporation, who conceived of "a completely planned and largely self-contained community" in Jackson Heights, Queens. He built what has been characterized as "the nation's first garden apartment suburb . . . for upper-middle-class New Yorkers." Like Jewish builders in their sections of town, the Protestant McDougall capitalized on the extension of rapid-transit links into the neighborhood that arrived late in the 1910s. By 1919, he was hatching a plan wherein his customers could buy, rather than just rent, their own apartments. Quickly, some six hundred families took up his offer. But none of these residents were Jews. Catholics and dog owners—the other two-thirds of the common troika of whites who were unwanted in supposedly "elite" neighborhoods—also had applications rejected. These exclusions did not approach the discrimination that African Americans faced but were nonetheless insulting to those who were denied entrance.[20]

McDougall hardly hid his intentions. His real estate code words—"Restricted Garden Residential Section" and "Social and Business References Required"—advertised who should not apply. Such admonitions not only appeared in Queensboro's promotional literature but were also posted on city buses, unquestionably to the chagrin of Jewish straphangers, including those who had no interest in Jackson Heights. If some determined Jews did not get that implicit message, they were curtly told at the rental office what were the unbridgeable realities. Such was the experience of "more than twenty-five prospective tenants of the Jewish race, of a class and character equal to that of people residing in Jackson Heights and with the financial means to carry out their contracts," who "applied . . . for acceptance as tenants . . . and were excluded upon the sole ground that they were of the Jewish race." The tension-laden scene unfolded as follows: "a man went there and applied for an apartment and would be then taken by the agent on the way to be shown the apartment. . . . He would give his name and if it was a Jewish name he was immediately notified that there was no use looking any further that they would take no Jews." That was just one of the revelations that became part of the public record when, in 1927, McDougall sued a Gentile contractor for his company's failure to fulfill a mortgage obligation. James Conforti's defense against foreclosure was that Queensboro's "act arbitrarily or capriciously in the selection or rejection . . . of tenants" had limited his requisite pool of applicants. Judge Burt Jay Humphrey sided with McDougall and affirmed his right to keep out "persons of Jewish name, origin or parentage who were otherwise desirable . . . and financially solvent." That decision and McDougall's and his counterparts' unending prejudices kept Jews out of Jackson Heights until the 1950s.[21]

Just a few miles from Jackson Heights, in the Forest Hills Gardens section of Queens, residential discrimination against Jews was subtler and less comprehensive. At its inception, this neighborhood was also envisioned as a "planned residential community." As early as 1907, the Russell Sage Foundation, an organization of Progressive reformers with seemingly the best of intentions and possessing a "broad mandate to improve social and living conditions in the United States," promised to build "attractive facilities in the suburbs for persons of modest means who could pay from twenty-five dollars a month upwards for the purchase of a home." Robert de Forest, an authority on city planning and tenement-house life, and Frederick Law Olmsted Jr., son of the architect of Central Park, were among its most distinguished officials. However, cost overruns pushed the foundation by the end of the 1910s to sell its finished garden-style apartments and one- and two-family houses to upscale customers. In the 1920s, its advertising emphasized that "lest confusion . . . exist as to just what Forest Hills Gardens is, . . . charitable and philanthropic objects . . . are not the aim. Forest Hills Gardens is a high-class suburban residential community." At that point, Forest Hills, utterly distant from the city, was enhanced by limited transportation consisting of railroad connections and a streetcar line that ran along Queens Boulevard to the Queensboro Bridge and on into Manhattan. Forest Hills did not become a "subway suburb" for people of more modest means until the mid-1930s, when the IND made its way from the city, sparking additional construction. In the meantime, Forest Hills Gardens' preferred clientele did not generally include Jews and Catholics. The foundation required that applicants provide references regarding their "character and business"—suggestive code words to deter the unwanted.[22]

Despite undertones and overtones of exclusion, some Jews broke into the restricted Gardens. In 1929, Lillian and Harry Mesard moved to 9 Archway Place, just a few blocks from the West Side Tennis Club and its stadium, the neighborhood's best-known landmark, even though "a neighbor hired a private service to investigate the new homeowners; the report stressed that they were of Hebrew extraction." More typically, Jews resided on the outskirts of the most desirable section. By 1930, some well-to-do Jews, including "businessmen and professionals" who had previously lived in older sections of Brooklyn and parts of the Bronx, settled just over the northern border of Queens Boulevard, within walking distance of the Mesards.[23]

Some of the wealthy were builders, such as Leo Wolosoff, who constructed a stately private home for his family and comparable accommodations for other Jews who could afford them. By a similar token, architect Benjamin Braunstein designed elegant apartments on the periphery of Forest Hills made to "resemble the . . . Gardens architectural pattern." Buildings with classy names like Devon Hall, constructed in 1927, boasted "Doric front columns, arched windows and colonial revival pediments." Braunstein bragged of his design at Holder Place with oak-paneled interior lobby walls and marble main lobby flooring. By contrast, local homeowner and entrepreneur Harry LeFrak focused his attention—when he was not concentrating on larger-scale projects in Brooklyn—on constructing apartments that middle-income and working-class families could afford. This family company's policy was magnified after World War II within LeFrak City.[24]

Some prosperous businesspeople and professionals stayed on the Lower East Side, while tens of thousands of their friends and relatives exited to the outer boroughs. Culture frequently influenced such decisions. Some who had succeeded economically may have not felt quite as comfortable any place other than downtown. Men of significant means also liked to be honored as patrons of some of the landmark immigrant synagogues that they could stroll to on

Sabbaths and holidays decked out in cutaway suits and top hats. The desire to walk to their jobs, yet another dimension of New York as a walking city, also had much to do with persistence. Even as many of their fellow New York Jews were comfortable with commutation, some of the well-heeled saved time and energy by living near their downtown places of employment.[25]

However, these better-off Jews who remained in the old neighborhood did not reside in the tenements that continued to billet the poor. Rather, those on the way up, but not out, benefited from new construction initiatives that changed the face of their surroundings. The walk-to-work scenario certainly applied to the occupants of the Ageloff Towers on Third Street and Avenue A, an eleven-story apartment building, built in 1929 at a cost of $2.5 million by Samuel Ageloff, who, with government assistance, also was building Brooklyn housing. This brick structure, with its ornate art-deco exterior designs, attracted "clerks, professionals and other white-collar workers," who held jobs both inside and outside the Lower East Side. Some even walked briskly to Wall Street employments, south and west of their homes.[26]

"Jewish" businesses similarly persisted in the old quarter. Starting in the 1920s, many of those who had moved away from the Lower East Side began to wax nostalgic about the streets they had left behind and returned on occasion to savor the sights, sounds, and products of their still-recent past. The special Lower East Side experience remained embedded in Jewish memories for several subsequent generations. This tendency led to throngs of Jews who reportedly had "not lost their taste for bargaining" to patronize—most notably on Sundays in blithe violation of city blue laws—"men's clothing stores on Stanton Street, women's clothing stores on Clinton Street, furniture stores on First Avenue." Those seeking religious articles also headed downtown to well-known spots on Essex Street. Purveyors of kosher provisions, such as wines and matzos, did particularly well before the Passover holiday. While kosher delicatessens thrived in local Bronx, Brooklyn, or Queens neighborhoods, for some Jews nothing quite matched a meal in an authentic "immigrant" restaurant.[27]

Second Avenue continued to entice crowds to matinee or evening Yiddish theater performances. The venerated venue continued to be the theater's "sacred grounds," even if there were "branches in Harlem, the Bronx, and Brownsville which presented melodramas, musicals, variety acts, and performers remaindered by Second Avenue." On occasion, these satellites "managed to entice a real star who had overplayed his hand in bargaining over terms and at season's opening found himself without a contract." Nonetheless, loyal fans preferred to attend a famous downtown playhouse, especially since theater producers, hoping to retain devoted patrons, constantly upgraded the artistic quality of presentations. During the 1930s, actor, director, and producer Maurice Schwartz, for example, brought to the Yiddish Art Theatre not only "Yiddish works of high caliber" but the oeuvre of Shaw, Tolstoy, Ibsen, and Shakespeare. In time, one of Schwartz's protégés, Muni Weissenfreund, moved on to Broadway and ultimately to Hollywood, where as Paul Muni he starred in such film classics as *The Good Earth, The Life of Emile Zola*, and *Scarface*. Molly Picon and Stella Adler similarly "crossed over to Broadway from the Yiddish stage." With the Yiddish theater still very much alive—albeit past its prime—as many of the younger generation preferred to go "uptown to American shows," it made sense for those who profited from fans' persistent allegiances to remain in the neighborhood so long as they could live in modern apartment buildings on Second Avenue. Decades later, "the playwrights, poets, journalists and publishers" who "lived and worked there too" would be remembered as a community of sorts, as "in the evening" they would "gather at one of the local cafes for a glass of tea," sharing smoky tables, reading the latest reviews, and critiquing the most recent performances.[28]

In 1931, just two years after the opening of Ageloff Towers, entrepreneurial Jews and their white-collar brethren found additional upscale housing near them in buildings supposedly designed for the neighborhood's laboring people. They eagerly snapped up apartments in the Amalgamated Clothing Workers Cooperative. The union headed back to the Lower East Side, its place of origins, to engage in early efforts in slum clearance and gentrification designed to help working-class New Yorkers. When two square blocks were cleared on Grand Street and the complex emerged, "it was as if," said one enthusiastic city reformer, "a fairy wand had been waved for there . . . stood a modern six-story elevator apartment building right in the midst of one of the worst tenement districts." For this observer, "a large central court which formed a charming garden, . . . a fountain in the center and shrubs everywhere, . . . represents the East Side of Tomorrow." But the cost of living there turned out to be beyond the meager means of downtown factory workers, who were worse off than other New York Jews. Soon, the endeavor that was open to all comers was critiqued as "too ambitious" for the poor. A *New York Times* article suggested that "there ought to be some middle ground between the old dumbbell rookeries east of Allen Street . . . and Park Avenue standards." The accoutrements of "garden courts, communal libraries, swimming pools, electric refrigeration are not essential." Still, they were important for civil servants, teachers, and especially the professionals and "businessmen" who could pay their carrying charges and made up half the tenants when the building opened.[29]

But did it make sense for owners of needle-trades factories who liked the downtown lifestyle to stay in the neighborhood when the industry that supported them moved out? In the 1920s, the Garment Center industrial mecca rose on the west side of Manhattan. The foremost New York Jewish line of work was now situated apart from its Lower East Side roots. Some thirty-eight large producers of women's clothing took over streets bounded by Thirty-Fourth and Fortieth Streets and Sixth and Ninth Avenues. Until the Garment Center Realty Company made its mark, this section of town was part of the notorious Tenderloin District, with its disreputable night clubs, saloons, and brothels. Now, every block acquired its own respectable niche in the ready-to-wear business. Coats and suits could be found along Thirty-Seventh to Thirty-Ninth Streets between Seventh and Eighth Avenues. For sportswear, the places were situated on Thirty-Eighth to Thirty-Ninth Streets between Sixth and Seventh Avenues. With the industry removed from its Lower East Side origins, this new area boasted "fancy showrooms in which to display its merchandise for the buyers," as the trade combined its manufacturing and sales components. Certainly purchasers from out of town—attracting them, along with local agents, was critical to success—appreciated the venue's proximity to Midtown hotels, short walks from where they entered the metropolis either at Grand Central or Penn Station. On their return trips, they took New York styles and collections all over the country. For several succeeding generations, this "place of trucks and bulky buildings, bolts of fabric, racks of dresses, drawing boards, sewing machines, showrooms and innumerable people in a hurry" made this Jewish creation in New York "a fashion headquarters second to no other city, with the possible exception of Paris."[30]

What this movement and excitement meant personally for the boss who patrolled both the new glass-enclosed display area up front and the reassembled production site in the back was that although he was not on the job as many hours as the hired help, he too would have to be a straphanger. If he remained downtown, the uptown-bound subway tacked on an additional half hour of riding to his workday. Perhaps, an Upper West Side residence—just a short fifteen-minute commute from work, one or two stops on an express train—offered the best solution, even if that relocation involved relinquishing past cultural comforts. One sample of Jewish West Side heads of households in 1925 revealed that half of them were "manufacturers of clothing or the sundries used by the garment trade." Ten years earlier, only 3 percent of the people in that section of Broadway, West End Avenue, and the adjacent side streets were such Jewish entrepreneurs. Such considerations, including daily transportation, where families chose to live, and more generally, what it ultimately meant to reside within sections of the city remained part of Jewish decision-making processes for generations to come.[31] However, in these decades relatively few differences separated apartment interiors, whether they were located in better buildings on the Lower East Side, the Bronx, Brooklyn, or Queens.

A promising young couple just starting out in the 1920s with abundant hopes and dreams, Solomon Novogrodsky and his wife, Sarah (née Lifschitz), wanted the best possible accommodations that they could afford. As high educational achievers, with attainable professional career horizons ahead, Ageloff and then Grand Street addresses were not beyond their reach. The Bialystok-born Solomon had been brought to the United States as an infant and had attended DeWitt Clinton High School before studying at the New York College of Dentistry. He had just hung out his shingle downtown when he proposed to Hunter College graduate Sarah, a botany major and education student, about to become a public school teacher. Born in Kaidenow, White Russia, her family had come to America when she was seven, and they settled initially on Monroe Street on the Lower East Side. The Novogrodsky's first homes—where Solomon grew up—were in tenements on East Third, East Fourth, and Henry Streets. With the couple intent on improving their residential lot, upon their marriage in 1929, Solomon and Sarah were among the first residents in Ageloff. Two years later, they moved into the Amalgamated on Grand Street, where their first child, Esther, was born. Shortly after a second child, David, arrived in 1933 and needing even more space for their growing family, they relocated to an apartment on Attorney Street in a house that the Lifschitzes owned.

Solomon and Sarah, who both lived close to a hundred years, never left the Lower East Side and raised three children in a series of comfortable neighborhood apartments. At the end of their lives, they resided in a three-bedroom, one-and-a-half-bath co-op apartment in the Seward Park Houses on Grand Street. Solomon and Sarah's religious values had much to do with their persistence downtown. They both possessed uncommonly strong religious training. As a young boy, Solomon had attended the Rabbi Jacob Joseph School, a yeshiva on Henry Street. Sarah had a Talmud Torah education, which was more than most girls of her era received. She studied conscientiously in this afternoon Jewish school that met after the public schools let out. Although successor Jewish neighborhoods produced comparable Orthodox institutions, the Novogrodskys preferred their downtown community. Family lore has it that toward the middle of the 1930s, when little David was ready for school, Sarah checked out the Flatbush Yeshivah. His enrollment would have caused the family to resettle nearby. But they decided to stay on the Lower East Side. Neither Solomon nor Sarah liked the idea of Solomon having to commute to his practice. The walk-to-work scenario carried much weight in a family's decision to remain downtown.

While the dentist and teacher disdained out-migration, Solomon's parents moved to the Bronx in the late 1920s or 1930s. Shimon Novogrodsky's job as an organizer of the Schohet's Union (kosher slaughters) took him, his wife Chanah, and the four younger children from East Broadway initially to Berretto Street in a working-class section of the Bronx. Many years later, in the early 1960s, after a thirty-year sojourn in that borough, when the union that Shimon helped organized forced him to retire and he and Chanah found it increasingly difficult to climb to their upstairs apartment on Topping Avenue, they returned to the Lower East Side. They were welcomed home by Solomon and Sarah, who helped take care of them. They were already looking after Sarah's widowed mother, yet another reason for these respectful grown children to stay downtown.[32]

The sentiments of filiopietism, familiar surroundings, and convenient access to the workplace that long influenced the Novogrodsky's decision to stay put were common concerns among many of those who could have left but who chose to remain in their area of first settlement. For all of the Lower East Side's persistent miseries amid overcrowded streets and despite the exodus of some two-thirds of its Jewish population as of the 1930s, this urban enclave preserved a measure of intimacy for longtime downtowners. They lived in a comfort zone of friends and family and the culture around them, even if in their professional lives they had become very Americanized.[33]

At the same time that second-generation Jews and some of their parents too were deciding whether to leave downtown, and if so, where to settle elsewhere in the city, thousands of new immigrants entered the United States. Despite the discriminatory quotas of the immigration laws of 1921 and 1924 that ended the unregulated flow of Jewish immigrants, approximately seventy to eighty thousand arrived in the late 1920s to begin their own American sagas. Many started out in the slum areas of the Lower East Side. In the first postwar decade, most fled persecutions facing Jews in newly reconstituted Poland. Though agreements signed in the wake of the Versailles treaty conference promised Jews protection, they suffered grievously as the Polish majority systematically reneged. While Marshall Josef Pilsudski, who ruled Poland from 1926 to 1935, opposed anti-Semitism, Polish Jewry, impoverished and oppressed, sought to migrate. In 1930, a typical year, of the roughly ten thousand European Jewish immigrants to the United States, forty-five hundred hailed from Poland. Over a thousand Jews from Romania similarly fled a country with a long history of Jewish persecution. Just like their predecessors who came in the years of mass migration, seven out of ten sought out New York's promised opportunities.[34]

The Lower East Side was not alone in housing the foreign-born and the poor; Williamsburg and Brownsville in Brooklyn and the South Bronx held many recent arrivals. In Williamsburg, 40 percent of the population were foreign-born, a similar percentage to the South Bronx. In Brownsville, the most predominantly Jewish section of town, close to one-half of all residents were immigrants. We cannot say for certain whether these Jews came directly from Europe to these outer-borough neighborhoods or tarried first in the Manhattan hub. Nonetheless, in each of these older Jewish neighborhoods, newcomers both supplemented and replaced those of longer standing in America, some of whom moved up to better sections of their boroughs.[35]

After 1933 and Hitler's rise to power in Germany, even as tribulations continued for Polish and Romanian Jews, German and Austrian refugees came to the United States. In the year ending in June 1938, after the Anschluss but five months before Kristallnacht, of some 20,000 Jews who gained admission to the United States, approximately 12,000 came from "Germany (including Austria)." By contrast, only 1,650 Polish Jews received visas to enter. Still, New York City remained the most popular destination for immigrant Jews, irrespective of national origins. However, Germans did not settle on the Lower East Side or in any established immigrant area but chose Washington Heights.[36] As of 1923, a decade before these refugees' arrival, this northwest section of Manhattan was a solid middle-class community. Jewish population in the neighborhood of 30,000 spiked with the building boom of the early 1920s. By 1930, the community held some 65,000 Jews, mostly the adult children of Russian and Polish immigrants. The transplantation from the Lower East Side in 1929 of the Yeshiva Rabbi Isaac Elchanan, with its newly established Yeshiva College, to the Heights signaled its emergence as a second-generation enclave.[37]

This established Jewish presence beckoned the 1930s German Jewish immigrants despite linguistic and cultural differences that set them apart from their American-born brethren. Washington Heights contrasted with less welcoming and more threatening Yorkville, Ridgewood, and Woodside, Queens, where German could be heard on the streets and where sympathies were sometimes openly expressed for the pro-Nazi German-American Bund. However, the availability of affordable housing in an unblighted area of town, as "the parks nearby and the cool breeze of the Hudson in the evening carried vague reminders of the bourgeois section of German cities" of their past, ultimately directed their settlement.[38]

Arriving at the depth of the Great Depression, these newcomers took advantage of a glut in the real estate market. Speculators had not properly gauged demand in the neighborhood and built too many apartments for too few middle-class occupants. Landlords desperately courted tenants with attractive prices. Some even tendered a month's free rent. Responsive to this offer, and using a classic working-class housing stratagem reminiscent of the South Bronx scene in the 1920s, German immigrants pooled the incomes of several breadwinners to pay the rent. Often, they were all members of an extended family, or they brought in boarders who occupied a part of the dwelling and shared food expenses. Once a foothold was secured, in typical fashion, a chain migration ensued.[39]

One young man recalled that when he and his parents arrived in America in 1936, they settled first in Marble Hill, just over the Harlem River in the Bronx. But his mother felt, situated as they were in a predominantly Christian section of town, that the family was missing out on Washington Heights' German Jewish environment. When they eventually moved and his mother was able to fit comfortably with her own kind, "at that time," she would say, "life began." Indeed, by the late 1930s, Washington Heights had acquired the moniker of "The Fourth Reich," speaking to the visible presence of German Jewish refugees.[40]

The economic catastrophe of the 1930s also transformed the way Jews lived in other neighborhoods. For most children of eastern European immigrants, the Depression ended that second generation's wanderlust. During this era of trials and "uncertain promise," they stayed where they were in the apartments that they had coveted in the 1920s—that is, if they could afford rents that had previously been manageable. The only significant exception to this pattern of inactivity took place in Forest Hills in the late 1930s. There, near the newly constructed IND lines, six-story apartment buildings with room for up to one hundred families each, attracted Jews—evidently those still of significant means—to a new "subway suburb." Some of the neighborhood's older, Gentile residents resented the newcomers and banded together as the Forest Hills Property Owners Committee in 1938; they said they wanted to "stop the unrestricted erection of apartment buildings which has grown so visible in the last year." One protestor complained to the press, "The streets don't present quite the same peaceful, suburban atmosphere they did when we bought property here." The ever-contentious Robert Moses, New York City's omnipresent parks commissioner, did not help intergroup relations much when he predicted that the community would soon resemble the Bronx, a borough with a majority Jewish population. Although he did not mention Jews by name, he agreed with the Owners Committee that the northern borough had been "despoiled by greedy apartment house builders who crammed buildings on every square foot of land that they could get away with." The quest among the majority of Jews and, for that matter, among most New Yorkers for the best possible physical environs for their families did not resume until after World War II.[41]

In the meantime, residents of the Grand Concourse or Eastern Parkway or Flatbush, not to mention the affluent Jews of Forest Hills or Manhattan's Upper West Side, did well to maintain their standard of living during the Great Depression. Generally, those with steady jobs survived financially, such as the "manufacturers and tradesmen, doctors, dentists, lawyers, engineers, school teachers, salesmen and minor executives" who lived in the better apartments of the Central Bronx. But on the other end of the financial spectrum, the 1930s exacerbated conditions for the poorest of downtowners who had suffered even during good times. In the Depression, the Lower East Side was second only to African American Harlem in the number of people on the federal relief dole. Concomitantly, many Jewish working-class families in the outer boroughs who had risen a few rungs up the economic ladder fell back down and were often unable to pay their rents in their Bronx and Brooklyn neighborhoods.

A popular family stratagem to cope with threatened evictions involved moving regularly to take advantage of landlords' offers of thirty to ninety days' free rent.[42]

Families in distress also looked to neighborhood merchants for credit to help tide them over stretches of unemployment. Those without resources appreciated when a landlord permitted them to fall months behind in their payments. However, Jews heaped scorn on real estate owners who put their neighbors out in the streets. Frequently, attempts by the police to evict those in arrears sparked protests. In Brownsville, one group of protesters kicked ash cans into the street to cause "a general ruckus" and to draw the police's attention. Meanwhile another group "would help the families put the furniture back."[43] Fighting evictions at times mobilized a neighborhood.

But what should a leftist Jewish "landlord"—seemingly an oxymoronic term—do with a comrade who could not keep up the rent? The Jewish cooperative movement of the 1920s struggled during the Depression's early years. For all the movement's excitement and emphasis on community, when the difficult days hit, these establishments could not pay their bills. But to pressure unemployed workers from their homes ran counter to every ideological teaching cherished by co-op leaders. An eviction, one resident warned as she "simply refused to pay her rent, would cause too much of a scandal if the [Jewish Socialist] *Daily Forward* found out." Some co-ops tried stopgap measures such as tendering several months' interest-free loans from their coffers to help those who were unable to handle carrying charges. But ultimately the national financial crisis engulfed their entire operations. One by one, these cooperatives descended into receiverships and were sold to independent landlords. The Sholom Aleichem Houses went first, going bankrupt in 1929 and under private ownership in 1931. Only the Amalgamated Houses survived the Depression untransformed.[44]

The demise of these housing ventures for workers only amplified the voices of those who were most dedicated to class justice. Even as their buildings fell into the hands of capitalists, Jewish Socialists and Communists on Sedgwick Avenue and on Bronx Park East redoubled their efforts to prevent evictions and force landlords to roll back rents. The aptly named "Great Rent Strike War of 1932" in the Bronx was the strongest of such citywide protest efforts. The Communist Upper Bronx Unemployment Council spearheaded battles that began on Olinville and Allerton Avenues and Unionport Road in the East

Bronx. With their foot soldiers drawn from the United Workers Houses, they rallied tenants to stop paying rents until landlords agreed to cut charges by 15 percent, to acknowledge tenant committees, and to make necessary repairs. When landlords responded through eviction notices, street struggles broke out. Mobs of protestors in the thousands fought pitched battles with police to prevent neighborhood people from being put out into the gutters. Comparable scenes took place that same year in the Morrisania, Melrose, and Crotona Park sections of the borough, and the movement spread to Boro Park and Williamsburg in Brooklyn. In each instance, Communist leadership attracted the support of fellow Jews who harbored no great partisan loyalties. The thousands of men and women in the streets simply empathized with suffering Jews.[45]

Whether rich or poor, advancing, struggling, or just surviving, New York Jews of the 1920s–1930s lived largely in distinctive, identifiable neighborhoods. In fact, this generation of immigrants' children was even more tightly ensconced in their multiple ethnic enclaves than were their newcomer parents, who settled predominantly on the Lower East Side and a few successor immigrant quarters. In 1920, just as the building boom began and new neighborhoods emerged, "only 54% of New York's Jews lived in neighborhoods that were at least 40% Jewish in population." Five years later, some two-thirds resided in their own ethnic areas. This era of profound intracity migration "produced the seeming paradox of concentrated dispersal," as "the process of migration intensified Jewish residential segregation."[46] When given a choice, most Jews stuck with their own kind, though restrictions denied them opportunities in Jackson Heights and Forest Hills, in Park Slope and Brooklyn Heights, in Riverdale in the Bronx, and in some "fashionable Park Avenue" Manhattan buildings.[47]

Yet Jews did not live totally apart from others in this ethnically and racially diverse city. Continuing an earlier downtown pattern in which Jews resided next door to Italian immigrants and Irish Americans, second-generation Jews concentrated near Germans, Irish, and Italians on the edges of a variety of neighborhoods. These groups often did not get along. During the Depression, economics and pressing world events exacerbated tensions that spilled over geographical borderlines, pitting "neighbors in conflict." Jewish difficulties with the Irish, and vice versa, were the most acute and of the longest standing. Both groups harbored mutual resentments over job opportunities that dated

back to the arrival of masses of eastern Europeans in New York. In the 1880s–
1890s, Italians and Jews also clashed over jobs in the garment industry, especially when Italians scabbed against incipient Jewish unions. But rapproche-
ments gradually occurred, due largely to the efforts of the International Ladies'
Garment Workers' Union to organize across ethnic lines. By the 1920s, Italians
and Jews frequently saw themselves as allies in recurring economic fights with
the Irish.[48]

The election of Yiddish-speaking Fiorello La Guardia as the first Italian
American mayor built bridges between Jews and Italians. But one of his major
governmental policies heightened tensions between Jews and the Irish. Born
of a Jewish mother and a lapsed Catholic father, he was very much at home
in Harlem and garnered support from Jewish voters. La Guardia proved his
multiethnic bona fides best during his 1922 campaign for the House of Representatives when he was accused by his opponent, Henry Frank, of being
"a pronounced anti-Semite." Offended, while at the same time understanding
how it might be used to his political advantage, La Guardia called for a debate
over his alleged "Jew-hatred." The battle would be conducted entirely in Yiddish. His Jewish Democratic adversary could not speak his own people's vernacular. Soon a Yiddish newspaper chimed in on the "Little Flower's" behalf,
characterizing the Italian American as pro-Zionist, knowledgeable of Jewish
history, an enemy of anti-Semitism, and a friend who "speaks Yiddish like a
true Jew."[49]

As mayor, La Guardia transformed government hiring practices. The reform of the civil service system was not explicitly designed to assist Jews, but
they benefited from the alterations, much to the resentment of their Irish
neighbors. Under many prior administrations, political appointments of police, firefighters, city-hired lawyers, and teachers went mostly to the Irish
through the patronage of Democratic Tammany Hall. Jews, Italians, and African Americans lacked political clout. When La Guardia entered office, patronage provided almost one-half of the civil service jobs. The new mayor changed
the system completely, championed competitive exams, and required candidates to possess a high school education even to sit for the entrance test. Jews,
with their diplomas in hand, were first on line for these jobs, at the expense
of the more poorly educated Irish. By 1939, three out of four civil service jobs
were awarded competitively.[50]

Irish women felt this shift most profoundly within the public schools, where for generations they had predominated. In the 1930s, under the new rules and with fewer posts available, Jews applied for these secure jobs in large numbers, displacing the Irish. Losing jobs to Jews fostered bitterness and anti-Semitism. Some Jews, especially men, turned to public school teaching because quotas at the nation's universities and academic anti-Semitism prevented them from seriously contemplating college teaching positions. By a similar token, quotas limited Jewish access to medicine and law. School teaching, especially in the newly expanded public high schools, offered a viable alternative for those who were marginalized. Jewish career frustrations garnered no sympathy from the Irish, who mourned their loss of control over school jobs, both a real and a symbolic part of the larger unemployment crisis that gripped their community.[51]

Such resentments contributed to neighborhood tensions and even street violence in areas where Jews and Irish lived near each other. Within Washington Heights, both groups controlled certain streets, with Broadway the boundary dividing Jew from Irish. On the east side of Broadway, Christian Front orators at their street-corner rallies made clear to angry Irish listeners that "the Jews" had all the good jobs since they controlled the American economy. On occasion, local vandals responded by retaliating against Jewish businesses and synagogues, and they attacked vulnerable youngsters who found themselves on the wrong side of the street.[52]

Father Charles Coughlin, the infamous anti-Jewish, anti-Roosevelt, radio priest, spurred on the Christian Front, an aggressively anti-Semitic group. He preached to millions, on a weekly basis, from his national radio pulpit in Royal Oak, Michigan. Beginning his attacks in 1934, his animus peaked in 1938, and despite censure from the Catholic Church, he continued even past December 7, 1941, when the Japanese bombed Pearl Harbor. Coughlin alleged that the Jews dictated the financial fortunes of America, controlled the government of the United States through their co-conspirator, FDR, and were leading the country to Socialism through the New Deal. Coughlin saw the Jews in the vanguard of spreading international Communism. He warned in the late 1930s that through Jews' internationalist and interventionist stances and propaganda, they were moving a reluctant America toward involvement in an unnecessary and ruinous European war on their own behalf. Energized by this rhetoric, resonating particularly to Coughlin's gut economic arguments, Christian Front activists and an even more violent group called the Christian

Mobilizers, with whom the Front had a tenuous alliance, applied these teachings enthusiastically to the mean street situations around them.[53]

So, in the South Bronx, where Jews and Irish lived in disharmony with one another, youngsters from hard-hit Irish families attacked Jews and their businesses. Some Jewish tough guys defended their people. When one Irish offender was arrested for his misdemeanors, he no doubt spoke for many when he complained that the Jews "seem to be taking everything away. . . . Most of the stores are owned by Jews. Practically everything is Jewish." Although this youthful miscreant did not explicitly reference a teacher contretemps in his neighborhood, possibly he recognized an ethnic anomaly in one school in the South Bronx that stirred antipathies. In Public School 9, off Brook Avenue, 75 percent of the teachers in this predominantly Irish district were Jewish. Most were, as the Irish saw them, recently appointed beneficiaries of new civil service protocols.[54]

As a citywide movement, the Christian Front and the Mobilizers sought to sink roots deep in every neighborhood where intergroup hostilities existed. The first steps toward the rise of the Front can be traced to meetings of agitators in Flatbush. In Brooklyn and elsewhere, Jewish groups responded with harsh words, bricks, and bats of their own. In 1938, the Jewish War Veterans chased their enemies off Flatbush streets.[55] But, neither the Front nor the Mobilizers gained much traction in Yorkville. At first glance, this section of Upper East Side Manhattan should have been prime territory. By the late 1930s, it was already one of the hotbeds of the German-American Bund, a rabidly anti-Semitic organization that from the rise of Hitler angled to be recognized as the Nazis' foreign-based representatives. However, its support emanated primarily from a circumscribed segment of the German American community: immigrants who had left after World War I due both to their country's economic calamities and their disaffection with Weimar democratic policies. Still closely tied to Germany and its anti-Semitic traditions, they embraced the ideology and practices of a revived Reich under Hitler. They were ready and willing to spread Nazism's messages in America.[56]

These newcomers agitated within Yorkville and petitioned for the right to march in full uniform regalia through the streets of Manhattan in 1937. This request troubled La Guardia personally and politically. Constitutionally, he could hardly deny these haters the right of free speech and assembly. Yet the Jewish community that long supported him pressured to have that basic guarantee revoked. To make matters worse, his mayoral opponent that year, Judge Jeremiah T. Mahoney, made much political capital of La Guardia's dilemma. His Honor let the parade go forward but did not allow the Bundists to march in their uniforms or to belt out their odious songs. Through all of this, native-born Germans either stood at the sidelines or actively opposed the radical rightists. They too were proud of Germany for reviving itself after the cataclysm of World War I defeat. But, at the same time, they did not want their ethnic group's good name associated with the bigotry of a foreign totalitarian power and as a potential threat to the United States, especially as America and Germany in the late 1930s seemed to be moving toward war footing.[57]

Senator Robert F. Wagner Sr., a long-term friend of Jews, personified that alternate and tolerant point of view. As a nine-year-old in 1886, Wagner had immigrated with his family from Nasttatten, Germany, and had gained first elected office in 1904 as a state assemblyman from Yorkville's own Sixteenth District. In 1926, New Yorkers elected him to the U.S. Senate. In that post, he championed the cause of Jewish refugees, most notably through his introduction in 1939 of the Wagner-Rogers Act, which attempted to admit, over restrictionist opposition, ten thousand German and Austrian Jewish children beyond the established quotas. But perhaps more important than Wagner's persona and these patriotic impulses, Yorkville's German American rank and file did not see Jews as intent on taking over the neighborhood. No matter the stresses of the Depression, they perceived their neighbors as fellow middle-class citizens. Not so the local Irish, who resented the Jewish minority in that community's midst and joined Yorkville's branch of the Christian Front. Decades later, in the 1970s, Joseph H. Lookstein, perhaps the neighborhood's most important rabbi, suggested that in the 1930s, his community had more problems with the Irish than with the German anti-Semites. He certainly was in a position to know. His synagogue, Congregation Kehilath Jeshurun, situated a mere block away from a Bundist stronghold, the New York Turnverein, never suffered from pro-Nazi vandalism.[58]

New York Jews had a different neighborhood relationship with African Americans. The 1920s–1930s marked an end to an era of residential proximity that had begun at the turn of the twentieth century when each group settled in its respective enclaves of Harlem. The Jews congregated primarily north of Central Park, from 110th to 125th Streets. Blacks predominated north of 125th Street, a major commercial thoroughfare that housed many Jewish businesses.

Except for economic interaction, with blacks proving to be steady customers for Jewish merchants, the two groups stayed largely to themselves, as Jews, Irish, Italians, and Germans did in other sections of the city. However, there was less intergroup tension in uptown Manhattan than elsewhere, though initially in their encounter, the West Side Improvement Association, which a black newspaper said was "composed in the main by Jews," attempted to keep African Americans from the western regions of the neighborhood.[59] Reportedly, the rationale for such behavior was not "prejudice against the race" but fear that "their presence in a neighborhood would cause the value of property to deteriorate." However, once Jews were settled, they avoided significant conflict with blacks because the two groups were situated on different rungs of the economic ladder and rarely competed over jobs. Upwardly mobile Jews did not jostle with blacks in day labor shape-ups, and African Americans did not work in large numbers in the garment industry.[60]

In the 1920s, Jews left Harlem but not because of any special aversion to living near or among blacks. Jews did better than most of their counterparts and possessed the means to move to new neighborhoods. Meanwhile, exclusionary racism of a kind that was far more pervasive than the anti-Semitism Jews faced in Jackson Heights or Forest Hills kept striving African Americans from leaving Harlem as it deteriorated.

Still, if Jews in the 1930s no longer lived in Harlem, their economic influence remained strongly felt and was often resented. For African Americans, the practices of Jewish owners of large local department stores were especially galling. Most notably, Blumstein's, on 125th Street, constantly courted black customers but did not employ black workers except for the most menial jobs. In 1934, African Americans initiated a boycott movement that focused on this store, the largest local retail establishment. The Citizen's League for Fair Play, which united black churches and women's organizations such as the Harlem Housewives League, along with community social, fraternal, and political clubs, energized by street-corner orators, impressed on its economically oppressed rank and file that it was critical not to patronize stores where their people could not work. An "honor roll" of picketers, up to over one hundred on some days, soon forced Jacob Blumstein to employ fifteen African American saleswomen and to promise to hire twenty more the following fall. However, this street victory did not endure. A year later, in 1935, the Citizen's League reported ruefully that Blumstein had not hired the promised additional employees and that, in fact, seven of those first hired had been laid off.[61]

These real economic concerns provided ammunition for neighborhood anti-Semites who magnified the tensions. Demagogues such as street-corner Muslim preacher Sufi Abdul Hamid and hate organizations such as the Harlem Labor Union shouted about Jewish economic control over Harlem, asserting that "Jews are the exploiters of the colored people" and that "Jews and leprosy are synonymous." Hamid and the Union also made rousing capital out of another tense, emotional point of black-Jewish economic interaction. African American domestic laborers, unable to find work in their own community, often traveled to the Bronx to what was called a "slave market" where Jewish housewives often hired them for pittances. When Hamid was interrogated by black writer Claude McKay about his sounding like a Nazi, he retorted that he had made himself aware of *Mein Kampf* to better comprehend the nature of anti-Semitism and that the allegations against him came from those same Harlem Jewish store owners who "did not want to face the issue of giving" his people "a square deal." The Harlem Merchants' Association, made up of Jewish business owners, refused to accept Hamid's apologia and denigrated its enemy as "Black Hitler." Concomitantly, a black organization, the Negro Labor Committee, averred that the Harlem Labor Union, its own longtime enemy, was instigating a "terroristic attack in Harlem against Jews" as well as against whites and the legitimate trade-union movement. Two eminent black newspapers, the *Amsterdam News* and the *New York Age*, supported the allegations against Hamid.[62]

Fortunately, harsh rhetoric and street demonstrations did not degenerate into intergroup violence. Perhaps the voices of responsible black journalists and sensible community organizers militated against physical neighborhood confrontations. When African American rioting that threatened local white businesses, including those that Jews owned, rocked Harlem in 1935 and 1943, explicit anti-Semitic sentiments did not fuel the core frustrations sparking the riots. After World War II, Jewish-black tensions in Harlem abated, due in significant part to the decline in neighborhood economic interaction. Many Jewish businesses relocated elsewhere, reflecting postwar economic upward mobility. But Jacob Blumstein did not. In 1949, the *Amsterdam News* praised him as one of the Jewish store owners who stayed, calling him one of Harlem's "top ten" leaders, the only white so honored. A generation passed, until the late

1960s, before a range of social and economic conflicts pitted African Americans and Jews against one another.[63]

Jewish journeys across the city brought them to new homes in neighborhoods that combined modern living with ethnic-group competition. In the prosperous 1920s, aspiring Jews managed to acquire a piece of New York City's expanding economy, together with other ethnic and racial groups that made up the city's diverse population. But the Great Depression strained families' economic resources, intensified competition for jobs and political influence, and provoked sporadic conflict between Jews and their neighbors. Such conflict dimmed the city's fabled promise, encouraging Jews to seek comfort among their own kind.

Antiwar rally at the City College of New York, circa 1938. (Courtesy of Archives, City College of New York, CUNY)

CHAPTER 2

Friends or Ideologues

Born in 1928, Adolph Schayes grew up on Davidson Avenue and 183rd Street, off Fordham Road and near Jerome Avenue in the West Bronx. For "Dolph," the son of Romanian immigrant parents, his neighborhood turf was the local asphalt-covered playgrounds. There he honed basketball skills that brought him honors at Mosholu Parkway's DeWitt Clinton High School and earned him a scholarship to New York University. He stayed at home because NYU's uptown campus was merely a short bus ride away at University Heights. After graduation, he capitalized on his athletic prowess in the early postwar years, becoming one of the great early stars of the National Basketball Association. Decades later, Schayes recalled, "As a kid I thought everyone was Jewish." He had good reason to feel that way. Though in 1930 and 1940 Jews constituted approximately 45 percent of the "Fordham" section of the borough, "sharing" the neighborhood with the Irish, everywhere Schayes turned he saw Jews and Jewishness around him.[1]

As a child, Schayes accompanied his mother to the Jewish-owned "little stores" in the neighborhood. They went to Kasowitz's fruit store, Israel's meat market, and Efron's bakery, with a stop at Zelesnik's candy store. As he got older, his peer group the "Trylons," an informal neighborhood street club named for the 1939 World's Fair centerpiece, consisted almost entirely of Jews, "with a token Irish" (youngster). They proudly walked through their streets wearing their dark-blue jackets with the club's name lettered in orange on the back. When they were not playing kick-the-can or stickball, these fellows simply hung out together, "meeting and talking." Though an intrusive beat policeman might on occasion suggest with his nightstick under his arm that they move off the corner, they were not a crowd of hoodlums in the making. They found their competitive edge in sports, not control of the streets.

Dolph graduated into a successor club as a teenager, another all-Jewish contingent called the "Amerks," that played more organized games against other Jewish teams and opponents from other ethnic groups. Schayes, who grew to be six foot eight and an outstanding athlete, recalled that the most challenging matches pitted them against Catholic teams at the St. Francis Xavier tournament. There he and his compatriots "suffered slings and arrows . . . [and] things thrown" at them by hostile crowds. But with Schayes leading the attack with his deadly set shot and hook shot, "the Jews always won."

Dolph Schayes also felt at home in his neighborhood public schools, with their large Jewish student bodies and many Jewish teachers. When in 1934 he entered PS 91, located on Aqueduct Avenue, only four blocks from his parents' apartment, most of the pupils had foreign-born parents, with those from eastern Europe, like his own, constituting the overwhelming majority. By contrast, there were but forty youngsters in the school from Irish and Italian immigrant families. Most of the Catholic boys and girls went to local parochial schools. Schayes found a similar ethnic student body at Creston Junior High School, PS 79, and one block east of the Grand Concourse. There, of the 1,087 children of the foreign-born enrolled, 666 (60 percent) came from Russian, Polish, and Romanian backgrounds. Only 67 Irish and Italian kids were in the halls and classrooms, a minuscule 5 percent of the students. In high school, Dolph found it easy "to hang out with Jewish guys," since there were over 1,500 students from eastern European immigrant homes at Clinton, four times as many as those of Irish and Italian extraction.[2]

The third dimension of Schayes's Jewishness, beyond the streets and schools, was his extended family. Aunts and uncles met once a month at his parents' home, or his folks trekked to visit the clan in Brooklyn. The elders played cards, enjoyed his mother's Romanian delicacies, and spoke of their affection for the "liberal" New Deal policies of President Franklin Delano Roosevelt.

None of Schayes's Jewish connections, however, derived from formal Jewish organizational life. He knew, as a youth, of the existence of the "large" Concourse Center of Israel and of other "store-front synagogues" in his neighborhood where some kids received religious training. But neither he nor his club friends ever set foot in these sanctuaries and schools. He "never even went to someone else's bar mitzvah." His neighborhood friends, schools, and family provided him with all of the Jewish identification that he needed or wanted. Schayes acquired a rich Jewish identity rooted in New York City itself.

During this same era, William Poster, future author and poet and dance and film critic for the *New York Times*, the *New York Herald Tribune*, and a variety of literary periodicals, similarly felt that his world, centered on Brownsville's Pitkin Avenue, was essentially Jewish. He later reflected that "up to the age of twelve," Brownsville boys like him "never really felt that the Jews were anything but an overpowering majority of the human race." So insular was their vision that they even believed that such great American heroes as "George Washington, Nathan Hale, Tom Mix, Babe Ruth and Jack Dempsey" had to be Jewish too. Within that intimate atmosphere, Poster's tightest ethnic circle revolved, as it did for Bronx boy Schayes, around his neighborhood club, another victimless street gang. Interwar Brownsville, the home of Murder, Inc., and such infamous criminals as Bugsy Siegel, possessed more than its share of Jewish toughs who preyed on the area. But within Poster's group, his friends, with such monikers as Yookie, Doodie, and Abie Kabbible, not to mention Irv, Joey, and Dave, all adhered to an informal network with "rules, aims and standards," none of which was outside the law. Both social and athletic clubs only included males. Neither Schayes nor Poster wanted girls as street companions. The Brownsville kids aimed to maintain sports supremacy over their block against all comers, Jewish and non-Jewish clubs alike, that invaded their space. Street competition was intense. Punchball games, on which they bet "with every cent [they] could muster, . . . were the gala events of the block." As these youngsters grew, athletic encounters became more organized. Like the Amerks of the Bronx, Poster's gang put together "half-uniformed athletic teams that participated erratically in interborough competition, though nearly all sports and social organizations were short-lived, breaking up in bitter conflicts over questions of power, privilege and obligation."[3]

Poster's buddies held stronger Jewish religious values than did Schayes. Although Poster reminisced that "many religious percepts were flouted with next to no concern," they drew the line when it came to "chalking up boxball boundaries on the Sabbath" because devout Jews would not write on the holy day. However, keeping that commandment "became amalgamated with [their] more fundamental preoccupation with prestige." To keep the game going, they usually "bullied . . . Cockeye Sidney, the lowest ranking member of the gang," into marking the boundaries and then "excluded him from the game he had made possible." For unfair good measure, they put him in his place, "if necessary, with a few kicks in the seat of his pants."[4]

Of course, if poor Sidney just wanted to play ball on the teeming Jewish streets of Brooklyn, all he really had to do was to get off his tenement stoop. As Gerry "Sheiky" Lenowitz recalled, "Back in Brownsville when you stepped out of your house there were forty or fifty kids on a corner. There were *always* some friends. You were surrounded by kids. You could round up fifteen at your beck and call for punch ball or stickball." For entrepreneurial-minded youths, the sidewalks also offered modest economic opportunities. During the Great Depression, when few families had phones in their homes, an ambitious kid could "hang around the corner drugstore and when there was a phone call . . . find the person, . . . get a nickel, three cents. If they were rich, . . . get a dime."[5]

At about the same time, another Brownsville boy, Alfred Kazin, who achieved far greater renown in the world of letters than Poster did, saw that same neighborhood as a part of town whose cultural borders set it apart from the larger metropolis. As he put it, "we were of the city, but somehow not in it." Kazin experienced Brownsville as an embracing home where everywhere he turned "men would stand around for hours smoking, gossiping, boasting of their children, until it was time to go home for the great Sabbath mid-day meal." But he also "saw New York as a foreign city": "that the two were joined in me I never knew."[6]

Eventually, Jewish boys started to pay attention to girls. During the 1930s, Crotona Park was the place to be for Irving Fier. It not only boasted of handball courts where Jewish men would "grunt, battle, sweat and curse" while Italians pitched their bocce balls along with their own epithets, but it was also a romantic preserve perfect for liaisons with the opposite sex. When Irving was not working in his father's dairy business, the teenager relaxed in one of the Bronx's great parks, on "a big lawn that thousands shared." Fier took his first date there. "If you wanted to make out, you walked through the park to Tremont Avenue, got a soda and then walked back." In time, the young man regularized his romantic routine, but so did other amorous Jewish boys and girls. Privacy, still a scarce resource, ultimately brought Fier and his dates to the semipublic intimacy of her apartment-house lobby.[7]

The Jewish neighborhood dating scene in Jamaica, Queens, remembered fondly as "stronghold of the Jews," had its own popular hangouts. A Saturday night might find teenagers lining up outside movie theaters such as the Hillside or the Savoy or the Merrick near Gertz's, a large Jewish-owned department store. Young men who went "stag" on those evenings might find entertainment at the Jamaica Arena, where for sixty-five cents they could enjoy a boxing or wrestling card, roller skating, or the roller derby. Afterward, Jahn's or Grossen's ice cream shops or the Concord Cafeteria tempted them for snacks and socializing. Jahn's offered a massive "Kitchen Sink Sundae," with a dozen scoops of ice cream, enough for the whole gang to devour. Those who had less money but much to talk about might buy a cup of coffee and a roll at the Concord and sit in its booths until closing time. Occasionally, as when *The Jazz Singer* played at their local movie theater, popular culture spoke directly to their personal concerns. How were they, as the sons and daughters of Jewish immigrants, to balance their ambitions with their parents' values?[8]

Fortunate youths who did not have to work on Saturday to help support their families could take advantage of the afternoon Sabbath promenade to socialize and hatch plans for the evening. Jews enjoyed seeing and being seen; it was part of urban life. Broad tree-lined avenues such as the Grand Concourse provided a perfect setting for this city pastime. The major Jewish holidays, most notably the fall High Holidays, intensified pedestrian traffic, turning Wilkins Street, near Crotona Park, into "the Rosh ha-Shanah gathering place for the neighborhood." A comparable parade convinced young Lillian Elkin that "the entire world was Jewish." When she was growing up in Brownsville, she "used to feel sorry for [her] Polish janitor because he did not share [her] holiday." At that juncture, she "did not realize that [she] was a minority and he was the majority."[9]

During the summer months, public beaches beckoned Jewish crowds. In 1934, Orchard Beach, in the northeast Bronx, opened for swimming, land sports, and socializing. It rivaled the Rockaways in Queens and Coney Island in Brooklyn as an uncommonly popular destination. One contemporary survey indicated that "on a normal hot Sunday or holiday these public beaches hold more than a million and a half persons. It is by no means stretching the probability to say that more than half of those come from the Jewish quota of the population."[10]

In each of these comfortable city spaces, this generation of Jews experienced what it meant to be members of a majority group. In this multiethnic city, the multiple ethnic groups inscribed their divisions on the streets. Beyond the metropolitan pale, Jews struggled for acceptance in America as a minority group. But within their home New York precincts, Jews owned their parts of town. Daily street interactions reaffirmed fundamental Jewish ties linking friends and family within urban boundaries and uniting a generation. As New York Jews routinely encountered each other on the block, a comfortable sense of belonging prevailed.

Possession meant that the sounds, smells, and sights of their own natural ethnic bonds abounded naturally and radiated joyously from the streets. On their own turf, they answered unselfconsciously to no other voices or commands. They spoke their own language, usually unaccented English flavored with Yiddish idioms, told their own insider jokes, relished their favorite foods, and socialized with friends who understood their idiomatic New York culture.

For youths of this era, a most popular topic of the day concerned what was going on in a very different type of Jewish neighborhood, one where no one actually lived. Ethnic ties and community pride in cultural and entrepreneurial achievement enhanced the day and night business comings and goings on Manhattan's west side, north of Forty-Second Street, the new home of Tin Pan Alley. The popular music writing and publishing business relocated in the 1920s from West Twenty-Eighth Street to be in concert with the expanding theater district. At a time when musical theater was the lifeblood of that entertainment industry, the talk of the town was how song writers interpolated ragtime tunes into Broadway hits. Irving Berlin—operating out of the Strand Building on Forty-Fifth Street, where he opened his publishing firm in 1919—knew that one or two first-rate songs could make a show. Residuals from the publication of his sheet music provided him with steady income long beyond the run of the theater production. In 1931, music publishers, both large and small, with similar aspirations, filled the upper floors of the Brill Building on Forty-Ninth Street. Morris Brill had his clothing store on the ground floor. Ambitious songwriters knocked on one door after another, eager to sell their wares. "The publishers were there, and if you had to be someplace else, you always wound up back at the Brill Building sometime during the day."[11]

By the end of the 1920s, some of the stars of Tin Pan Alley expanded its reach beyond New York. For generations, Jewish popular music composers and publishers had provided songs for the nation. At the turn of the century, Harry Von Tilzers, arguably "the most prolific song writer in the annals of Tin

Pan Alley," wrote "Wait Til the Sun Shines, Nellie." A parody of this ballad titled "Wait Til the Sun Shines, Frisco," was sung by relief workers hoping to cheer up the citizens of San Francisco after the 1906 earthquake. In 1911, Harry's brother Albert wrote the anthem of the national pastime, "Take Me Out to the Ball Game," though he had never attended a baseball game. Now, Hollywood lured some of the best talent. By the mid-1930s, renowned New York composers and lyricists George and Ira Gershwin, Jerome Kern, Richard Rodgers, and Lorenz Hart, along with Irving Berlin, had joined the movie scene, though they frequently returned to their homes on Broadway. Their fans, sitting at Jahn's and tapping out their favorite tunes, using silverware as their instruments and plates as their tin pans, rhapsodized about what successes these fellow Jews had made of themselves. Walking through Crotona Park, a young man and his date fantasized that they were Fred Astaire and Ginger Rodgers, "dancing cheek to cheek," a song that they knew Berlin wrote for the 1935 hit movie *Top Hat*. Most did not know that his most famous song, "God Bless America," was written before World War I. But Jews swelled with pride when Kate Smith belted out Berlin's alternative national anthem, at both major political conventions in 1940. It remained an enduring example of Jewish affection for America, "the land that I love."[12]

Ambitious, bright Jews next encountered each other in the classrooms, cafeterias, and alcoves of the city's colleges and universities, particularly its free, municipal-run institutions. For most of these first-generation college students, a combination of prejudice and penuriousness brought them to local schools of higher education. But friendly associational ties, rooted in enduring neighborhood relationships, ran deep even as the intellectual foment and political influence of the most outspoken among them pervaded undergraduate life.

Informal and formal quota systems severely limited the numbers of Jews who attended the nation's elite schools. The paltry and declining numbers of Jewish admissions to Ivy League colleges in the 1920s–1930s chilled the dreams of many high school valedictorians. Even if a youngster changed his name on his application and fibbed in answering other personal information questions, his Eastern Parkway address, a photograph that revealed to close-looking admissions officers his "semitic features," and his Boys High School transcript were dead giveaways that he was Jewish. Even at Columbia, the Ivy League school in New York City, discrimination reduced the percentage of Jewish students from 40 percent in the early 1920s to 22 percent ten years later.

Communal pressures kept 20 percent of Harvard's student body Jewish, far above the 10 percent at Yale.[13]

Other, less prominent schools accepted Jewish students. Land-grant universities such as Pennsylvania State or Ohio State University opened their doors, as did, remarkably, the University of Alabama. Infamous for segregationist policies that it maintained against African Americans into the 1960s, the University of Alabama has been described as "the most noticeable southern shelter for beleaguered potential Jewish university students in the 1930s with Tuscaloosa the most popular destination for both men and women." But it took both an adventurous, self-confident, and perhaps most importantly, sufficiently affluent young man or woman to seek these frontiers of learning, far away from the neighborhood. When New York Jews did arrive on these campuses and walked up fraternity or sorority roads in search of friends, they found that Jews from other parts of the country rarely welcomed them. Other Jews considered New Yorkers "undesirable." They were deemed "loud, unrestrained, poor (or "new rich"), lower-class, un-American, . . . and either too traditionally religious or politically radical" to fit in. Still a combination of overcrowding, competition, and quotas prompted one out of every ten New York college aspirants to enroll out of town.[14]

Back home in the city, New York University, taking cues from Columbia, tendered a mixed reception to Jews. Actually, that school "represent[ed] probably," said two journalists who surveyed anti-Semitism in the 1920s to early 1930s, "the most striking dualism, a house divided against itself, to be found in the academic world." The school possessed a bucolic Bronx campus, a preserve on University Heights set apart from the larger city; it was founded in 1894, before the borough became so Jewish, "as a men's country college, with the good old American collegiate spirit." Women were not admitted to this enclave until the late 1950s. However, the so-called old guard at NYU saw their "quiet, retired hill-top" world changed and, to their minds, undermined in the 1910s when "aliens," many of them Jews, began to attend. Not only did they lack proper breeding—renowned racist sociologist Henry Pratt Fairchild was a faculty eminence—but these Jews espoused unpatriotic radicalism. At least, that was the opinion of student and alumni groups who made the newcomers feel quite unwelcome during the 1919 Red Scare. Anxious to restore the school's presumed racial-religious balance, school officials in the early 1920s instituted "personal and psychological" tests to weed out Jews. Quickly, Jewish percentages at the College of Arts and Pure Science dropped "from nearly 50 percent to less than 30 percent . . . during the early and mid-1920s." When Dolph Schayes applied in the mid-1940s, receptivity toward Jews had improved. The exigencies of Depression economics helped, as NYU, strapped for funds, looked to attract more tuition-paying students, with less regard for their origins. But then again, Schayes also was an ideal candidate, a fine student and an outstanding athlete. One of the persistent critiques against Jewish students was that they lacked the good old American collegiate spirit because they were not varsity men. Dolph Schayes became an All-American basketball star.[15]

The "other" NYU—particularly its undergraduate Colleges of Commerce and Education and its Washington Square College—in Greenwich Village, where the school first began back in the 1830s, extended a more hospitable welcome to Jewish men and women. In the 1920s, James Buell Munn, dean of the liberal arts college, Washington Square, spoke warmly of a mission to provide children of immigrants of both genders with "natural cultural opportunities" within his school. He wanted it to be a "laboratory" for inculcating American values while pupils strived to fashion productive careers. Whether or not Jewish undergraduates resonated to this assimilatory message, they understood that they were accepted downtown. They flocked to the commerce-business curriculum, for teacher training, and for liberal arts educations. Friendly relations between Munn, a wealthy descendant of *Mayflower* Americans, and his poor Jewish students has been celebrated, perhaps hyperbolically, as "an episode in the emergence of an ethnically-diverse, cosmopolitan, largely urban intelligentsia in the United States." Munn facilitated that process not only with his vision but with the money he invested in his charges from his inherited fortune. As of 1931, approximately 64 percent of Washington Square College students were Jewish, from the "East Side, Williamsburg, Brownsville and the Bronx." Downtown residents had a particularly easy commute to the Greenwich Village campus since it was less than a mile away from the Lower East Side.[16]

These downtown undergraduates felt at home among their own kind, though occasionally Jewish fraternities blackballed some Jewish undergraduates of eastern European heritage because they "looked too Jewish." Between classes, they clustered within the "Jewish cafeteria, . . . three delicatessen shops whose *chef d'oeuvre* [was] hot pastrami and two street vendors of *halvah* and Indian nuts." Still, most college-bound Jews of this era aspired to gain acceptance at the city's own competitive municipal colleges, especially the City College of New York (CCNY), "the Cheder [Jewish school] on the Hill," in St. Nicholas Heights in Upper Manhattan, north of Columbia University.[17]

These "sturdy sons"—as the school's alma mater described them—did not care that anti-Semitic rhetoric had it that their school's acronym stood for "College of the Circumcised Citizens of New York." City College was their "Proletarian Harvard." In the interwar period, close to 90 percent of the student enrollment at CCNY was Jewish. Those who got in understood what it meant to be beneficiaries of their school's century-old tradition of free tuition. Future *New York Times* editor A. M. Rosenthal may have captured the decision-making processes of most of his City College contemporaries best when he recalled, "When I was a senior at DeWitt Clinton High School," six years before Schayes, "I had absolutely no conversations with any of my classmates or with my parents about what college I would enter or try to enter." For this Depression-era youth seeking to get ahead, "there was only one choice. You either got into City College or you looked for a job in the Post Office."[18] At no other place in America did the total daily cost of college attendance reach "about 30 cents, . . . 10 cents for the round trip subway ride and about 20 cents for food." One luncheon staple, a "generous and highly seasoned chopped liver sandwich," cost fifteen cents, leaving a nickel for a soda or coffee.[19]

During the Depression, the financially strapped municipal government seriously contemplated imposing tuition at CCNY. In 1932, there was talk of charging fifty dollars per year or, perhaps, two dollars and fifty cents per credit. Such exigencies actually led to the closing, at least temporarily, of city colleges in other municipalities whose low tuitions attracted the children of the poor. But CCNY remained open and free largely due to the efforts of a galvanized student body that rose as one to protest the city's attempt to "save $1,500,000 at the expense of the City College students." In a most impassioned plea, they argued that the "establishment of fees would seriously cripple" the school's "enviable reputation" for "intellectual vigor," transforming a college renowned for the "mental ability" of its students and bringing it "a step nearer to some of our country club establishments."[20]

The best CCNY students more than rewarded their alma mater for its uninterrupted largesse. A year after the tuition threat passed, three young men from poor Jewish families enrolled who subsequently won Nobel Prizes in the sciences. Herbert Hauptman and Jerome Karle shared the award for chemistry, and Julius Axelrod won in medicine. They were among seven CCNY men who were so honored for scientific research during the generation that spanned the Depression and the early postwar years. Kenneth Arrow, class of 1940, received his prize in economics. But perhaps Jonas Salk most epitomized how New York City through its distinctive educational promise to its people benefited the nation and the world.[21]

The research physician who ended for millions the scourge of polio entered the St. Nicholas Avenue campus as a high school student at the age of twelve. He had skipped several grades in elementary school, a common leap forward among New York's gifted public school youngsters, before gaining admission to Townsend Harris High School, essentially a publicly funded prep school. Every year, thousands applied for the two hundred coveted spots. If a student survived the pressures to succeed there, where four years of secondary training were crammed into three, he was virtually assured a seat at CCNY. Salk did just that and started college just after his sixteenth birthday, initially aspiring to be an attorney. But poor grades in the humanities and pressure from his domineering mother moved him to the premed program, where he excelled. The only "science" course that he struggled with was "hygiene" (gym).

While an undergraduate, Salk was the consummate "grind." A biographer noted that he focused intently on "class work, preparation and exams. . . . He joined no clubs, held no offices, won no honors, played no sports," and unlike most CCNY fellows, "made no life long friends." But upon graduation in 1933 at age nineteen, he had prepared for medical school. More than two decades later, when his vaccine first became available, New York City's Mayor Robert F. Wagner Jr. crowed, "We are all quite proud that Dr. Salk is a graduate of City College."[22]

The tenor of seriousness that students such as Salk brought to the campus resembled the mien of most classmates intent on graduating, desiring to secure decent employment during these difficult times. Living at home and commuting to school, they rushed back to their part-time jobs in the neighborhood with no time for undergraduate hijinks or even more serious extracurricular activities. "Around C.C.N.Y.," wrote one chronicler of college life at the start of the Depression, "there flock no romantic legends. There are no dormitories here. . . . No voices group under a moonlit elm to sing the glories of the College and the bullfrog on the bank." The reality was, he observed, "students are here a few hours and they are sucked back into the city from which they come.

The boys at City College do not even drink, as all hilarious college cut-ups do. The reason is simple. . . . They just can't afford it. Three-quarters of them work to keep themselves in school."[23]

Jewish women at Hunter, like their brothers at CCNY, found college life highly "transitory." During the Depression, Jews made up 80–90 percent of the student body at Hunter.[24] A college report in 1938 revealed that such "girls spend more than half as much time in their underground campus—the subways—as they do in classes, lectures and laboratories." A student who lived in Brooklyn "puts in forty minutes in trains, buses and trolleys for every sixty minutes she attends classes." The quantification added "to the 89.2 twenty-four hour days of class room attendance during the four years at college 1,650 hours, or 68.75 full days of traveling." During such journeys, female students at Hunter and at Brooklyn College, which opened as a coed institution in 1930, perfected "the art of studying while straphanging." Good manners were not alive and well beneath the city streets. "Even with the help of an armful of books and a weary countenance," none of the Hunter coeds interviewed "could remember having had a seat offered her more than twice." But while these women chafed at the lack of chivalry, they knew that they were themselves a privileged minority. In other families, sisters sacrificed their chances at higher education to afford their brothers the opportunity to work only part-time while attending school. They contented themselves with jobs as book-keepers, salespeople—"salesgirls" as they were then called—or secretaries. A 1935 study determined that Jewish male high school graduates were twice as likely as females to continue on to college. Jewish men attended graduate and professional schools at a ten-to-one ratio to Jewish women.[25]

Returning to their neighborhood daily after dark, the men and women of the city college system might occasionally come back to school as daters on "Saturday night in December and [walk] across the cement campus" on St. Nicholas Heights to hear "the *Allegaroo*" (CCNY's idiosyncratic cheer, "baffling to etymologists"), urging on the basketball team to "yet another victory." To this day, no one has precisely defined what an "Allegaroo" is. These fans applauded their own student-athletes from their neighborhoods who spent their own meager extracurricular time perfecting their sports skills and taking off time from their own part-time jobs to give the lie to allegations about Jewish lack of American athleticism. As one memoirist put it, "Our victories were important beyond the actuality of the score; immigrants or (mostly) sons of immigrants, we triumphed over the original settlers . . . whose forebearers (some of them, anyway) had landed on Plymouth Rock."[26]

For all of students' efforts to satisfy academic requirements—and the dropout rate for economic reasons was quite robust—those who attained degrees did not necessarily rise above their fellows or move beyond their neighborhood and friends. Once again, a combination of poverty and prejudice told the tale. During these difficult times, it was not necessarily "CCNY or the post office" but perhaps CCNY and then the post office. After completing four encumbered years, a college alumnus might line up against high school graduates in competition for a coveted civil service post. La Guardia's merit-based appointment system may have benefited Jews in their battles for city jobs against the Irish who lacked academic credentials. But with Depression cutbacks, neither a high school diploma nor a college sheepskin guaranteed employment. A Jewish Brooklyn College graduate who became a policeman recollected, "Back . . . in the 1930s, when there was a Depression on, the biggest factor in anyone's life was job security. So I guess it was everyone's duty at that time to take every civil service exam that came along." In his case, he became one of twelve hundred appointees out of thirty-eight thousand who sat for the exam.[27]

Even professional degrees did not promise prosperity. A Jew with a law degree, having passed the so-called character hurdle to gain admission before passing the bar, could not aspire to a high-paying post in a prominent law firm. Those positions were off-limits to most Jews. Those who broke through even more difficult barriers and became physicians and dentists, similarly, did not get coveted and lucrative positions. Often these professional practitioners relied on an informal network, as Jews turned to other Jews as clients, patients, and customers. Solomon Novogrodsky, for example, had very few non-Jewish patients.[28]

Jonas Salk, brilliant and lucky, gained admission to NYU's School of Medicine, where "tuition was comparatively low; better still, it did not discriminate against Jews." This exceptional talent secured an internship at Mount Sinai Hospital, where "out of 250 who sought the opportunity, only a dozen were chosen." But anti-Semitism almost denied him more advanced research opportunities. Rockefeller University turned him down. A non-Jewish former mentor, Thomas Francis, secured him a position at the University of Michigan, thanks to a National Research Council fellowship. To get his disciple the grant,

Francis had to refute the contention that Jews did not possess the bedside manner required of physicians. Francis affirmed, "Salk is a member of the Jewish race but has, I believe, a very great capacity to get on with people." Francis's admiration for Salk's abilities directed his young colleague to his initial work in combating infantile paralysis. From 1942 to 1947, Salk worked under Francis at the University of Michigan, "moving up the academic ladder—too slowly he felt—from a research fellow to a research associate to an assistant professor of epidemiology." In 1947, he left for the University of Pittsburgh to direct its new viral research program. Eight years later, his merit and perspicacity rewarded, he won international acclaim as "the man who saved children."[29]

What of the trying career paths of men and a few women who pursued graduate education in the humanities and social sciences? CCNY was also proud of the disproportionate number of its alumni who earned doctorates. During the 1920s–1930s, Jewish students saw in philosopher Dr. Morris Raphael Cohen a consummate academic role model. However, few of the young men whom he challenged in class to dedicate themselves, as he did, to "the full-blooded life of the mind" could hope to follow in his professional footsteps. There were few posts available even at "Jewish" schools such as CCNY, Hunter, and Brooklyn College. A 1938 Jewish communal survey reported that "while Jews constitute a considerable proportion of the student body in the colleges and universities, . . . they represent but an insignificant proportion of the faculties. . . . The belief is universal that it is folly for any Jew to strike out for an academic career." Discriminatory policies only changed after World War II. For career opportunities, these best of the Jewish brightest looked to secondary school teaching. Such realities also connected Jews with other Jews despite competition for scarce opportunities.[30]

While most young people saw their neighborhoods as secure places to articulate personal aspirations or to express nagging frustrations, a vocal and highly dedicated minority of Jews dreamed that the streets of Jewish New York and its college campuses could become ideological strongholds. Each in their own ways, religious leaders of the faith's several movements, radicals of differing stripes, and Zionists anxious to strengthen their footholds in America wanted those among whom they lived to share their deep concerns. They engaged in quests to alter fundamentally the destiny of their people, if not the direction and fate of all humankind. But the masses that they hoped to lead were only episodically interested in the activists' messages. More often than not, most Jews tendered tentative, intermittent assent to the campaigns when the arguments and agitations touched their gut needs and emotions.

In many ways, second-generation youth continued patterns of halfhearted allegiances that characterized New York's immigrant Jewish community. In the religious realm, for example, back at the beginning of the century, downtown appeared so devout on the High Holidays, when Jews in the tens of thousands flocked to synagogues. The demand for seats often exceeded capacity, leading to the emergence of a cottage industry of "mushroom" or "provisional" synagogues. To the great consternation of many neighborhood people, too many of these "Temporary Halls of Worship" contributed to "the abuse of religion," as "self-styled, . . . irresponsible . . . Holy-day Rabbis," often bereft of credentials, rented "halls and sold tickets of admission." These abuses capitalized on a seasonal demand among "customers" wrought by a combination of nostalgia, awe over the days of judgment, and a desire to be among their fellow Jews and to be seen in the best finery they could afford. But these temporary allegiances also underscored the reality that even if synagogues were open for prayers three times a day, seven days a week, they were often half filled Saturday morning because so many potential worshipers went off to work.[31]

Similarly, most immigrant families demonstrated a lack of commitment to Jewish education. The "one room school house" in the tenement hovel, manned by a poorly trained but also often abusive *melamed* (teacher), did little to inspire ongoing interest in its students. Community-run Talmud Torahs that emulated public school pedagogy while teaching traditional Jewish ways emerged as early as the 1890s. But by World War I, after nearly a decade of modernization efforts, "less than 24% . . . of Jewish children of elementary school age" received any form of Jewish education, including the "private teachers" and the "one teacher schools, or 'Chedarim.'" If these youngsters were touched at all by religious life, it occurred when they showed up outside synagogues on the High Holidays and conversed with fellow Jews who had their same low degree of interest in their faith.[32]

Early twentieth-century Jewish radicals had no sympathy for the problems rabbis and other religious communal figures faced. Those on the left frequently launched disparaging barbs at the values and practices of the devout, attacks that were returned in kind. Although these ideologists never acknowledged a common dilemma, they too struggled to strengthen the uncertain allegiances of masses that were rarely steadfast in their support. The most committed considered the transplantation of revolutionary thoughts and actions an act of secular faith. Radicalism thrived on sweatshop abuses, long hours, paltry wages, and unsanitary conditions. But even when Jews joined the Socialist Party, they often avoided full-fledged ideological commitment.[33]

Despite these difficulties, radicals and unionists dominated much of the street culture downtown. They succeeded in mobilizing workers, putting strikers out in the streets in legendary proportions. Yet the 1909 "Uprising of the 20,000" shirtwaist makers and the 1910 "Great Revolt" of sixty thousand cloak makers rarely translated into electoral success.[34] Some of the most supportive immigrants out in the streets could not vote. Male newcomers had to wait at least five years before gaining that right. Immigrant women, often the most committed demonstrators, did not possess the franchise until 1917. In addition, Jewish workers wanted to act like other citizens and so refused to vote for Socialist or Socialist Labor candidates. Republicans and Democrats courted Jewish voters, sending an implicit message of acceptance and a promise of integration.[35]

Radicals could not count on steadfast support. As historian and Socialist Irving Howe has pointed out, Jews attended meetings, lectures, and rallies that highlighted the problems they faced. They read the radical press regularly, if not religiously, and gratefully accepted the fraternal benefits, mutual aid, and emotional succor of the Arbeter Ring (Workmen's Circle). But, like Jews who in the small downtown synagogue found homes and companionship amid the trials of immigrant life, those at the Workmen's Circle meetings came to fraternize and to contemplate but not necessarily to act on their secular movement's ideology. "To be active in a Socialist branch," Howe has written, "to pay dues, attend meetings, hand out literature," all required a "disciplined commitment" from the Jewish worker. It was a degree of "intens[ity]" that "even left-leaning immigrant workers" would not dedicate to radical agendas.[36]

Second-generation Jews continued this pattern of unrequited allegiance to both the religious and the radical. On the religious front, boys and girls evinced more disinterest than disdain for synagogue life. The "eighty-three synagogues . . . and dozens of Hebrew and Yiddish schools" that were crowded into a "less than two square mile" section of Brownsville usually stood empty. Few boys "continued their Jewish education or frequented synagogues past the age of thirteen." A 1940 neighborhood survey confirmed these impressions. It determined that "only nine percent of adult males in Brownsville attended a synagogue with any regularity." We do not know if that paltry percentage might have included some members of William Poster's posse, who did not write on the Sabbath but forced poor Cockeye Sidney to do so. While the High Holidays witnessed closed stores and empty public schools and thousands promenading in the afternoon, more Jews stood outside the synagogues than prayed within.[37]

This phenomenon of "attending synagogue on the holidays, *sometime*" (emphasis mine), held true citywide. A study of metropolitan young adults also published in 1940 indicated that 72 percent of Jewish men aged sixteen to twenty-four had not attended any religious services that year. Five years earlier, in 1935, another survey showed that attending religious social activities —not to mention services—ranked dead last among some fifty leisure-time activities for Jewish teens, males and females, and those in their early twenties. Many enjoyed simply "walking or hanging around," presumably on their Jewish blocks.[38]

Although religious leaders of all Jewish movements bemoaned the empty seats in their sanctuaries, Rabbi Mordecai M. Kaplan proffered the most creative solution to this dilemma. Although he was not the first to hit on the concept that young people could be attracted to sanctuaries through a variety of ancillary portals, his Synagogue Center idea popularized the strategy that those who came to play might in time be convinced to stay to pray. His initial home base, The Jewish Center, was founded in 1917 within the emerging community of the Upper West Side. Kaplan's formula called for the "translat[ion]" of the synagogue into "a synagogue center . . . where all the members of the family would feel at home during the seven days of the week. There they could sing and dance and play." The method was to sustain that social momentum, using it to make participants more religiously committed Jews. Israel Levinthal, a Kaplan disciple and, beginning in the 1920s, rabbi at the Brooklyn Jewish Center, believed there was "magic" in this methodology. It would come into play when a "young man, entering the gymnasium class, would notice the announcement on the bulletin board that on the next evening a meeting would be held in the interest of Jewish refugees or for relief." With his "interest aroused," he would then come to a weekday Forum lecture. "The chairman would announce that on the coming Friday eve, the rabbi would speak on this or that subject. . . . He would come to the services. If the services appealed to him, he would come again."[39]

This pray-through-play posture became the communal calling card of a string of interwar synagogue centers in New York, from the Jacob H. Schiff Center and Temple Adath Israel in the Grand Concourse region of the Bronx to the Brooklyn and Ocean Parkway Jewish Centers, all of which were tied either personally or ideologically to their teacher and leader. Kaplan divorced himself from the Orthodox Jewish Center in the early 1920s, publicly separating himself from traditional faith, and founded the Reconstructionist movement. However, The Jewish Center and the Orthodox Institutional Synagogue, located in Harlem until the late 1930s, maintained gyms and/or pools in their shuls.[40]

For all of Kaplan's and his followers' enthusiasm, this endeavor fell short of inculcating staunch religious allegiances in many members. The naysayers who questioned, from the outset, whether athletes or artists or dancers or music lovers would ever find their way from the synagogue's gym, studio, or auditorium to its sanctuary had a point. Brooklyn rabbi Harry Weiss believed that those who attended the fun and games part of Jewish life were likely to "feel that . . . [their] duty towards a Congregation is fully performed and the Friday night and Saturday morning services are of necessity neglected." Statistics that Rabbi Alter Landesman offered in 1928 supported Weiss's impressions. From his post at the Hebrew Educational Society in Brownsville, Landesman's survey of national trends in "synagogue attendance" revealed that "experiences with synagogue centers thus far have been negative or very slight . . . in augmenting attendance in religious services." If anything, during the 1930s, with so many people with time on their hands, synagogue centers became even more popular as secular Jewish retreats. From 1931 to 1935, "more than four thousand new members came to use the gymnasium" at the Brooklyn Jewish Center, and others flocked to its manifold other recreational and cultural activities. Singers such as Sophie Tucker and Belle Baker performing at a congregational benefit packed the house and contributed toward filling strapped coffers. But such events that "blurred the boundaries between the world of Broadway and the world of the synagogue" did little to increase regular religious attendance. In the Bronx, Schiff Center officials spoke of four thousand Jews attending High Holiday services, not to mention those who, as always, congregated outside. But during the year, it was the same old story of half-empty sanctuaries.[41]

These realities were not lost on Kaplan, who in 1935 allowed, "At first I thought if the synagogue were transformed into a center that would house the leisure activities of our people, the problem of Jewish life in this country would be solved."[42] But such had yet to be proven the case. Throughout the interwar period, his initiative really only produced yet another comfortable venue for Jews to interact with each other. They took their strong neighborhood ties indoors.

Radical groups held greater expectations that their efforts would garner sustained allegiance to their causes. They did not have to seek out the neighborhood masses. Their several Bronx cooperative apartment endeavors brought potential comrades into daily contact with those who preached world-changing ideologies. But here too most Jews did not become political activists unless a campaign touched them personally, even those who believed in the causes and appreciated what the unions, Socialists, and Communists promised and delivered.

House painter Louis Myerson and his wife, Bella, exemplified this reality. Among the original owners within the Sholom Aleichem co-ops on Sedgwick Avenue, they purchased their five-room apartment in a four-story walk-up in 1926 for $1,000. Nine other family members—siblings and in-laws—joined them in this close family circle. As working-class Jews, they imbibed radical rhetoric, distrusted the capitalist system, and inculcated these values in their three daughters. Helen, Sylvia, and Bess attended the two Yiddishist schools on co-op premises after the neighborhood public schools let out. One of the "schules" was Socialist, the other Communist, but the girls hardly learned the differences. They received little clarification at home, as Louis Myerson's "political policy was to participate in everything and commit to nothing." Bess once quipped that her father joined "the IWO" (the Communist International Workers Organization) because of its "excellent burial program." He stayed clear of the great debates that roiled the co-op, such as the battle royal between the Communists and Socialists, particularly the Labor Zionists, over the 1929 Arab riots in Palestine. The Stalinists backed the Arabs; the Zionists supported the Jews. A biographer of the Myerson family considered Louis's position "common among thoughtful moderates," individuals whom Irving Howe described as "non-party leftist[s] engaged in cultural activities."[43]

If hard-line neighborhood radicals were disappointed with the tepidness of the Myersons' involvement, less doctrinaire Yiddishists, who strove to perpetuate that Yiddish language and culture, welcomed the family's willingness to teach its daughters the Jewish vernacular. Many American Jewish families disdained their ancestral tongue, fearing that it smacked of unpatriotic radi-calism and posed a barrier to becoming true Americans. Some worried that speaking too much Yiddish would make youngsters sound like immigrants and retard their integration. Even Abraham Cahan, the formidable editor of the Yiddish *Daily Forward*, advised in 1931 that since "young college-educated men and women are being disqualified as teachers because they speak and conduct themselves like foreigners," it was an "absolute necessity" to raise youngsters with "thoroughly American pronunciation, intonation and ges-tures." A Jew could do well in the civil service exam and then fail the oral exam for public school teaching because of accented English. Cahan opposed such Yiddish schools. But the Myersons' middle daughter, Bess, did not suffer for her attendance at the Sholom Aleichem schools. In 1946, when she became Miss America, she spoke perfect English to the judges in Atlantic City.[44]

There was, however, one gut issue that hit home with the Myersons. In 1932, a year after the co-op went bankrupt and was sold to private investors, forty tenants were tossed out of their apartments for nonpayment of rent. The three sisters, surely with parental assent, worked the picket lines as a rent strike, championed by radical leaders, erupted on Sedgwick Avenue. Beyond that, leaders and youngsters alike helped their neighbors, assuring that "no co-op member ever wandered homeless."[45]

There were certainly youngsters who rose out of these same Bronx streets who were fully swept up with the excitement and promises of left-wing move-ments and dreamed of influencing their peers and ultimately changing the world. One of the most iconic of these youths, having grown up in the "Jewish slums of the East Bronx," Irving Howe recounted, "I wandered into the ranks of the Socialist youth and from then on, all through my teens and twenties, the Movement was my home and passion, the Movement as it ranged through the various left-wing, anti-Communist groups." Here, too, ideologically commit-ted Jews felt secure amid their own kind, as children "from immigrant Jew-ish families." Howe recognized, "the Jews still formed a genuine community reaching half-unseen into a dozen neighborhoods and a multitude of institu-tions, within the shadows of which we found protection of a kind." Only on occasion did they venture beyond their home base to preach their gospels to other, often unreceptive groups, such as to the tough Irish kids on Fordham Road. They did better talking up social justice issues to poor blacks in Harlem. Notwithstanding this "protective aura," street bona fides still had to be earned among real laborers of their parents' generation. "You might be shouting at the top of your lungs against reformism or Stalin's betrayal," Howe recalled, "but for the middle-aged garment worker strolling along Southern Boulevard, you were just a bright and cocky Jewish boy, a talkative little *pisher*."[46]

The young Daniel Bell, the future social theorist and later professor of social sciences at Harvard, first learned of socialism at home. His mother joined the International Ladies' Garment Workers' Union, always voted the Socialist Party line, and read the *Forward* "religiously." By thirteen, her son was ready to tell the rabbi who had trained him for his bar mitzvah, "I found the truth. I don't believe in God. I'll put on *tefillin* [phylacteries] once in memory of my dead father, but that's all." The rabbi apparently retorted, "*Yingle* [literally "little boy," a cleaned-up version of *pisher*], you don't believe in God. Tell me, *you think God cares*." Though divorced from the faith, Bell later admitted that he gleaned much from Jewish tradition. Soon, he was applying "the same kind of thinking you learned" in analyzing the Bible or Talmud to Karl Marx's "torah" as a teenage member of YPSL (Young Peoples' Socialist League). He and his comrades went from "corner to corner" on the streets of his Lower East Side neighborhood preaching. To gain attention, they used "a sort of stepladder" and began "gathering a crowd until [the] main speaker would come along and talk." Bell "was usually the first one up the ladder."[47]

Howe, Bell, and those of comparable keen political persuasions reached their majority as CCNY students. Gathered in the alcoves of the school's cafeteria, these doctrinaire advocates did their best to convince others of the rightness of their cause, hoping to recruit followers for on- and off-campus campaigns. CCNY's indoor Jewish street possessed many kiosks, each manned by competing ideologists who engaged in legendary debates with Jewish spokesmen for different brands of radicalism positioned provocatively in the next alcove. One memoirist has recalled that Alcove #1 was the province of a mix of "right-wing Socialists" and "splinters from the Trotskyist left wing" and an even more "bewildering" array of "Austro-Marxists, orthodox Communists, Socialist centrists, . . . etc.," not to mention "all kinds of sympathizers, fellow travelers, and indeterminists." When these peripatetic debaters were not battling among themselves, starting out with a civil call—"let's discuss the situation"—they engaged in intellectual combat with those in Alcove #2, the home of the pro-Stalinist Young Communist League, headed by Julius Rosenberg.[48]

For those who took up the cudgels for their deeply felt convictions, the alcove arena mattered more than any class. Irving Howe showed his priorities through a "device of checking in at the beginning of a class when a teacher took attendance . . . and then slipping out to the bathroom and coming back at the end of the hour and meanwhile spending that hour in the alcove."[49] Howe and his confreres—who included, among others, Daniel Bell ('39), Irving Kristol ('40), and Nathan Glazer ('44)—honed skills as debaters and dialecticians that shaped their lives as major American Jewish thinkers. These self-assured men in the postwar era became renowned political thinkers and cultural arbitrators, characterized as the "New York Intellectuals."[50] In their college days, they "declared themselves citizens of the world," cosmopolitans who set themselves apart from parochial sympathies and patriotic American realities. In the postwar years, their consciences raised by Communist aggression, by Soviet anti-Semitism, and most profoundly by the horrors of the Holocaust, which reminded them of their ancestral ties, they refashioned themselves as loyal Jews. Some of them, most notably Irving Kristol, refocused completely as intellectual cold warriors and formative influences on American neoconservatism, whose influence was yet so powerful within turn-of-the-millennium American politics.[51]

While these advocates were still in their radical phase, however, holding forth from their cafeteria soapboxes, they were voices to reckon with on campus. They attracted many students who gravitated to the alcoves to listen in on a point well struck. "When that happened," one veteran of these battles recalled, "a crowd gathered around the contestants, the way kids do, waiting for a fight to explode. But there were no fist fights, even when the provocations seemed unbearable." However, when the noise and excitement died down, as debaters were known to engage one another "at the top of [their] lungs," listeners who did not share the depth of the alcove spokesmen's concerns, drifted away to their worldly pursuits, their classes or part-time jobs.[52]

Occasionally the call of the classroom interfered with students in the maelstrom of intellectual combat. In one unforgettable contretemps, at least for Nathan Glazer as he described it, one of his colleagues in Alcove #1 "held forth for something like six or eight hours as various people" from the Communist Alcove #2 "rose up against him, then had to go to class. He decided to drop his classes, I suppose. And people would come and go and he was still holding forth, he was still going hammer and tongs." Yet Irving Kristol has noted that, on the one hand, "because of the kinds of kids that went there, . . . at least eighty-five to ninety percent Jewish," from working-class backgrounds, possessed of some degree of radicalism in their families' traditions, "the entire student body was to one degree or another political." On the other hand, "most were passive politically": "the active types numbered in the hundreds."[53]

This endemic passivity frustrated radicals seeking to take their fights out of the alcoves and into the streets beyond CCNY. The thousands on campus were potential shock troops for revolutionary change. If harnessed, they could do more than debate the world; they could change it. How grand would it be if hundreds of students might be convinced to put down their books and pressing personal concerns to trek to Kentucky in 1932 to support striking miners and to protest police brutality? Such an expedition promised an ideal opportunity to "expose capitalism at its worst" and to demonstrate how young people "could act effectively on behalf of those victimized by the Depression."[54]

Future renowned Marxist economist Harry Magdoff was one such instigator. This Bronx-born house painter's son came from a home "environment in which class problems—unemployment, seasonal unemployment, negotiations, problems of the union"—were the talk around the kitchen table. His first formal exposure to radical teachings took place at his local Sholom Aleichem school, where he read the literature of the European Left in Yiddish. Daily reading of the Yiddish press fostered these beliefs. As a high school student, he struggled to convince his classmates to take class conflict seriously. Looking ahead at the college scene, he chafed over "the indifference of U.S. college students to poverty and politics," while there were "student riots over social issues in Hungary, maybe Romania." When he enrolled at CCNY in 1931, he immediately joined the Alcove #2, Communist, Social Problems Club and edited the organization's magazine, *Frontiers*. A year later, in 1932, he went off campus to be part of the inauguration of the National Student League and the Youth League Against War and Fascism. All of his efforts, starting with editing an unauthorized magazine and culminating with leading a rally against autocratic CCNY president Frederick B. Robinson, ultimately led to his expulsion. He finished his bachelor's degree at NYU.[55]

However, Magdoff admitted that he and his comrades often stood alone. While many students sympathized, the vast majority focused on preparing for careers at a school that was, as this campus activist once put it, "horrendously competitive, terribly competitive in terms of class work." One historian has explained that "City College's low-income students responded to the Depression not by embracing radicalism, but by buckling down in their academic work, hoping that by performing impeccably at college they would improve their chances for employment in the dismal job market." Moreover, many impoverished students, even those who understood the issues as Magdoff saw them, simply did not have spare time to hang around for rallies and protests when part-time job responsibilities hung over their heads. Magdoff recalled the pressure to secure any job, no matter how menial: "When an announcement was posted stating 'Jobs available-Part-time for Chemical Engineering Students,' . . . everyone was envious." The employment was only "to shovel snow. There was a heavy snow fall in New York. They knew that if they announced snow shoveling jobs they'd have a thousand guys applying." To keep the numbers down, they limited the offer to chemical engineering students. Still, men like Magdoff soldiered on. As one of his non-Marxist contemporaries at CCNY later observed, with some degree of admiration, "Communists in the student body, although only a handful, . . . were the most dedicated and aggressive missionaries challenging teachers and deans whenever the occasion presented itself but concentrating especially and relentlessly on skeptical and or indifferent fellow students."[56]

Women radicals at Hunter College similarly endured disappointment with their rank and file's inability or unwillingness to commit fully to their causes. The most dedicated members of its Young Communist League (YCL) endeavored to do it all. They traveled long distances back and forth from home, held part-time jobs, distributed party literature, solicited names on petitions, sold the *Daily Worker* on Manhattan street corners, and attended interminable political meetings on campus. For Lucy Schildkret—the future historian of the Holocaust Lucy Dawidowicz—and her "circle," she recalled, "the YCL took precedence over our classes especially required courses which we cut a lot." She "was in search of a utopian solution to earthly ills," and her "goal was nothing less than a secular version of the eternal Jewish striving for a Messianic world." Schildkraut's "particular vision was colored red, the color of blood and of revolution": "We believed that the future was ours." But she also recognized, to her dismay and chagrin, that she and her comrades were "a tiny minority among the student body." Most other Hunter students "kept their noses in their books and tried to have some fun." Schildkraut especially dismissed as "frivolous, even irresponsible" activities such as "Senior Hop and SING," sports teams, and the college's eighteen sororities, "surprisingly for a public college with a subway student body." There were also some who agreed with activists' feelings about changing society and who might have taken to the streets but feared that if word got out that they were troublemakers, they might lose their part-time jobs. A student-librarian knew that if she were arrested at a demonstration, she would forfeit her position. Aspiring teachers understood that if the Board of Education's Board of Examiners designated them as a "potential threat to the school system," they would be denied their coveted pedagogue's license. Challenged and conflicted, the majority of Hunter students remained on the sidelines at critical protest moments.[57]

Socialist Hal Draper first spoke out at Brooklyn College and remained with radical movements long enough to link up with New Left operatives in the 1960s. Looking back at his and his comrades' efforts to create ideological strongholds in New York City colleges in the 1930s, he has suggested that where and when he was a student, only 1 percent joined the student groups. But their impact, he proudly believed, extended to "concentric rings of influence embracing different portions of the student body" around them. Some supported particular campaigns when the issues touched home; others would have become more involved had they the time. The National Student League and other such leftist organizations found their widest and staunchest support at CCNY, Hunter, and Brooklyn College in 1932, when they championed the student bodies' ultimate gut issue, the aforementioned crusade to maintain free tuition. Draper has also argued that even those who never showed up at meetings and kept solely to their books and jobs "could not help absorbing the climate of ideas which pervaded the political life of the campus as a part of the larger society." For him, even the masses of students who did not break with their daily routines to take part in the National Student League's "National Scottsboro Week" teach-ins in 1934 had their consciences raised. They learned not only about this specific travesty of justice in Alabama, where nine young black men were convicted and sentenced to death on trumped-up charges of raping two fellow hobos on a freight train, but also about "all that was wrong with the Jim Crow system everywhere," even on their own campus.[58]

Notwithstanding these claims of cultural suzerainty, many CCNY students ignored the radicals' causes, such as "partisans" of the sports fans' alcove who "fought over the relative merits of the Dodgers and the Giants" baseball teams. Others actively opposed the leftists on campus.[59] The most aggressive opponents enrolled in the Reserve Officers Training Corps (ROTC). Like all organizations at the school, ROTC consisted predominantly of Jews, who hailed from the same Jewish neighborhoods as the Socialists and Communists.[60] These students opted to take two basic courses in military science as part of their college curriculum. From 1917 to 1928, such training had been imposed on all students because CCNY president Sidney Mezes deemed it "beneficial to the students' health and patriotism," part of a national move toward uniformity that grew out of the era of World War I. By the mid-1920s, however, widespread student opposition led to the abandonment of this requirement. From 1928 on, students could take two semesters of hygiene instead. Still, a CCNY man could enroll in ROTC, continue with the program throughout his four years in school, and upon graduation earn a commission in the U.S. Army. The corps—a competing campus community of its own— also had its extracurricular component, including its band, its own monthly, *The Lavender Cadet* (a reference to the CCNY school colors), and a rifle team, and it conducted review parades through campus.[61]

Some students signed up because grading was apparently higher in military sciences courses than in hygiene. In 1931, the student newspaper noted "the remarkable eagerness" of enrollees and bemoaned the "disparity" that "impels students fearful of low grades and rigid requirements" to don the uniform on campus. But others became student soldiers because they agreed with the administration's social and political values. They also shared common cause with CCNY's athletes, another highly visible segment—mostly Jews too —members of the College Athletic Association and its Varsity Club. Two hundred lettermen of the Varsity Club, fellows such as baseball players Lou Trupin and Arthur Koenigsberg and lacrosse stars Cohen, Gottfried, and Rosenberg, vigorously applauded the proposal of Major Herbert M. Holton, associate professor of hygiene, at a sports dinner that "City College athletes organize a vigilance committee to eradicate 'rowdyism'" on campus. In the 1930s, CCNY, the renowned radical campus, had "the largest voluntary [ROTC] unit in the nation."[62]

Radicals saw the presence of ROTC at CCNY as a major provocation. They opposed participation in any future capitalist- or fascist-inspired war. On this issue, Magdoff and his National Student League found allies within more moderate campus elements, such as the student editors of the *Campus*. In May 1935, for example, the editors spoke of their own efforts "to combat the forces making for war and fascism." Their sentiments aligned with those sixty thousand young men and women who, less than a month earlier, had signed an American version of the Oxford Oath during a national daylong student strike for peace. In 1932, several hundred pacifist members of the Oxford Union had foresworn fighting for "King and Country." They promised not to fight in another war. Radicals frequently disrupted military reviews, turning them into antiwar demonstrations. Protesters at what they called the "Jingo Day" event in May 1933 ended up in a melee with the police who had been called in to break up the battles between students. Those arrested—only the leftists were incarcerated—accused President Robinson of personally joining in the struggles, wading in with his umbrella as a weapon. Subsequently, Magdoff, his Social Problems Club, and their newspaper were all suspended. This first major infraction of college rules eventually led to his expulsion. But protests continued. In 1935, fifty adamant protesters broke up a Charter Day event commemorating the founding of CCNY. The *Campus* editorialized that "the ROTC is a disgrace to a liberal institution of higher learning and that a color guard composed of ROTC men is distinctly out of place in the Charter Day exercises."[63]

However, in May 1940, when three hundred student protestors carried signs into Lewisohn Stadium that read, "Down with ROTC" and "To Hell With War," they received a mixed reception on campus. It was one thing to continue to reject the American military's presence at CCNY and quite another to oppose the European war, with the Nazis overrunning western Europe and ghettoizing Jews in eastern Europe. Such antiwar sentiments smacked of the isolationism of the right-wing America First Committee, a movement that attracted more than its share of anti-Semites. But most committed Socialist and Communist students held true to their beliefs, following their parties' lines even if Alcoves #1 and #2 vigorously debated justifications for the Hitler-Stalin pact of 1939, which cleared the way for the Nazi invasion of Poland. The beginnings "of the war in Europe" contributed to an increase of 154 students in ROTC over the previous semester, and enrollment reached 1,204. Perhaps, these Jewish student volunteers anticipated what Hitler's war would mean both to America and to the Jewish people. Preparedness could be considered a virtue since eventually the United States too might have to fight for democracy. An uncompromising evil warranted military readiness.[64]

Four students, Bronxites Irving Cohen and Milton Miller, Fred Bloom of Brooklyn, and Fred Brooks, who lived on Manhattan's Upper West Side, were arrested for their disorderly efforts attempting to break up field-day events. Their remonstrations did not deter the twelve hundred cadets who marched that day. That predominantly Jewish parade of students included Milton M. Wiener, also of the Bronx, who was honored with a gold medal from his home borough's Reserve Officers Association. ROTC identity led to recognition for fellows with Jewish-sounding names from such groups as the national society Daughters of the American Revolution, a nativist group that often portrayed Jews as radicals. These explosive contretemps between students demonstrated that New York's Jewish neighborhoods produced young men who matriculated at CCNY with either strong revolutionary or "patriotic" proclivities, though most of their classmates observed from the sidelines and kept their political views to themselves.[65]

Committed Zionists focused their efforts to construct their own ideological strongholds primarily in Brooklyn. They built on an early heyday around World War I. Initially, the Jewish national movement experienced great difficulties gaining traction. Its European predicates, that the bounties of emancipation were ultimately illusions and that Jews could only be free and secure in their ancient homeland, did not resonate with immigrant Jews. They had chosen America over Palestine and had found both liberty and opportunities for individual advancement in the United States. However, around World War I, under the auspices of the Federation of American Zionists and subsequently within the Zionist Organization of America, a new attractive definition of Zionism evolved, spurred on by the advocacy of the famous Jewish jurist Louis D. Brandeis. Often referred to as "Palestinianism," it emphasized the obligation of American Jews to assist their European brethren who were settling in the home land. This philanthropic ideology provided Jews who were estranged from Judaism with a new ethnic identity congruent with the American values of cultural pluralism. Articulated by the Jewish philosopher Horace Kallen, cultural pluralism emphasized the importance of maintaining a group identity in the United States. It thus behooved American Zionists to study their people's history, to learn modern Hebrew, and to attend rallies that glorified heroic Jewish pioneers in Palestine, similar to America's own legendary frontier settlers.[66]

Palestinianism crested during World War I, especially after the Balfour Declaration of 1917. It served as the basis for the British Mandate over Palestine. With the guarantee of a national home in place, committed Zionists faced the challenge of sustaining the movement's momentum. They aimed to create a strong and enduring modern Hebrew culture within second-generation communities.

Children ideally imbibed these lessons in a number of all-day Jewish elementary schools that sprung up in several Brooklyn neighborhoods. At the Etz Hayim-Hebrew Institute of Boro Park or the Shulamith School for Girls or the Crown Heights Yeshiva or the Yeshivah of Flatbush, families enrolled their sons and daughters in modern Jewish educational settings dedicated "to engender[ing] in them a love of their people and its cultural heritage and a strong attachment to the Zionist way of life," while upholding Americanized versions of religious Orthodoxy. Neighborhood supporters of these schools, primarily the parents who paid tuitions, hoped that they would become "a training ground for future leaders in Jewish life both in America and Israel." Some of these youngsters did find their destiny ultimately in the State of Israel. Others joined the American Zionist movement. They spoke modern Hebrew, read Hebrew books and magazines, promoted Jewish nationalism as a means of group identification in America, and passionately supported the Jewish settlement in Palestine.[67]

Intensive Jewish elementary education inspired a handful of young adults to become rabbis and educators. They turned to Yeshiva College and its Teachers Institute, which proffered staunch religious Zionism. Others, men and women both, enrolled in the Jewish Theological Seminary of America, which offered similar careers of service to the Jewish people. However, women could not aspire to be rabbis.[68] The fictional character Reuven Malter, one of the heroes of Chaim Potok's novel *The Chosen*, exemplifies this cohort. Malter, the son of a noted Hebraist and Judaica scholar, learns cultural Zionism at home and as a student in a modern Jewish day school in Brooklyn. Dedicated to the Jewish national cause, he strives to help the endangered fledgling Jewish state. Eventually he decides to study for the rabbinate at a fictional college depicted as a hybrid institution combining educational and theological elements of both Yeshiva and the Jewish Theological Seminary of America. One can imagine an older Reuven Malter becoming a Modern Orthodox or Conservative rabbi in the postwar period, emphasizing Zionism and Israel as a major building block of Jewish identity.[69]

However, without gainsaying the involvement of real-life versions of Malter —Potok was quite like him, though he grew up in the Bronx—most neighborhood youths were neither intrigued with nor engaged in this expression of Jewish politics and culture. American Zionism in Brooklyn and elsewhere in the city received an additional boast in the 1930s when the public school system, in a remarkable turnaround from its long history of undermining Jewish identity, countenanced Hebrew as an accepted Regents foreign language. A supporter of cultural pluralism, John Laughan, a principal at Christopher Columbus High School in the Bronx—presumably a Gentile—welcomed the move. In introducing Hebrew into his school, he stated, "Young people should be urged to preserve their racial heritage particularly when, as Hebrew, that heritage is culturally valuable and historically important. Our American democracy will be enriched and strengthened by the perseveration of this cultural heritage." In 1940, thirty-two hundred junior high and high school students chose this course of study, yet they constituted less than 5 percent of Jewish enrollment in city schools. And both the Hebrew course and the two-semester overview of Jewish history proffered at Boys High School were not restricted to Jews.[70]

For all the efforts of those who were engaged in promoting Jewish ideologies on the streets of New York, "very few Jewish youth," a survey in 1940 concluded, "belong to clubs connected with their religion." The same held for affiliation with radical groups too. "Although the Young People's League of the United Synagogue," the report continued, "is reported to have 10,000 members in New York City, the Youth Zionist movement other thousands, and there are smaller groups of Jewish youth organized to promote understanding of Jewish traditions and religion, the total number of members hardly makes an impression on the estimated nearly one-third of a million young Jews under 25 who live in New York."[71]

Throughout this era, the most successful ideologues were groups of strictly Orthodox Jews who maintained staunch enclaves in their parts of Brooklyn. A remarkable set of first- and second-generation Jews, they had avoided the lures of Americanization and calls for cultural change that had captivated most others. Instead, they maintained a strictly separatist social profile that stood out on the neighborhood scene. Within Williamsburg in Brooklyn, amid the "dance halls and poolrooms for the young," lived an aggregation of "really *baale-battishe* [religiously upstanding] Jews and many *talmidei chachomim* [truly learned individuals]." In this milieu of the meticulous, Sabbath-observant families dominated. According to a scholar of that time and place, a "representative" family was headed by a father who "did not let a day pass without praying with the minyan in the synagogue" and who "attended a regular *shiur*, a Talmud study class after his hard, long hours in the sweat shop." His wife kept a house that "was a model of kashruth, [where] the Sabbaths and holidays were celebrated with the proper ceremonies." More important, their children followed suit. A comparable pocket of piety existed in Brownsville as well as in East New York and Bensonhurst.[72]

These strictly Orthodox Jews focused their efforts on their yeshivas, most notably the Mesivta Torah Vodaath on Bedford Avenue, the most comprehensive of five borough schools for boys and young men. It placed the highest premium on the transmission of traditional Torah and Talmud learning, showing only marginal interest in modern Jewish subjects, such as the study of modern Hebrew, and frowned on the teaching of Zionism. A similar mission motivated the leaders of the Yeshiva Chaim Berlin, situated in neighboring Brownsville. It too "aspire[d] to reproduce in this country, the old type of observant God-fearing Jew devoted to the ancient ideals of learning and piety [who would] exhibit the diligence, sincerity and other-worldliness of the traditional *yeshiva bochur* [along the] model of the *yeshivoth* of Poland, Lithuania and Jerusalem, . . . extreme and uncompromising in its Orthodoxy." These schools discouraged students, as far as was possible, from pursuing secular education beyond the high school years mandated by state law. If their disciples really desired a college degree, to help them earn more money, they attended Brooklyn College at night. There they endured fewer challenges to their faith, and most evening students had no time for secular protests. Nowhere else in the United States, not even on the Lower East Side, were there so many young Jews studying more of the Torah and less of the secular world than in Brooklyn.[73]

These religious hubs did hold on to many of their youngsters, but they were limited enclaves. Despite efforts at isolation, some young people drifted away from their parents' worlds. Some made common social cause with the equally small day-school crowd of young men and women, to the chagrin of yeshiva officials. Others chose to cross bridges into Manhattan and beyond to study secular subjects. Still others left to prepare for careers of service to modern Jews, enrolling at Yeshiva College or the Jewish Theological Seminary. These moves resembled the peregrinations of Potok's other fictional character in *The Chosen*, the yeshiva student Danny Saunders. Potok's novel takes him from his rabbi-father's roots to encounter the world of psychology at Columbia

University. Though Potok dressed up the conflicted rebbe and son as Hasidim at a time when, historically speaking, they were a small minority of the extremely devout in Brooklyn, contentions over what secular subjects might be studied, not to mention debates over Zionism, roiled these religious realms.[74]

Finally, other scions of the borough's faithful Jews broke almost completely from traditional religious values. One bittersweet dynamic took place within that aforementioned "representative" pious Williamsburg family in which the father and mother personified unfailing devotion to old religious ways. One son and a daughter followed in parental footsteps, as "good and upright" second-generation Jews. But a second son wanted to "become a man of the world." As his still-observant brother later told an investigator, "[After] his return from the wars [World War I], he began to mock some of our customs and criticized our rigid observance of the traditional laws. . . . It was only a question of time till he would go his own way." After marriage to a Jewish woman from Brownsville, who evidently shared his declining religious commitments, and then blessed with financial success, the young couple left the neighborhood and Orthodoxy. They headed to a "swanky neighborhood in Forest Hills," Queens, where he became, according to his saddened brother, "what we at our Shul call a 'high-holiday Jew.'" Thus, he anticipated that large cohort of former Orthodox families that expanded after World War II.[75]

But while these separatist communities suffered attrition, their numbers grew exponentially during and after World War II. Their neighborhoods' commitment to resistance was intensified. Survivors of the Holocaust and refugees from Soviet domination of eastern Europe—many, but not all, of Hasidic stock—made their way to the United States and gravitated to these indigenous Orthodox enclaves. There they began their American experiences as Jews who endeavored to live socially and culturally apart from secular and irreligious Jews. In time, their values and perspectives, preserved and protected within their ideological strongholds, reverberated both in the tenor of Brooklyn life and on American Jewry well beyond their immigrant hubs.

New York Jews transmitted and transmuted their neighborhood experiences beyond the boundaries of the city through intellectual creativity, political radicalism, and Jewish activism. Although only a minority of New York Jews established reputations outside their local milieu, they drew sustenance from the ethnic worlds of their youth. Emboldened by experiences on the city's streets and nurtured in the city's free schools and colleges, they honed their intellectual, political, cultural, and religious commitments through conflict with other Jews. New York City provided just this blend of intimacy and opportunity, fashioning multiple forms of Jewish and American identity. Looking back, many who succeeded even beyond their dreams recognized the debt they owed to the city's ethnic neighborhoods.

Red Cross Surgical Bandage Division of the Jewish Community House of Bensonhurst, Brooklyn, February 6, 1945. (Courtesy of the Sephardic Community Center
of Brooklyn)

CHAPTER 3

During Catastrophe and Triumph

Jews of New York lived at the center where American Jewish responses emerged to the cataclysmic events that decimated their people in the decade of the Holocaust. Their location placed them in the midst of decisions leading to the rise of the State of Israel. More than any community in America, New York was the hub of national Jewish organizational life. Hundreds of Jewish political, social, and religious groups, across the broadest of spectrums, had offices in the metropolis. Although the seat of American government was 250 miles away, seemingly all major deputations to influence leaders in Washington, D.C., originated in New York. Between 1938 and 1948, Jewish organizations spread within Midtown across Forty-Second Street, east to west, were positioned to garner public attention. Two major defense organizations, the American Jewish Congress and the American Jewish Committee, with often polar-opposite approaches to Jews' monumental problems, stood at opposite sides of the famous New York street. The Congress, a Zionist mass-membership organization that advocated public remonstrations to its government to champion Jewish plights, made its headquarters off Eighth Avenue. The Committee, a bastion of elite leadership, prized quiet diplomacy and commanded space on Lexington Avenue. They did, however, walk together in harmony on those occasions when they were given the opportunity to speak to government. Jews who set foot among the powerful, they believed, had to do so with respect and dignity.

The offices of the Joint Distribution Committee and the American section of the Jewish Agency for Palestine faced each other across the street between Park and Madison Avenues. The Joint acquired renown for securing or secreting supplies to Jews in eastern Europe before, during, and after the war. The Zionist organization's most dynamic publicity arm, the American Zionist Emergency Council, and its primary fund-raising group, the United Palestine Appeal, shared space with its parent organization, the Jewish Agency, the pre-state Jewish government in Palestine, first at 41 East Forty-Second Street and later a block or so away at 342 Madison Avenue.[1]

Future leaders of American Judaism's movements also located in Manhattan. Rabbis and religious teachers in training at the Orthodox Yeshiva Rabbi Isaac Elchanan and its undergraduate school, Yeshiva College, studied in Washington Heights. Sixty blocks south in Morningside Heights, the men and women of the Jewish Theological Seminary of America prepared either to become Conservative rabbis or, in women's cases, to graduate as Hebrew teachers. On Sixty-Eighth Street, off Central Park West, stood the Jewish Institute of Religion, a Reform rabbinical school led by Rabbi Stephen S. Wise, who was also president of the American Jewish Congress.

Volunteer workers and advocates for Zionist organizations with very different strategies for how Palestinian Jews should fight for their freedom, and varying visions of what sort of state Jews might create, passed one another daily on the way to their offices on Twenty-Sixth and Twenty-Seventh Streets in the Chelsea section of Manhattan. At lunch time, Madison Square Park, off Fifth Avenue between Twenty-Third and Twenty-Seventh Streets was a fine location for unscheduled waxed-bag debates between supporters of the David Ben-Gurion–led Histadrut, the "umbrella framework of the Labor Zionist movement in Palestine," and the confrontational New Zionist Organization. In the critical first postwar days of 1945–48, the backers of the Histadrut pleaded that the British could be convinced through diplomacy and cooperation to exit Palestine. Their interlocutors, Revisionist Zionists, sought to drive out the English through violence and intimidation. For longtime observers of these ideological conflicts, this Palestine debate represented but a continuation of wartime disputes between Wise's Congress, allied with Ben-Gurion, and the Revisionists over how to approach the government to rescue Jews. The transcendent disagreement was over whether the Roosevelt administration had Jewish concerns at heart. Wise believed in and trusted FDR; the Revisionists did not. If the Congress spoke to the powerful with respect and regard, the Revisionists—who rarely could get audiences with government—harangued and condemned.[2]

In another part of the park, Mizrachi members spoke passionately to those who might listen about the glories of a future Jewish state rising in "the Land of Israel, for the people of Israel, in the spirit of the Law of Israel." These Religious Zionists munched on sandwiches from home or foods purchased at Lugee's Kosher Restaurant, located four bocks north of Madison Square.[3] Yet aside from a common Jewish background, they shared little with comrades of the Jewish People's Committee, a Communist organization that also worked in offices in 1133 Broadway on Twenty-Sixth Street. Although both were Jewish groups, they held uncompromising divergent views of their people's destiny. The antireligious and antinationalist Communists dreamed that Jews would join an international workers' revolution, even if in the meantime, the organization religiously observed directives sent from Moscow.[4]

A mile or so south on Lower Broadway, near Washington Square, the Agudath Israel, representative of Orthodox rabbinical refugees and their followers who had recently established themselves in the city, also operated on its own. They did not share the Mizrachi's vision of the role Orthodox Jews had to play in the restoration of their people to its ancient homeland. But they certainly were attuned to the tragedy unfolding in Europe and were deeply committed to saving remnants from the Nazis' hands.

As the nation's media center, New York was critical to American Jews for disseminating information and for molding sympathetic public opinion first about terrifying news about the Holocaust and then of compelling reports about the birth of the Jewish commonwealth. These efforts began with gaining space in the city's newspapers, its weekly and monthly magazines, and through its radio outlets. America's information capital published nine English-language dailies, from the popular tabloid the *Daily News*, with close to two million readers, to the "newspaper of record," the vaunted *New York Times*. Borough-based organs such as the *Brooklyn Eagle*, the *Long Island Press*, and the *Bronx Home News* had their own loyal subscribers. David Sarnoff's National Broadcasting Company (NBC)—the country's largest radio outlet, with twenty-five affiliates from coast to coast—operated out of Manhattan, as did its competitor the Columbia Broadcasting System (CBS). NBC's listeners tuned into its Blue Network for the most up-to-the-moment information. Entertainment was the medium on its Red channel. Scores of periodicals, from the news weeklies *Time* and *Newsweek* to the photojournals *Life* and *Look*, published out of the metropolis. Jewish media followed suit.

The city housed the all-important Jewish Telegraphic Agency at Park Avenue and Fortieth Street. It fed reports to the four Yiddish dailies and a myriad of journals and the Anglo-Jewish periodicals. Operatives of the Jewish Labor Committee, which before and during the war was one of the most aggressive Jewish organizations dedicated to "fight Fascism and Nazism" and "to prevent the spread of Fascist propaganda in America," did not have to go far to hear the most important reports. Its offices rented space in the *Forward* building on East Broadway, home of the most renowned Yiddish daily.[5]

The city, particularly Manhattan, also provided a prime venue for Jews to speak out publicly. Madison Square Garden became the ideal place for protest rallies with its approximately twenty thousand seats within the main arena and room for thousands more under its famous rotunda and out on to Eighth Avenue. There, in March 1938, the Jewish Labor Committee and the American Jewish Congress joined forces to brand "Hitlerism" as "the gravest menace to peace, civilization and democracy." At that mass meeting, the two groups renewed their pledge to keep the economic pressure on the Third Reich. They had been cooperating since 1935 in prosecuting, with the help of sympathetic longshoremen, a boycott of German products and services at the port of New York. In November 1938, in the aftermath of Kristallnacht, "more than 20,000 persons paid 25 and 40 cents each" to attend "a mass meeting that unified a varied group of organizations," Jewish and non-Jewish, the "majority of them from the side of the working class," to "protest Nazi outrages." The side streets were filled with thousands who listened through loudspeakers. At the podium, representatives of the World Zionist Organization and the Jewish People's Committee stood shoulder to shoulder with those from the American League for Peace and Democracy, the Transport Workers Union, and the International Labor Defense, among others who called for the end to persecutions. Two years later, in December 1940, after the Nazis had overrun all of western Europe, the Labor Committee and the Congress engineered another ecumenical gathering as Christian and Jewish leaders declared their opposition to both "Nazi terrorism and Soviet aggression." However, the Communist Jewish People's Committee would have no part of that pronouncement since the Hitler-Stalin pact was still in effect. In 1942, as rumors of the systematic destruction of European Jewry in the death camps filtered into the city, the Labor Committee, the Congress, and the B'nai B'rith gathered even more solemnly to decry the murderous onslaughts and to hear a message from

President Roosevelt, who promised that "the American people would hold the perpetrators of these crimes accountable on the day of reckoning."[6]

On March, 9, 1943, a week after the Congress packed the Garden for a "Stop Hitler Now" rally that beseeched FDR to rescue Jews remaining in Nazi clutches, the Emergency Committee to Save the Jewish People of Europe took over the arena. There they staged a dramatic, emotional pageant titled "We Will Never Die." For Revisionist Zionist leader Peter Bergson and his aggressive followers, this event, which was staged twice over successive days to sold-out audiences and with thousands more in the streets, represented the culmination of a yearlong media torrent designed to energize supporters to embarrass the American government into making saving European Jews a priority. Previously, the Emergency Committee had taken out full-page ads in the *Times* and elsewhere that proclaimed, "AT 50$ A PIECE GUARANTEED HUMAN BEINGS," pleading with the Allies to ransom Jews. Now, the Committee presented a cantata that Hollywood screenwriter Ben Hecht wrote and Broadway impresarios Moss Hart and Billy Rose directed and produced. In its most evocative moment, child actors dressed as shadowy shrouded figures representing the doomed called out "remember us" to a hushed gathering. After the recitation of the Kaddish, memorializing the dead, attendees filed out silently as if they were leaving a cemetery. After the pageant's New York opening, it carried its message nationwide to other venues, including the Hollywood Bowl in Los Angeles.[7]

The Garden provided a venue too for rallies of a very different sort, designed to send opposing messages to the American government and people. The most disturbing event, from a Jewish point of view, was the German-American Bund's February 1939 "Americanism" rally and "Washington's Birthday celebration." Through the visual pageantry of uniformed marchers carrying swastikas and the Stars and Stripes together to the podium, these American Nazis projected themselves as patriotic defenders of the United States. A crowd of twenty-two thousand heard group leader Fritz Kuhn recite a list of Jewish leaders who he said controlled America, its media, and its president, all part of the Jewish conspiracy, "the driving force of Communism" in the country.[8]

As an international political center, Midtown Manhattan was also the site of turning-point moments in the Zionist endeavor to secure international recognition and ultimate guarantees for the establishment of a Jewish state. In

May 1942, at a low point in the war, the Biltmore Hotel accommodated the Extraordinary Zionist Conference. There six hundred delegates from every American and world Zionist organization—with Wise in the chair and Chaim Weizmann, president of the World Zionist Organization, and David Ben-Gurion, in his role here as chairman of the Executive Committee of the Jewish Agency, eminences in attendance—demanded that "the gates of Palestine be opened." Three years had passed since the infamous British White Paper of 1939 limited Jewish immigration to Palestine. In anticipation of an Allied victory, which was then far from certain, the gathering proclaimed "that Palestine be established as a Jewish Commonwealth integrated in the structure of the new democratic world." At that moment, Zionism reached its full maturity as its advocates articulated their movement's ultimate goal of statehood. Less than a year later, in January 1943, as Allied armies made gains in North Africa, hundreds of delegates from virtually every Jewish organization in the United States descended on New York's Waldorf Astoria Hotel to attend the American Jewish Conference. There, by an overwhelming vote of 478–4, an almost unified American Jewish community agreed to prod its governmental officials and members of the international community to support a Jewish commonwealth in Palestine.[9]

Through all of these activities to rouse co-religionists and fellow citizens everywhere in the nation to Jewish suffering, the city's Jews were especially important. They were almost two million strong in number with the closest proximity to the scenes of action. They possessed the potential to fill the Garden, and perhaps to do much more, to prove that American Jews cared about the fate of European Jewry and the destiny of Jewish Palestine. In some cases, extraordinary measures were taken to emphasize how grave the situation was during the Holocaust. In January 1941, two Brooklyn Orthodox rabbis, emissaries of Agudath Israel's Rescue Committee, known as the Va'ad ha-Hatzala, drove around the wealthier sections of Flatbush on a Saturday to solicit badly needed funds. Their seeming violation of Sabbath strictures was understood correctly as far from a transgression. They were acting appropriately, within the spirit and letter of Jewish law, to save lives in a critical emergency. The sight of these pious Jews in their cars on the holy day made clear how desperate the situation was for their doomed brethren.[10]

In autumn 1942, a group of students at the Jewish Theological Seminary of America, shocked by public confirmation of the death camps and determined to do more than just attend Garden rallies, reached out to both synagogue- and churchgoers in the city and beyond. Under the auspices of their own European Committee, they organized, in February 1943, an Inter-Seminary Conference of Christian and Jewish Students. Meeting at the Seminary, these future leaders of many faith communities called on the United States to throw open the nation's doors to Jewish refugees who had successfully eluded the clutches of Hitler and to create temporary internment camps within the United States. The students' call for greater activism, published in *The Reconstructionist*, Rabbi Mordecai Kaplan's publication, spurred support by the Synagogue Council of America, an organization of rabbis and lay leaders of all Jewish movements. The Council called on some three thousand synagogues and Jewish schools nationwide to use the *Sefira* period, the weeks between Passover and Shavuot, days historically associated with Jewish tragedy, to observe special memorial days and partial fast periods, to raise additional funds for relief organizations, and to curtail "occasions of amusement" during this time of contemporary tragedy.[11] Subsequently, the European Committee called for a rabbinical march on Washington, a move that came to fruition in 1943 when five hundred Orthodox rabbis cried out on the steps of the Capitol.

Rabbi Baruch David Weitzmann, who took part in the Orthodox rabbis' march on Washington, acted on his own to issue a rabbinical ruling to his congregation effectively extending "*Sefira*-like" restrictions indefinitely. He determined, "because we have to feel the *tsa'ar* [pain] of the Jews who are being killed in Europe, there can be no festivities, no parties, no music." This edict even extended to weddings in his community. Throughout the ages, traditional Jews have not held weddings during *Sefira*. Now similarly in Weitzmann's shul in Brownsville, Brooklyn, "if someone wanted to get married, they came to [the rabbi's house]; there was a little *chuppah* [wedding ceremony], some cake and soda, nothing more; no celebrations, no dancing." Jewish life in America had to go on; there would be nuptials, but with none of the usual attendant gaiety. The rabbi decreed that "you cannot celebrate when other Jews are dying."[12]

On Washington's Birthday, 1943, the New York Jewish Education Committee conducted a "Children's Solemn Assembly of Sorrow and Protest." Some thirty-five hundred preteens, teenagers, their teachers and leaders from community Talmud Torahs, congregational schools, and religious Zionist day schools and youth movements descended on the New York City Center on Fifty-Fifth Street in Manhattan. Through a massive display of both grief and anger featuring children crying out about the calamities befalling their fellow Jewish youngsters in occupied Europe, melodramatic scenes, much like the Bergson group was to do in the Garden two weeks later, attempted not only to deepen the students' and their parents' awareness of the dimensions of the Holocaust but also to enlist the sympathies of all New Yorkers. The proceedings were broadcast live on WNYC radio, and the next day newspaper readers saw the participants' anguished faces. This New York protest model was replicated subsequently in Chicago, Boston, Detroit, Philadelphia, Cleveland, Detroit, and Rochester.[13]

Rabbi Joseph Lookstein of Yorkville's Kehilath Jeshurun, who presided at this impressive youth gathering, also determined to sensitize his congregants to the fate of European Jewry. In April 1943, at the traditional *Yizkor* (holiday memorial service) at the conclusion of Passover, he distributed "black ribbons" to his congregants, "who were asked to wear them during the period" of *Sefira*. Similarly, he called for increased contributions to the United Jewish Appeal—American Jewry's "Community Chest"—and directed his followers to recite special prayers at "the close of the main meal in every home." Passover 1943 was a particularly poignant moment because Jews in the Warsaw Ghetto had begun their courageous revolt against their Nazi oppressors. In May 1943, a "special meeting for prayer and intercession" brought more than five hundred Orthodox, Conservative, and Reform rabbis and over a thousand lay participants to his main sanctuary.[14]

Nonetheless, despite all of activists' efforts, they failed to enlist consistent widespread support. Even the trumpeted Garden events were occasional, less than a score of nights in seven years (1938–45). A key stumbling block to galvanizing continuous community engagement was the unbelievable details and extent of the atrocities. How else to explain, in light of what the Nazis were actually doing, publication of a whimsical mock article in the Yeshiva College student newspaper in February 1942? *Commentator* writers poked fun at their administration, as they always did on Purim, that joyous feast day that commemorates the saving of Jews from Haman, an ancient evil Persian prime minister. The headline read, "Adolf Hitler Was Once Teacher Here." The spoof continued with a report that "Professor Hitler was considered quite a man by many members of the faculty who tried to emulate him as best they could." For "Dr. A Litmus," it was said, "in many ways Adolf resembles my good friend Benny Spinoza," the seventeenth-century Jewish heretic. A year later, all too many students still ignored the unfolding Holocaust. In March 1943, student leaders publicly deplored those fellow schoolmates whom they critiqued for their "seemingly frightful indifference to the unparalleled plight of their people." Minimally, said these activists, letters should be written to elected officials calling on them to support rescue efforts.[15]

Retrospectively, alumni of the Jewish Theological Seminary of America "insist that despite reports most students did not really know about the mass murder until after the war." During the war, even their own president, Rabbi Louis Finkelstein, it has been said, "probably had not yet internalized the reality of the assault, . . . did not have a clear sense that European Jewry would not be able to reconstitute itself," and "misunderstood the reasons for the Nazi assault on the Jews, blaming it on Nazi animosity for the monotheistic idea." Finkelstein "neither responded to direct appeals to participate in protest actions . . . nor involved the Seminary in any public activity about the Holocaust." And this religious leader, his students, and their rank-and-file counterparts at Yeshiva College could be counted among the Jews of New York most deeply committed to their people's destiny. Moreover, they were living in the American and Jewish media capital.[16]

But then again, while the *New York Times* published during World War II some 1,147 stories about the destruction of European Jewry, basically "a story every other day on . . . the Holocaust," it never "presented the story of the persecution and extermination of the Jews in a way that highlighted its importance." Laurel Leff, who waded through *Times* articles that appeared during the 2,077 days of the European war, has determined that "what was happening to the Jews was never the lead story even when American troops liberated the Buchenwald and Dachau concentration camps." Accounts of the "discrimination, the deportation and ultimately the destruction of the Jews" appeared on the front page only twenty-four times and never "back to back . . . or over a span of a few days." Perhaps, more important, the leaders of this newspaper that was then deemed to be to "U.S. journalism . . . what Harvard is to U.S. education and the House of Morgan has been to U.S. finance" only "intermittently editorialized about the extermination" and rarely highlighted it in the "Week in Review" or magazine sections. In other words, with Holocaust stories "often no more than a couple of paragraphs long" and tucked away "on inside pages amid thirty or so other stories," all but the most acutely aware readers "would not necessarily focus on the stories because they were not presented in a way that told them they should."[17]

More than most New York Jews, Seminary and Yeshiva students may have accessed Jewish media reports that placed the Holocaust front and center. From the very start of the war in September 1939, the Jewish Telegraphic Agency fed verified reports and eyewitness testimony that was consistently picked up by Yiddish dailies and not long thereafter by the English-language Jewish press. Still, seemingly for most students, even for those with these terrifying reports in hand, there remained a gap between hearing and reading and believing and acting.[18]

Meanwhile, theological and political disagreements among New York–based Jewish organizations and leaders who clearly understood the dimensions of the Nazis' murders stymied unified communitywide efforts. While thousands of schoolchildren, including pupils at Religious Zionist schools, assembled at the City Center, those who attended the Brooklyn yeshivas did not. Their schools' leaders affiliated with the Va'ad ha-Hinuckh ha-Haredi (Council of Orthodox Jewish Schools) refused to cooperate in an event that included non-Orthodox and nonreligious Jewish schools. The organizers of the gathering harbored their own political prejudices. The Revisionists, whose political affect was always confrontational, were, early on, disinvited from participating, as they were deemed "embarrassing" to the organizers.[19]

Religious antipathies, likewise, undermined the May 24, 1943, interdenominational prayer meeting at Kehilath Jeshurun. It was the third venue considered by the Synagogue Council and its local supporting organization, the New York Board of Rabbis. Some members and officials at the West Side Institutional Synagogue and the Spanish-Portuguese Synagogue, sites originally considered, chafed at having "non-Orthodox rabbis" such as the Reform Wise or the Conservative Israel Goldstein address the gathering. They "would have preferred to have the convocation a purely Orthodox service." The Lower East Side–based Agudath ha-Rabbanim, solidly in league with the Agudath Israel, explicitly rejected participation. Just like the Va'ad ha-Hinuch ha-Haredi, an aligned organization, theological scruples prevented them from assenting "to the proclamation of the *Sefira* days as a period of mourning and to the summoning of a rabbinical convocation" if Reform and Conservative rabbis would be participating and sharing the pulpit with them.[20]

While these difficulties contributed much to uncertainty among New York's Jews about what they should or could do—and how, and with whom, to remonstrate—they knew for sure their obligations as loyal citizens. The United States demanded that they actively participate in the war effort, a commitment they enthusiastically assumed. As patriots, first and foremost, young men in the thousands signed up for the military, and some women joined the WAACs. Many more fellows responded affirmatively to their draft notices. In some families, volunteering created tensions between dedicated boys and their parents, who not only feared for their sons' safety, as all American mothers and fathers did, but who also had yet to overcome a Jewish historical repugnance to army service. How many of these elders knew of someone, if not themselves, who had fled to America to avoid the terrors of Tsarist conscription? But for this new generation of Jewish men, this was an entirely different army and a very different war. While most non-Jewish soldiers were motivated primarily to defeat the Japanese for their attack on Pearl Harbor, Jews in the barracks wanted to take on Hitler. On the most visceral level, they saw themselves fighting for their people and against Nazism, and doing so as real American men. It was also their opportunity to answer canards that American Jews were slackers during a national crisis. One Yeshiva College student felt precisely this way, disdained the opportunity to garner a divinity student deferment, and enlisted. He did so despite knowing with certainty that his act would distress his widowed mother. Ultimately, however, most parents with lumps in their throats and tears in their eyes accorded these decisions "controlled silence," even as perhaps they felt pride well up in their hearts.[21]

For some Jewish men who took up arms, the exigencies of the day trumped politics. One CCNY graduate, who as a left-leaning student in the late 1930s had taken the Oxford Oath, reneged on that pledge to take on a greater enemy than war: Nazism. Though he had a high draft-lottery number and an essential home-front job in the Army Signal Corps, he eventually forsook his potential exemption and was called up. Other, more doctrinaire former students, particularly the anti-Stalinist Trotskyists, who in the prewar years dominated their CCNY alcoves, bristled at these ready transformations. For the budding intellectual Irving Howe, the war was "the literal last convulsions of capitalist interminable warfare. . . . Both sides fight for the retention of their reactionary status quo." The ideologue wrote these and other words against FDR, Churchill, Hitler, and Stalin for the radical journal *Labor Action* under the pseudonym

L. Fahan, while serving as PFC Irving Horenstein, stationed for most of the duration in Alaska.[22]

Once in the army, Jewish soldiers, not unlike most GIs, received support from their families and communities. Publicists debate whether the owners of Katz's Delicatessen on the Lower East Side's Houston Street coined the ditty "send a salami to your boy in the army" when the Katzes' own three sons were in the service. Another version has it that Louie "the Waiter" Schwartz of the Sixth Avenue Deli came up with the idea. In any event, this ad capitalized on the desire of Jewish folks on the home front to take care of their own. The arrival of such packages also helped their boys cope with culinary difficulties on military posts. Army rations did not include kosher food, and pork was a popular source of daily protein. Eating ham was a cultural taboo even for many young men who were not particularly concerned about the regimens of the kosher laws.[23]

When Jews on the home front were not focusing on their own husbands, sons, or brothers, they took part enthusiastically in neighborhood war drives. They bought war bonds, gave blood, rolled bandages, collected scrap metals, organized block observances memorializing those who had fallen, and attended first-aid and civilian-defense activities. A rabbi who worked in Brownsville during the war has emotionally recalled that "when the stars started to twinkle in the windows, denoting children in service, and flags bearing the names of servicemen began to appear in the halls of every organization, those left behind (particularly the mothers) could not rest." They "left their homes to work for victory," rallying in the community's streets.[24]

Several local Jewish organizations used patriotic naming opportunities to fund-raise for America and to demonstrate to people around them how engaged they were in the war effort. In April 1943, five days after Treasury Secretary Henry W. Morgenthau called on all New Yorkers to "start digging down into their pockets" to raise billions for the war-bond drive, a chapter of the American Jewish Congress in the Parkchester section of the Bronx contributed its first $5,000 toward financing "a bomber bearing the name 'The American Jewish Congress.'" In the Syrian Jewish community of Bensonhurst, members of its Magen David congregation demonstrated their loyalty by raising $300,000 to name a two-engine B-25 Mitchell bomber that carried the name "Spirit of Magen David" into battle. Its community organ, the *Victory*

Bulletin, proudly exclaimed in October 1943, "This Is the Bomber Your Money Bought." Their achievement resulted from a yearlong campaign that began on the anniversary of Pearl Harbor in December 1942. Congregants were admonished, "With every American city, every American church and every American synagogue . . . planning some sort of observance on that day . . . don't you be the one person in our community who did not have the time to attend a rally during the all-out war." In 1943, the Yeshiva College Student War Council Committee, cooperating with the Metropolitan Inter-Collegiate War Council, linking students from many local colleges and universities, set off to raise $100,000 for an army ambulance plane to be called "The Spirit of Yeshiva College." The Committee did not quite meet that goal, but by 1945 it had raised $70,000 and had the satisfaction that it had solicited hundreds of pints of blood from students as part of its "Gallantry in Giving" program.[25]

Jews also challenged fellow Jewish neighbors to avoid any exploitation of wartime shortages. During Passover of 1943, peak season for kosher meat sales, "150 Bronx kosher poultry retailers" participated in a "selling strike" initiated "to force wholesalers into lower price levels." On an ongoing basis, butchers showed awareness of wartime needs by collecting cans of fat from their willing customers. Now they closed their stores for three days, and "prospective customers [who] appeared were advised to stay away" to force "wholesalers [to] sell at prices" in accord with the Office of Price Administration (OPA) regulations, which monitored rationing of consumer goods during the war. The members of the poultry dealers organization also picketed the stalls of two operators who refused to cooperate. Eventually, Bert Weiner of Lydig Avenue in the Pelham Parkway section of the Bronx submitted and "reduced his prices and closed shop." Jack Glicker, who worked a few doors over also on Lydig, "kept open but reduced his prices."[26]

The local regional director of the OPA, with the assent of Mayor La Guardia, did his utmost that Passover to provide feasting Jews with as much meat as was legally possible to relieve what was called hyperbolically "a near famine . . . said to affect 1,600 of the 4,000 kosher butcher shops in the city." Not that observant Jews of New York requested special consideration. In the fall of 1942, Rabbi Israel Goldstein, president of the Synagogue Council, made clear that "under present circumstances, . . . when nationally ordered, . . . indispensable and immediately essential Jewish personnel" were permitted to "work on holy days in aircraft war production." To his way of thinking, such laborers resembled Jewish soldiers on the front lines in defense of the country who were excused from—if not commanded to dispense with—Sabbath and holiday work restrictions.[27]

Among New York's Jewish neighborhoods, Brooklyn's Syrian community actively threw its support for its young men and women in uniform and demonstrated unwavering patriotism. Their proud fund-raising for a bomber in Magen David's name represented one type of mobilization. As a closely knit community, Syrian Jews sought anxiously to keep tabs on their soldiers, exalting in their courage and relieving any homesickness. Under the leadership of a remarkable women's group, the Girls' Junior League, the *Victory Bulletin* was created, and they led efforts to maintain lines of communication with the estimated one thousand of their boys, and some girls, in military service both stateside and overseas. Many of these young women discovered the transforming effect of their activism, perhaps "equal in impact to that of the boys who went off to fight a global war." These activists broke out of longstanding and passive female roles and assumed leadership positions to a degree previously unseen within this traditional Jewish community.[28]

The activists did much to galvanize community support for their soldiers. Every issue of the monthly *Victory Bulletin* contained a "Roll of Honor" of combatants, and subscribers were implored to write to their heroes. Upon receiving the newsletter, service members who were posted far away also read comforting accounts of local communal activities, including street gossip. In August 1942, a Syrian Jewish GI stationed in Fort Jackson, South Carolina, wrote back, "Receiving the *Victory Bulletins* . . . has really pepped me up quite a bit not only for the news and gossip about our community but because it proves that our community is an American community doing all it can for us." If he read the bulletin, three months later, in November 1943, soldier Joseph A. Cohen likewise would have been gratified to be informed about Esther Levy, who "decided to make good use of her idle hours" and "organized eight children . . . into a scrap-collecting Junior Commando group."[29]

From the *Victory Bulletin* editorial desk, Girls' Junior League leaders, speaking to readers in Bensonhurst, reminded them of their ongoing obligations as patriotic Americans to show unquestioning support for the war effort. There was no place among them, as there was no room in the Bronx among those Jewish butchers and their customers, for exploiters. "A consumer on the home front who patronizes the black market," they declared, "is in effect helping the Axis. Any mother, father or friend of a man in uniform, who hoards one can, one suit or one anything (except War Bonds) is in effect stabbing that soldier in the back." Through all the twists and turns in the priorities and conduct of the war, the *Victory Bulletin* expressed only total support for FDR and his administration. The president was lauded as "literally the only man in public life in whom the whole nation can confide leadership. Thank your lucky stars that the United States has a Franklin Delano Roosevelt." When it came to controversial war policies, such as when and where to open a "second front," an allied invasion from western Europe to complement the Soviet Union's titanic struggle with the Nazis from the east, the *Victory Bulletin* instructed its readers to write to Roosevelt and tell him, "I am behind you in your efforts. . . . I am willing to sacrifice and do anything that is asked of me to help win this war." Similarly, any American who questioned Washington's war objectives, who, for example, "attempt[ed] to obscure the essential truths of the war" (i.e., total, unconditional victory), was deemed a "pettifogger," borrowing the White House's term. So conditioned, in the one article that during the war explicitly discussed the verified reports about the destruction of Jews under Hitler, the *Victory Bulletin* aimed no criticism at FDR or his subordinates. But it did pillory the Red Cross for its failure to "utilize their financial resources and power to their utmost." And it called on the Allied nations "to threaten a terrible vengeance should such a crime"—the murder of an estimated four million additional Jews—"be perpetrated." The *Bulletin* contended in March 1943, sounding much like the United States' own war officials, that there was only "one sure way of averting this tragedy and at the same time insuring a speedy victory." That strategic second front had to be opened. The *Victory Bulletin* did not call for extraordinary measures to rescue doomed Jews.[30]

The Syrian community's unwavering support for the president paralleled the sentiments of most New York Jews. Although Peter Bergson's group of Palestinian Jewish activists and American supporters relentlessly criticized the administration, they were an outspoken minority. Most American Jewish leaders, beginning with Congress president Stephen S. Wise, trusted FDR, as did many New York Jews. Indeed, a pervasive street tradition of belief, if not love, for Roosevelt flourished among them. When the president died, Wise eulogized him as "a beloved and immortal figure" who "felt the misery of the Jewish people in Europe" with "compassion" and with a "resolute will if possible to bring them healing and redress."[31]

New York Jews had joined FDR's bandwagon in the late 1920s, helping to elect him governor of their state. During this decade, American Jews entered the Democratic political column en masse and became loyal members of an emerging urban coalition of minorities that backed candidates who favored social welfare legislation. Many of them saw their politics as congruent with normative, American ways of acting. They continued to support policies championed by neighborhood Socialists for several generations without casting votes for a minority, radical party. Most Jews remained with the Democrats for the rest of the twentieth century. Support for FDR spiked even more after New Deal legislation became a reality. Roosevelt appointed unprecedented numbers of Jews to high administrative offices, further increasing support. Jews commended his courage in choosing financier Bernard Baruch, political adviser Samuel Rosenman, and Treasury Secretary Henry Morgenthau, among others, especially since their presence provided grist to anti-Semites who charged that "Jew Deal" operatives controlled Washington. By the early 1930s, even many longtime committed Socialists lined up with FDR. Abraham Cahan's appeal to his comrades to "give up their theories and back Roosevelt's specific polices" resonated in the streets and at the ballot boxes. And beginning in 1936, those who refused to vote the Tammany party ticket could support Roosevelt on the American Labor Party line. New York labor leaders David Dubinsky and Alex Rose, in consultation with Labor Secretary Frances Perkins, established this so-called Jewish third party to garner moderate left-wing backing for the administration. By the 1944 election, the ALP captured within one heavily Jewish Bronx neighborhood some 40 percent of the vote. The ALP contributed a substantial component of the 90 percent of New York Jewish votes for FDR. Only the most hard-boiled Socialists and doctrinaire Communists, as well as a staunch minority of Republicans, stood apart from this Jewish political alliance with the White House.[32]

Yet wartime anxieties as both Americans and as Jews did not erase desires to live as normally as possible under the circumstances. These trying concerns —worries about family, fear over what was really happening to Jews in Europe, struggles to cope with consumer deprivations, demonstrations of their loyalty to America, and eagerness to trust the administration—coexisted with mundane daily realities. In extraordinary times, New York Jews also lived ordinary lives. Jews of Parkchester displayed a mixed set of priorities, balancing wartime concerns with local community needs. In 1940, before the United States entered the war, some who contributed to Morgenthau's government loan campaign also endeavored to create a new congregation in this section of the Bronx, the Young Israel of Parkchester. Although there were already at least three synagogues nearby, two that were Orthodox and one Conservative, the Young Israel's founders felt the need for "a social center in Parkchester in a refined Jewish environment where . . . young men and women, boys and girls, and small children too, can find a source of recreation and relaxation as well as spiritual and cultural development." To make the congregation's social and religious objectives better known, in September 1940, after five months of "ardent activity," the group sponsored a "Dutch Supper and Card Party." To celebrate its first anniversary, in April of that year, organizers held a "Mah Jong and Card Party." Successful in its initial efforts to gain neighborhood traction, in November 1941, the synagogue acquired its first permanent home on White Plains Road, on the outskirts of a large apartment-house development.[33]

Less than a month later, when America entered the war, these Parkchester Jews embraced the patriotic mood along with their neighbors. Two days after Pearl Harbor, board members decided to call off their planned New Years Eve Affair at the Hotel Capitol both because of "bad outward appearance of a gala affair in these times of emergency" and as "precaution for air-raid." They also recognized, "Wardens may be asked to serve that evening and a number of our members are wardens." Their decision was facilitated by the information that "the Hotel may refund" their deposit and by their acknowledgment that "from a practical side, hardly any tickets ha[d] been sold." That same New Year's morning, January 1, 1942, the congregation heeded FDR's proclamation of a "day of prayer" for the nation. In June 1942, sixteen members volunteered to assist the USO in its "house-to-house-canvass," ringing bells on every floor of the Parkchester project's apartment houses, requesting donations. Similarly, the synagogue took part in the United Victory Committee of Parkchester and participated in 1942 in a communitywide United Nations Victory rally at the local public school. Like the Syrians in Brooklyn, these Parkchester Jews did their utmost to keep in contact with their valiant boys and girls in uniform. The War Work Committee wrote personal letters to GIs not only informing them of local gossip but also reporting excitedly about war-bond sales achievements. The Committee forwarded election ballots, reminding service members to "take advantage of this privilege." The young men and women in uniform were constantly asked to write back to their "anxious" community. At war's end, in 1945, the congregation reviewed its "war effort" and proudly reported that its "first concern [to] help the war effort" had led to selling more than $75,000 in war bonds.[34]

But notwithstanding these efforts to be part of a patriotic American community, on balance, this religious group focused primarily on building their congregation as "the happiest Jewish community in New York." When in 1942 the synagogue's financial secretary contacted members who had "not been attending . . . meetings," he emphasized the need in Parkchester for "a militant Jewish group." But for him, militancy meant people "dedicated to [their] faith in a true community spirit." He specified, "We need a model synagogue, a Talmud Torah, a social center, a club house for the men and a meeting place for the women. Our young boys and girls want dances, handicraft, ping pong, etc." This local social militancy did not translate into Jewish political involvement. Although the shul's newsletter spoke of its desire to keep informed of events beyond Parkchester's border, there was but one terse and statistically inaccurate mention, in December 1945—six months after V-E Day—of the calamity that had befallen European Jewry. In an article titled "Did You Know That . . . ," mention was made that "over 1,300,000 Jews fought in the armies of the United Nations. *Four million Jews* were murdered in Europe during the Nazi siege." And throughout the war, there was no call for Young Israelites to leave the neighborhood to participate in rescue protests and projects of any sort.[35]

Comparable sets of concerns about the community's soldiers, the war front, and the progress of institutional life also characterized a sister congregation on the Lower East Side. At the Young Israel of Manhattan on East Broadway, home of that movement's first affiliate, the dual page 1 headlines of its January 1942 bulletin announced the congregation's organizing a "defense unit" and reported on the success of its "30th Anniversary Dinner reunion." When it came to "sale of bonds and stamps" and first-aid and knitting classes, the bulletin crowed that the "name of 'Young Israel' is synonymous with that of 'Young America' and it is to the interests of all Americans to 'keep 'em rolling' as well as flying." With religious concerns at heart, the monthly proudly printed two letters from servicemen who were successfully navigating military experience while retaining a strict fidelity to Orthodoxy. One navy man wrote back from Charleston, South Carolina, reporting, "Thus far, I haven't eaten any *trefus* [unkosher foods] and I haven't missed a single day of *davening* [praying] or putting on *tefillin* [phylacteries], no matter whether I was on a train, a truck, camp, tent or barracks." He prayed that such remain his fate: "in keeping up with my past orthodox habits."[36]

During the war years, the Young Israel's organ, *Viewpoint*, reported to its predominantly Bronx, Lower Manhattan, and Brooklyn readers about Nazi atrocities primarily within a column called "Recent News of Jewish Interest." However, the horrific stories were intermingled among other items of a very different moment. In November 1941, a report about pogroms in Lithuania in which four thousand Jews were killed in Kovno, Vilna, and Shavli was mixed into a long column that spoke also of the relief that New York police were according Sabbath-observing merchants hurt by blue laws. The *Viewpoint* only rarely headlined the destruction of European Jewry. In October 1942, it deviated from its usual pattern to inform readers, under the headline "Death over Europe," about the seven hundred thousand Jews starved to death in Warsaw. It detailed as well the doomed who were marched off to their deaths in the Belzec death camp. Perhaps the editors surmised that their readership was current about the ongoing devastation from the Yiddish press's stories and from other Jewish media.[37]

In June 1943, the president of the National Council of Young Israel, J. David Delman, submitted a thirty-two-page annual report to delegates at their convention at the Pine View Hotel in Fallsburg, New York. The lead item, the group's "war effort," occupied a full eleven pages of his activity summary. Delman particularly enthused over two soldiers and one sailor who had written to him about conducting services for their fellow Jewish comrades. The Young Israel president had far less to say about and was decidedly downbeat in discussing organizational support for "emergency committees like the Vaad Hahatzalah [*sic*] to movements for the building of Eretz Yisroel, and particularly to two recently-organized communal endeavors, . . . the Vaad L'Pekuach Nefesh, and the American Jewish Conference." This Vaad Pekuach Nefesh, he explained, was an Orthodox group dedicated to "rendering all possible financial and diplomatic aid on behalf of thousands of Jews in Germany and in German-occupied countries who have not yet succumbed to the fate of the more than two million Jews who have been cruelly slaughtered."

These remarks were subsumed, however, within a long paragraph item titled "Young Israel in Its Relationship to the Jewish Community." The group's rescue activities mostly entailed "preparing certain memoranda to be presented to officers of the State Department and to members of the House of Representatives and the Senate." While Delman promised, "Our attempts at rescue will not cease until something definite materializes," he acknowledged with frustration, "The trend of events in the war has made action along these lines extremely difficult. We have seen . . . how ineffectual many of our petitions have been."[38]

Delman did not mention the Council's motivating its members, most of whom were New Yorkers, to turn out en masse for Wise's or Bergson's protest meetings. In fact, only once, in February 1943, did the *Viewpoint* even note that one such rally was in the offing. Then among its "Council Jottings" feature, it observed that "'action not pity' is the slogan of the committee"—most likely the Bergson group—"sponsoring a rally at Madison Square Garden. . . . The purpose is to further the campaign for a Jewish army."[39]

If anything, Delman had his own personal problems with the tenor of street demonstrations, even with the 1943 Orthodox rabbis' march on Washington. Subsequent to this emotional outpouring by leaders whose religious authority he revered, Delman wrote in his monthly "President's Column," "It is true that many of our greatest Orthodox rabbis participated, . . . but yet we feel that in a great measure this incident is yet another sign of chaos in Jewish community life in this country." He noted, "The rabbinical group, acting independently, decided upon this march [after] three different delegations [had] already been to Washington and [had] spoken to our highest authorities." And although "when so many lives are at stake, no stone should be left unturned in the attempt at rescue," still, he said, "we honestly feel . . . that the method chosen in this instance was not the proper or dignified one." As he saw it, "Washington has enough turmoil at the moment without the confusion caused by a mass march on the White House." He felt "certain that President Roosevelt and Vice-President Wallace would have received a delegation of five or six rabbis, . . . even if they were not backed by 500 or a thousand additional rabbis on the spot." Delman "prefer[red] that the world understand" that in their demands, they were "not represented by individuals or individual groups who act at will."[40]

The ambiguities of communal life—the mixed priorities of commitment to weighty Jewish rescue concerns and addressing the realities of an American war while attempting to maintain institutional equilibrium—appeared as well at Congregation Kehilath Jeshurun. There, as noted, on Passover 1943, Joseph Lookstein impassionedly summoned his congregants to wear black arm bands and to pray daily for the salvation of European Jewry. It is not known how many men and women in the pews heeded his call. Nor do we know if any of those so deeply moved turned out for major city-based rallies. Congregational organs did not tell them to mark their calendars and show up. However, there is one indication that his message did not sink into the hearts of many of those who heard him. Two years after his outcry, Lookstein publicly upbraided his flock for its tardiness in responding to his Passover 1945 appeal on behalf of the Va'ad ha-Hatzala, "the one organization that is effecting the rescue through heroic underground methods." He was deeply chagrined that his call was "very disappointing in its results": "Only $1,400 have been raised out of the badly needed $5,000." The rabbi minced no words when he observed, "Delay at a time like this is hazardous. Neglect is sinful."[41]

What is certain about life at Kehilath Jeshurun during the war is that its rabbi's pleas and reminders of Jewish exigencies did not cast a mournful pall on synagogue life. Its for-men-only "Annual Smoker" of January 1944 went off as scheduled. The assembled enjoyed "smokes, drinks, refreshments" and heard "a three man team" of "famous radio funsters." The next night, couples attended "a sellout" theater party at the Alvin Theatre on Broadway. Such events, not to mention the congregation's annual dinner and Purim and Chanukah parties, followed emphases its synagogue president articulated back in 1941. As the congregation made plans to celebrate its seventieth anniversary, Max J. Etra asserted, "Our common prayer should be that neither personal sorrow nor universal hardship may mar our proposed celebration and that it may be observed amidst a world enjoying the blessings of peace."[42]

Although the Agudath ha-Rabbanim never accused its followers of complacency, in February 1945, weeks before Lookstein unburdened himself, it requested of the faithful to seriously contemplate how well they were performing as "their near and dear ones fell victims in the gas chambers through the brutality of the enemy." In declaring Wednesday, March 14th, "as a Fast day for Jewry throughout the world," the sponsoring body of the Va'ad ha-Hatzala called on Jews, "Gather in our places of worship to meditate and to search our hearts and souls" to ascertain "whether we have fulfilled the great responsibility to our unfortunate brethren." Specifically, the rabbis asked, "Did [we do] enough to save those who pleaded to us? . . . Did we give maximum support to organizations such as their Emergency Committee?" Beyond "seek[ing] our God and implor[ing] his forgiveness," the "Rabbinate call[ed] upon all members of the Jewish race to give the traditional 'Tithe' or ten percent of their income . . . for work of rescue, relief and rehabilitation."[43]

During World War II, Sylvia and Jack Goldberg harbored no strong Jewish organizational ties. Perhaps the story of what concerned them and how they coped, more than the saga of activists and of those with conflicting communal priorities, ultimately exemplified the quintessential New York Jewish home-front narrative. Residing on the outskirts of Parkchester, their local religious involvement consisted of Jack's accompanying his wife's stepfather on the High Holidays to one of the older Orthodox synagogues in the neighborhood. In thinking about those days more than half a century later, Sylvia insisted, "We had absolutely no idea [about the Holocaust]. The press did not write about it and we read the papers every day." Nor were they aware of Wise's or of Bergson's public efforts. Their issue during the war was not even the war effort, although they surely were patriotic. Rather, they wanted Sylvia to live a normal life raising their infant child, Linda May, while Jack, drafted in 1943, served in England and then in France and Germany with the Third Army. He did not see his daughter until he was discharged in 1945.[44]

Fortunately, Sylvia lived with her doting mother. More important, she participated in an informal support circle of eight Jewish couples from the neighborhood who helped each other out. In addition to keeping daily tabs on each other while three of the husbands were in the service, they met, as they had done before the war, on a monthly basis at each other's homes. Their friendship had blossomed in the 1930s on the handball courts of the Castle Hill Pool, a blue-collar Jewish swim and sports club. Many of the men and women had competed there against one of the greatest star Jewish athletes of the time, "Hammerin'" Hank Greenberg, the future Hall of Famer first baseman for the Detroit Tigers. Jackie Goldberg, who also was a fine athlete, alleged, years later, that Greenberg was a "bit of a klutz" (uncoordinated player) when he was still a Bronx boy. Yet they, like most American Jews, were proud that Greenberg, a guy from the neighborhood, had stood up strongly for his faith, when he absented himself from an important game in the 1934 pennant race because the matchup against the New York Yankees took place on Yom Kippur. (Thirty-one years later, in 1965, another transplanted New York Jewish athlete—this time a fellow from Brooklyn named Sandy Koufax—sat out the first game of the World Series because it took place, likewise, on the holiest day of the Jewish year, to the acclaim of both Jews and Gentiles alike. But then again, the L.A. Dodger hurler played during an era of much greater tolerance toward Jews and their holidays than did Greenberg.)[45]

Beyond the home gatherings, the Castle Hill Pool couples occasionally repaired to the Catskills for a weekend of rest and recreation. It helped them to cope with their daily cares and floating anxieties about their loved ones at war. They obtained a group discount by calling themselves "The Sylvia Goldberg Association," since she made the reservations. Sylvia paid her bill because she lived rent-free in her parents' apartment and received an army family stipend. Sylvia recalled that despite wartime shortages, "times were not bad, . . . much better than the Depression." Then she had been the prime breadwinner, working as an office manager in a textile firm, while Jack struggled from "job to job" before finally securing a forty-dollar-a-week position in the post office. Comfortable in this upstate bucolic Jewish space, as they ate to their hearts' content from a Borscht Belt menu, they put their cares behind them. At least temporarily, they did not worry about the fate of their loved ones in uniform. One of the Goldbergs' friends was fully conscious of how they had found personal normalcy during these extenuating times. She took as a souvenir a dinner menu from the hotel that listed a mélange of Jewish delicacies and wrote a comment that found its way into a family picture album. It read, "Would you believe this is war time?"

After the war, activists in New York focused on achieving Zionist demands articulated at the Biltmore and American Jewish Conferences for the establishment of an independent Jewish commonwealth in Palestine. The first priority was to secure and sustain the American public's and its governmental officials' support for the cause. The American Zionist Emergency Council, energized after the American Jewish Conference and headquartered within the nation's media capital, took the lead in highlighting Palestinian Jewish aspirations, denigrating British opposition and linking these issues to the now commonly recognized dimensions of the horrors that had befallen European Jewry. From this metropolitan base, the Council reached out and organized hundreds of local emergency groups all over the country. It enlisted sympathetic Christian groups and together advocated with national and local political parties for resolutions calling for Jewish statehood. It also squelched any oppositional voices among American Jews. Though the Council had some internal ideological and tactical disputes, it integrated both the American wing of the Jewish Agency and the Bergsonite Revisionist Zionists. One barometer of their successful propaganda was that from 1945 to 1948, "twice as many —and later three times as many—Americans sympathized with the Jews as with the Arabs."[46]

As Palestine convulsed with violence, with the British mandate unraveling and Jewish and Arab forces battling for territorial control against each other and against the British, American activists sought to arm Zionist fighters with funds and weapons. The wealth of the city's Jewish population and its location as the foremost East Coast port made it the prime venue for fund-raising and surreptitious paramilitary operations. Far less unity of purpose and conduct existed in this work because militant groups often skirted American laws. American friends of the Haganah found ways to ship weapons and materiel to troops loyal to the Jewish Agency and future prime minister Ben-Gurion. U.S. backers of the Irgun, the Revisionist Zionist strike forces, did their utmost to support these irregulars loyal to Menachem Begin.

Both groups canvassed Jewish neighborhoods to solicit funds. The Revisionists used a "Fighting Zion" sound truck to belt out their message, and when the sound died down, they appealed to passersby to drop their dollars and cents into their charity baskets. These activists also took their message to the Catskills Jewish hotel region to induce those on vacation to donate their monies to the cause. A particularly striking event was a third Passover seder held in April 1948 at Manhattan's Paramount Restaurant, where for fifteen dollars those interested could participate in a "freedom seder."[47]

In 1946, Haganah operatives fashioned an "Institute" that held weekly briefings on developments in the Middle East for New York Jewish businessmen, first at the Hotel Astor and then at the McAlpin Hotel. The waiters who set up the buffets before retiring thought these gatherings little more than standard men-only luncheons where entrepreneurs could make their deals "without the distractions of their wives, relaxing among men they could feel were their equals." In fact, after receiving their insider updates, participants were not only asked to contribute their own monies but also were cajoled to become fund-raising leaders in their fields. The Institute recruited "key men in industries previously untapped, dairy products, radio, sewing machines, advertising." Those who desired to do more "arranged bank credit, office and warehouse space, meetings with ship brokers, . . . or they transferred funds through their own accounts." In direct competition with Bergson's American League for a Free Palestine, the Institute also established its own Americans for Haganah. This advocacy group "rounded up celebrities and held its own mass meetings."[48]

In providing Jewish fighters with weaponry desperately needed to hold off their enemies, both American Haganah and Irgun supporters violated the U.S. embargo. They manufactured or purchased all sorts of military materiel from former War Assets Administration stockpiles and then smuggled arms to the Middle East. The road to Haifa began at the docks and warehouses of New York, with its 771 miles of water frontage and two hundred piers. To ease their way through this maze of laboring humanity, each of the pro-Palestinian groups formed alliances with longshoremen and their bosses. Both payoffs and appeals to Irish dockworkers, who harbored their own anti-British feelings, brought results.[49]

Eager for support irrespective of its sources, Revisionists welcomed the help of some unconventional contributors to their efforts. At one point in their campaign, the Manhattan office of the American League was surprised and pleased to receive a check for $25,000 from crime boss Meyer Lansky. (There is also a story that Ben "Bugsy" Siegel, Lansky's colleague in crime, once volunteered to "bump off" Ernest Bevin—an opponent of the Zionist cause—when the British foreign minister visited the United States in 1947. The Jewish Agency quickly dispatched the young Conservative rabbi, and future major American Jewish religious thinker, Arthur Hertzberg to Los Angeles to talk Siegel down.) Reportedly, when Lansky turned philanthropic, it was not the first time the New York–born mobster showed some strong Jewish colors. In the 1930s, elements of Murder Inc., Lansky's so-called commandos, had broken up German-American Bund rallies in Yorkville in Manhattan, Ridgewood in Queens, and Staten Island and extended their fight to Hoboken and Bergen County, New Jersey. To Lansky's great chagrin, he later recounted that he received no credit from respectable Jewish leaders for his stand. "They wanted the Nazis taken care of but were afraid to do the job themselves. I did it for them. And when it was over they called me a gangster. No one ever called me a gangster until Rabbi [Stephen S.] Wise and the Jewish leaders called me."[50]

Now more than ever before, rank-and-file New York Jews unabashedly identified with their people's heroic aspirations. Formal affiliation with the Zionist movement peaked between 1945 and 1948. Local Jews could be accounted as a major component among the more than seven hundred thousand who enrolled in Zionist organizations in America, compared to less than four hundred thousand at the end of the war and well under one hundred thousand before 1941. For many new members, "interest in Zionism [took] on a greater sense of urgency during those years." It offered partial consolation for what Jews had lost during the Holocaust. It answered the frustrating problem of the hundreds of thousands of displaced persons still adrift and suffering in Europe. America's gates remained largely closed to survivors and refugees. These mixed emotions of trauma and triumph, tragic memories and immediate concerns, swirled around the reported twenty thousand ticket holders who on May 16, 1948, packed Madison Square Garden and the fifty-five thousand others who stood out in the rain during New York's inaugural "Salute to Israel" rally. They were moved beyond words when they heard the Hatikvah, the Israeli national anthem, sung; they responded with a heartfelt "Amen" to the traditional Jewish blessing of thanksgiving to God for having "kept us alive and having brought us to this day." They also rejoiced in proclamations of support for Israel that emanated from a range of government officials who called for an end to the arms embargo to help Israel survive and for the quick admittance of the Jewish state to the United Nations. They left the Garden that night understanding, as more than one Jewish leader emphasized, that they had witnessed "the culmination of 2,000 years of exile and anguish for the Jewish people."[51]

While these cathartic crescendos energized many within New York's Jewish community, the early postwar years were also, on a mundane level, a time for personal readjustment and planning. Like millions of their fellow Americans, a generation of Jews who had been veterans of Depression and war began a quest for stability in their lives for themselves and their future children. They sought a place in the sun within a changing and expanding U.S. economy and society. Often that meant migration to new suburban locales. But to do so required their leaving the world and culture of the metropolis behind them. This decision proved to be quite challenging.

"For the First Time in Queens . . . at Fashionable Forest Hills . . . Elegance Comes of Age," real estate ad for Parker Towers. (*New York Times*, April 12, 1959)

CHAPTER 4

Élan of a Jewish City

Jewish GI Eddie Zwern grew up on the Grand Concourse, but World War II found him stationed briefly in California en route to the Pacific theater. Zwern discovered a new land of promise in a sun-bathed milieu far removed from the harsh New York winters of his youth. He vowed to return should he survive military service. Upon discharge, true to his word, he hustled back to the Golden State. His wife, Pauline, soon followed, and quickly they became boosters of life in Los Angeles, a city bursting with economic opportunities for ambitious entrepreneurs. Although the couple initially settled in a modest furnished apartment, they also knew that Eddie could take advantage of the benefits of the Servicemen's Readjustment Act of 1944, which assisted former soldiers to purchase homes. Six months after making his move, Eddie reappeared on the old Bronx streets to settle up with his former landlord. Proud of his risky decision, he talked up the bounties of a new and better life three thousand miles away. The young couple's word-of-mouth up and down Fordham Road sparked a chain migration. When relatives subsequently came "out to visit, next thing you know, they're making plans. You'd come out in January, and you'd leave snow-filled streets of New York." Eddie and Pauline proudly claimed that they enticed more than 250 fellow Jews to L.A. Still, it took a measure of boldness to strike out for this new locale. Migrants were bidding farewell to their comfortable Jewish neighborhoods. To mitigate homesickness, some of these erstwhile New Yorkers, acting in classic migrant fashion, created social societies to ease adjustment to the foreign culture around them. Los Angeles may have been part of the United States, but it felt strange and different. So CCNY and public high school alumni associations sprung up in Los Angeles and also in Miami, the other popular Sunbelt destination for Jews. Eventually, the Amerks, Dolph Schayes's old group, reassembled in Florida and retold tales of the Bronx, even if their most famous member chose to live out his life in snowy Syracuse, New York. Dolph and Naomi Schayes would reconnect with his friends on their trips down south.[1]

Tastes and smells of the old neighborhood also nurtured connections among displaced New York migrants. In L.A., the owners of Lax's Delicatessen on Hollywood Boulevard and Joseph's Delicatessen in western Hollywood knew that there was something distinctive about the Jewish delicatessen that those from back east still relished. Catering to their customers' wishes and memories, they advertised their restaurants as featuring "choice Eastern delicacies." Longtime Angelinos also flocked to this New York contribution to local culinary diversity. Eating in the deli became a ritual: "Jews could celebrate being at the forefront of popular culture and yet also eat the foods they loved from childhood."[2]

However, on balance, most Jews chose suburbia, a more modest move within commuting distance to the city and not far from their parents' urban neighborhoods. The suburbs of Nassau and Suffolk Counties on Long Island and Westchester County north of the city, characterized in 1959 as "bedroom boroughs," beckoned New York Jews: 329,000 Jews settled in Nassau County, more than a quarter of its population. Levittown, situated just twenty-five miles east of Manhattan, was the best-known community. With government assistance, through the GI Bill or with a Federal Housing Authority loan, young couples purchased a Cape Cod–style house for $7,900 or a ranch for $9,500 in "the largest housing development ever put up by a single builder."[3]

Across the Hudson River in New Jersey within Bergen County, Jews found new homes in townships such as Englewood, Fair Lawn, Teaneck, and Fort Lee. One local rabbi discussed why Jews moved to his community in Fair Lawn —though he was unquestionably speaking for other places as well—explaining that those "who take up residence in the suburbs . . . were seeking a more wholesome environment for their children." Many had "chosen to move to a suburban community primarily because friends and relatives, who preceded them, recommended suburban living"—another instance of chain migration.[4]

For a few suburban-seeking Jews, the welcome wagon stopped short when they approached the Westchester community of Bronxville. In a distant replay of the 1920s era of residential anti-Semitism, local residents perpetuated into the early 1960s a social covenant that dated back generations to keep their town free of those who "may have different views on religion." Jews were "unwelcome, except as visitors or customers." But where most New York Jews sought to sink their roots, they were quietly tolerated.[5]

Acceptance, however, posed new social threats to Jewish suburbanites. Although many New York Jews established strong, informal relationships with each other within these suburban developments, they did not congregate, as they once had, in tightly knit Jewish neighborhoods. Their worlds were no longer totally Jewish, particularly since they now perceived their non-Jewish neighbors as friends and not as enemies. They wondered how they could still express to their children, in an agreeable way, a sense of Jewish difference from those with whom they lived. One 1950s parent, writing from his home in a village in mid-Westchester, articulated his family dilemmas: "Somehow," he wrote, "we do not worry so much in the city about the problem of children's identifying themselves with the Jewish community." Thinking back on his own youth in the city, he continued, "On the street, in the school, among their friends—and even in the home—they found out who they are and what it means." But "when your street, counting both sides, has twenty houses, twenty families and only one other than your own child is Jewish, you wonder and worry."[6]

Such apprehensions, fear of loss of Jewish street ties and connections, caused tens of thousands of other New York Jews, no less able economically to make the break to suburbia, to think twice about migration. They ultimately stayed within the city's limits, but they moved to new neighborhoods. As a perceptive Jewish social scientist explained, even if in "the mass-produced Levittown-type suburbs . . . their neighbors were still close by, . . . on the other hand, there were no hallways, or lobbies, as in apartment houses, for chance meetings, no elevators for quick exchanges of gossip and news, no corner luncheonettes for ready sociability," in short, "no street life to speak of." Jews, who still "look[ed] for urban virtues" and suffered "a real deprivation . . . of the Jewish urban scene," considered the elegant and convenient sections of Queens, sometimes referred to by real estate promoters as "suburbs," as an ideal destination. Between 1940 and 1950, Queens' Jewish population jumped from 115,000 to 223,000. In the succeeding seven years, 1950–57, it almost doubled again. By that decade's end, 100,000 more Jews lived in Queens than in Manhattan. As of 1950, in some neighborhoods, such as Rego Park and newer sections of Forest Hills, Jews

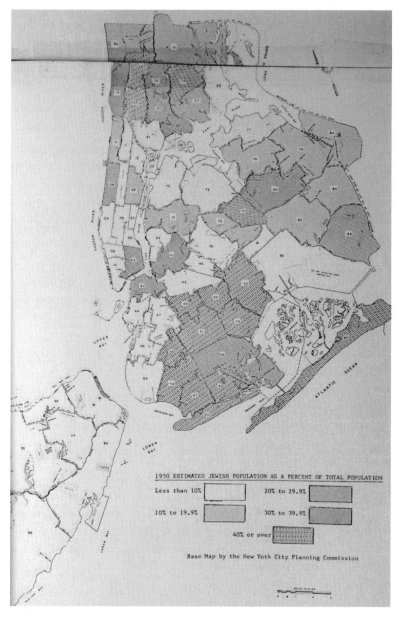

1950 ESTIMATED JEWISH POPULATION AS A PERCENT OF TOTAL POPULATION

Less than 10%

10% to 19.9%

20% to 29.9%

30% to 39.9%

40% or over

Base Map by the New York City Planning Commission

Map of New York City showing the population distribution of Jews. (From C. Morris Horowitz and Lawrence J. Kaplan, *The Jewish Population of the New York Area, 1900–1975* [New York: Federation of Jewish Philanthropies, 1959]; reproduced with permission from United Jewish Appeal–Federation of Jewish Philanthropies of New York, Inc.)

constituted more than 40 percent of the total residents. Seven years later, Jewish density increased: two out of three residents were Jews. Meanwhile, by the end of the 1950s, similar proportions of Jewish residents characterized Bayside, Whitestone, and Hillcrest, as well as within Douglaston, Little Neck, and Bellerose, situated on the very end of the city line.[7]

Reminiscent of the earlier interwar period, real estate operators, many of them Jews, played a crucial role in building these new urban landscapes. Queens Boulevard joined "the great boulevards of Brooklyn [and] the Bronx" as "essentially 'Jewish' avenues, built by Jewish developers for a Jewish clientele." As early as 1942, the *New York Times* reported on "suburban apartments which provide open-air balconies or terraces . . . and garage spaces for tenants' automobiles," not only on Long Island but within Queens. Owners Herbert Kronish and Harold V. Kalikow took particular pride in the "Normandy" on Queens Boulevard, Forest Hills, "near the Continental Avenue [subway] station." This six-story structure, for 130 families, boasted beyond the balconies and parking spots, "suites . . . in size from two to five and a half rooms" with the "land around the building . . . beautified with gardens and lawns." Concomitantly, work was almost complete at Flushing's Murray Hill Terrace Apartments, "built about a central garden court below which will be a tenant garage, being constructed for use as an air raid shelter."[8]

In 1947, builder Max Levine boasted that his Parkmore Realty Corporation set a "postwar record" in completing a six-story elevator apartment house in only four months. Financed in part from sale of his DeWitt Homes in the Bronx, Levine and his associates constructed the Rhoda House (probably named for his wife) on Booth Street in Forest Hills. Each of the forty-two apartments was outfitted with "new postwar household appliances, such as refrigerators and modern kitchen ranges." Builders lured well-heeled migrants to Queens with residential improvements comparable to "luxury-type apartments on Park Avenue" without paying Manhattan prices. In 1948, Sam Minskoff and Sons conceived of just this type of attractive option for some two hundred families at their Park Crest Terrace, a "multi-family development" at Booth Avenue, in Forest Hills. Close by, the developers of the Parker Towers on Yellowstone Boulevard pitched their enterprise in the mid-1950s as offering "many improvements used in luxury type apartments on Park Avenue" and other elite neighborhoods in Manhattan, but with only a brief subway ride "to the office, the Fifth Avenue shops, the theatre." When the development was completed in 1962, they described their "three luxurious 21 story skyscrapers" as "an entire suburb within a suburb" but without the hassle of commuting. Sagaciously, they capitalized on the prime flaw of suburban life, the daily trek of breadwinners to work in the city. Parker Towers, located just "16 minutes from midtown," evoked "the distinguished tradition of East End Avenue, Sutton Place, Beekman Place," highly coveted addresses in Manhattan. It advertised "78% of the land given over to landscaped private grounds, malls, fountains!" —accoutrements reminiscent of locales outside of the metropolis. All apartments possessed "unobstructed views, . . . covered balcony terraces, . . . Westinghouse air conditioning," and "uniformed doormen."[9] Residents "marked their upward passage by moving from elevator buildings to so-called 'luxury apartments.'"[10] Each item—balconies, views, air-conditioning, and uniformed doormen—signaled status within reach of middle-class Jews, much as elevators, windows in every room, light, and air promised modern American living for aspiring immigrants and their children in the 1920s.

If Jewish builder Jack Parker sought to attract the most affluent customers to his sections of Forest Hills, the Muss family built on their Jewish family tradition, dating to the 1920s, of constructing small, affordable homes in other sections of Queens for working- and lower-middle-class people. In the years before the Depression, immigrant Isaac Muss and his sons Charles, Alex, and David had constructed Independence Homes in Bayside, a community of approximately fifteen hundred six-room, three-bedroom houses. After falling on hard times in the 1930s, the family reentered the industry in 1947 with one hundred modest two-family homes in Bayside. Two years later, they put an additional four-hundred single-family units on the market in Whitestone and College Point, Queens. Looking to suburbia simultaneously, in 1952 they opened a 360-unit garden-apartment complex in White Plains.[11]

A decade later, in the early 1960s, the LeFrak family built extensive construction projects in Rego Park for, as advertised, "the masses not the classes." They, too, drew on a heritage dating to the early years of the century, when immigrant father, Aaron, and his son, Harry, focused on housing for working-class Jews, first on the Lower East Side and then in Brooklyn. Their most ambitious early effort was the construction of "small houses and walk-up apartment buildings" on De Kalb Avenue in Brooklyn. After the war, the family, now headed by Harry and his son Samuel, shifted their attention to Queens, starting off in 1951 with a 136-family complex named the Colorado, on Yellowstone Boulevard. With the rise of LeFrak City—construction began in 1960 and concluded by decade's end—the family acquired a reputation of "giving the people what they wanted, at a price that they could afford to pay." Monthly rents of "$40 a room or $120 for a one-bedroom apartment" provided tenants with "total facilities for total living," which included shopping, tennis, and swimming, amenities reminiscent of suburban locales.[12]

While the growth of Queens did not halt a Jewish march to suburbia, by the early 1960s, the city's dynamism and the borough's attractions and convenience to work actually lured back some families who had tried suburban living. In 1962, a group of families, who had once lived in inner-city apartments, rattled off for a reporter why they "had given up their own homes" in places like North Plainview or Oceanside or Bethpage on Long Island "to move into six-story apartment houses" in Queens. They spoke of "convenience, more relaxation, transportation problems, inadequate facilities for teenagers and loneliness." The Rabinowitzes explained, "Suburbia was fine while our children were growing up, it turned to a nightmare when they reached their teens. There just wasn't any place for them to go unless they had their own cars." The Joel family, late of Bethpage, said it was their sense of loss of the best of city life that had moved them "back home." They complained that for eleven years they "had to forego attending the theatre" in Manhattan.[13]

Nonetheless, the neighborhood culture of Jewish Queens, characterized in 1955 as a "midway point" between "the Big City and suburbia," was still not the Bronx or Brooklyn. Jewish identification did not radiate as naturally from these streets. In a section such as Hillcrest, Jews, mostly business people, "manufacturers and wholesalers, . . . a number of lawyers, physicians," lived in suburban-like homes, "neat rows, each exactly the same distance from the sidewalk, with little space between, looking very much alike," but "only a five minute ride to the last station on the Independent Subway" line. For many families who "came from Brooklyn and the Bronx" with concerns about group persistence, "settling . . . involved a new adventure in Jewishness, expressing itself in formal affiliation, for the first time in their lives, with a Jewish community institution." Like those in suburbia, Hillcrest Jews lived in a tolerant environment, where they watched a strengthening of social ties between their children and their Christian friends. Anxiety that "the kids marry properly" (i.e., with other Jews) lurked in the back of many parents' minds. Concerned adults trusted in a burgeoning Hillcrest Jewish Center to entertain their children. They hoped that rather than congregating with a mixed crowd "at the neighborhood movies or ice-cream parlor, hanging out on the corner or even in the basement playrooms of one another's homes," Jewish boys and girls would gravitate to the Center. Borrowing a page from Mordecai Kaplan's book, Rabbi Israel Moshowitz strategized, "If we can get the young people here for one reason, the dances and the sports, they'll start coming for religious reasons as well." A sympathetic reporter thought in 1955 that his game plan was gaining traction. "On Friday nights and Saturday mornings," the rabbi noted proudly, "several hundred persons usually are present. At these times, the services include Bar and Bas Mitzvahs, of which there are almost always three or four." He carefully avoided activities in the sanctuary or elsewhere on the premises that smacked in any way of "the store *cheders* of the Bronx and Brooklyn," venues that so many congregants had stayed away from as youths.[14]

Increased synagogue affiliation, growing out of a search for sustained group conviviality, also characterized postwar experiences of Jews in Forest Hills, although many of these residents experienced the intimate ambiences of apartment-house life. That neighborhood's foremost touchstone institution, the Forest Hills Jewish Center, dated to the 1920s, when Jews, then a small minority, kept a low social profile. The Center's heyday began right after World War II, with the emergence of Forest Hills as a distinctively Jewish area. Still, a residue of "unfriendly and biased attitude[s]" endured among non-Jewish neighbors. In response, Rabbi Ben Zion Bokser expanded the Center, between 1949 and 1952, to include a commodious sanctuary, an auditorium for social activities, and a youth center. Some thirty social clubs and basketball, swimming, and boxing leagues attracted almost seven hundred children to its Hebrew school, with many bar and bat mitzvahs every week.[15]

While Conservative congregations relied on a synagogue-center model to reach youth, Orthodox Jews in Queens addressed identity issues less through their synagogues than through an emphasis on modern day schools. These differed from the elementary yeshivas and day schools of the interwar period. In 1937, the day school movement moved beyond its core constituency of parents committed to Jewish identification and largely bound to traditional religious observance. With the opening in Manhattan's Yorkville section of the Ramaz School, concerted efforts recruited youngsters from families that were not particularly concerned with rigorous ritual performance. Ramaz convinced them of the value of daily separatism, which was explicit in attending even the most upscale Jewish parochial school. One of the impressions that had to be over-come was that notwithstanding the bounties of Jewish knowledge and iden-tification offered, in the end such institutions left their charges socially and culturally disadvantaged.[16]

Four years later, the Yeshiva of Central Queens brought this type of Jew-ish education to Queens. Samuel Spar recruited six youngsters from observant families, starting with his son, to a fledgling school situated at Rabbi Solo-mon Gordon's Talmud Torah Mishkan Israel synagogue. The school offered a modern religious Zionist orientation similar to that of Shulamith School or Flatbush Yeshivah of Brooklyn. The school grew slowly, and by 1948, when it acquired its own building on 150th Street in Jamaica, it had seven grade lev-els. Initially, the yeshiva relied to a great extent on the enrollment of children of Orthodox refugees from Hitlerism or survivors of the Holocaust who had settled in Queens. Soon they were joined by pupils from "non-Orthodox" homes or from families that were once quite observant but were no longer so inclined. In 1954, principal Rabbi Bernard (Baruch) Charny told a Jewish magazine correspondent, who happened to be a school parent, that "most of the children in his institution came from homes of young parents, between thirty and forty, who are not particularly religious or observant." Charny also publicly allowed that the "majority of students" hailed not from Orthodox but "from Conservative congregations." The Jewish religious diversity at the Ye-shiva of Central Queens spurred the founding in 1953 of the Yeshiva Dov Revel in Forest Hills, which attracted a larger percentage of its pupils from observant Orthodox homes. Four years later, "with classes from the nursery through the eighth grade," Dov Revel enrolled some 450 students, who came "from all types of neighborhoods in Queens."[17]

The religious heterogeneity created tensions within the Yeshiva of Central Queens. The school day opened with recitation of morning prayers from the siddur, the Orthodox prayer book; grace was recited after meals; boys wore yarmulkes and tsisith. However, Conservative families objected strenuously when in the late 1950s the school administration "introduced segregation of the sexes . . . not only in the class room, but also in the dining room and play-ground." Temporarily, "the resistance of the parents was so great" that it led to the abandoning "of the policy of segregation in the school." Ultimately, those who "desire[d] a more liberal approach to Jewish education" determined that they had to have a school of their own. Guided by Rabbi Bokser of the Forest

Hills Jewish Center, whose son had been a student in Central Queens, they established the Solomon Schechter Day School of Queens in 1957, "under the sponsorship of nine Conservative congregations in the area."[18]

Bokser sought to provide his movement with "an important reservoir of intensively educated men and women who will become the informed Jewish lay leaders, the teachers, the rabbis and scholars of the future." He reaffirmed that the "strength of Conservative Judaism has been the Synagogue Center," and he asserted, "The afternoon religious school will remain our basic educational agency for the great majority of children." But he placed his ultimate faith—just like the Orthodox—in "the development of the vital field of Jewish education which the day school represents." Subsequently, Conservative day schools all over the country turned to this New York Jewish educational initiative as a model.[19]

As postwar migrants to Queens adjusted to new conditions and identity concerns, the textures of Jewish life did not change in the Bronx. These Jews saw no reason to leave their neighborhoods. It is true that some of the neighborhoods were getting older and were somewhat run-down, but memoirists reflected warmly on continuities in lifestyle and street culture. For Ruth Glazer, who in 1949 was doing research and editorial work for the Amalgamated Clothing Workers Union, there was "more life, vigor and excitement in one single Bronx apartment house at six o'clock in the evening than in a thousand elm-lined Main Streets on a Fourth of July." She described the West Bronx as a "community whose residents seem occupied full time in discovering the wonderful things produced in the world that can be had for even the moderate amount of money at their disposal." Like those who rhapsodized in the 1920s about all that was right in their neighborhood, Glazer wondered "what streets anywhere can match them in their sheer number of food stores, ice-cream parlors, delicatessens, restaurants, specialty shops for women and children." In these venues, neighbors enjoyed sociability. In the butcher shops, "a leisurely, almost club-like atmosphere" flourished among women, especially on Thursday mornings, when Sabbath shopping began. "Then the butcher holds court, announcing his opinions on the world, commenting on departing customers." Just as in the past, "the role of the Concourse in Bronx life, like its geographical location is central." While "its once aristocratic buildings have become shabby and it no longer has its former prestige," still "it is a name to conjure with." For "at one end of the Concourse there is a small but intricate park, complete with bandstand and Sunday afternoon concerts." And "there is the middle section where one may see and can be seen." Ultimately, for Glazer, "the present generation is only the continuator and the embellisher of the Bronx style. It does not revolt against the given. It does not seek for new modes of expressions in its domestic arrangements." Glazer concluded, "The younger generation . . . has not exhausted the present pattern."[20]

Writer Vivian Gornick evoked similar streets scenes within the West Bronx. Everywhere she turned there "was Jewishness in all its rich variety. Down the street were Orthodox Jews, up the street were Zionists, in the middle of the street were shtetl, get-rich-quick Jews, European humanist Jews." She did not stop to reflect on how committed these segments of the community were to each of these expressions. In any event, "Jewishness was the leveler." Gornick recalled that "observance" was looking at other Jews on the avenue on Passover and Yom Kippur. "The whole world shut down, everyone was dressed immaculately and a sense of awe thickened the very air we breathed; the organic quality of the atmosphere told us who we were; gave us boundary and idiomatic reference, shaped the face of the culture in which each one of us assumed a vital albeit, primitive sense of identity." When Gornick was ready for college, she followed the generation that preceded her to CCNY. The college became fully coeducational in 1951. She took the standard oath of allegiance: "For us, it was City College or nothing." And "on the surface," attending City, as it had been for thousands before her, was hardly a journey away from the "working class immigrant neighborhood in New York City" where she was born. "You still used the subways, still walked the familiar city streets between classes, still ate in grubby luncheonettes, returned to the old neighborhood each night, talked continuously to your high school friends on the block who had not gone on to college, felt the steady flow of the city's current running through the dailiness of your life." But Gornick refused to assume the occupation after college that her parents had envisioned for her. As an English major, she dreamed of becoming much more than just a teacher. The Jewish aspiration, "my daughter, the teacher," seemed to Gornick's mother appropriate for "a girl child sent to school."[21]

Gornick's Bronx contemporary Ralph Lauren (né Lifshitz) spent his class time daydreaming at CCNY's night school about his own distinctive career path, a vocation for which there was no training offered within the business school's curriculum. While still a high school student at Clinton, where he publicly fantasized in his senior yearbook that his life's goal was to become a "millionaire," the future fashion designer already aspired to dress like one. He haunted Paul Stuart and Brooks Brothers, among the most upscale haberdashery stores in the city, sampling suits, jackets, ties, and other accessories traditionally fit for the British aristocracy. Finding the styles wanting, he began to sketch his own clothing lines. At age twenty, he dropped out of CCNY to pursue his ambition, catching on initially as a salesman at Brooks Brothers and later at A. Rivetz and Co., another stylish menswear establishment. In 1964, his "professional touch" attracted initial media attention. The *Daily News Record* wrote enthusiastically about his corduroy riding pants, suits, and double-breasted jackets. Though it took several more years before Lauren earned his first million, he was heading up and away from his Bronx origins.[22]

Unlike Gornick and Lauren, most Jewish students at the "proletarian Harvard" saw their alma mater as an accepted vehicle for achieving more than their working-class parents had. In 1962–63, five years after Gornick graduated and three years after Lauren dropped out, Jews still predominated at CCNY. They made up almost 60 percent of the twenty-nine thousand total enrollees, even if New York Jewish children of "middle class rank" increasingly chose "education away from home." They matriculated either in the moderately priced, growing state university system or in private institutions that once discriminated against Jews. NYU was still the city's second-largest Jewish school, with its sixteen thousand Jewish students uptown and downtown, 40 percent of the forty-thousand-member student body. Columbia enrolled some sixty-five hundred Jews, 25 percent of its undergraduates.[23]

In 1960, *Fortune* magazine featured this palpable sense of calm and continuity among Jews and within their longstanding neighborhoods. Noting the "Jewish élan" in New York that still contributed "mightily to the city's dramatic character—its excitement, its originality, its stridency, its unexpectedness"—the article emphasized a "condition of non-crisis" among postwar Jews, "occupying as they frequently do in a residential area or in an industry, a majority position and exercising such wide influence." Persistence was visible almost everywhere. The Grand Concourse remained "the only place in the world where . . . you can pick up a girl by whistling a Beethoven quartet at her." Within that "main artery" of the Bronx, Jews constituted 48 percent of the population, within "a solidly middle-class society," comfortably "inhabiting large old-fashioned apartments in large, old-fashioned buildings."[24]

Focusing on stability within that middle-class enclave, the article did not note comparable residential continuity within the longstanding co-ops. They had moved solidly into their second generation, despite the anti-Communism of Cold War America. Some vociferous, if ultimately passive, Jewish Communists still held forth on Bronx Park East, "arguing the fine points of Marxism" on park benches across the street from the buildings on Barker Avenue. But others still deeply committed to the cause did more than just talk. In 1953, they mobilized to save two of their own through the National Committee to Secure Justice in the [Ethel and Julius] Rosenberg Case, even if advocacy marginalized these radicals from other New York Jews. Most New York Jews, and especially major Jewish organizations, distanced themselves from the Rosenbergs and their defenders. "Opposition to Communism [became] a criterion of Jewish communal membership," at a time when the Anti-Defamation League of B'nai B'rith willingly shared its documents on Communists with the House Un-American Activities Committee. In fact, in this city of many Jewish voices and opinions, some Jews even celebrated at a block party on the night of the Rosenbergs' execution for conspiracy to commit treason. In Bensonhurst, Jews sitting among their Italian friends, as a television set "faced the sidewalk so all could watch the live broadcast from Sing Sing prison," felt a palpable sense of relief as "they put aside the painful case that separated them from their neighbors" and had threatened the good name of American Jewry. Watching as closely as anyone this "Jew against Jew" dynamic while sitting in the jury box—as the judge, the prosecutor, the defendants, and their lawyer were all Jews—the foreman, a Gentile, observed, "I felt good that this was a strictly Jewish show. It wasn't the Christians hanging the Jews." And if dedicated radicals, long after the executions, continued to revere the Rosenbergs as "icons, big-eyed, tragic victims," other erstwhile Jewish Communists in this highly charged political atmosphere, intimidated by the wide scope of McCarthyism, lowered their profiles. At that point, the Bronx Park East co-op library, "which already had a remarkable collection of radical books, . . . found itself with sudden donations from people who did not feel safe with a collection of Lenin's works in the apartment." Indeed, many "coopniks," from oldsters who "remained factory workers" to the younger breed, "teachers or lawyers or operators of small businesses," became "Democratic voters" not unlike Jews raised "in the apartment house of a capitalist landlord in Brooklyn."[25]

At the same time, new building construction added depth to Jewish neighborhoods. In the late 1940s and early 1950s, the Van Cortlandt section of the Bronx welcomed two large-scale, high-rise additions to its Amalgamated co-op section. Government aid and union activism reminiscent of the scene in the 1920s spurred co-op construction. Builders willing to put up with "the annoyances and hazards of bureaucratic FHA [Federal Housing Administration] supervision" were assured a "builder's profit" on their investments. Workers in search of affordable housing relied on the United Housing Federation headed by Abraham E. Kazin, "a former garment union employee who [had] lived and breathed cooperative housing for the last 32 years," since the start of the co-op program in 1927. The Federation was "ostensibly . . . a clearing house" for "labor unions, neighborhood associations, fraternal organizations and other nonprofit groups interested in developing middle-income co-ops." Endeavors such as these received an additional boost in 1955 when the New York State Limited Profit Housing Company Act, better known as the Mitchell-Lama law, was passed providing for "forty per-cent tax abatement on city-approved middle-income co-ops or limited dividend rental projects." Jews as builders and residents took advantage of these new regulations and helped their city maintain its reputation as "the unrivaled co-op housing capital of the nation."[26]

Occupationally, *Fortune* found that while citywide Jews were approximately one-quarter of the population, they made up "45 percent of the proprietors and managerial category and 33 percent of the professional and semi-professional categories." An additional 15 percent worked as civil servants, ranging in occupations from teachers to minor city officials, such as clerks in municipal departments, and including police officers and firefighters. The "enterprising garment industry" continued to carry a Jewish stamp, even if fewer Jews were involved in making clothing on Seventh Avenue. "Merchandising of products, . . . retailing," was part of the "Jewish élan in the principal class merchandising streets of the city," from Fifth Avenue department stores to Fifty-Seventh Street specialty shops to cut-rate operations on Union Square. "In high fashion, most of the city's leading designers [were] Jewish." It did not take an overabundance of capital to gets one's start as an entrepreneur, just a modicum or courage and/or gall (i.e., *chutzpah*). Jews had those requisites. Social critic Daniel Bell mused in 1961 that it was still possible to survive and advance through "ingenuity, 'shmearing,' cutting a corner, trimming a margin, finding some other way to make a fast buck in the swift race."[27]

At that point, Bell surely had heard neither of the young Ralph Lauren nor of Calvin Klein, who attended the same Bronx elementary school as Lauren. But a combination of talent and cutthroat business aggressiveness applied to their entrepreneurial initiatives. Unlike Lauren, Klein aspired to design women's clothing. His maternal grandmother, a seamstress and later an owner of a notions store in the Bronx, was his role model. Predictably, the young man's unconventional occupational desires did not play well on Mosholu Parkway streets among neighborhood boys who thought of becoming doctors, lawyers, or civil servants. His effeminate mannerisms also did not garner much in the way of street credits, though his homosexuality was fully closeted, a common lifestyle choice for gay men in the 1950s–1960s. Klein abandoned his neighborhood, at least by day, when he enrolled in the High School of Industrial Arts in Manhattan and subsequently matriculated at the Fashion Institute of Technology on the Lower West Side. Each evening, however, he endured catcalls that he was a student at the "Fairy" Institute of Technology. While often restless, Klein developed a more sophisticated appreciation of styles, fabrics, and colors that helped him in his future career.

Upon graduation, Klein hooked up with the Millstein outfit, one of the top "cloak and suit houses" in the fashion district of Seventh Avenue. After two unsatisfying and financially unrewarding years, he moved on to the even more prestigious Halldon Ltd. There he met another former Millstein employee, a patternmaker, Abe Morenstein. They temporarily joined forces. According to Klein's biographer, Morenstein shared Klein's ambition of creating his own firm but had been deterred by his sense that "his thick Polish-Jewish accent and lack of cosmopolitan air would defeat him in the image conscious marketplace." Calvin Klein "was the perfect front man." Neither man had sufficient capital, however, to fulfill their dreams. So Klein returned to the Bronx. He turned to a Jewish boyhood friend, a supermarket owner who had given him part-time work when he started out with the penurious Millsteins. With Barry Schwartz's money, Morenstein and Klein established an unofficial partnership. In return for Schwartz's backing, he desired a large piece of the enterprise. In 1967, Calvin Klein incorporated Calvin Klein Ltd. with Schwartz as a 50 percent "silent partner." He cut Morenstein out, a move not unprecedented in the highly competitive world of Seventh Avenue. Less than a year later, Schwartz became far more than a disengaged investor. When his Sundial Supermarket in Harlem was ransacked in the riots following the murder of Dr. Martin Luther

King Jr., Schwartz directed his energies to the Jewish garment industry. Ten years later, both men were annually drawing salaries in excess of $4 million.[28]

Jews made their presence felt throughout the city's cultural worlds. They owned or managed "perhaps a third of the city's art galleries"; Jewish "owners, producers, playwrights and actors" kept Broadway booming. One proud New York Jew asserted that "the city could still be intrigued by the flavor of the East Side when recaptured by playwrights, novelists, and musicians." He considered it ironic that while "immigrant parents and Jewish garment workers have almost vanished from real life, sentimental portraits of their idiosyncrasies and relations with American-born children and grandchildren have become more common." What he dubbed "matzo-ball soup operas" achieved Broadway success, with a dozen plays reaching the Great White Way in the late 1950s and early 1960s. "American-born Jewish audiences and large numbers of non-Jews too" had "made these productions great successes."[29]

Perhaps Paddy Chayevsky's *The Tenth Man*, which from 1959 to 1961 ran on Broadway, with more than six hundred shows, resonated most with Jewish audiences. Many connected and mused knowingly about the premise of this updated version of the "dybbuk" story, a staple of the Yiddish theaters that either they or their parents had attended years earlier on Second Avenue. The direct linkage between downtown and Broadway existed through casting Jacob Ben-Ami, long a star of the Yiddish Art Theatre. In Chayevsky's modern incarnation of the folk drama, a demon invades the soul of a young woman who lives in Mineola, Long Island, and must be exorcised. A tenth man to fulfill the quorum for prayer has to be found within this suburban community. That mystical religious quest provides the Bronx-born Chayevsky with an opportunity to sympathetically contrast the values of old-timers in that congregation—characters drawn from men he knew in the old neighborhood—with the vacuous and materialistic attitudes of younger members of the synagogue and their "go-getter" rabbi. "This conflict between older, devout Jews and a younger generation in whom faith has grown dim," as one critic described the play's ultimate theme, portrayed suburban versus urban Jewish ways of looking at life.[30]

Jews continued as leaders in radio and the growing television industry. But they were far more than just owners. Through these media, Jewish actors in shows on Jewish themes both entertained and educated Americans coast to coast about Jewish social life. The most popular of these, the *Goldbergs*, starred

Gertrude Berg as the irrepressible Molly Goldberg. The television version, which premiered in 1949, represented the third incarnation of this saga of an immigrant Jewish family making their way in New York City, adjusting to the promises and challenges of America. The radio series began in 1929 with the Goldberg family already settled in their East Tremont apartment home in the Bronx. Often scripted discussing upcoming major Jewish holidays, they acquainted listeners with some of the basic rituals and customs of Judaism. Several times, the television show placed the Goldbergs in a synagogue on Yom Kippur, treating viewers "to an elaborate liturgical service." In 1948 and 1949, a Broadway production, *Me and Molly*, flashed audiences back to 1919, with Molly assisting her husband to establish himself in the garment industry. The packed houses saw how perceptively and perspicaciously she hit on the idea of producing half-size dresses "for neighbors with the same problem she had." Viewers of the television treatment went back to 1038 East Tremont Avenue, where they immediately grasped the informal community life still part of the Jewish Bronx. Every episode opened with Molly rolling down her kitchen window and unselfconsciously calling out her hello ("Yoo hoo, Mrs. Bloom!") to her neighborhood friend. In 1954, toward the end of the show's run, the Goldbergs moved to suburbia, at the behest of apprehensive network executives who wanted the series to be more reflective of the emerging American scene. The Goldbergs moved to Haverville—as in "have it all." Still, in those episodes, the newly arrived family addressed, in its own comedic way, one of the weighty dilemmas of the decision to leave the city. One student of the show's approach has explained that "inherent in the *Goldbergs*" is the idea "that even though a family has moved to the suburbs, it's still possible to have good neighbors and be a cohesive family." That medium's message was a "reassuring" one "for a recently-mobile populace anxious about the advantages of moving to the suburbs and breaking ties with extended family members."[31]

In New York City, an ongoing nexus existed between Jewish business spirit and Jews' willingness to consume culture. One leading sociologist emphasized that "large symphony orchestras, the theatres, trade-book publishing, the avant-garde magazines, the market for drawings and paintings, all have as their principal audience and consumer, the Jewish middle-class." This was made possible largely by "the entrepreneurial wealth of small-unit firms."[32]

From dress circle seats at Carnegie Hall—and as of September 1962, also at Lincoln Center—Jewish subscription holders not only enjoyed the New York

Philharmonic's performances, but they also took pride in its Jewish conductor and music director. Professional promises and opportunities had drawn the Boston-bred Leonard Bernstein, son of Russian-Jewish immigrants, to the metropolis. When in 1943, the Harvard University and Curtis Institute of Music maestro ascended the stage and tapped his baton for his inaugural concert at Carnegie, as a last minute substitute for the ailing renowned German Bruno Walter, newspapers noted that this was the first time an American-born conductor had reached such an august position. Bernstein represented an American Jewish success story. He brought to the Philharmonic's performances dynamism and even an athleticism that captivated audiences. One local newspaper wag who reported on Bernstein's surprise first appearance depicted it in competitive sports terms as "a shoestring catch in center field: . . . make it and you're a hero, muff it you're a dope. . . . He made it." The morning after his opening triumph, glowing reports reached the front page in several New York newspapers. Years later, Burton Bernstein, looking back on his brother's achievements, suggested that Leonard's elevation to music director in 1958 was "a watershed moment in American history, . . . [a] singular cultural, sociological event," comparable—as he saw it—to Jackie Robinson's joining the Brooklyn Dodgers eleven years earlier. Hyperbole aside, it was a signal moment not only in his life but also in the city's cultural history.[33]

While Bernstein's philharmonic concerts consistently thrilled New York regulars, from his start he played to national audiences. A longstanding New York Philharmonic radio network hookup broadcast his inaugural concert, and many subsequent performances were heard across the country. In the 1950s, he turned to television to reach audiences. At a time when critics of the tube, such as Federal Communications Commission chairman Newton N. Minow, characterized the medium as a "vast wasteland," Bernstein frequently contributed to the best television had to offer. For close to a decade, Bernstein used the ninety-minute award-winning *Omnibus* series not only to present his music but also to instruct his viewers about the nuances of classical music. Beginning in 1958, the New York–based teacher turned to educating the nation's children through the first of fifty-three Young People's Concerts, live from Carnegie Hall. Adult viewers, wherever they lived, brought their youngsters close to the set and closer to high culture; together they watched Bernstein patiently explain to enraptured New York children "What Is a Concerto" or "Humor in Music" or "The Sound of an Orchestra." In time, the series was broadcast to twenty-nine countries, a major New York contribution to the world of the performing arts. In turn, this American cultural mecca made Bernstein "a household name even to people who only dreamed of visiting the city, who never set foot in a concert hall or went to a production on the Great White Way."[34]

Like so many immigrants, Bernstein, the New York newcomer, gave much back to his adopted city. On Broadway, this multitalented composer entertained his public with depictions of the metropolis's postwar promises. In 1944, he collaborated with writers and lyricists Betty Comden and Adolph Green and choreographer Jerome Robbins, three other children of Jewish immigrants in the midst of establishing distinguished careers in the performing arts, to stage *On the Town*. The musical celebrated the excitement, vitality, and opportunities of New York through the adventures of three sailors who careen through the city during their twenty-four-hour shore leave. Though the play ends on a serious note, since the young men have to return to war duty, audiences remembered from the production that opened on December 28, 1944 —at a time when Americans were intensely focused on the Allies' breakout of the Battle of the Bulge—that New York was "a helluva town with the Bronx up and the Battery down, with people rid[ing] in a hole in the ground." That image of a "fun, . . . gay" city that "takes neither itself nor the world too seriously" ran for over four hundred performances on Broadway. In 1949, *On the Town* found its way to the Hollywood screen and reminded a national audience how dynamic was New York City.[35]

However, Bernstein recognized that prejudice tarnished New York's promises. In 1957, he collaborated again with Robbins and two other New York Jews, playwright Arthur Laurents and a newcomer, lyricist Stephen Sondheim, in producing *West Side Story*. Through a retelling of Shakespeare's *Romeo and Juliet* in contemporary New York ethnic terms, the four men tried to raise public consciousness about the blight of youth gang warfare in the city, tinged with racial overtones. In its original iteration as *East Side Story*, it focused on the conflict between a Catholic and a Jewish family on the Lower East Side, with anti-Semitism directed at a Jewish gang by the Italian American "Jets" as a central theme. However, the initial collaborators, Bernstein, Robbins, and especially Laurents, ultimately felt that such tensions had already been portrayed theatrically. Laurents noted in his memoir that as early as the 1920s a long-running Broadway show, *Abie's Irish Rose*, had dealt with family tensions over a Catholic-Jewish intermarriage. The prescient Bernstein considered racial more than religious tensions as the future problem. He referenced news-paper reports of the late 1940s to the mid-1950s about marauding youth gangs on the West Side and in L.A.'s barrios, to emphasize the need for "an out and out plea for racial tolerance." The play's protagonists thus became a Puerto Ri-can young woman and her ultimately doomed Italian boyfriend, victims of senseless animosities. That warning about New York's present and future ran on Broadway for over seven hundred performances. In 1961, a movie version of *West Side Story* appeared. Ironically, it was filmed on location in a tough working-class West Side neighborhood just before its tenements were torn down to make way for Lincoln Center, where Bernstein would long be the consummate star attraction.[36]

Notwithstanding suburban migration, the first two decades after the war witnessed much continuity between generations of New York Jews. Ensconced in their old Bronx neighborhoods or living in other long-term enclaves in the city, Jews continued the style of life inherited from their parents. Although pre–World War II interethnic tensions, especially with the Irish, diminished, definable turfs within and among neighborhoods endured. Youth gang war-fare, however, largely occurred in other parts of town. Jews were neither prime antagonists nor victims. They kept to themselves. One study has shown that a dozen years after the end of World War II, "more than one of every four New York Jews lived in a neighborhood that was over half Jewish in composi-tion." In fact, these figures may even underestimate the extent of Jewish self-aggregation, "as residents of larger neighborhoods tended to cluster in smaller areas by ethnicity."[37]

Racial segregation likewise characterized New York City. At least it pos-sessed that feel for most Jews. As of 1957 on the Grand Concourse, African Americans constituted only 3.5 percent of its population, even if their num-bers, in the prior seven years, had grown fivefold, from approximately 1,400 to around 6,700. Jews made up still two-thirds of the neighborhood's popu-lation. A comparable story could be told in Brooklyn, where almost no Af-rican Americans lived in Boro Park, only 200 or so in total, when 63,000 Jews constituted 55.2 percent of the neighborhood. Similarly, in Flatbush, where some 123,000 Jews resided, only 3,000 blacks also lived. By contrast, in Bedford-Stuyvesant, 166,000 of its 253,000 residents (66 percent) were black, while only 11 percent of the population in that very poor neighborhood were Jews. Despite a population divided between Jews (40 percent) and African

Americans (24 percent), Crown Heights appeared to harbor few black residents in Mark Naison's memories. This historian recalled that "there were only a sprinkling of black families in the fifteen blocks between Eastern Parkway and Kings County Hospital," his key neighborhood landmarks, "most of them seemed solidly-working class." He frankly allowed that most blacks in Crown Heights were seen only by day as domestics, "girls" who "arrived in a group on the Kingston Avenue bus from Bedford-Stuyvesant and left by the same route in the evening." To the extent that there were subsurface racial issues in the neighborhood, he added, they "did not have much impact on my early childhood."[38] Jewish children growing up in New York City in the 1950s lived in a multiethnic city, but most of them remembered instead a secure childhood in largely Jewish neighborhoods.

New York Jews, comfortable where they were and among whom they lived, took the cheap and quick, if often crowded, subways together to work, as their parents had before them. Researchers in the late 1950s observed that these residential areas "linked to the central business district by the extraordinarily rapid transit facilities" were "the real 'bedroom communities,' . . . even more so than the classic suburban county of Westchester." As late as 1948, a single ride cost but five cents, and the fare rose above fifteen cents only after 1966. Bronx subway commuters—cutters, pressers, or finishers—could leave their homes at 7:30 a.m. and be certain to punch the clock in the Garment Center by 8:00. They returned home to shop and socialize on their Jewish streets. On occasion, they might go back to Midtown to enjoy the metropolis's cultural spots. An inexpensive night out on a warm summer's evening might take a couple or a family to a free open-air concert at the hard stone seats of CCNY's Lewisohn Stadium. The New York Philharmonic performed outdoors during those months. Alternatively, local movie theaters offered double features in air-conditioned comfort. Or Jewish New Yorkers might "gather in groups on weekday evenings to watch their favorite shows." Brill Building artists still churned out popular tunes to sing on the streets and "platters" to buy at local record stores. Careful listeners to one of Brooklyn-born Carole King's early records might have noticed that "Pleasant Valley Sunday" critiqued suburban life in what she called "status-seeker land," even if she was not a year-round city dweller. This daughter of a New York school teacher and firefighter had a summer bungalow in Connecticut within a community founded by the Ner Tormid Society, the Jewish firefighters' fraternal organization.[39]

During the school year, King's parents and other Jewish adults watched their youngsters learn in the public schools, usually taught by Jewish teachers. The highest achievers passed entrance tests for the elite High School of Music and Art, Hunter College High School, the Bronx High School of Science, Stuyvesant, and Brooklyn Tech. In the late 1950s, Jews constituted as much as 70 percent of those schools' student bodies. From there, it often was a natural and convenient step to CCNY, the school their fathers might have dropped out of during the Depression. Music and Art was located within City's St. Nicholas Heights campus. Some of these parents gave their children a more extensive supplementary Jewish education than they had received. A 1954 report revealed that the overwhelming majority of Jewish youngsters who went to a Jewish school, irrespective of neighborhood, attended either Sunday school or afternoon Hebrew schools for at most four hours a week. Despite the growing popularity of day schools, they enrolled only a small minority of Jewish children. Most New York Jews celebrated but did not strictly observe the major holidays, when they saw and were seen with other Jews inside and outside of the city's synagogues. Attendance figures in these houses of worship for 1960 read very much like those of the 1920s and 1930s, despite a decision by the New York City Board of Education to cancel classes on Rosh Hashanah and Yom Kippur, due to the large numbers of Jewish teachers in the public school system. Yet more than half of all New York Jews only went to synagogue "a few times a year," and 19 percent completely ignored organized Jewish religious observance. This survey included newly arrived immigrants, many of whom were highly observant.[40]

In the early postwar years, these immigrant newcomers, refugees from diverse lands of oppression and survivors of the Holocaust, carved out their own niches in the city. Following in the footsteps of millions of their fellow Jews, they established themselves within this metropolis of promises. Close to half of all Jewish immigrants to the United States from the late 1940s to the mid-1960s settled in the city. Their presence contributed to Jews continuing to constitute 30 percent of New York's population. But more than just replacing those second- and third-generation Jews who opted for suburbia, these new arrivals brought new attitudes and practices to their neighborhoods.

Five years after the war, the foreign-born constituted a full one-third of the city's Jewish population. The overwhelming majority, 450,000 of these 700,000 immigrants, hailed initially from Russia, Poland, and other eastern

European states; as survivors of the Holocaust, tens of thousands of them obtained their visas while billeted in displaced persons' camps in Europe. Many more eastern Europeans would have settled in America if not for immigration laws that continued to discriminate against applicants based on country of "national origins." Though some special legislation was passed in the late 1940s to ease a fraction of the pain and frustration of the victims of Nazism, not until the administration of Lyndon B. Johnson in 1965 did the quota laws change. Soviet policies locked the doors in Russia as well as satellite countries behind the Iron Curtain, preventing additional numbers of Jews anxious to seek American shores from leaving.[41]

Ironically, immediately after the war, survivors from Germany and Austria found their own paths to America hindered by legal and bureaucratic definitions that included them as among unwelcome refugees from a former enemy state, even though these so-called German expellees had had their citizenship stripped from them by Nazi edicts. Only in 1950 did the United States ameliorate this patent mischaracterization by amending displaced-persons legislation to allow approximately 55,000 of these unfortunates to enter on a nonquota basis. Many of them gravitated to New York and made up a large proportion of the some 130,000 German and Austrian Jews in the city.[42]

Anti-Semitism of a different sort brought thousands of Sephardic Jews to America and especially to New York in the late 1940s and 1950s. Popular animosities and governmental policies driven by Arab anger and frustration over the rise and successes of the State of Israel forced Jews from Syria, Lebanon, Iraq, and Egypt—particularly during the regime of President Gamal Abdul Nasser—to flee. Special congressional legislation passed in 1957 to help "victims of persecution"—designed to assist Hungarian victims of Communism—eased the way for Egyptian Jews to enter the United States.[43]

Upon arrival in America, these Jewish newcomers, like so many immigrants before them, sought out familiar faces, essentially those men and women who shared their ethnic, social, and religious sensibilities. Orthodox Jews from eastern Europe gravitated to Brooklyn neighborhoods. The co-ops of the Bronx welcomed those who espoused socialist traditions. German Jews reconnected with refugee establishments in Washington Heights, while others settled on the west side of Manhattan and Jackson Heights in Queens. Sephardim moved into other Brooklyn enclaves, especially Flatbush and Bensonhurst, and a limited number found homes in Forest Hills. Most noticeable of these newcomers were the varying sects of Hasidic Jews. They established themselves in Williamsburg, where they intensified Orthodox Judaism in that settlement.[44]

One observer of that postwar transformation observed that rather than conform to existing mores, these newcomers "preferred to adjust the standards of the community to their own particular pattern of religious life." Following their rabbis' commands, they not only "established their own new religious and communal centers" but "changed the appearance of the neighborhood by their insistence on maintaining . . . the habits and customs" of their European traditions. One sign of the changing times was the conversion of local movie theaters into store-front yeshivas. These devout Jews disdained secular amusements, and they needed space for their growing educational network. Under Hasidic sway, the streets filled daily with "men with long beards, kaftans, and all varieties, types and sizes of black hats, and women with wigs or kerchiefs and dark stockings." To the uninitiated, all of these Hasidim looked pretty much alike. But discerning observers noted that while the Satmar from Hungary were the largest new group in Williamsburg, the neighborhood now housed more than a dozen sects from different parts of eastern European, each proud of and eager to maintain its own distinctive customs and clothing. Propinquity heightened another European tradition: disputes and rivalries among different Hasidic groups, each loyal to its own religious leader's ideologies and practices. The leaven for controversy rose out of the city's ecology; "members of [Hasidic] courts," be they from Klausenberg or Belz or Munkac or Vizhnitz, among other vicinities, "that had once sprawled from Bratislava to Odessa were now located a few streets from one another or only a brief car ride apart."[45]

As these newcomers changed the neighborhood's character, they hastened the relocation of many erstwhile Jewish residents of Williamsburg, including those who were quite observant themselves, to other parts of the city and suburbia. Certainly those "who had been forced to stay on during the years of the war housing shortage" eagerly packed their belongings for new homes in Queens or Long Island or even just a few miles away in Boro Park or Crown Heights in Brooklyn. Eventually these Americanized Jews relocated again, after Hasidim from Williamsburg settled en masse in Boro Park in the 1960s. While they might have looked back with some disdain at an enclave that they now referred to derogatorily as "refugeetown," their exodus opened up the neighborhood to even more Hasidim, who flocked to newly vacant apartments, precisely to be among their fellow sectarians and under their rabbis' wings. By the mid-1950s, this new Williamsburg was "a different neighborhood." One former resident, who came back to visit "after years of living in Boston," saw an endearing vitality to the neighborhood. "Life, Jewish life," he remarked, "seems to be bubbling over in these streets. And one feels good to see all this, after one has been away from any kind of concentrated community life as long as I." While acknowledging that Williamsburg had lost its "calm, dignity," he appreciated something special about the "lower-class type of activity that fills the street, louder and full of hustle."[46]

In the early postwar decades, Crown Heights also become a Hasidic hub, home to the most renowned sect, the Lubavitchers. whose influence on Jewish life extended well beyond their neighborhood. Here, too, a transfer of Jewish populations occurred but at a slower pace than in Williamsburg. While Lubavitchers flocked to the neighborhood with the arrival of their leader, Joseph Isaac Schneersohn, in 1941, through the 1950s they still shared the streets with Americanized Jews and other ethnic groups. The neighborhood even absorbed some Jews from a changing Williamsburg who opted for the still middle-class section of Crown Heights. As the Lubavitcher presence expanded during the 1960s, Crown Heights became a mecca for Jewish visitors. Both the faithful and the intrigued came to hear and see Rabbi Menachem Mendel Schneersohn. Upon assuming the helm of his sect in 1950, he transformed the *farbrengen*, his public lectures, into popular staples of his inspirational message to his followers and of his outreach efforts to all Jews. Thousands crammed into the headquarters at 770 Eastern Parkway to listen and be inspired. Eventually the world became his neighborhood, as he broadcast his discourses first on radio and then on television.[47]

But back home, by the mid-1960s, there were major problems within the neighborhood that threatened the continuity of the community. For a variety of social, economic, and political reasons, Crown Heights was racially transformed. Its Jews eventually found themselves entangled in the city's emerging crises as their postwar era of continuity and cachet dissolved into times of strife and conflict. Jewish concerns, immersed in a larger urban malaise, ultimately clashed with African American aspirations and anger. It is to the bitter battles of the 1960s that we now turn our attention.

Confrontation between the members of the United Federation of Teachers and the Ocean Hill–Brownsville Community, 1968. (Photograph by Sam Reiss; Sam Reiss Photographs Collection, courtesy of Tamiment Library, New York University)

CHAPTER 5

Crises and Contention

When Molly Berg wanted America to feel the vibrancy of New York Jewish neighborhood life, she projected 1038 East Tremont Avenue as the quintessential windows-open, door-unlocked, Bronx apartment-house community. Helen Lazarcheck, who really lived in that area, felt that warm embrace. "Everyone seemed to help one another. If there was trouble, everyone would do something for you if they could. They were always coming in and sharing what they had." Not that the Jews of East Tremont agreed on political issues. "The Yiddishist and Hebraist each had his following, with a supporting system of cultural clubs, bookstores, debating societies," as did the hard-core radical, the Socialist and Communist. And the rabbis of the neighborhood's seven synagogues competed for the allegiances of the religious. Jews debated competing worldviews on weekends or on Jewish holidays at the crowded park benches of Crotona Park or Southern Boulevard. But a palpable feeling of belonging united the neighborhood. Patterns of street life reassured everyone. Continuity characterized this place where they had grown up and were raising their children and where they expected to grow old among friends. That was, until the all-powerful city official Robert Moses set his sights on a one-mile strip of territory that cut through their homes.[1]

While most New York City Jews in the 1950s lived securely and comfortably among friends and family in their own enclaves of long standing, residents of that targeted area felt the tremors of crisis. A massive city project, destined to change the face of the entire metropolis, was to obliterate their neighborhood. For Moses, who at one point reigned simultaneously as head of some dozen city and state offices, from chairman of the Triborough Bridge Authority to

New York City parks commissioner, this land was an essential link in his master-builder road plan. He aimed to construct the Cross Bronx Expressway, connecting the city with New Jersey, Long Island, and New England, later known as the "I-95 corridor." He had been at work on this megaproject, beginning the digging in the late 1940s, in less populated sections of the East Bronx and had been frequently chafed that federal, state, and municipal dollars had not materialized as quickly as he desired. Now, he refused to hear alternatives on how and where work in East Tremont might proceed. His foremost argument was that "every time a project was delayed by hearings and rerouting, funding was also delayed and costs increased." Accordingly, in December 1952, in dictatorial fashion—his customary mode of operation—Moses, from his post as city construction coordinator, curtly informed 1,530 families housed in some 159 buildings that they had but ninety days to move out of their condemned buildings. This edict ignited a half-decade battle between neighborhood activists and this metropolitan mogul. Ultimately historians have argued that because the city, under Moses's decisive hand, undertook massive public works projects, including an "arterial highway system," New York in future decades was able to claim—as it always had—"that it was the capital of the twentieth century, the capital of capitalism and the capital of the world." But during the strident and sometimes ugly skirmishes of the 1950s, no one in East Tremont was looking so far ahead, at a master builder paving the way for the future. Rather, they were focused on an autocrat who could resort to cutting off heat and hot water in some protestors' buildings. In the end, as was the case in most of Moses's fights, "city hall" won.[2]

The removal of these five thousand displaced people, most of them Jewish, marked the beginning of the end of the neighborhood. As construction of "Heartbreak Highway" ensued, starting with noisy, dirty, and toxic excavation work, some ten thousand additional East Tremont residents moved out. Those with more money, mostly the younger generation, looked for housing in the suburbs or the suburban-like community of Riverdale. That enclave in the northwest corner of the Bronx began earning a reputation as an up-and-coming Jewish neighborhood after World War II, particularly after Fieldston, its most expensive private-home section, dropped its anti-Semitic restrictions. By 1957, there were eight thousand Jews in the neighborhood—approximately 20 percent of the residents—and religious institutions were established.[3]

As Jews vacated East Tremont's apartments, many of the city's poorest of the poor, mostly African Americans, moved into the increasingly dilapidated buildings. Families on welfare found shelter in the neighborhood, having been sent by social welfare agencies. Fears and realities of muggings, robberies, break-ins, and violence reverberated through the neighborhood, sparking a chain migration out of the area. As each additional group of Jews left a building, word spread next door and then around the corner. By the mid-1960s, the community's Jewish era had ended. The luckier ones found refuge in the borough's "decent areas," as one former East Tremont resident put it. Co-ops and other middle- and lower-middle-class developments absorbed those who could flee. But the poor and elderly remained trapped in what was later described as "ravaged hulks," with residents "barricaded in their freezing apartments." Ultimately, other sections of the Bronx replicated the East Tremont template of turmoil—physical deterioration, initial departures, arrival of minorities, fears, and sometimes the realities of criminality, further evacuations, and intensified deterioration of the neighborhood, leaving behind only the most disadvantaged. East Tremont produced a compelling formula for the next decades of urban crisis.[4]

By the late 1950s, similar distressing scenarios began to trouble Jews in Brownsville. They, too, started to move out of their apartments, similarly adumbrating future citywide neighborhood predicaments. Never an elite economic enclave, Brownsville, as previously explored, was always rich in Jewish population and street culture. In the early postwar years, those with money departed for suburban Long Island and New Jersey. Or they took the intracity migration route, settling in Queens or filling in new areas in Brooklyn such as Canarsie or Mill Basin, out "in the boon docks" along Jamaica Bay. One satisfied settler later claimed, "Once we made it to Canarsie, we finally had a little piece of the country." Those remaining in Brownsville lived much as they had before the war, albeit with greater financial security. For some, a steady income allowed them to send their daughters to college and not just their sons. Brooklyn College, accessible and affordable, beckoned. When students returned home from day classes, they reentered the Jewish atmosphere that had long pervaded their safe streets. One woman memoirist recalled, "We spent our time in the streets. We went into the yard calling up to our friends. We didn't have a telephone; we didn't have to be formal." Another remembered how "provincial" Brownsville still was: "Everything was in a small nucleus. I was taught in Brownsville, met a boy from Brownsville." She married him and then faced intense separation anxieties when he received a fellowship to study at Duke University in North Carolina. "How could I leave my mother?" she recounted. "I couldn't have a baby without my mother nearby." Sounding much like those who lived in Brownsville during the interwar years, a spokeswoman for that group argued that in the 1940–1950s, "it was possible to think everyone was Jewish. They were not outsiders; the rest of America was made up of 'the others,' *der anderers*—the goyim—often to be ridiculed and often feared but usually just avoided."[5]

However, as an area with the reputation and reality as a working-class and poor, deteriorating neighborhood, as the 1950s progressed, Brownsville was chosen for a massive incursion of the most indigent minorities. African Americans and, to a lesser extent, Latinos fundamentally altered the social chemistry of the community. Actually blacks lived in Brownsville as early as the interwar period, and particularly Socialist and Communist Jews accepted them, adopting an egalitarianism in contrast to other areas, where whites did their utmost to keep blacks out of their neighborhoods. As of 1940, 13,000 blacks lived among 145,000 Jews, and by the end of World War II, blacks actually predominated on some blocks. Studies showed that from 1940 to 1950, Brownsville's black population doubled (to 24,000), and seven years later, their numbers stood at approximately 38,000.[6]

Many new African American arrivals settled in Brownsville after migration from the South during and after the war, in search of economic advancement and social and political equality. More than a million and a quarter African Americans made the city their home from 1945 to 1970. Initially, these newcomers migrated to longstanding black sections of the city, such as Harlem and Bedford-Stuyvesant, before coming to Brownsville. Caught in the web of dilapidated environs, they struggled to gain a financial foothold. However, they found that discrimination had followed them north. Men and women in search of employment encountered a declining market for their skilled and semiskilled occupations. Segregated unions denied them entry into existing jobs. Those domestic "girls" working in Crown Heights homes might have become "secretaries or sales clerks" if racial barriers had not forced them to slop pails and brooms. Unemployed or underemployed families doubled up in cramped quarters to pay their rents, contributing to further overcrowding and exacerbating neighborhood decline by straining local resources. Parental desertions, broken homes, and juvenile delinquency were also part of the unfavorable social mix.[7]

Champions of urban renewal urged the city to tear down the worst dwellings. But what of those who were displaced? Seemingly little, if any, thought was given to the time lag between the destruction of portions of neighborhoods and the construction of improved housing. Instead, urban renewal empowered city officials to increase residential segregation. The all-powerful Robert Moses, as head of the New York City Housing Authority, determined that the Brownsville "community would be a dumping ground for those displaced by the renewal of other [middle-class and white] areas." He used the false promise of large-scale public housing.[8]

Ironically, back in the 1940s, when such ideas were first discussed, Brownsville's Jewish residents had supported that type of housing initiative. They imagined public housing, such as the projects built across the East River on the Lower East Side, as better than the tenements that blighted the area. But the buildings turned out to be deficient in many ways. The contractors used cheap materials, providing for only small, narrow apartments devoid of many amenities and without sufficient recreational areas around the high-rises. Yet when the first large-scale developments, the Brownsville Houses, opened in 1948, they provided space for thirteen hundred families. Jews occupied the majority of the units; African Americans lived in the others. However, soon, these new apartments became launching pads for the "working poor." In the years that followed, those Jews who ascended the socioeconomic scale moved out. Strict income limitations forced out the most successful. In their stead, a different class of blacks, who previously had lived in even worse conditions, settled in. The racial balances started to tip. City housing regulations contributed to additional imbalances, giving preference to those who were displaced elsewhere (i.e., indigent blacks), including many who were referred to euphemistically as "problem families." Criminality, both juvenile delinquency and gang violence, was the most visible and fearful social pathology that gradually infected these "projects."[9]

Prejudice also deterred those African Americans who might have acquired the economic wherewithal to create a stable middle-class presence in the locality. The same Federal Housing Administration programs that provided white former GIs with mortgages to live in a suburbia off-limits to blacks

denied African Americans opportunities to purchase homes within existing neighborhoods. Through policies known as "redlining," Brownsville and
other comparable inner-city neighborhoods were foreclosed federal mortgage
insurance, and new private investment or capital improvements were ren-
dered impossible.[10]

For those Jews remaining in Brownsville by the early 1960s, a combustible
combination of floating fears and realities of crime stoked yet another round
of white flight. Crime numbers horrified many. Stories of attacks against Jews
in the public housing units traumatized more than just the immediate victims. As in East Tremont, once word and fear spread, one family's departure
inspired others. In time, a crescendo of concerns motivated additional families
to seek shelter elsewhere in the city. Again the elderly, who were often destitute, were left behind. With these spiraling dynamics in play, a community
that in 1957 was 66 percent white and heavily Jewish became, in just five short
years, 75 percent African American and Latino.[11]

By 1962, this compound of poverty, violence, fears, and flight, exacerbated
by unscrupulous real estate operators who capitalized on these tensions,
ended vibrant Jewish life in Brooklyn's East New York, threatened continuity
in Crown Heights, and over in Queens, changed Jamaica. "Blockbusting" by
aggressive agents seeking to "flip" houses warned those who owned residential properties that it was essential to sell out before the entire neighborhood
turned black and their life's investments would be lost.[12]

Although these neighborhood transformations surely engendered strained
relations between Jews and blacks, the absence of expressed, intense racial
animosities tapped down their volatility and limited the spread of antipathies
beyond local communities. Thus, whatever was then happening in Brooklyn stayed largely within circumscribed confines. A historian of the tenor of
these times in Brownsville has pointed out that while Jews who remained in
the area in the early 1960s "felt increasingly uncomfortable in a sea of black
and Latino faces, . . . there were no race riots or significant confrontations."
Perhaps the hardest feelings that were exposed publicly emanated from the
streets of Crown Heights. There in 1964, a local Hasidic rabbi, Samuel Schrage,
organized the Maccabees, a Jewish street-patrol group. By that time, the once
middle-class neighborhood was in the throes of change. Poorer blacks were
migrating in large numbers from Brownsville and elsewhere in the borough.
Blockbusting in a neighborhood where Jews often lived in private homes and

not in apartments was prolific, and street crime escalated. But even as Crown Heights was changing, Rabbi Schneersohn told his followers that come what may, the Lubavitchers would not leave an enclave that they had labored to build up. They would not abandon its network of schools, shuls, shops, and other communal institutions. Rabbi Schrage, following his rebbe's decision and anxious to protect fellow Hasidim, organized patrols, with their walkie-talkies in hand, to create a neighborhood watch. But to many blacks in Crown Heights, the Maccabees' activities smacked of vigilantism that targeted their people all too indiscriminately. Conversely, some Jews saw criminals as more than just a reprehensible underclass but as anti-Semites. It remained for a City Commission on Human Rights investigation to attempt to set that record straight. It determined that muggers, burglars, and other criminals were essentially opportunists—black and white—who had invaded the neighborhood. The commission's analysis also made clear that street patrols included both Jews and blacks. Schrage eventually changed his group's name to the Crown Heights Community Patrols, helping to calm angry community voices.[13]

Racially tinged skirmishes occurred elsewhere as well. The writer who rhapsodized about the late-1950s Jewish élan in town and its condition of "non-crisis" admitted "that there had been a number of 'incidents'" that had made race relations "anything but easy." He noted that in 1958, the *Amsterdam News* "denounced the Jewish principal of a Bronx school in a predominantly Jewish neighborhood for accepting five classes of Negroes from a nearby school, but isolating them on a separate floor." This *Fortune* feature story also pointed to misunderstandings in Harlem, where the NAACP initiated a campaign against neighborhood liquor stores—most, they said, were owned by Jews—that were "closed to Negro salesmen." Local residents expected more out of Jews than from the general white population, because "the Jewish attitude on integration [was] more liberal than Protestants and Catholics." The article noted that in testifying before the city's Commission on Intergroup Relations, a spokesman for the black group "expressed amazement" that given "the closeness that has existed between Jews and the Negro community," Jewish store owners did not immediately accede to their requests.[14]

However, during the 1950s and early 1960s, blacks and Jews, living in a highly segregated city, largely did not confront or even engage one another. In most parts of town, few pressure points existed to produce conflagrations. Eli Lederhendler, a historian of postwar Jewish New York, in writing about his youth recalled, "I (and many others) lived in a kind of conditioned ignorance where black-white relations in our city were concerned. . . . Certainly nothing explicit was ever mentioned to me that was anti-black. In fact, as far as I could pick up from people of my parents' generation (relatives, friends, teachers), there was an active desire to put things right," that is, with regard to "principled politically sanctioned segregation between people of different backgrounds." However, back then, the question of "just why basic services like public schools should have been inadequate to those [black] children's own home environment, or why de facto residential segregation by color was a way of life in New York . . . would have taxed my limited powers of analysis and my limited awareness of racial thinking at that age." Apparently it "only barely registered" on him at the time that his "own mixed Jewish-Catholic, middle- and lower-middle-class neighborhood constituted a pocket of relative privilege, at least in quality-of-life terms."[15]

I grew up, at precisely the same time, in Parkchester, a working- and lower-middle-class section of the East Bronx, just a few miles from where Lederhendler was raised. My experiences with blacks were even more limited. Like most New York Jews of the time, as Lederhendler has aptly described them, I was "blithely unaware . . . of others' situations." Parkchester, a complex with fifty-eight apartment houses that housed fifty thousand people, owned and operated by the Metropolitan Life Insurance Company, was racially segregated. The Met maintained similar policies toward blacks in Stuyvesant Town and Peter Cooper Village in Lower Manhattan. A City Commission on Human Rights report charged in 1968 that from its opening in 1941 until 1963 not a single African American family rented an apartment in the neighborhood. From 1963 to 1968, only twenty minority families secured housing there. I can testify that as a child and later as a teenager (1949–1968), I never saw a young black face in the playgrounds. It was the Jewish minority against the Irish majority, with whom we played and against whom we sometimes fought. The ethnic composition of the area, we were told as kids, was "90% Irish and 10% Jewish and almost nobody else." Actually, "Parkchester was 35% Irish, with heavy concentrations of Jews and Italians." I did have one friend of German American extraction. A rather large fellow, he aligned himself with the Jews in pickup games and helped even out the score in the playground.[16]

As a student who commuted daily to a Jewish day school in Yorkville, I never saw a black student in my classes. They lived in the Soundview and

Hunts Point sections of the Bronx and in East Harlem, serviced by stations that my "express" subway train passed on the way into "the city." When we took the "local," parents admonished us never to get off at stops in these "poor" neighborhoods. But even most of my Jewish playground teammates had only handfuls of black kids in their public elementary and junior high school classes. They were outsiders bused over from Hunts Point. For some Parkchester Jewish students, the racial calculus changed in high school. Depending on where they lived in the complex, they might have been assigned to the well-integrated James Monroe High School in Soundview, while others went to the predominantly white Christopher Columbus High School in Pelham Parkway, if they did not pass the entrance exams to elite public schools.

Like the Lederhendlers, my family believed in social justice, but we never really acted on that viewpoint. We kept ourselves fully up-to-date about protest marches in Selma, Alabama, and efforts to integrate the South. We habitually watched it all on the evening news at dinner hour, applauded Dr. King's efforts, took pride that Professor Abraham Joshua Heschel, the eminent Jewish philosopher and social activist, stood next to King on his marches and mourned the trio of martyrs Goodman, Schwerner, and Chaney during the "freedom summer" of 1964 in Philadelphia, Mississippi. But we had little sense of any racial tensions between Jews and blacks in our city. Effectively, we were part of that last generation of New York Jews who believed in the existence of a special relationship and a commonality of fates that linked us with African Americans, even if our social and economic positions both in the city and nationwide differed radically and our commitments were never tested.

In that same "freedom summer" of 1964 in Mississippi, race riots broke out in Harlem and in Bedford-Stuyvesant. The violence began on July 18, when New York City police lieutenant Thomas Gilligan killed a fifteen-year-old African American, James Powell. After a protest at the Harlem police station, thousands of angered residents became rioters as they "raced through the center" of the neighborhood, "shouting at policemen and white people, pulling fire alarms, breaking windows and looting stores." This initial conflagration resulted in thirty arrests. Violence continued for two successive nights in Harlem. By the third day, Bedford-Stuyvesant erupted. In that poorest black neighborhood in Brooklyn, one thousand protestors gathered on Fulton Street and Nostrand Avenue, shouting "killer cops." Soon "bottles began raining on the police," and attacks occurred on local businesses. In the aftermath of the violence, white store owners in Harlem and Bedford-Stuyvesant tallied up their losses. The rioters seemingly targeted "only businesses owned by white persons." In Harlem, the damages from the first night were estimated at $50,000, while in Brooklyn, owners of a looted furniture and appliance store put losses at more than $10,000. They sued the city and its police for failure to protect their property against the rioters.[17]

In the days that followed, instant analysts and more detailed examinations made clear that the root causes went well beyond neighborhood revulsion at alleged police brutality. Rather, the violence "reflected deep-seated grievances," a litany of social and economic abuses that resembled those pushing Harlem residents into the streets in the 1930s and 1940s. As in the earlier conflicts, "squalid living conditions and barriers to employment" had "created . . . despair" that contributed mightily to anger and ultimately to attacks. *New York Times* editorialists minced no words when they opined that "the deepest reason for the rioting" was "the horrible ghetto condition, . . . stinking tenements, the lack of good schools, the inadequate recreational facilities, the shortage of job opportunities that condemn thousands to life on a near-animal level." Just as in the past, high on the list of malefactors were rapacious landlords and storekeepers, "greedy white folks," and "prejudiced employers." All of these enemies were routinely characterized as part of the "white power structure" intent on "keeping us [African Americans] down." Nonetheless, for all of the raw emotions that were then expressed, neither in the rhetoric of the rioters nor in the criticisms of the commentators did anyone suggest that the riots were directed against Jews, as opposed to whites, even if Jewish names abounded on lists of local entrepreneurs whose places were looted. "No observer at any of these first series of riots recalled hearing anti-Jewish slogans," wrote a sociologist several years later. For her, such silence contrasted pointedly with the strident voices heard during the "troubles of 1965–1967" that began in the Watts section of Los Angeles and ended in Detroit. In these later encounters, "increasingly intermingled with the cries of rage against whitey were words of hatred reserved just for the Jew." At no point during New York's first "long hot summer" outbreak did a contemporary street-corner counterpart of Abdul Hamid project "the Jews" as Harlem's problem.[18]

The Jewish Telegraphic Agency (JTA), in reporting on nights of violence in Brooklyn to its national Jewish readership, also detected no widespread anti-Jewish sentiments on the streets, even as it noted that some "anti-Jewish slogans [were] yelled." JTA quoted Maccabee leader Rabbi Schrage alleging that "a number of Arab students . . . entered the area to stir up trouble against the Jews" but admitted that "the rioting did not appear to be directed at the stores because they were Jewish-owned, because the rioters also stormed and ransacked stores owned by Negroes in the section, which still had a heavily-Jewish population." The Brooklyn-based *Jewish Press*, an organ hypersensitive to any manifestations of anti-Semitism, shared JTA's viewpoint. While four weeks earlier its headlines reported, "racial crisis in U.S. brings increase in anti-Jewish bias"—although the haters in that piece were the Klan and the American Nazi Party—and a week later it highlighted that boxer "Cassius Clay had pledged to fight with the United Arab Republic in any future war against Israel," its July 31, 1964, edition simply reprinted the JTA's release. Its editorialists, who in future strident black-Jewish confrontations were habitually outraged, did not comment on the 1964 riots. Nor did any of its readers care, in subsequent editions, to offer views on the outbreak of urban violence.[19]

The turning point in black-Jewish relations in New York occurred in 1968 as a battle ensued in Brooklyn over community control of the Ocean Hill–Brownsville public school district. Then the two groups first openly confronted each other on issues that not only hit home on the local neighborhood scene but also resonated throughout the city and beyond. The confrontations elicited vituperative anti-Semitic and racist sentiments from both sides. Angry feelings and misunderstandings that had previously bubbled beneath the city's surface percolated up to large-scale consciousness. The prime combatants pitted the largely Jewish United Federation of Teachers (UFT) union against local black parents, even if neither group precipitated the dispute.

In 1967, the president of the Ford Foundation, former Kennedy and Johnson administration national security adviser McGeorge Bundy, turned his attention to ameliorating the most pressing domestic issue of the day, racial inequality. Focusing on New York City, he was keenly aware that students in poor neighborhoods did not receive the same level of education as their white counterparts did elsewhere in the metropolis. Schools in these slums were underfunded and overcrowded, and their pupils were dispirited and underachieving. An advocate of community control of local neighborhoods and self-empowerment, Bundy authored a plan to turn control of schools in such areas over to local leaders and to parent groups in three sections of the city, including Ocean Hill–Brownsville. Mayor John V. Lindsay, anxious to tamp down racial tensions, welcomed Bundy's involvement and the Ford Foundation's financial support. Few issues provoked passions as much as the blight of inadequate schooling. As one impassioned mother put it, "I do not want my child to grow up in the same ghetto as I did." For her, quality public education held the key to opportunity and mobility.[20]

Initially, the teachers' union leaders supported decentralization plans that promised to revitalize depressed schools. Some even walked arm in arm with local parents to the 110 Livingston Street headquarters of the Board of Education to advocate for more funding. For UFT head Albert Shanker, who was soon pilloried by black activists and Jewish critics alike for harboring racist sentiments, these early protests reflected his past pedigree of support for civil rights. He had marched in Selma. However, when the Bundy plan was implemented in the Ocean Hill–Brownsville experimental school district, it immediately led Shanker's unionized Jewish teachers into a confrontation with neighborhood people and with their advocates both within and without the district.[21]

District unit supervisor Rhody G. McCoy provoked the first emotional flash points. The word on both the black and Jewish streets was that McCoy was a follower of Black Nationalist Malcolm X and associated himself with black activists or provocateurs—that designation depended on what side of the racial divide an observer stood—such as Sonny Carson and Les Campbell. The former, head of the Brooklyn chapter of the Congress of Racial Equality, was renowned, or notorious, for his physical intimidation of white opponents. The latter led the African-American Teachers' Association and spoke angrily of the "death for the minds and souls of . . . black children" due to "the systematic coming of age of the Jews who dominate and control the educational bureaucracy of the New York public school system." McCoy, in accord with these radical sentiments and determined to assert his authority within the district, moved to fill administrative vacancies with blacks who shared his sentiments. The union quickly protested that he did so without following promotion guidelines. The union was also troubled by the decidedly antiwhite and frequently anti-Jewish rhetoric that permeated Ocean Hill–Brownsville schools in the days after the assassination of Dr. King in April 1968. But McCoy's unilateral move of summarily dismissing nineteen teachers and administrators in May 1968 galvanized union opposition and greatly exacerbated racial tensions. All but one were Jewish, and many closely aligned themselves with the UFT.

They had been deemed "unsupportive or ineffective" in meeting community needs. On their way out, McCoy threatened, "Not one of these teachers will be allowed to teach anywhere in the city. The black community will see to that."[22]

The UFT initially prosecuted its defense of its members in the courts, which granted relief to the terminated teachers because of lack of "due process," only to have the mayor refuse to implement the decision. Shanker, now at odds with both City Hall and his African American opponents in Brooklyn, called his rank and file out on the first of three strikes that effectively closed down the entire city school system for close to three months. During this time of troubles, spewed charges and countercharges of anti-Semitism and racism fouled the city's air. An unsigned letter that found its way into the mailboxes of UFT teachers in one of the Brooklyn district's schools exacerbated matters. It read in part, "It is Impossible for The Middle East Murderers of Colored People to Possibly Bring To This Important Task" of teaching "African American History and Culture . . . to our Black Children. . . . The Insight, The Concern, The Exposing Of The Truth That is a *Must*." Shanker quickly distributed half a million copies of this letter, which angered Jews throughout the city. Jews picked up black anti-Semitism from two other local sources, one that was related to the school fight. Late in December 1968, on WBAI-FM radio, Les Campbell read a poem "dedicated" to Shanker written by a fifteen-year-old schoolgirl. The young author, reportedly "sick of hearing of [Jewish] suffering in Germany . . . and of the Jews' hatred for black Arabs," rhymed the following: "Hey, Jew Boy with that yarmulke on your head / You pale-faced Jew boy—I wish you were dead." A month later, many New York Jews took deep offense at an introductory essay to a catalogue from a "Harlem on My Mind" exhibit at the Metropolitan Museum of Art. The essay quoted another black teenager: "behind every hurdle that the Afro-American has yet to jump stands the Jew who has already cleared it."[23]

Throughout the school ordeal, which only simmered down in the winter of 1969 when the school district in turmoil came under a state trustee, national and international developments intensified city-based black-Jewish tensions. Most critical was the impact of the Six-Day War on both communities. That anonymous letter writer's referencing "Middle East murderers" and the young poet's comment about the "Jews' hatred for black Arabs" reflected a growing African American identification with the Third World and denigration of Israel as a colonialist state. Bringing these perceptions back home, blacks projected Jews as oppressors wherever they encountered them. For many New York Jews, by contrast, the Israeli victory inspired them to emulate their courageous brethren and to stand tall against all enemies foreign and domestic. Bringing that attitude back to their own urban realities, they "concluded that they could and must fight like hell for themselves"—specifically in the school teachers' case, for their jobs and, more largely, against anti-Semitism—and they needed to "stop worrying if others saw them as pushy, rude or unreasonable." Reading public opinion polls that found, in 1968, that "49 percent of African Americans in New York believed that 'Jews are irritating because [they are] too aggressive' [and] 39 percent thought Jews were 'too ambitious for their own good'" only intensified their concerns. For Shanker's supporters, "he was one 'tough Jew,'" a battler for his people in New York civic life.[24]

If these late-1960s conflicts underscored the reality that while Jews and blacks lived in the same city, they lived largely in different economic, social, and political worlds, these tensions also revealed serious fault lines within the Jewish community. There were Jewish teachers who hardly perceived Shanker as a hero. Though their presence was barely noted, UFT opponents of long standing, erstwhile members of the far-left Teachers Union, identified with black aspirations. Many of the Teachers Union's rank and file lost their jobs during the McCarthy Red Scare of the early 1950s for their alleged, or real, Communist affiliations. Some refused to sign loyalty oaths that were demanded of teachers. But others within this graying cohort soldiered on in the system even after their labor organization disbanded in 1964.[25]

More significantly, young Jewish teachers—40 percent of the replacement cohort that McCoy brought into the district in 1968—publicly denied that anti-Semitism pervaded Ocean Hill–Brownsville. A twenty-three-year-old recent graduate of Long Island University who secured one of those jobs characterized his group as "younger and better educated" than UFT stalwarts, "with less experience in working for the system and more in working against it, . . . nearly all . . . 'committed' to social change." He thought the UFT had made "skillful use of the issue of . . . anti-Semitism . . . to intensify the fears of the liberal Jewish community." Older strikers were offended by this youthful rhetoric of "social change" and rejected the allegations that the UFT was distributing hate literature. As they reviewed their own lives and careers, they contended that they were drawn back to a neighborhood that was once "theirs" to teach a new group of underprivileged youngsters. They had empathized with their charges because they, too, had been poor children of immigrant newcomers to New York, growing up in Brownsville and adjoining Brooklyn neighborhoods. In the spirit of egalitarianism that had long permeated these once Jewish streets, they had cooperated with responsible local black parents in attempting to improve students' lives. Now, arrogant young colleagues chastised them while black anti-Semites pilloried them as racists.[26]

Ira Glasser, executive director of the New York branch of the American Civil Liberties Union, strongly seconded the younger teachers' sentiments. As he challenged the UFT's motives and methods, he pointedly "blamed Shanker for whipping up the anti-Semitism issue" in order to undermine the entire decentralization effort. As far as black anti-Semitism was concerned, the liberal organization alleged that the UFT's evidences were "half truths, innuendoes and outright lies." Concomitantly, Jewish left of center social commentator Nat Hentoff, from his desk at the *Village Voice*, not only "opposed the union stance and its supporters" but addressed the alleged volatility of the collateral incident at WBAI. As a civil libertarian par excellence, Hentoff upheld the station's right to permit its shows' hosts and guests to speak their minds. While the rhetoric was unfortunate, ultimately he expected that the discussion that ensued around the poem would make clear that Jews were not the blacks' real enemy. Others in his office opined, "would the critics of WBAI prefer that we made a compact (or law) to pretend that anti-Semitism does not exist and let the virus spread in darkness and silence?"[27]

Meanwhile, operating out of a totally different Jewish space, Rabbi Meir Kahane, founder and leader of the Jewish Defense League (JDL), projected his people as under existential attack. Stimulated during the Ocean Hill–Brownsville difficulties, JDL initially followed in the footsteps of Rabbi Schrage's Maccabees street patrols but with no ambiguity about their enemies. From his pulpit as managing editor of the *Jewish Press*, Kahane constantly argued that the anti-Semitism that emanated from the teachers' strike was but the latest manifestation of black antipathies suffered by his Jews of Brooklyn. He ridiculed the "establishment" Jew as "a rich Jew who lives in Scarsdale or some other rich suburb" removed from the realities of city life and without any feeling for what the "grass-roots" was facing. Kahane viewed the city as "polarized beyond hope" with "anger, hate, frustration." In the Jewish neighborhoods that he championed, "integration," that liberal byword, had occurred because wealthy Jews had abandoned their lower-class and lower-middle-class fellow

Jews, precisely those whom Kahane sought to mobilize. "Militant blacks there," he said, "practice terror, extortion and violence." To protect his own kind, Kahane and his paramilitary activists used every means to answer anti-Semitism both within and without Brooklyn. They picketed WBAI's offices, calling on the Federal Communications Commission to revoke its license. They rallied on Fifth Avenue at the Metropolitan Museum of Art, demanding that the "Harlem on My Mind" exhibit be taken down. They even extended their fight in Manhattan to the steps of Temple Emanu-el, protesting this liberal Jewish congregation's invitation to a member of the Black Panther Party to present his claims for reparations from whites for the exploitation of blacks. One of Kahane's lieutenants warned that "heads would have been broken" if the event had gone off as scheduled. In his view, "if they could extort money from one synagogue, black extremists all over the country would do the same thing."[28]

The Jewish Defense League also pilloried Leonard Bernstein and his wife, Felicia, when, in January 1970, they hosted a fund-raising gathering in their Park Avenue duplex in support of the (Black) "Panther 21" on trial for conspiring to blow up the Bronx Botanical Gardens. For Kahane, the maestro epitomized the elite and naive "radical chic" New York Jew at the center of "liberal and intellectual circles [who] lionize the Black Panthers." While Kahane asserted that his organization defended "the right of blacks to form defense groups," Bernstein and his friends, in his view, went "beyond this to a group which hates other people. . . . Bernstein and other such intellectuals do not know this, they know nothing."[29]

Kahane's rhetoric, and especially his methods, did not capture the hearts and minds of the vast majority of the city's Jews. But his articulation of dichotomies of Brooklyn versus Scarsdale or, for that matter, Brooklyn versus affluent Manhattan reflected real disagreements among Jews. The splits actually measured the comfort level of Jewish groups and enclaves within the metropolis. All Jews seemingly agreed that black anti-Semitism was increasing. The Anti-Defamation League, which before the strike had proclaimed that there was no "organized anti-Semitism in New York" and that blacks generally were less anti-Jewish than whites were, now noted, "Raw undisguised anti-Semitism . . . is at a crisis level in New York City schools where, unchecked by public authorities, it has been building for more than two years." But levels of anxiety over this threat varied. Depending on where Jews lived, they held fundamentally different views of the role the municipal government was playing, or abdicating, in addressing their concerns. One sociologist has argued that the Brooklyn school events of 1968 transformed "outer borough Jews" from "optimistic universalism" to "nervous parochialism," while inner-borough cohorts maintained their longstanding personal equanimity and liberal equilibrium.[30]

A public opinion poll conducted half a year after the strike picked up an even more complicated and nuanced range of attitudes across the city. Every calculus of concern showed Manhattan and Brooklyn Jews in fundamentally different places. For example, the proposition that "blacks tend to be anti-Semitic" was "emphatically denied by Manhattan Jews . . . but was solidly believed by Brooklyn Jews." In similar fashion and degree, less than one-half of the Jews in Manhattan perceived a rise of "anti-Jewish feeling in the city," while almost two-thirds of those in Brooklyn felt the increase in such tensions. The Brooklynites also "tended to deny that discrimination against blacks takes place . . . and tended to believe stereotypes against blacks, . . . while those who live in Manhattan . . . tended to disagree with their co-religionists." Comparably, twice as many Manhattan Jews agreed that African Americans were "justified in [their] demands" than did their Brooklyn counterparts. While those in Manhattan expressed significant reservations about the state of their urban enclaves—26 percent said that their neighborhoods were "going down"—a full one-third of them enthused about where they lived. They perceived that their areas were "getting better." Almost no Brooklynites felt very good about where they lived. The most that they would say in a positive tenor was that the "trend was staying the same," for better or for worse. On one of the fundamental questions that revolved around the crisis between the UFT and the Ocean Hill community, the perception that "white teachers discriminated against black youngsters," more than a quarter of Manhattan Jews agreed with the allegation. Almost no Brooklyn Jews concurred with that provocative statement.[31]

This Louis Harris poll also ascertained that not all outer-borough Jews agreed on other compelling issues. Those in Queens generally mirrored the perspectives of those in Manhattan. They, too, rated the state of their neighborhoods favorably; in fact, they were the least likely New York Jews to worry about "going out on the street at night." Similarly, fewer Queens Jews estimated a "rise in anti-Jewish feeling" citywide than did their coreligionists elsewhere. "Manhattan and Queens Jews were most agreed that anti-black discrimination does exist," and the majority of Queens Jews felt that blacks in the city were "justified in [their] demands."[32]

Perhaps most interesting were the attitudes of Jews in the Bronx. On the one hand, they appeared to be the most apprehensive about the future of their residential areas. Even more than those in Brooklyn, "they expressed dissatisfaction with their neighborhoods," seeing them as "going down." Some 70 percent of those polled felt that way. This trend, it was surmised, stemmed from "a recent influx of blacks and Puerto Ricans." In other words, as the 1960s ended, their sections were changing more rapidly than any other borough was. But when it came to attitudes toward these newcomers, on several questions, those in the Bronx responded much like their fellow Jews in Manhattan and Queens. Of all New York Jews, as an aggregate, those in the Bronx were the least pronounced in their estimate of "anti-Jewish feeling in the city." Like those in Manhattan and Queens, their majority perceived that blacks suffered from discrimination and that they were "justified in [their] demands." For the surveyors, the Bronx Jews were a major part of "the balance in the center of the Jewish community."[33]

Ultimately Bronx Jews were of two minds because by 1969 there were two textures to Bronx Jewish life. In older sections such as the Grand Concourse, which was in the early throes of its decline—aging both in the length of Jewish presence in the area and of its inhabitants—Jews expressed concern about "inundation by recently arrived blacks and Puerto Ricans." Those Jews pointed out that "affluent Jews who live in expensive apartments in Manhattan do not have to worry about the likelihood of a large-scale black influx." But they could have said the same thing about the "under thirty-five," upwardly mobile, "well educated" Jewish crowd that populated the growing Riverdale section of the Bronx. Though the surveyors did not break down attitudes by specific neighborhoods, this new generation of Bronx Jews identified with the social values of those in Manhattan and scored high on every quotient of tolerance. They might even respond affirmatively to the theoretical concept of blacks moving into their neighborhoods, assuming these newcomers were of the same socioeconomic class. Meanwhile, in a place such as Parkchester, there was no racial turmoil because as late as 1968, its owners kept it segregated.[34]

The diversity of Jewish opinions on where the city was heading and their place within the changing urban mix became even more apparent in the fall of 1969 when Mayor Lindsay ran for reelection. In 1965, New York Jews had split between those who voted for one of their own—Controller Abraham Beame would have been the first Jew to occupy Gracie Mansion—and those who voted for the young Republican John Lindsay, who was also the standard-bearer of the Liberal Party. The major issues that time around had been "fiscal responsibility," due to a significant budget gap left by the incumbent Wagner administration, "political extremism," and "police misconduct." Only the third consideration smacked of race, as it was just a year after the murder that led to the Harlem riots. Lindsay supported establishing a civilian police review board, while his opponents demurred. But that issue did not turn the election. Actually, more blacks voted for Beame than for Lindsay. As far as political extremism was concerned, that highly charged item related to the views and associations of the Conservative Party candidate, the widely quoted intellectual William F. Buckley Jr., whom Beame and Lindsay both linked to the John Birch Society, an anti-Semitic and racist organization.[35]

For Jews, the choice came down to ethnic heritage versus reform politics and a perceived new start for New York. Beame, who prized his independence, was unfairly cast as a relic of old-time city politics, though he had been elected controller just four years earlier as a "reform" candidate. Almost no Jews voted for the archconservative Buckley. In fact, as Election Day grew closer, Beame's appeals to group pride, or even his failure to formally distance himself from such endorsements, fell flat among many Jewish voters, as the Protestant outsider picked up traction among portions of the controller's natural constituents. Lindsay campaigned vigorously for Jewish support, his nylon yarmulke perched high on his head. When the votes were tallied, Jewish districts in Manhattan and Queens leaned toward Lindsay, while some Brooklyn neighborhoods, such as Williamsburg, supported Beame. One pollster declared that the Jewish Democrat was "clobbered . . . in upper-income professional Jewish areas of Reform Democratic persuasion." But Beame held his own in "Jewish middle-income, non-professional neighborhoods." While class-based distinctions appeared, this election was not a referendum on the place and comfort of Jews in the city.[36]

In 1969, the city's exploding racial tensions lodged firmly in Jews' minds when they went to the polls. Now, the incumbent faced Democratic challenger Controller Mario Procaccino and Republican and Conservative candidate John Marchi. Lindsay retained only his Liberal line. To so-called outer-borough Jews, His Honor was no friend of theirs. Had he not sided with the blacks against the Jewish teachers, not to mention mayoral missteps and slights that seemed to reflect an anti-Jewish mien on the mayor's part? His

proposal to enforce alternate-side-of-the-street regulations on the High Holidays angered those constituents who would not move their cars on Rosh Ha-
shanah or Yom Kippur. Many Jewish residents of Queens also felt that the administration failed to provide proper city services. Hundreds of thousands of
them had been stranded during the winter storm of 1969 when sanitation department snowplows never made it to their homes and offices. The candidate's
every effort to apologize for his mistakes and to deny favoring blacks over
Jews did not mollify this constituency. But Lindsay retained the allegiance of
"Manhattan" Jews and their compatriots in other boroughs for whom Lindsay still stood for a progressive, compassionate, and ultimately optimistic vision of the city's promise for all groups. The incumbent also wisely interjected
a national-international concern into his campaign that appealed to young,
liberal Jews. He spoke out strongly for an end to American involvement in
the Vietnam War. Procaccino lampooned these Jewish voters and their Christian counterparts as "limousine liberals," a caricature of those who it was said
were insulated by wealth and position from the traumas of crime, neighborhood change, and racial extremism. That image of privilege and naiveté about
the urban crises around them played well among Jews and others whom the
mayor's postures and policies had alienated. Jews divided their votes. Affluent Jews who resided largely in Manhattan and those "who lived in Brooklyn and Queens and still worked as schoolteachers, wholesalers, accountants,
and dentists" made different choices in an election in which "for the first time
in New York City's history . . . racial conflict became determinative for the
city's politics."[37]

These acute differences appeared when Jewish votes were analyzed. "Upper-
income and [luxury] apartment-dwelling Jewish areas voted to re-elect
Mayor Lindsay, while middle-income and [modest] home-owning Jewish areas tended to favor Mr. Procaccino." The victor carried three-quarters of the
predominantly Jewish vote on the Upper West Side and Upper East Side of
Manhattan, including Yorkville, and ran well in Flatbush's Forty-Fourth District, "with perhaps the best incomes for Jewish residents" in that borough.
Similarly, "the well-to-do and largely Jewish [areas] of Forest Hills and Kew
Gardens" went for the incumbent, but he lost the "middle-income and lower-
income" Jews in the Rockaways and elsewhere in Queens. In the Bronx, the
two tenors of Jewish attitudes played out, as Riverdale, "the highest-income
section" of the borough, chose Lindsay, while "middle-income areas" preferred

his opponents. Ultimately, "an unusual combination of support from higher-income New Yorkers and low-income Negroes and Puerto Ricans" propelled Lindsay back into office. Better-off Jews, content with their lot in the city, lined up with blacks and Latinos, while their less affluent brethren voted with other white ethnic groups unhappy with New York's direction and priorities.[38]

Just a few months after this hotly contested election, these profound attitudinal differences resurfaced as the crux of an intense internal Jewish debate over the future of Forest Hills. The controversy arose in reaction to a Lindsay plan to build low-cost housing in the neighborhood. The city proffered as its "moral imperative" the end of tacit racial segregation in the city, with access for all to improved educational, recreational, and social outlets. But opponents heard "projects" when the city contemplated a plan to construct 840 apartment units within three twenty-four-story buildings in their neighborhood. The government's arguments that the new construction would also avail deserving elderly did not dampen objections. Nightmare fantasies imagined poor newcomers bringing crime and racial turmoil, elements it was claimed that had undermined other Jewish enclaves. Many of the protestors saw themselves as "refugees" from Bronx and Brooklyn communities that had "turned" due to governmental tampering with their streets. The leader of those who were outraged, for example, had been born and raised in Williamsburg. One of his supporters asserted, "Many of us come from formerly Jewish communities in the Bronx and Brooklyn where an influx of low-income people meant that our children could not play safely in the streets and grown men were afraid to go out after dark." They carried those last memories from earlier happier times in their old neighborhoods. Now they perceived themselves as victims of an insensitive, if not cynical, Lindsay administration that had taken for granted their supposed unalterable Jewish liberalism. Had not most of the Jews of Forest Hills stood with the mayor in the election that had just passed? Notwithstanding his widely critiqued record on black-Jewish relations, he had garnered six thousand more votes than Beame had in that district. Those who now increasingly felt at odds with their city's policies and its lack of concern about their needs also noted that Gracie Mansion had backed off from comparable initiatives in adjoining predominantly Italian enclaves because the politicos understood that that ethnic group would not stand for unwanted black incursion.[39]

But Rabbi Ben Zion Bokser, spiritual leader of the neighborhood's largest congregation, stood apart from his community and absorbed much criticism for his liberal stance. In sermons and in essays in his synagogue's bulletin, he consistently supported the Lindsay plan and forthrightly addressed its racial subtext. Sanguine about what changes would mean in improving Jews' lives in Forest Hills, he once allowed, "The initial impact [of] more contact with Negroes in our places of business, in our schools, in our home neighborhoods will produce many incidents of tension, but in the fullness of time this will be a source of blessing to all of us." He continued, "Integration . . . will give each of us unanticipated opportunities to widen our understanding of life."[40]

As the debate continued, predictably both "Manhattan" and "Brooklyn" Jewry's views were heard. The Midtown-based American Jewish Committee and the Anti-Defamation League of the B'nai B'rith echoed Bokser's sentiments, although these defense organizations were appalled by the city's racial polarization. However, the ADL did have a problem with its Forest Hills representative, who stood up at its annual meeting against the "overwhelming" majority of its "national chapters" that voted "to pass a resolution in support of the low-income project . . . and its goal of integration." In response, the meeting's chairman spoke of his Queens community having been "agitated out of all proportion into baseless fears." On the other side of this debate, the Jewish Defense League prepared to fight forced racial integration. Kahane recognized how the political perspectives of Forest Hills' Jews had been changed by crisis at their doorsteps, and he turned them toward militancy. He mused, "It's easy for the Jew in Forest Hills to be liberal in Mississippi, [but] when a low-income housing project comes to Forest Hills, suddenly all these Jews that used to get up in the Forest Hills Jewish Center [Rabbi Bokser's congregation] and say that JDL uses violence and they're bad, come over to me and say, 'Listen, if that housing project goes up, can you blow it up?' "[41]

Though not advocating violence, Rabbi Harry Halpern of Brooklyn's Flatbush Park Jewish Center confided his fear to Bokser. "People have a right to be alarmed by the influx of such a large number of low income residents. I know that in schools where there has been considerable bussing there are numerous threats against children who will not yield their money to those who wield knives." From a very different part of Manhattan, the racially changing Upper West Side neighborhood, came a warning from Rabbi Joseph Sternstein of congregation Ansche Chesed: "I have served . . . inner city temple[s], . . . and I was in the thick of many controversies . . . and had my family exposed to the conditions of the city. . . . If you do not want Queens Boulevard to be transformed to Upper Broadway, where Jewish women cannot walk down the street unmolested, you will reverse your opposition on this Forest Hills project."[42]

Mediation efforts of Queens lawyer and future governor Mario Cuomo, together with intercession from the federal government, eventually transformed the project into a cooperative endeavor that stilled the angry voices.[43] But as the 1970s began, New York Jews walked away from these disputes increasingly of several minds over how comfortable they were, unsure of whether promises or nightmares would be theirs in their city. In the decades that followed, Jews in each of the boroughs, indeed in every neighborhood, told varying stories, from how frightening to how exciting life was in the metropolis in an era of urban decline and revival.

Embattled Mayor Abraham Beame with famous *New York Daily News* front page: "Ford to City: Drop Dead," November 3, 1976. (Bill Stahl Jr. / *NY Daily News*; reprinted with permission)

CHAPTER 6

Amid Decline and Revival

With the eyes of millions of viewers coast-to-coast on the screen watching the second game of the World Series, commentator Howard Cosell looked beyond the diamond to the view outside Yankee Stadium: "Ladies and gentlemen," he announced in his acerbic fashion, "The Bronx is burning!" A controversial Jewish sports commentator who saw himself as a transcendent social critic, Cosell prided himself on telling it "like it is." So although he mis-identified the source of the conflagration—he said it was an apartment build-ing, but it was an abandoned school—Cosell, with a mien of extreme gravitas, pointed out to the nation that his native city was ablaze, a blighted, steeply declining metropolis under siege. Cosell did not pause to note the symbol-ism of the action on the field. The October 11, 1977, game pitted the Los An-geles Dodgers—that once-adored neighborhood-hugging franchise that had, in 1958, abandoned Brooklyn and contributed to a decline in the borough's self-esteem—against the Yankees, long emblematic of the city's power and dominance but presently rife with internal strife and controversy. For Abra-ham D. Beame, the city's first Jewish mayor, New York City needed such nega-tive publicity like a hole in the head. But Cosell's pronouncement etched itself into national consciousness. Everyone now saw New York as a city of bro-ken promises.[1]

Cosell's stinging jab came just a few days after President Jimmy Carter had made a surprise visit to the South Bronx. Newspapers and television reported that "he viewed some of the country's worst urban blight." Carter delivered a powerful media blow to the city Beame led. Arriving by way of the south-ernmost part of the Grand Concourse, described as "a decaying remnant of a once fashionable boulevard," he walked on Charlotte Street, near Crotona Park, "through two blocks of rubble that looked like the result of wartime bombing." Less than two years earlier, a *Daily News* headline screamed, "Ford to City: Drop Dead." While President Gerald Ford took offense at this tabloid's characterization of his response to New York's appeal to the federal government to "underwrite the city's debts" to prevent municipal bankruptcy, Ford asserted strongly that the "people in New York have been the victims of mismanagement."[2]

Beyond the injurious rhetoric lay unavoidable realities that a confluence of social, economic, and political crises had brought the city to the brink. Unlike earlier periods in New York history, in this century seemingly there was no escape. When Beame took office in January 1974, the explosive, explicit racial name-calling of the late 1960s had abated, but underlying tensions from long-existing problems of urban decline persisted. The compromising controller had won election after outlasting Herman Badillo, the first Latino to run for mayor, in a Democratic primary runoff and then defeated Republican John Marchi and Conservative Mario Biaggi in the general election.[3]

Under Beame's watch, the "lag" ended on many interconnected fronts "between the time when destructive forces" began to work and "the time when the effects" became visible. The metropolis's years as a light manufacturing center ended. Jews for generations found work and prospered in the city's industries, but neither their children nor new immigrants managed to compete against cheap, nonunionized labor and tax incentives in Sunbelt states. New York's garment trades, printing industries, and food processing migrated south, the first stop before leaving the country. Located near superhighways, these businesses had plenty of room to expand operations, and goods could be easily transported to, rather than from, old large-city markets. As the city's revenue base declined due to out-migration of businesses, short-sighted increases in municipal corporate taxes on the firms that remained and the always annoying permit and inspections fees further exasperated manufacturers.[4]

A significant worldwide recession began in 1973, exacerbating matters. Many major commercial banks, concerned with their own liquidity, demanded that the municipality pay back loans that they had for years encouraged New York to assume. These lending institutions also pushed strongly for greater government responsibility, calling for diminutions in city services, freezes and reductions in city jobs, and the rolling back of longstanding municipal labor benefits. Attempting to respond, the Beame administration instituted a wide range of budget cuts that engendered hard feelings citywide. Several firehouses were closed. Police and teachers were laid off. In 1976, the City University ended its 129-year tradition of no tuition. The city found little sympathy in Washington, D.C., where there was a sense that the metropolis was being repaid for its longtime irresponsibility and arrogance, even if no one actually told the city to drop dead.[5]

The abandonment and destruction of housing in expanding poor neighborhoods was an even more profound example of how governmental "sins of the past"—and some very recent transgressions—were being visited on "the population of today."[6] For more than a generation, critics of municipal policies had warned of the unintended consequences of rent-control laws, initiated during World War II to keep landlords from capitalizing on the housing shortage. Observers raised concerns about "the rent control trap . . . that distorts its housing market and creates new slums." Because landlords were blocked from garnering reasonable returns on their rent-frozen property, "a nibbling deferment of maintenance" ensued, as owners were "discouraged from repairing the leaky roof before it rots out beams and ceilings." Predominantly white, working-class residents put up with these inconveniences while paying very low rents until the early 1960s, when the fortunate ones relocated to suburbia or other new urban neighborhoods. Jews, too, increasingly decided to leave the city, abandoning mostly their elderly. Jewish communal discussions ignored these indigents until the 1970s, when crusading journalists focused attention on their problems. In the meantime, those left behind shared these buildings in disrepair with the city's poorest, if these Latinos and African Americans did not opt for the "projects," which possessed their own problems.[7]

The collapse of the manufacturing job market brought massive unemployment to recent immigrants and African Americans. Those who had never shared equally in the city's economic promises found fewer opportunities than ever within the depressed pool of entry-level industrial occupations. Many tenants were unable to pay their rents unless they were supported by the Welfare Department. People doubled up in apartments, as others had done during the Depression. Streets teemed with youth, and some turned to peddling drugs as addiction and crime rates increased. Landlords, seeking a way out of their financial holes, decided to take advantage of an ill-advised vacancy decontrol law of 1971 to extract whatever money they could from their poor tenants. The law allowed owners to hike rents every time there was a turnover in what were increasingly becoming transient populations. In each instance when a welfare family was moved in and out, fees and charges could go up without any improvements on the property. Yet if a landlord desired to up-grade the holdings, "redlining" by banks prevented the requisite extension of loans and mortgages.[8]

But after a certain point, landlords escaped this spiral of deterioration by abandoning their buildings to avoid real estate taxes. On the way out, the most unscrupulous were complicit in torching their investments to collect insur-ance. Nefarious "finishers" found lucrative opportunities to help complete the job. Before the suspicious fires, these criminals stripped the building of salvage-able parts, while the destitute still lived there. The epidemic affected neighbor-hoods all over the city, from the Lower East Side to the Bronx, to Brooklyn's Brownsville, Crown Heights, and Flatbush. As the housing problems spread, they often reached the outskirts of previously middle-class communities.[9]

Such was the fate of the wide expanse of the Grand Concourse. In Decem-ber 1970, an aide to Bronx Borough President Robert Abrams complained to a reporter that while the media was keenly aware of housing problems else-where in the city, he "sure would like to dramatize the abandonments" in his borough: "But we can't get the newsmen to come up to blocks like Charlotte Street." Seven years later, he and his bosses and City Hall leaders had their fill of the writers and cameras. Then the news media chronicled how the eco-nomic and social distress of Charlotte Street and its South Bronx neighbor-hood was leaping north and west, consuming the once-elite Concourse and its side streets. New York provided the classic city-in-decline scenario: rent-control conundrums, white working-class exodus, job loss, drugs, crime, and abandonment of housing. By the mid-1970s, "the boulevard," wrote one dis-mayed observer, "had become a major thoroughfare of a slum." Then in the hot summer of 1977, physical decimation intensified beyond all limits. During a regionwide electrical-grid blackout, marauding gangs of youths, who were angrily characterized by some people as "vultures" or as "jackal packs," looted much of the area's remaining businesses. Several months later, when Cosell spoke out, the designation "South Bronx," with all its negative connotations, applied to much of the Grand Concourse and its neighboring streets.[10]

These years severely tested the faith of New York's Jews in the metropolis's promises. More than in any prior era of their history in the city, the issue centered on whether they still felt safe, secure, and comfortable. Differences in perspectives between optimistic "Manhattan" and pessimistic "Brooklyn" Jews, and their counterparts in other boroughs, appeared in the sharpest relief. Tens of thousands answered the basic existential question of whether they belonged in New York with an unqualified no. They joined and indeed constituted a significant component in the middle-class exodus of the 1970s–1980s. The numbers show a net loss of one hundred thousand Jews from the five boroughs, with their prime destination nearby suburbia. Now, for the first time, Jews were as "equally suburbanized" as the general population was. The Bronx suffered the steepest decline. By 1981, fifty thousand fewer Jews lived there than ten years earlier. Congregations folded. The Tremont Temple ended its more than half century of service to the Grand Concourse community. As late as 1966, the congregation still had "200 families with 120 children in its school." Nine years later, membership had evaporated "down to fifty—most of who live[d] north of area." At that point, it merged into the Scarsdale Synagogue.[11]

Among the most dissatisfied Jews on the move were those with preteen and teenage children, who saw no future for the next generation in the old neighborhood. They worried about the education their youngsters would receive in city schools and with whom they would sit in classes. Longtime Jewish public school teacher and administrator Berl Sternberg recalled that in the 1960s, during his first decade as an assistant principal at Junior High School 45, located off Fordham Road, perpendicular to the northern section of the Grand Concourse, half of his students were of Italian ancestry, a third were Jews, and only 15 percent were black or Latino. By the early 1980s, only 5 percent of his pupils were white. School statistics verify shifting enrollments. As of the 1971–72 academic year, within District 10, where Sternberg worked, some 60 percent of the students were either black or Latino.[12]

The arrival of Jewish refugees from the Soviet Union and Muslim countries along with expatriates from Israel mitigated the substantial decline of New York Jews. Rough estimates suggest that from 1972 to 1984, fifty thousand Jews from the USSR, one-half of those allowed to immigrate to America, settled in New York. Approximately the same number of Jews came to the metropolis from Iraq, Syria, and most notably Iran, where Jewish life declined precipitously after the fall of the Shah in 1979 and the rise of the Khomeini regime. In addition, by the early 1980s, no fewer than fifty thousand and perhaps as many as one hundred thousand Israelis lived in New York. Such common immigrant impulses as "economic and professional problems or temptations" motivated their migration, as did interest in advanced educational training and a desire to "get out and see the world." A minority emigrated because of concerns over Israel's security and personal military obligations in a country constantly threatened by war. Each of these groups settled in Brooklyn and Queens and helped to maintain a Jewish presence. Starting out from their own enclaves, the newcomers began their quests to see what New York, even in decline, had to offer.[13]

Some Jews who stayed in New York City nonetheless shared their suburban compatriots' pessimism about the destiny of the city. In the 1970s, many Canarsie Jews felt alienated from the metropolis, although their Brooklyn enclave had been spared much of the worst of urban blight. Those who worked in service industries among the poor or as city employees, social workers, and most notably, teachers encountered daily the economic and social problems just beyond their borders. Everyone seemed to know someone who had been victimized elsewhere in the city. However, though fears of African Americans pushed those with money to move to the suburbs, many more determined to stay. They decided to protect their neighborhood by forcefully limiting the numbers of blacks and Latinos around them.

"We ran once but we have nowhere else to go," one Jewish community leader explained. The earliest postwar Jewish settlers came to Canarsie from Brownsville and East New York during calmer times in the 1950s. But by the 1970s, the sense on the Jewish street was that they were part of a "Diaspora," unwilling exiles who had been forced out elsewhere in Brooklyn. "Not rich" but fortunate enough to have found a refuge, "a sanctuary," in Canarsie, they refused to surrender their piece of the borough.[14] Jews struck alliances with their Italian neighbors, who occupied the vanguard of community backlash. Jews eschewed the vigilantism that some Italians resorted to and were often apologetic and circumspect when they explained their stance to family and friends who lived outside of their threatened neighborhood. But on key gut issues, the two white ethnic groups found common cause, even if they failed to "achieve a seamless identity."[15]

In the critical housing arena, Jews and Italians worked on convincing those who might put their properties on the market—often the elderly with longstanding ties to the community—to sell only to the "right kind of buyers." They implored these neighbors that advertising be placed only in "Jewish, Italian and *Chinese* papers" and not in the *New York Times*. In courting that Asian minority, they reasoned that if the neighborhood was destined to change its color, "Orientals"—as they were called—who "mind their own business, . . . respect you as an individual and their morals are good" were far more acceptable than blacks and Latinos were. Local residents created neighborhood buying services to bring customers to sellers. No one wanted "for sale" signs posted outside. Block associations patrolled the community to forestall panic selling, to fight blockbusting real estate agents seeking to "flip" houses, and to impress on those contemplating a move their continuing obligations to those who would remain. Some Jews turned to the nearby Brighton Beach community to recruit coreligionists from the former Soviet Union who had acquired the economic wherewithal to purchase their first homes in America.[16]

Defense of turf also spurred Jewish and Italian activists, with widespread support among their neighbors, to stand as one against the busing of even a limited number of black youngsters into a Canarsie junior high school. Parents boycotted during the 1972–73 academic year and succeeded in keeping 90 percent of the students out of school for more than two weeks. In asserting his community's right to control its own public schools, one local rabbi reminded his public that just two years earlier, during the fractious New York City teachers' strike, black parents had claimed just that right. His "what's good for the goose is good for the gander" rhetoric resonated in a community where more than 10 percent of the Jewish residents in some sections were teachers, administrators, or paraprofessionals. An Italian resident spoke of an inescapable irony that "blacks wanted decentralization in Ocean Hill–Brownsville. But then 80 percent of the fired . . . teachers came to Canarsie and now the blacks want to come here." Concerted efforts led the city school board to halt its busing initiatives.[17]

The Jews of Co-op City hoped that come what may to their old neighborhoods, they could live comfortably and securely in new environs in the city. However, that promise was only partially fulfilled. They had been lured away from their stable and affordable communities, most notably from the Grand Concourse, by a gigantic 15,400-unit apartment complex in a northeastern corner of the Bronx. The dream was to construct, in the spirit of the Amalgamated initiatives of decades earlier and under the name of the United Housing

Federation, a bucolic residential environment "for friendly people living together." Supported by Mitchell-Lama subsidies, these apartments included free electricity and air-conditioning. Previously Jews had sprawled on fire escapes or sat on park benches long into the summer nights, the best way to stay cool. The planned community for working-class people and their children boasted shopping centers, schools, parks, and abundant parking, in effect offering residents suburban amenities within the metropolis. Attracted by these offers and often frightened by African American and Latino migrations into their erstwhile neighborhoods in the late 1960s–early 1970s, between twenty-five and forty thousand Jews (estimated as 50–80 percent of the initial residents) made Co-op City their home.

Moving there made abundant sense to "the salesmen and civil servants, the accountants and bakers," many approaching retirement age, who perceived their new homes as "the only way station between the decaying neighborhoods they escaped and the affluent suburbs they cannot afford." They hoped to re-create at least part of the friendly street culture of the old neighborhood. And indeed, when the complex opened, "long after night fall elderly men and women [would] stroll along the expansive greens or chat on benches." On the Jewish holidays, residents promenaded in a style reminiscent of the Grand Concourse of old, even if one of the early arrivals described that street scene as not New York but "a little Jerusalem." There were "no iron gates on the stores" and "no graffiti." Co-op City boasted "one of the lowest crime rates in the city, second in the Bronx only to Riverdale." A thirty-five-man "security force armed with night sticks" enforced an eleven o'clock weekday and midnight Saturday curfew, which annoyed youngsters but kept them in line. Occupants could pretty much have it all for "an average carrying charge of $31.71 a room (including utilities) after a down payment of $450 a room." It appeared to be a Jewish working-class haven. An early resident who had paid "$83 a month rent plus gas and electric for four rooms" in the West Bronx now expended but "$130 a month utilities included." Moreover, she, an office employee at Mt. Sinai Hospital, her postal employee husband, and their two sons had a terrace in an apartment that they owned with open spaces around them.[18]

Some older Jewish residents of Parkchester also moved to Co-op City, even though it represented but a half step up. Fear did not motivate their move. The youngsters chased by Parkchester private cops from locked playgrounds after closing time were their own. But while their buildings were well maintained, the prewar structures lacked air-conditioning. Sitting outside with friends until late at night during the summer was no substitute for the promises of Co-op City. Parkchester's vacant apartments attracted some Jews who fled the South Bronx. They joined aspiring working-class blacks and Latinos, who now could rent apartments in Parkchester, and Irish and Italians in composing its new core constituency.[19]

The adult children of Parkchester residents who made it to Co-op City, having outgrown their mischievous moments with the neighborhood's security force, did even better than their parents. They settled either in suburbia or in Riverdale. By the mid-1970s, Parkchester's Jewish heyday had ended. If Jews chose Riverdale, they discovered an "island entirely of itself, . . . in the city yet not of it," a new-era urban bedroom community tucked away from New York's decline. They could even pretend to be, as one critic put it, "a rich nephew who doesn't recognize his ragged old uncle." In 1972, this articulate Bronx partisan who apparently lived in Kingsbridge, a few blocks east and down the hill from that "rocky escarpment," wanted those privileged denizens to be more engaged in their borough's concerns. He noted that while Riverdale "prides itself" as a "cultured, progressive and liberal community," it had "resisted, successfully so far, any attempts to build low-income and even Government-subsidized middle-income housing projects." By the 1980s, whether they were socially committed, elitist, or apathetic, thirty thousand Jews lived in Riverdale.[20]

But while middle- and upper-class Jews sank secure roots in Riverdale, so that by 1991 they constituted a full third of the neighborhood and their percentage of the population grew steadily, poor planning plagued Co-op City. Both United Housing Federation leaders and government officials badly underestimated expenses in building and maintaining the state-assisted endeavor. Carrying costs, which included mortgage payments and rising fuel prices, became an increasingly onerous burden on residents who had qualified for apartments under Mitchell-Lama precisely because of their limited incomes. In the early 1970s, fifteen thousand (40 percent) of the occupants were over sixty-five years of age, and many of them lived "on pensions and Social Security." However, although they were aging, these "cooperators" had not lost their combative spirit, honed for decades as unionists. In 1975, when the United Housing Federation board attempted to impose a 25 percent rent increase, residents took to their own streets and withheld monthly payments, setting off a thirteen-month rent strike. They demanded that the government increase its subsidies. This protest had some of the trappings of past consumer revolts. Reportedly 80 percent of the people joined in the protest. Driving around the complex, block captains, elected by a steering committee, boomed out announcements as bedsheets supporting the effort hung from windows. Strike leaders collected some $15 million in rent checks, which they kept secretly. There was even a sort of underground newspaper. With constituents showing their lack of confidence, if not outright contempt, the United Housing Federation directors resigned. In June 1976, an initial compromise solution was reached whereby a new resident-elected board would endeavor, with government help, to "seek to implement economies and find new revenues." But without a program for ongoing rent stability, the cost of living in Co-op City remained a burden for many residents. Israel Schwartz, who moved into the complex soon after it opened late in 1968, in looking back on his experiences after ten years there asserted, "It's a dud, a complete dud. We were taken in, suckered right from the start. We were promised the Garden of Eden, but they inveigled us to get us in and then started to pile the charges on."[21]

By 1979, when Schwartz was interviewed by the *New York Times*, he and his elderly confreres also complained that their buildings were not aging well. Just two years earlier, there was a six-month dispute with the State over construction defects. These ranged from falling bricks to shifting land under the buildings that occasionally caused gas leaks. The word on Co-op City streets in the mid-1980s was that " 'CD' does not mean 'compact disk' but 'construction defect.' " By the end of that decade, naysayers described this neighborhood as "a dream gone sour." As the citywide crack-cocaine epidemic entered its buildings, Co-op City lost most of its Jewish residents. Rabbi Solomon I. Berl, struggling to keep his Young Israel of Co-op City going, attributed the decline of his "once-vibrant congregation [to] the three Ms, mortality, move-outs and Miami Beach." When he relocated from the East Bronx some twenty-one years earlier, his congregation had seven hundred families. In 1989, he ministered to less than two hundred. Among those who remained—as well as those who belonged to the complex's four other congregations—were those who did not feel his acute sense of abandonment. They acknowledged that their numbers constantly were dwindling, but they lived harmoniously, in their relatively low-crime area, amid the new majority of African American and Latino families, whose aspirations reminded some Jewish old-timers of their own years earlier. The most contented among them even felt that gradually the upkeep of Co-op City improved. But no young Jewish families moved in.[22]

While Riverdalians felt right at home, Co-op City families wondered about their decisions, and Canarsie Jews struggled, other New York Jews in the 1970s evinced unbridled confidence that the city still possessed, as it always had, so much to offer. These upwardly mobile singles and couples without children scorned suburbia. They found both comfort and excitement in the metropolis. Even at the very nadir of New York's decline, social commentators noted the beginnings of an alternate urban dynamic. "Behind the empirical city lurks *another* city, a city of wonders and dreams," wrote one scholar in his 1977 paean to a New York that had "kept all of its promises" to him. Another sociologist concretely observed that "despite the exodus to the suburbs and changes in the ethnic configuration of the city," it was home to "a sizable middle- and upper-middle-class" that had decided that the "city's amenities outweigh, or at least compensate for, its disadvantages." Economist John Kenneth Galbraith explained that "the suburban movement was the response of the older city dwellers to the poverty and indiscipline of the new arrivals" and predicted, "As that shock effect loses its relevance, the superior quality of city life will naturally assert itself." Members of this "new elite" made "the entire city their bailiwick." Not tied to a specific neighborhood, they frequented chic cultural, culinary, and high-class entertainment throughout the metropolis. Still, when they ended their days and nights out, they returned to communities that benefited from their presence. In 1978, it was noted that "young people who two decades ago would have settled in a Levittown are gravitating towards neighborhoods like Soho and Brooklyn Heights." In some cases, these "trend-setting gentrifiers" or "urban homesteaders" began to turn once dismal districts into "delightful neighborhoods." Observers marveled that Manhattan's Columbus Avenue, once run-down and dreary, possessed "colorful shops and restaurants." With the right bottom-line bank accounts, and perhaps also the right pigmentation, they found banks ready and willing to extend to them the necessary lines of credit to assist their initiatives.[23]

Young Jews participated in the emergence of this other optimistic New York scene because so many of them had escaped the occupational downturn in their city. Part of a new generation, no longer working class, they possessed

financial security. They had choices and could move around the city's neighborhoods. They proved that the old adage about American Jews, romanticized
as early as the 1920s, that eastern Europeans were "neither the sons nor the
fathers of workers," had now come true on a large scale.[24]

By the early 1970s, union by union, officials reported, as did the leader of
the Knit Goods Union Local 155, "The Jewish parents used to send us their
children and ask that we give them jobs. Now they no longer come." This once
predominantly Jewish garment industry had employed Jews as "pressers, cutters, knitters, finishers." Now half of the union membership was black or Latino. Within the Amalgamated Clothing Workers Union, the only Jews in the
factory were approaching retirement age. The same held true among those
who worked in bakeries. Local 51 of the Bakers' and Confectionary Workers' Union noted "a steady decline in Jewish workers from about 70 percent
to 35 percent." Young Jews were also far less likely to seek civil service jobs,
except public school teaching, or to stand behind counters in retail stores. As
of 1970, only a quarter of the members of District Council 37 of the American Federation of State, County, and Municipal Employees Union were Jews,
mostly secretaries and supervisory clerks. Likewise, at large department stores
such as Gimbels and Bloomingdales, only 25 percent of employees were Jews.
A quarter century earlier, the figure approached 50 percent. These firms even
saw a "decline in the number of Jews entering the executive ranks." Citywide
numbers confirmed these trends. As the 1970s opened, 55 percent of Jewish
men were employed in "professional, technical, managerial or administrative"
posts. Some 20 percent were in sales and clerical positions. Only a quarter
of them were involved in any working-class occupation. If they were self-
employed, argued one demographer in 1972, they would be in "accounting,
business advisory services, . . . law" and not in the "Mom and Pop store."[25]

This younger generation had taken full advantage of the increasing openness of American society toward Jews. Academic achievers, they contributed
to the statistic that by the close of the 1970s more than half of New York Jewish heads of households were college educated. In Manhattan, a borough described as home for over a decade to "an influx of socio-economic 'upscale'
individuals," more than one-third of Jewish men and 29 percent of Jewish
women possessed graduate degrees. They had studied for their advanced degrees and elite professions not only at the City University but on campuses
across the country.[26]

In New York City, at Columbia and Barnard, as of 1969, rough estimates placed their percentage of undergraduate Jewish students at approximately 30 percent. These numbers included New Yorkers and others enrolled at these universities that recruited nationally. Fourteen years later, the percentage increased to a full one-half of the student body.[27] Some of these Jewish students of the late 1960s and early 1970s became prime provocateurs of campus protest. It was as if the spirit of the 1930s alcoves and the locus of the student leadership in the National Student League had moved from CCNY to Columbia, where Jews played leading roles in such organizations as Students for a Democratic Society. When Nathan Glazer analyzed "the Jewish role in student activism" on college campuses, he noted Jews' commanding presence at the University of California–Berkeley, the University of Wisconsin, and the University of Michigan, but not at his alma mater. When CCNY did erupt in protests, as so many campuses did during the Kent State–Cambodia crisis of 1970, some radical Jews shared the rostrums with other ethnic groups. But Jews were not identified as the most outspoken elements. Two years earlier, a Jewish physics professor at CCNY, described as "close to the radicals" on his campus, reflected, "Most of the kids here are, in some ways, like the parents of the Columbia students." In his view, "their prime concern is mobility, to get a professional skill." And, "as in past years, most of City College's undergraduates climb into subways and return home by dusk."[28]

But in the 1970s, this quintessential city commuter school lost much of its cachet among local college-aged Jews. Their percentages dropped precipitously from almost 75 percent of the student body in 1969, including both those enrolled at the main Harlem Heights campus and at its Baruch business school branch in Murray Hill, to only 20 percent of the uptown student population ten years later. By 1982–83, another informal study suggested that only 950 Jews (8 percent) attended an institution where they once predominated. These declines are attributable, at least in part, to a perception that the school no longer stood for academic excellence. In the spring of 1969, a city university systemwide fight over "Open Admissions" focused on CCNY. This policy granted a seat in any unit to all New York high school graduates regardless of grades. Those who objected to the plan argued that it meant bringing young men and women unprepared for higher education into advanced academic environments. While "Open Admissions" was mandated citywide, it did not deter Jews as much from attending a now freestanding Baruch

College or Queens College and Brooklyn College. While the Jewish percentages at Queens dropped from an estimated 46 percent in 1969 to 36 percent in 1979, four years later, the Jewish presence on campus crested at 50 percent. Perhaps here, young men and women from less affluent Jewish families still gravitated to the promises of the city's higher education system, even if tuition was imposed in 1976. But they no longer competed to enter CCNY in Harlem Heights. Many other New York Jews opted for moderately priced, academically respectable New York State system schools and the possibility of attending a college "away from home."[29]

After graduation, these Jews obtained jobs offering more financial security than their parents had achieved. Such jobs opened doors to any number of attractive neighborhoods. Jews enjoyed their city, optimistic about its future. When queried at the start of the 1980s as to whether they were "very satisfied with the safety of the streets and with the cleanliness of their neighborhoods," only a small minority of Jews in Manhattan, not unlike those in the outer boroughs, responded positively. But when further interrogated as to whether they thought their neighborhoods would be "better" within the next three years, 40 percent, twice as many as even those who lived in suburban Nassau and Suffolk Counties, answered positively. They planned to be part of the expected "neighborhood revival." Less than one in seven were then looking "for a new place to live."[30]

As these young people enthused about their prospects, more than one hundred thousand needy, elderly Jewish New Yorkers struggled to survive in "this huge concrete and steel and garbage city which consumes lives." For them, wrote a sympathetic observer in 1973, "New York is an ambiguous lover. It promises riches. It steals them away. . . . It was a city that symbolized 'the American dream.' Now it is this city which typifies the American nightmare." A full decade after economist and social critic Michael Harrington exposed the existence of an "other America, the America of poverty, . . . hidden today in a way that it never was before," the plight of similarly afflicted "socially-invisible" New York Jews finally attracted public attention. The Federation of Jewish Philanthropies quantified the extent of their predicament. It reported that "272,000 individuals or 15.1 percent of the Jewish population . . . are poor or near poor." Most of the seniors, 86,000 of them, lived in "15 of the city's 26 designated poverty areas . . . frequently . . . in a religiously hostile environment."[31]

In many cases, these men and women were remnants of the Jewish laboring class. They were too old to continue working, or their jobs had evaporated as the city's manufacturing base shrank. Thousands of foreign-born Jews also possessed few marketable skills. Often these seniors were widows and widowers whose children or other relatives had left the old neighborhood. Some were socially and psychologically unable to leave their apartments in crime-ridden environs, despite repeated family entreaties. These "holdouts . . . just put another lock on [their] doors."[32]

Yet, occasionally, Jews remained for other reasons. One group of elderly South Bronx Jews stayed in their neighborhood not because they had no alternatives but because their perseverance provided "a sense of dignity and self-worth," permitting them "to feel brave and resourceful when others [saw] the area as too dangerous to visit, let alone inhabit." For them, "rejecting their children's offer to house them or shunning homes for the aged" represented "a personal protest against passivity." Anthropologist Jack Kugelmass discovered these staunch "hold-outs" within the Intervale Jewish Center, the last synagogue in the so-called Fort Apache section of the Bronx. By the time Kugelmass arrived in 1980, the area had risen somewhat from its mid-1970s nadir. "The fires had stopped. The gangs had disappeared. The drug addicts had died." Still, these stalwarts said that even during the toughest times of the prior decade, when one member recalled that "the fumes [from fires] were so bad you couldn't breathe at night," they had been committed to keeping their minyan [prayer quorum] alive. What kept them going was "a lust for the 'good fight,'" taking on "the challenge to overcome adversity by actively imagining reality and imposing their will on it." Their "charismatic leader" and "acting rabbi" personified this vision. Moishe Sacks linked their fortunes and fate to a future messianic era, when the destroyed Holy Temple in Jerusalem would be restored. A gifted storyteller, he inspired the handful of neighborhood survivors to paint the building and fix the roof. Sacks, who earned his livelihood as a baker, once quipped, "When the Messiah comes, all of the synagogues will pick themselves up and be transported to Jerusalem. I want this place to look nice, and besides, we shouldn't have leaks during the rainy season there."[33]

Hasidim within their several Brooklyn settlements—the Satmar in Williamsburg, Lubavitchers in Crown Heights, and a myriad of other sects in those neighborhoods and in Boro Park—awaited the coming of the messiah far more reverently. In fact, so convinced were the Satmar that divine intervention alone would bring Jews back to their holy land that they violently opposed the return of Jews to the State of Israel. Their anti-Zionist stance set them at ideological odds with other Hasidism and the overwhelming majority of Jews worldwide. However, while the Redeemer tarried, Hasidim determined not only to fortify their enclaves in the Brooklyn Diaspora, even as some relocated within concentrated, insulated communities in Rockland and Orange Counties, but also to advance financially. Pursuit of New York's economic promises while avoiding its secular culture required a strategy of engagement with New York politics. They formed a dedicated voting bloc to ensure that government would address their needs. Politicians learned quickly that a Hasidic rebbe's endorsement meant that his followers would turn out at the polls for the chosen candidate. Soon a new urban rite of passage for those in search of votes emerged: the pilgrimage to be photographed with a nylon yarmulke on their heads next to Hasidic rebbes.[34]

Beyond the fear of crime, poverty plagued Hasidic communities. In the early 1970s, Hasidic indigents, "many of them with young families," constituted "the third largest poverty group in New York." Their problems stemmed from dilemmas that troubled all newcomers to the city, including the African American and Latino minorities among whom they lived. Many Hasidim possessed few marketable skills in a declining manufacturing center. Their resistance to American mores, which was highly esteemed in their community, severely limited their economic mobility. Often they acquired minimal secular educations. English was at best a second language. Their dress and demeanor and their high level of observance, including utter avoidance of work on the Sabbath, limited their attractiveness to employers. Fidelity to traditional bans on birth control led to large families with concomitant burdens of paying for yeshiva education. A 1972 statistic indicated that "the larger families" among the Hasidim—families of six or more—were disproportionately represented among "the poor or near poor. . . . About 25% of all such families are below the near poverty level." There were also many unemployable elderly in these communities.[35]

Hasidim sustained a distinctive local economy that provided steady and sometimes lucrative incomes for owners and operators of kosher butcher shops, bakeries, restaurants, and Judaica stores. These businesspeople also served observant Americanized Orthodox Jews elsewhere in the city and nation, whose next generation was not interested in these occupations. Communication and confidentiality within families, coupled with international group connections with Hasidim in Belgium and elsewhere, helped others succeed in the diamond industry. Brooklyn Hasidim entered Manhattan's Forty-Seventh Street, the heart of the city's jewelry district, in pursuit of customers of all backgrounds and ethnicities. In the back of their stores, friends and relatives worked as cutters and polishers of gems. Satmar Hasid Israel Goldstein became a legend for his entrepreneurial acumen, not for selling jewelry but for electronics. By the late 1980s, Goldstein's 47th Street Photo grossed more than $100 million annually and employed around three hundred of his fellow Jews. Most of his customers from all over the country who never set foot in his four stores probably were unaware that Jewish religious scruples governed his business hours, although he advertised that "47th Street Photo was closed Friday afternoon and all day Saturday." Goldstein and other financially successful figures supported Hasidic institutions and the poor. Still, despite philanthropic generosity, Hasidic leaders sought government aid. Their pragmatism overcame the religious communal norm of Jews caring for their own without outside assistance or interference. Hasidim's optimism or pessimism about New York's future directions and their place within the city would not be tied to any citywide economic and cultural renaissance. Rather, their range of sentiments depended on the municipality's ability to keep them safe and solvent.[36]

Syrian Jews, in their own sections of Brooklyn—Midwood, Bensonhurst, and Flatbush—also came to terms with the city. Their social mores did not appear to separate them from other New Yorkers. In their dress, speech, and public demeanor, they resembled those around them. Moreover, with entrepreneurial skills from Aleppo or Damascus, they carved out successful business niches and engaged customers of all backgrounds. Often relying on friends and relatives for start-up cash, a time-honored tradition, they achieved prominence in discount store operations. In the 1970s, Ezra Antar was their best-known success story, until he ran afoul of the law. Known around town as "Crazy Eddie" due to his wild television ads, in which an actor portraying him shouted at the top of his lungs that his low "prices were insane," Antar became a discount electronics sales giant—that is, until sadly for him and his community, he was charged with a variety of securities violations, including schemes to "overstate company income and benefit from stock sales." More typically, law-abiding Syrian Jews exploited New York's economic promises while cultivating an "in-group and clannishness syndrome" to limit their engagement with New York's wider cultural scene. A community insider noted how both older and younger generations largely avoided social intercourse with Gentiles and non-Syrian Jews. Gradually, these patterns changed in the 1970s. Young men and women broadened their social circles by attending colleges and universities. Many chose Brooklyn College close to home, but "the more venturesome went outside of Brooklyn and out of town." Some aspired to professional careers. By the 1990s, Syrian Jews included a cadre of their own physicians, attorneys, and accountants. Some of these college-educated sons and daughters married a non-Syrian Jew and never came back to Brooklyn except to visit. Others sought advanced degrees in business administration to help them in the local family enterprise. Within the Midwood, Bensonhurst, and Flatbush enclaves, notwithstanding increased exposure to a more diversified social and intellectual world, social insularity reigned, maintained more by communal pressure than explicit religious edict.[37]

Differences in attitudes among New York's Jews toward their city, and their sense of place within it, grew more striking during the recovery decade of the 1980s. Metropolitan fortunes began to change under the first administration of Mayor Edward I. Koch (1978–82). The new Jewish incumbent and his constituents rode the crest of an improving national economy and benefited from the energetic efforts of Governor Hugh Carey that started even before Koch took office. Albany marshaled a group of investment bankers to create regulatory agencies such as the Municipal Assistance Corporation and the Financial Control Board, which projected an aura that the city's finances were secure. The mayor amplified practically and psychologically the city's renewed cachet. When he appeared before congressional committees seeking financial assistance, he pointed to his aggressive posture in dealing with municipal unions, whose longstanding sweetheart contracts had burdened the city. As important, as the quintessential unmarried Manhattanite, he made a point of personally being out on the town. He personified the advertising slogan "I Love New York." Frequenting upscale restaurants, night clubs, and athletic events, including those at Yankee Stadium, he constantly asked, "How am I doing?" Without waiting for a reply, he let anyone within earshot know that he and New York were doing just fine.[38]

By the middle of Koch's second term, 1982–87, his ebullience seemed to have rubbed off on his fellow New Yorkers. While harboring "an acerbic portrait of metropolitan life," they were not "nearly as gloomy about the city's future as in years past. . . . Fewer residents dream[ed] of moving to more placid places." "A quirky pride in their city" was also palpable. Three out of four New Yorkers polled in 1985 "repudiated the notion" that their fellow citizens, including the mayor, who had a biting tongue, were preternaturally unpleasant to strangers. "It's survival not rudeness," retorted one interviewee who found the "attitude amusing and feisty." The most upbeat people, such as His Honor, "explore[d] the city's variety—attending plays, concerts and sports events, . . . museums, parks and libraries."[39]

Indeed, New York was rebounding, with revenue streams flowing in because of "the post-industrial revolution." While the metropolis continued to be "a headquarters city" for national and international firms, the city's service industries rather than manufacturing or distributing companies generated the jobs and income. Between 1977 and 1988, New York lost 112,000 jobs in manufacturing but increased by 271,000 the number of spots in "telecommunication, air transportation and transportation services, commercial and investment banking, legal services, advertising, computer services, accounting and business consulting." Manhattan became "the world's largest shopping center" for such activities. People with proper training and motivation made their fortunes in these exciting, when not cutthroat, pursuits. When their long-before-dawn-to-postdusk workday ended, they repaired to their favorite restaurants and bars for respite, before perhaps returning to work into the wee hours. Working with clients and customers around the world, they transformed New York into a global city.[40]

Young associates at an aggressive law firm such as Skadden, Arps, Slate, Meagher and Flom never had a free lunch. Under the leadership of managing partner Joseph Flom, a Jewish CCNY night-school student with a Harvard law degree but without either the social graces or Christian faith, in the 1950s, to step into an established WASP "white shoe" law firm. Skadden earned a reputation for its high-volume work ethic as specialists in litigating hostile corporate mergers. One veteran of the booming 1980s, when this outfit grew to more than one thousand attorneys, recalled that when he "went out [with clients] for very fancy dinners and drank very expensive wines," a boon in its own right to these restaurateurs, he always chalked it up to "billable time."

With a long work night still ahead of him after his expensive business meal
—dinner at ten p.m., back to the desk at midnight—it made sense to live near
the office, even if private car services also flourished in that labor-intensive
environment. Gentrification crescendoed as former loft manufacturing space
morphed into luxury residences to serve ambitious lawyers.[41]

In 1982, the *New York Times* advised people thinking of living in Chelsea
that "rundown buildings that used to be single-room-occupancy dwellings are
being converted into luxury cooperatives. . . . Seedy blocks once distinguished
most noticeably by their derelicts now boast shops selling expensive cheeses,
exotic coffee beans, pates and pasta salads." The boom in real estate resonated
beyond Manhattan. "The restless ranks of the ambitious but not yet affluent,"
who could not yet afford Chelsea's "skyrocketing rents," were "colonizing fresh
territories across the bridges." But as "new districts of prosperity" were expanding, displacing underclass and working-class New Yorkers, pioneers of
neighborhood improvement also had to move. Artists who initially had used
these former manufacturing lofts as home and studio now fled upscale prices.
"There's always been room in this town for the dreamers and the poets," complained one critic. "Sadly, it seems that the weavers of dreams are becoming
expendable." Some compared the potential departure of "the New York arts
community into the arms of the Mayor of Jersey City" to the departure of the
baseball Giants and Dodgers a generation earlier.[42]

While these young professionals were on the make, frustrations and foibles
troubled them. These social pathologies garnered their greatest public exposure through the artistry of a filmmaker who shared their problems. Woody
Allen was the "reigning *auteur* of yuppie angst, in fact of all varieties of urban
angst, during the eighties," even if his work focusing on this contemporary
metropolitan scene had begun a decade earlier. Like many who were born in
Brooklyn, the Bronx, or Queens, Manhattan was New York City. The "Manhattan" Allen satirized was "inhabited mainly by Jews and WASPs—there are few
blacks, or Hispanics, Italians, Chinese, Irish or Haitians." His city dwellers are
affluent: "the people generally have income, a sense of style and good taste,"
and his scene settings are often yuppie haunts, "all infused with [his] sense of
excitement of the city and the reassurance that provides for ceaselessly varied
life going on in all its urban permutations." One analyst of the locations that
Allen uses to tell the story of *Hannah and Her Sisters* notes that Allen's 1986

movie identifies no fewer than thirty venues. These range from a loft on Grand Street to the Carlyle Hotel on Madison Avenue, to restaurants in Soho, to the jogging track and Sheep Meadow in Central Park, places that his subjects, like Allen himself, frequented. The film *Manhattan* (1979) located the geographical hub of Allen's central character, a semiautobiographical figure, on "the East Side extending from the forties to the nineties." But many of these young men and women appear unhappy with their lives of material achievement. In these movies and in *Annie Hall* (1977) and *Crimes and Misdemeanors* (1989), Allen demonstrated how attuned he was to their, and his own, feelings of acute anxiety over "the competitiveness of their jobs, . . . guilt over their greed and meaningless acquisitiveness." In their quests, as Allen portrays them, these "self-seekers" end up in troubled relationships with their backgrounds and families in the neighborhoods they had left behind. One critic lauded Allen as "the urban poet of our anxious age—skeptical, guiltily bourgeois, longing to answer the impossible questions." Another observer credited him with possessing a keen sense for "some large philosophical dualities" that undermined the lives of these men and women who had broken from their pasts but were uncertain about their futures. Reflecting on his own cinematic achievements, and his own endemic frustrations, Allen has allowed that he was "sensitive to the reflectiveness of modern life, focusing upon inner tensions and anxieties exacerbated by the pressures of urban living."[43]

There was, however, an even darker real-life side to "generation greed" when competitiveness for acquisitiveness crossed legal lines, leading the unscrupulous to commit high-profile white-collar crimes. In 1986, corporate takeover kingpin Ivan F. Boesky was fined $100 million for illegal stock manipulation based on insider trading. A man who, just a few months earlier, had told an eager young audience at the University of California that "greed is healthy, you can be greedy and still feel good about yourself" was sentenced to two years in federal prison. While Boesky served time, fictional character Gordon Gecko borrowed the line "greed is good" in the 1987 movie *Wall Street*. Boesky's fall from grace embarrassed several major Jewish charities that previously had courted his generosity. At a time when other rich Jews were showing how much they desired upper-class acceptance through identification with the philanthropies of high society, organizations such as the United Jewish Appeal and the Jewish Theological Seminary of America had been very pleased that

Boesky had not forgotten his own people. He also sought to promote Jewish life at Princeton. The Seminary moved on after Boesky's release, when "acting on his own request, [he] took his name off its $20 million library," which he largely endowed.[44]

As with all ethnic and racial groups, Boesky and his ilk were exceptional notorious figures. Most young Manhattan Jews did not emulate the felon, even if during his rise his picture was on the cover of *Time* magazine. Rather, they fit the profile of those New Yorkers most energized and excited by a revived city who did so well within the law. In the early 1980s, this borough was deemed "the pre-eminent home of the never-married," as "fully one half" of young Jewish singles in the metropolitan area lived there. Substantial numbers of childless young marrieds joined them in their upscale neighborhoods. These were upper-middle-class professionals earning salaries far in excess of those in other boroughs, and only some older affluent Jews living in Westchester or Nassau Counties outstripped them financially. These young Manhattanites grasped "the opportunity to live near people in similar family circumstances," handled high housing costs, and enjoyed "the proximity to expanding sources of business and professional employment and the cultural richness of the center city."[45]

Some Jews struggled with personal difficulties, as captured in Allen's movies, but did not emulate Boesky's unbridled rapaciousness. More generally, they blended their success story with that of members of diverse ethnic backgrounds to create a new cultural texture to New York Jewish neighborhood life. This new Jewish generation did not sense that its whole world was Jewish or desire that it be that way. When surveyed, close to half indicated that their three closest friends were not Jewish. They did, however, maintain one long-standing tradition, widely observed years ago on the Grand Concourse and on Eastern Parkway. They shunned local synagogues eager to welcome them. In 1981, more than 40 percent of these young men and women never attended religious services, and another quarter appeared only on the High Holidays. Merely 16–18 percent attended any more than a few times per year. Perhaps, as in past eras, some of them could be found promenading around their neighborhood in their holiday finery on Rosh Hashanah. But their crowd likely included non-Jewish friends and, increasingly, relatives.[46]

Creative religious leaders attempted to use modern publicity methods to fill empty seats in their sanctuaries. In 1980, the Lincoln Square Synagogue of the Upper West Side initiated its "Turn Friday Night into Shabbos" program, with a plan that smacked of Madison Avenue's advertising firms. Its pitch to those who frequented local singles bars was, "How about sharing red wine for Kiddush instead of white wine for cocktails?" Or "How about a $10.00 ticket for a Shabbos meal instead of a $40.00 ticket for the Theater?" The program that enveloped the liquor and tasty food offerings promised not a formal service but instead a "real Shabbos meal, . . . lots of singing, maybe some dancing" of the Jewish, and not disco, variety. Once those young "curious residents" were attracted, the congregation's rabbis worked slowly and subtly to convince them to "usher in the Sabbath in the same way their ancestors have ushered it in for centuries."[47]

Ten years later, perhaps due in part to these and similar efforts among all Jewish denominations, a discernible surge occurred in affiliation on the West Side and in other Manhattan neighborhoods. Approximately one-third of the families had "someone who is a synagogue member," although regular attendance remained unmeasured. Changes in demography may better explain this partial turn toward the synagogue. These communities were still youthful: "persons living alone account[ed] for nearly half of Jewish households" in Manhattan, and some one-fifth were "married without children." But increasingly young children appeared on neighborhood streets. Demographers suggested that "having children in the household correlate[d] with more extensive Jewish social ties, and with greater organizational affiliation."[48]

During this same era in the West Village, homosexual and lesbian Jews who desired to affirm Jewish identity and spirituality but were alienated from synagogues that did not countenance their sexual preferences created their own alternative religious community. Beth Simchat Torah, founded in 1973, brought together for religious devotion and camaraderie a largely professional and artistic class of Jews who had helped to gentrify the area of town. For some, a gay synagogue reflected an attitudinal shift from a need to rebel against convention to a desire to belong. While sexual orientation united them, the shul remained primarily a spiritual space. Their congregation was more than a site where people came to see and be seen. Rather, said one founding member, "We wanted a shul. . . . Anything else, if it interferes with the service we say 'No!' Those who leave . . . say that we are too traditional, which means we are not a social center." Congregation Simchat Torah grew from a few hundred members in the early 1980s to over one thousand by 1991 and inspired comparable gay religious efforts across the country and internationally.[49]

The excitement of the city scene in the 1980s and the new neighborhood dynamic of sharing space among others while deciding how and when to identify as Jews was largely lost on those who continued to be part of that "other" Jewish New York. The elderly poor, widowed, or divorced still struggled, though their numbers gradually declined. Throughout the 1980s and into the early 1990s, the Bronx (except Riverdale) remained the borough of Jewish seniors. Surviving stalwarts witnessed some improvement in their lives due to both the efforts of Jewish community social service agencies and the beginnings of a physical revival of their neighborhoods. Still, while a bit more comfortable where they resided, though always wary of their surroundings, with their days numbered, they did not expect to live to carve out new Jewish places for themselves if, and when, gentrification arrived.[50]

When Jack Kugelmass paid a return visit to the Intervale Jewish Center in the early 1990s, he found these actuarial, social, and attitudinal dynamics in play. Many of those whom the anthropologist "knew and cared about" were gone. Kugelmass reflected that whereas ten years earlier "death lurked in the background, showing its face now and then but always dispelled through blind determination," now "death . . . parades itself haughtily," challenging but not defeating the spirit of people such as Moishe Sacks. Those for whom the South Bronx would always be their homes lived in somewhat more salubrious conditions. Thanks to the infusion of billions of dollars in state and federal housing grants, 225,000 units of affordable housing were built. No foe of hyperbole, Koch crowed in 1989 that these endeavors constituted "the greatest construction program since the Pharaohs built the pyramids." The reality was more modest. While the Bronx, south of Fordham Road, lost more than 300,000 residents in the 1970s, roughly 40 percent of its population, between 1980 and 1990, 26,500 people moved in, some of them Jews. Working- and middle-class families were resettling the neighborhood. Still, the South Bronx was a work in progress. Crime continued. The era of arson had passed, but the pathology of drug-sales-related violence endured. The Intervale group made the best of these shifting circumstances and persevered even as their "rabbi" died on January 12, 1995.[51]

Hasidic communities in Brooklyn scorned the bright lights of a changing Manhattan. They preferred their traditional way of life, preserving the tenor of communal existence. Except for proselytizing Lubavitchers, most Hasidim evinced no interest in having other Jews join their ranks. Proud of their social insularity, they were heartened by their strength of numbers, which contributed to their borough maintaining its reputation as "a virtual demographic heartland of New York's, indeed, the nation's Orthodox community." The faith of the devout in neighborhood continuity expressed itself in investments in educational and cultural institutions that under the sway of the community's religious leaders kept more affluent Hasidim in the neighborhood, supporting the poor. Still, many families struggled to maintain an adequate standard of living. A survey of Jewish poverty in 1991 ascertained that while "there are fewer poor Jewish households in the New York area than there were ten years earlier, . . . they are heavily concentrated in Brooklyn because the average household size has increased (from 2.11 in 1981 to 2.8 in 1991)." These very observant Jewish families typically had far more than two children. While they were not among the poorest of New York's indigent, in a neighborhood such as Boro Park, only one-half of Jewish families described themselves "as at least 'reasonably comfortable' financially," as opposed to 45 percent indicating that they were "just getting along." Committed to maintaining their enclaves, Hasidim demanded that the municipality secure and enhance their living conditions.[52]

The parochial agenda of Hasidim appeared in their political choices when they became the quintessential "Koch Democrats." When Koch ran for reelection in 1981, the mayor faced no strong opposition since he received credit for successfully steering the city's fiscal recovery. Only black voters questioned his sensitivity to their concerns. Still, they too voted for him, although not with the enthusiasm of his overwhelming white majorities. Flush with his triumph, Koch sought, a year later, to capture the statehouse. However, his complete and unapologetic identification with New York City's ethos damaged his candidacy upstate and in the suburbs. He lost a hotly contested primary to Mario Cuomo, whom he had defeated five years earlier for the mayoralty.[53]

During Koch's second term in Gracie Mansion, he remained popular, benefiting both from the positive tone he had previously set for city life and the reality that his administration had upgraded city services to pre-fiscal-crisis levels. There was much money around within government, and affluent New Yorkers were conspicuous in their consumption. Lost from view, but noticeable to those who walked the city, was the suffering of an underclass of homeless people, many of them African American. Their fate, said their advocates, little concerned the mayor. Race relations—the calmest critics spoke of economic disparities among groups; others shouted racism—became an issue in the 1985 campaign. As that political battle approached, blacks and this Jewish mayor also sparred over the rise of Rev. Jesse Jackson as a national political candidate. African Americans reacted excitedly to Jackson's aspiration to capture the Democratic nomination for president. They resonated to his message that they whose ancestors "once picked cotton could now pick a President." Koch heard Jackson differently, taking great umbrage at his earlier characterization of this most Jewish city as "Hymietown." The mayor interpreted this remark as proof positive that Jackson was no friend of Jews. Never one to mince his words, Koch positioned himself on the other side of the political barricades as an unintimidated Jewish advocate. But when it came back to local politics in 1985, Koch's enemies were unable to mount significant opposition to his reelection. In the Democratic primary, he easily defeated Manhattan Assemblyman Herman "Denny" Farrell, an African American, and a liberal opponent, City Council President Carol Bellamy. In the general contest, the incumbent easily trounced the Republican challenger, Diane McGrath. Like two of his predecessors, Fiorello La Guardia and Robert F. Wagner Jr., Ed Koch had been returned to Gracie Mansion for the third time. He did not win a fourth election.[54]

During the mayor's final four years in office, a confluence of problems made him politically vulnerable. A series of citywide corruption scandals undermined his standing. The October 1987 stock market crash ended a period of unbridled optimism about the city's progress, a mood on which he had capitalized. Ongoing racial tensions that he had not effectively mitigated were exacerbated by events that made New Yorkers angry and suspicious of each other. In 1986, a white mob in Howard Beach, Queens, killed a black youth and injured two of his friends. A year later, a black teenager, Tawana Brawley, constructed an elaborate hoax, aided and abetted by black militants posing as family "advisers," asserting that she had been abducted to Dutchess County, where she was raped by a group of white men, including police. When a special prosecutor refused to indict the alleged perpetrators, strident voices in the black community warned that with "no justice" there would be no peace. Koch incited black-Jewish tensions in the summer of 1988, when the Democrats convened in his city to select their presidential nominee, saying that "Jews and other supporters of Israel would have to be crazy to vote for Jackson," at a time when Jackson elicited pride among black New Yorkers.[55]

Two Jewish candidates arose to challenge Koch, arguing that his tenure had lasted long enough. They preached good government practices and pledged to clean up City Hall. Harrison J. Goldin, four-term controller of New York through good and bad times, projected himself as a calm, efficient alternative to the bombastic Koch. Businessman Richard Ravitch, a key figure in the city's fiscal revival who also headed the Metropolitan Transportation Authority and was an ally of Koch in chairing a charter revision committee, spoke of himself as a city manager par excellence. But African American Manhattan Borough President David Dinkins mounted the strongest opposition to an incumbent prepared to take on all comers.[56]

Dinkins secured support in the African American and Latino communities. To white New Yorkers, Dinkins projected reconciliation and moderation, a stance that previously had held him in good stead. One election earlier, he had garnered one-half of the Jewish vote in the Manhattan borough president's race as he roundly defeated a Jewish candidate. Dinkins spoke warmly of his city being made up of a "gorgeous mosaic" of peoples.[57]

In 1989, Dinkins emphasized to Jewish voters his outright condemnation of Nation of Islam leader Louis Farrakhan. Moreover, Dinkins pointed out his long and enthusiastic support for Israel, his concerns for the freedom for Soviet Jews, and his own dramatic travel to West Germany to protest President Reagan's wreath-laying ceremony for members of the Waffen SS. However, Koch's supporters exploited Dinkins's largely symbolic cochairing of Jesse Jackson's primary campaign to question whether Dinkins's election would free the city from future turmoil. To one interlocutor, Dinkins responded testily, "I'm not . . . asking you to vote for Jesse Jackson. What in blazes does that have to do with whether I should be mayor of the City of New York?" But the vision of Jackson's influence in the city concerned many Jews. They feared that under Dinkins blacks would be favored over whites. When these voters approached the polls on primary day, their choices came down to those who felt "enough already," who were "embarrassed by [Koch's] constant 'shtick'" (his idiosyncratic if not undiplomatic behavior), and those who worried about what was called "the Jackson factor." Others opined that the election highlighted the differences between those on the "traditional liberal Upper West Side" and those "who have always voted conservatively," protective of their turfs, such as "Orthodox Jews, who make up 12 percent of the city's Jewish population (27% of Brooklyn Jews)."[58]

Primary results bore out these variances. Koch carried by very large margins "five hard-core Democratic Brooklyn and Queens" areas "with largely Jewish" and Catholic populations. But in "other predominantly white areas," Dinkins did well enough among these constituents, who joined with his African American and Latino base to carry him into the general election.[59]

Fear of Jackson as a hovering presence versus the promise that New York under Dinkins would be a gentler, quieter, and more inclusive city divided Jewish voters during the general election campaign. Earlier apprehensions that had kept such voters close to Koch were now rearticulated forcefully by the Republican designee, Rudolph Giuliani. Brooklyn Jewish neighborhoods heeded his warnings, despite Dinkins's repeated efforts to calm antagonistic Orthodox Jews. Dinkins made far more than just the expected courtesy calls on local rabbis to allay community suspicions. But his efforts did not avail him on Election Day. Giuliani swept heavily Hasidic neighborhoods of Brooklyn, such as the Forty-Eighth Assembly District, which gave him 20,494 votes and Dinkins a mere 4,049. Similarly, Jewish sections of Forest Hills and Kew Gardens went for the Republican by a three-to-one margin.[60]

But Dinkins won the election, albeit by the smallest percentage in the city's history. His winning coalition included approximately 40 percent of the Jewish vote, primarily in liberal Jewish neighborhoods. In Manhattan, Dinkins won assembly districts that included Greenwich Village, Chelsea, Central Park West, and the Upper West Side and was barely bested in Sutton Place. The only heavily Jewish area in that borough that went strongly for Giuliani was the Upper East Side–Central Park South. Even there Dinkins garnered a full third of the votes. In the Bronx, Dinkins ran extraordinarily well in minority communities, capturing in some places eight to ten times as many votes as his opponent. But he also did well in the untroubled Riverdale section and in the racially harmonious Co-op City–Pelham Parkway region, winning almost 40 percent of the vote. Dinkins succeeded with an electoral coalition reminiscent of the groups that secured John Lindsay's reelection some twenty years earlier: liberal, higher-income Jews, along with some similarly disposed, affluent Catholics and lower-income minorities. In retrospect, Dinkins's victory revealed that "despite deep racial cleavages within New York City," this town differed "from other older industrial cities," due in part to its large, if variegated, Jewish population. An effective black politician on the scene where "racial mistrust was far from universal," who articulated a "bi-racial rhetoric," received a fair hearing. Dinkins appealed to "cosmopolitan white young professionals dwelling in places like Manhattan's Upper West Side and Brooklyn's Park Slope," who proved to be critical.[61]

In those districts, Dinkins also may have tapped into a distinctive attitudinal trait that made these voters especially receptive toward his persona and message. More than any other city in America, New York housed nonprofit foundations, many attuned to "social and urban issues." In fact, "one-third of the largest foundations in the United States" had offices in Manhattan, and "vast sectors" of those who worked for these organizations possessed a positive "orientation towards social justice and urban issues rather than merely economic issues." Beyond casting their own votes for Dinkins, these liberal constituents, comfortable and confident about their place in the city, might have brought others out to the polls with them, including their corporate-lawyer neighbors, who took off the legally allowed time to fulfill their civic duty before returning to their case loads.[62]

Dinkins's promise to fashion a gorgeous urban mosaic was marred, however, and his reputation for fairness irreparably damaged in 1991 when Crown Heights erupted in a bloody black-Jewish confrontation. The violence began after the death on August 19 of seven-year-old Gavin Cato, a child of Guyanese immigrants, killed in a traffic accident by Hasidic driver Yosef Lifsh, who was part of an entourage escorting the Lubavitcher rebbe through neighborhood streets. Incited by local demagogues to avenge Cato's "murder"—rumors quickly spread that Hatzolah, the Jewish-run volunteer ambulance corps, had rushed Lifsh to Methodist Hospital, where he received eighteen stitches, but had left the young boy to die—bands of enraged black youths rampaged through the night attacking Jews and police and destroying property. The mob caught twenty-nine-year-old Yankel Rosenbaum, who, though not a Lubavitcher, was identified stereotypically as an Orthodox Jew by his beard, dark clothing, and visible *zizith* (the ritual fringed undergarment). He was beaten and stabbed. He died at Kings County Hospital, the same place where Cato was pronounced dead. Rosenbaum's death did not restrain the still-outraged bands. This outbreak lasted for three days. Confederates from outside the neighborhood joined local rioters. Not just Cato's death but a number of unmitigated points of tensions fueled the attacks.

The Lubavitchers' effective manipulation of the city's political system chafed their neighbors. To help their own poor, the Hasidim had effectively gained control of a local community planning board and directed public funds their way, to the exclusion of needy blacks. Seeking to expand their presence in Crown Heights, Hasidim had used government monies to purchase and rent houses and apartments. Blacks resented when Lubavitchers literally knocked on their doors asking whether their houses were on the market. The angriest black voices spoke of "Jewish expansionist aggression." Jews, on the other hand, worried about rising crime and laid the problem first at the doorsteps of their neighbors and then at the police for insufficient protection. But African Americans still thought that Jews engaged in racial-profiled vigilantism as they had during the early era of Rabbi Schrage's Maccabees of the 1960s. They also resented apparent special treatment accorded the Lubavitcher rebbe. Though Koch had removed the police post from outside the rebbe's international headquarters at 770 Eastern Parkway, the entourage that followed him through the streets on that fateful day in August 1991 had a police patrol-car escort. Ironically, this sort of protection, which began in 1981, reflected concerns over violence arising from intra-Jewish struggles between the Lubavitchers and their Satmar enemies from Williamsburg.

Mayor Dinkins failed as a conciliator in this time of testing. While he distinguished between the youngster's accidental death and the murder of Rosenbaum and called for restraint, many within the Jewish community claimed he intentionally delayed ordering the police to stop the rioting. Brooklyn's *Jewish Press*, ever sensitive to anti-Semitism and protective always of the interests of its largely Orthodox readership, publicized widely a troubling alleged conversation between the mayor and Governor Cuomo. Dinkins purportedly intimated that he had accorded "a sort of day of grace to the mob" on August 19, the very day that Rosenbaum fell victim to its criminal intentions. At that critical juncture, through Dinkins's inaction, it was said that he had shown his true colors as a coddler of black perpetrators and as unconcerned with the safety of Jewish constituents. His most virulent critics called him an anti-Semite.

For the Jews of Crown Heights, the riot and perceived governmental indifference had a transcendent meaning beyond the immediate traumas of the days of terror and their sorrow over Rosenbaum's murder. It spoke to them about their sense of place within this American Diaspora and questioned the most basic promise of New York. They called the attack a "pogrom," because it reminded them of what their people had suffered elsewhere from mobs as police stood aside. It told them that wherever Jews might live, eventually they would be victimized. New York City was no different from Kishinev; America was just like Russia. Possessed of a totally different vocabulary for describing what had transpired, Crown Heights blacks characterized the violence after Cato's death as a riot. They saw it as a "rebellion" emanating from within their midst against racism and prejudice in their neighborhood; it "resonated with a history of injuries black communities in the Americas have suffered at the hands of callous and indifferent whites." For them, the young boy's death did not just happen; it was not an "accident."

The Lubavitchers garnered sympathetic expressions from most corners of the New York Jewish community. Gadfly liberal rabbi Arthur Hertzberg was a rare voice asserting that historical trauma lay behind black rage. He wrote in the *New York Times* that the motorcade evoked "ghosts of slave masters riding into their quarters and not caring whom their horses might trample." By contrast, some modern Orthodox activists from Riverdale who agreed with the Lubavitchers that the riot was a pogrom rushed to the scene to support their brethren. And a rump organization, the Jewish Action Alliance, kept up pressure on Dinkins to bring Rosenbaum's killers to justice.

As the investigations and recriminations proceeded, another fault line appeared, separating these Brooklyn Jews, and their allies, from Jewish Manhattanites, or at least from a segment of influential spokespeople who operated out of Midtown headquarters. This establishment group included not only the longstanding American Jewish Committee, the American Jewish Congress, and the Anti-Defamation League of the B'nai B'rith (ADL) but also the Jewish Community Relations Council (JCRC), an agency established after World War II to advocate for Jewish rights on local fronts. Brooklyn Jews charged that each of these organizations had been either silent or hesitant to address the plight of fellow Jews in Crown Heights. They allegedly constrained themselves because of their overwhelming desire to maintain good relations with African Americans at the expense of their own kind. One angered Jew from the Bronx damned the ADL as "just a bunch of indifferent yuppies" and asserted, "We need some real leadership."

In response, the executive vice president of the American Jewish Committee contended that organizations such as his had "worked feverishly behind the scenes" in order to end the violence. Two advocates for the JCRC took on their critics, pointing out that among other initiatives their agency had posted a $10,000 reward for information leading to the arrest and ultimate conviction of Rosenbaum's murderers. However, the head of the ADL broke from the solid defensive pack and admitted that his and his colleagues' organizations did indeed harbor "a strange sort of color-consciousness [that] may begin to function when the problem is [black] anti-Semitism." Reflecting on what he saw as these groups' endemic reticence, one sociologist suggested that there was another crucial factor in play here that went beyond a "hesitan[cy] to disrupt the already fragile black-Jewish coalition in the city." For Jerome Chanes, those powerful "Manhattan" Jews—my term, not his—"were generally distant from the Hasidim and ambivalent toward them." Editorialists for the *Forward* —that classic critic of establishments, even if it had, by the 1990s, moved from its socialist moorings—went further in pillorying the powerful. For them, such "sluggishness [was] at best an unwillingness to revise sentimental notions about black-Jewish relations [and] at worst an aversion to the plight of so conspicuous and fervent a population as the Chasidim," these most Jewish of New York's Jews.

Meanwhile, journalist Sidney Zion placed this "Brooklyn" versus "Manhattan" split within a provocative historical context. While he did not mention either Stephen S. Wise or Peter Bergson by name, inaction by the resourceful yet apprehensive reminded Zion of the Holocaust years, "when Jewish organizations joined in the conspiracy of silence dictated by the Allied powers with Franklin Roosevelt at the helm." Certainly, those Jews who took to the streets in Crown Heights, criticized the establishment, and attacked the mayor considered their actions inspired by the failure of Jews to act during the Nazi era. In this spirit, too, supporters of the late Rabbi Meir Kahane, who had been assassinated in a Manhattan hotel ballroom just a year earlier, reiterated his "Never Again" slogan and brought his ethnocentric approach back to the streets.

But Crown Heights only made more visible deep divisions among New York Jews. For close to two decades, groups and individuals who rallied under the banner of militant activism, despite all of their own differences, had contended with Midtown leaders over tactics in advocating for Jewish causes all over the world. Even amid their city's wild ride of decline and revival in the 1970s–1990s, New York held on to its keel as a center of Jewish communal activity and dynamism.[63]

Student Struggle for Soviet Jewry, Freedom Day Rally at the Soviet UN mission, May 1, 1988. (Photo taken by Abraham Kantor; courtesy Judith Cantor, Student Struggle for Soviet Jewry Records, Yeshiva University Archives)

CHAPTER 7

Renewed Activism

When Congresswoman Bella Abzug ran for mayor in 1977, she understood the frustrations her generation of New York Jews felt toward their native city's faltering promises. To a great extent, she shared their values and experiences. A child of the working class, she had earned her labor bona fides Saturdays at her father's butcher shop, the Live and Let Live Meat Market on Ninth Avenue, in the Meatpacking District. A product of the South Bronx during its Jewish interwar heyday, she lived at home while attending Hunter College. Like so many who shared her roots, the "abandonment" and "debris around those places" she once called home saddened and angered her. She articulated plans such as "reviving the port, increasing public transportation, collecting some $590 million in uncollected real estate taxes, and lobbying the federal government" to restore New York. She cared about the city's future. But there was far more to Bella Abzug that set her apart from those who focused narrowly on specific crises. She aspired to be not just someone who would improve city conditions. Pundits pointed out that her palliatives differed little from those of the six other candidates originally in the race for the nomination. Rather, she desired, through a stint in Gracie Mansion, to cap her career as a transformative figure, a catalyst for a more egalitarian society within and without the metropolis. Once again, out of New York Jewry arose a driven activist bearing promises of transcendent change. Her supporters in this campaign recognized that quintessential quality. It was "not so much what she . . . promise[d] to do for New York as her image as a fighter" that propelled her as a compelling figure. One local politico understood Abzug as the uncommon leader who "stirs up the people who want to kick the backsides of the powerful."[1]

By the time Abzug aspired at age fifty-seven to the municipality's highest office, she had distinguished herself as an aggressive advocate. She had earned high marks as a lawyer in labor and civil rights cases in the 1940s, as a defender of Senator Joseph McCarthy's targets in the 1950s, and as a founder of Women's Strike for Peace in the 1960s. She demonstrated for a nuclear test ban treaty and protested against the expanding war in Indochina. An unabashed liberal, she proved to be an attractive representative to residents of Chelsea, the West Side, Greenwich Village, and the Lower East Side, who elected her to Congress in 1970. Women's Strike for Peace recognized her election as a turning point. After "a decade of struggle," it "moved from seeking to influence the men in Congress to do the right thing to electing one of its key women." Once in the House, she championed legislation that women needed most: securing reproductive rights, banning gender discrimination, and helping women gain child care. Abzug served three terms and barely lost the New York State Democratic primary for Senate in 1976 before entering that crowded mayoral contest a year later.[2]

Abzug failed in that citywide contest. Detractors suggested that her unyielding, uncompromising style, dubbed by her opponents as "inflexible," limited her appeal.[3] Still, for her devoted followers, she remained an iconic figure who personified a world-altering cause that extended beyond the city's immediate concerns. Her life story bridged generations in the struggle for the liberation of women. This movement possessed deep New York roots and a profound Jewish texture.

Abzug followed in the footsteps of exceptional Jewish women from New York who in prior generations had risen within and then beyond their neighborhood surroundings to fight their own battles for women's rights. Back in the 1910s–1920s, Clara Lemlich Shavelson—best known for her fiery speech at a labor protest meeting at Cooper Union in 1909, which inspired tens of thousands of young women garment workers to support a general strike—helped to found the Wage Earners' League for Women Suffrage. Rose Schneiderman —famous too for her role in putting young women out in the streets in the monumental "Uprising of the 20,000," a strike that was instrumental in the growth of the International Ladies' Garment Workers' Union—linked arms with Shavelson and others in organizing the Wage Earners' League. They reasoned that the vote would facilitate their "taking control of their own lives." Their concerns as working women differed from both those of working-class men and middle-class suffragists. Tensions existed over priorities between the uptown "mink brigade activists," who were animated by unequal gender relationships within their powerful social circles, and these Jewish leaders of working women, who focused on the needs of poor factory girls sweating over sewing machines. Suffrage was essential, said Schneiderman, in order to secure fundamental human entitlements that included "the right to be born well, the right to a carefree and happy childhood, the right to education, the right to mental, physical and spiritual growth and development."[4]

Unlike Abzug, Betty Friedan grew up outside New York. Friedan claimed that until she began work on *The Feminine Mystique*, she was not even "conscious of the women problem." She lived in a New York suburb, a housewife like millions of her fellow American sisters struggling with the "problem that has no name." The title of her book gave that festered social pathology a name. Notwithstanding her academic degree from Smith College and her aspirations as a professional writer, Friedan asserted that she had become victimized within her rocky marriage, forced into a "comfortable concentration camp" of a bored, unfulfilling life of affluent routine. Historians have interpreted Friedan's life differently, arguing that she was "no ordinary suburban housewife and mother" but possessed an activist, radical political past with decades of "prior engagement with women's issues." But once she gave voice to dilemmas with which so many identified and her 1963 book rose to become a perennial best-seller, she and her family returned to Manhattan's Upper West Side, the neighborhood she and her husband, Carl, a theatrical producer, had abandoned for the suburbs. In 1966, Friedan founded the National Organization of Women (NOW), serving as its first president. Three years later, she and Carl divorced. In the early 1970s, she became a major spokeswoman in the National Women's Political Caucus (NWPC). There she worked with Bella Abzug and black congresswoman Shirley Chisholm, who represented Bedford-Stuyvesant and was the first African American woman to serve in Congress.[5]

Competition as well as cooperation characterized the women's movement. Gloria Steinem joined her sister Jewish activists in promoting women's liberation, when she was not wrestling with them for the primary leadership position. Steinem was a cofounder and editor of *Ms.* magazine, which began publishing in 1971. Also a Smith College graduate like Friedan, Steinem aspired to be a writer and journalist, but unlike Friedan, she did not marry and suburbanize. Steinem moved to the city to pursue her career, only to find doors closed to serious employment opportunities. Furious at the marginalization of women, Steinem worked as a Playboy Club bunny in 1963 and then wrote a damning piece exposing the sexist exploitation of these underpaid waitresses. With the emergence of *Ms.* magazine, Steinem found a feminist pulpit to galvanize women across the nation.

This triumvirate of activists differed over directions the movement should take and who should be its spokeswomen. Friedan often attacked Abzug for "invading her turf" and took on Steinem for allegedly "ripping off the movement for personal profit." Abzug, in turn, publicly questioned Friedan's claim to the "motherhood" of feminism. Still, for all of their jealousies and misunderstandings, they were united by another form of marginality, anti-Semitism. They were lumped together as "leaders of the Jewish conspiracy to destroy the Christian family" and accused of using "Jewish International Communist ideas to destroy America." For Steinem particularly, born to a Jewish father and Christian mother and baptized as a Congregationalist at age ten, responsiveness to this animus was a major component in her Jewishness. She averred, "Never in my life have I identified myself as a Christian, but wherever there is anti-Semitism, I identify as a Jew."[6]

Not only did Steinem, Abzug, and Friedan have to contend with antipathies from antifeminists, but they also confronted prejudices from those within their own movement. In 1975, even with Abzug as chair of the American delegation to the First United Nations International Women's Decade Conference, they witnessed Israel pilloried as a racist state and their, and their country's, support for the Jewish state roundly denounced. They endured similar calumnies five years later in Copenhagen, where delegates angrily contended that "Gloria Steinem, Betty Friedan and Bella Abzug all being Jewish gives the women's movement a bad name." Friedan recalled with outrage and sadness how a PLO hijacker was lauded as the conference's "heroine," while Leah Rabin, the wife of Israel's prime minister, was attacked for her nation's alleged "imperialist aggression." Retreating to a church away from the official gathering to express her views, Friedan reflected ruefully on how far their enemies had strayed from a promised sisterhood of unity designed to ameliorate the real problems of women worldwide.[7]

Back home, however, their trials and steadfastness only enhanced their standing among other New York Jewish feminists, who had long been impressed with their dynamism but whose personal and communal goals differed. In most cases a younger cohort, they sought the transformation of gender power relationships within American society. But they also wanted to change attitudes toward women within Judaism. For many feminists of that era, "Christian as well as Jews, . . . patriarchal religions were simply a source of oppression and hence irrelevant to their lives." These young Jewish women "could not define themselves solely through their feminist ideology and affiliations." Jewishness was fundamental to their identities. Rather than reject Judaism, they determined to free themselves from constraints that the tradition had imposed on women's participation in religious rituals and leadership. "Well-versed in and committed to the women's movement just as they were to the Jewish tradition, . . . their loyalties" were on "a collision course." The solutions that they articulated percolated far beyond New York and transformed the way Jewish women and men ordered their religious and communal lives in America and around the world.[8]

Most of these activist women found each other and coalesced into an influential community on Manhattan's Upper West Side, the same neighborhood that housed young Jewish professionals who were increasingly disengaged from their faith. Some were pursuing graduate study at nearby Columbia University and at the Jewish Theological Seminary of America (JTS) in Morningside Heights. In the early 1970s, JTS, the flagship school of the Conservative movement, admitted women to its graduate and teacher-training programs but not to its rabbinical school. Jewish feminist activists considered this situation discriminatory and worked to change it. Many belonged to the New York Havurah, an experimental Jewish religious community. Ironically, there, within a supposed open Jewish environment, Havurah membership raised their feminist consciousness by forcing them to confront patriarchal prejudices.

Products of the Jewish counterculture ethos of the late 1960s, havurahs attracted committed college-age students who chafed at what they perceived as the shallowness of synagogue life. In their quest to change the Jewish world, they sought kindred spirits eager to experiment with ritual, in song and liturgy, to imbibe an authentic communal experience at Sabbath and holiday meals, and most important, to engage Jewish texts by applying modern methods and sensibilities to received teachings. True to the havurah mission, the feminists, "dissatisfied with the strong bias in Jewish religious learning," established a study group "to subject the Jewish tradition to serious scrutiny as women react[ed] to God-concepts, liturgy and sex roles." Hopefully, as they learned more about themselves and about women's historical role within the faith, they expected to convince the men around them to appreciate these issues. This would be a crucial first step toward consciousness raising throughout the wider Jewish community. But to their dismay, these women of the New York Havurah found that while their male counterparts, leaders of their movement, were determined to find new ways of living and acting Jewishly, they did not perceive the amelioration of female concerns as prime, or even worthy, objectives. Out of these painful gender conflicts, the women realized that they had to work for change on their own.[9]

Well educated and raised in the Conservative movement, these women trained their fire directly on the Jewish Theological Seminary of America. As girls, many of them had been groomed to be the future intellectual and communal leaders of their branch of American Judaism. They had been the star pupils in Conservative religious schools, regular attendees at services, participants in the movement's United Synagogue Youth groups, and campers and counselors at Camp Ramah, its renowned summer educational program. In all regards, they were educated like their brothers, even so far as to enroll in JTS's coeducational undergraduate program. But gender equality ended when it came to full participation as adults in religious observances. As important, they were barred from rabbinical and cantorial careers.

Paula Hyman explicitly articulated the conflict the women faced: "between the way we are educated [Jewishly] and the kind of role we are allowed in the Jewish community." A student of modern Jewish history who came to Columbia after taking her undergraduate degree at Radcliffe, Hyman had turned with her sisters in arms to the sources in classic havurah style for religious validation of their discomfiture with the status quo. She observed that "when tradition was incompatible with your sense of self, and some of your basic ethics, then you have to go back and examine the tradition." In March 1972, Hyman joined others in drafting a manifesto, the Jewish Women's Call for Change.

It demanded inter alia that "women be counted in a minyan," that they have full equality under Jewish law, that they have decision-making power in synagogues and general communal activities, and that they "be permitted and encouraged to attend rabbinical and cantorial schools, and to perform rabbinical and cantorial functions in synagogues." Hyman subsequently wrote on behalf of the New Jewish Sisterhood to the Committee on Law and Standards of the Rabbinical Assembly, the Conservative movement's religious authority. When the letter urging acceptance of the Call's provisions was summarily rebuffed, the Sisterhood concretized into an ongoing advocacy group, Ezrat Nashim. The name literally means "aid to women," but it also denotes the subordinate women's section of the traditional synagogue, away from the liturgical action and powerful domains occupied by men. Self-empowered, the women decided to confront the rabbis directly and drove up to the rabbis' convention in the Catskills. There they distributed their Call and held "countersessions" —a tactic of their times—within earshot of the delegates. This bold move was applauded by at least the 130 delegates and their wives who sat in at their educational forums.[10]

As Ezrat Nashim's spokeswomen asserted themselves, they readily acknowledged that just as Abzug followed Shavelson, and Friedan implicitly picked up after Schneiderman, they too walked in the footsteps of exceptional Jewish women who strove to reorient traditions, efforts that possessed national ramifications. Henrietta Szold was their most iconic historical figure. When in the summer of 1973 *Response*, largely the journal of the New York Havurah, devoted an entire issue to essays on "The Jewish Woman," it featured a profile of Szold. The volume subsequently became a widely disseminated group study guide. As Szold's story was told through feminist eyes, she "by the standards of her time . . . was blessed with an intellectual and professional freedom, which only a handful of women enjoyed in her era." But "by the standards of the current Women's Liberation movement, she was exploited and harassed throughout the best working years of her long life." She "harbored two ambitions—one for a brilliant career, the other for a brilliant marriage." These dreams, her biographer quickly noted, "many 'liberated' women today will tell you are incapable of peaceful coexistence in a 'male-dominated' world." Pursuit of a calling in Jewish communal leadership and scholarship prompted her to write articles from her Baltimore birthplace for the *Jewish Messenger* (New York) under the pseudonym "Shulamith." In these pieces, she attacked Reform Judaism as a threat to Jewish survival. But she also expressed her reservations about the gender limits of traditional Judaism. Most poignantly, she asserted her right and obligation to say Kaddish, the memorial prayer, for her own mother rather than to have a man recite it in her stead. Scrutinizing rabbinic law, she observed, "Elimination of women from such duties was never intended by our law and custom." Szold inspired a new generation of feminists.[11]

Szold's sad saga of frustrations and exploitation at JTS also resonated with the members of Ezrat Nashim. Like her spiritual descendants, she moved to New York for advanced Jewish training. This first woman in the rabbinical school "was accepted for admission to some classes only after she assured its administration that she would not use the knowledge she gained to seek ordination." So she assisted male classmates with their writing assignments. Later in her career, she similarly served as the "literary secretary" of the Jewish Publication Society, where, for close to thirty years, she aided "men who picked her brain and sapped her strengths, . . . took her for long walks, . . . thanked her with all their hearts and [then] married other women." Longing for a family and a husband, the resolute Szold adopted the health needs of Palestinian Jewry as her own. Returning to New York in 1912 from her first visit to the new Jewish settlement she founded Hadassah, which not only rose to become Palestine's and later Israel's foremost social welfare agency but also provided an autonomous leadership venue for American Jewish women.[12]

The women of Ezrat Nashim recognized as well that they benefited personally from an accommodation of Judaism to feminism that had occurred fifty years earlier only a few blocks away from where they now lived on the Upper West Side. The tradition of the bat mitzvah that some of these 1970s feminists had celebrated as girls began in 1922 when Rabbi Mordecai Kaplan's oldest daughter, Judith, read a section of the weekly Torah portion at the Society for the Advancement of Judaism. Rabbi Kaplan considered this innovation as but part of his challenge to Judaism's status quo on many theological and ritual fronts, leading eventually to the rise of Reconstructionist Judaism. But it also reflected, as Judith Kaplan Eisenstein recalled decades later, "a conscious feminism" in the Kaplan household, a sensibility spurred by the women's suffrage amendment in 1920. The Kaplans were far ahead of their time, and the bat mitzvah did not become commonplace for several decades. Still, their voices publicly called out for changing "women's place in a synagogue," a cause that Ezrat Nashim emulated.[13]

As these activists demanded change primarily within the Conservative movement, Reform Judaism's contemporary pathbreaking step in empowering women heartened them. Unbound theologically by the strictures of religious legal precedent, Reform Judaism had always been capable, according to its own Jewish system, of ordaining women as rabbis. Frequently during earlier decades of the twentieth century, ambitious women and their male supporters had petitioned for female admission into the Reform Hebrew Union College for rabbinical training and ultimately into its clergy. But the weight of unyielding social mores within Reform leadership and its congregational ranks had stymied all initiatives. In 1972, however, the Cincinnati branch of the Hebrew Union College–Jewish Institute of Religion ordained Sally Priesand as its first woman rabbi. Her first pulpit position brought her to the Stephen S. Wise Free Synagogue as an assistant rabbi and to the Upper West Side, maintaining the neighborhood's tradition as a locus of Jewish change. Ezrat Nashim happily monitored Priesand's career path even as it worked to transform all segments of American Judaism.[14]

In February 1973, Ezrat Nashim participated in the call to New York of five hundred delegates to the first National Jewish Women's Conference. There the issues that had initially energized the women of the New York Havurah became the articulated goals for a national movement. The unequal power relationships between men and women in Judaism had to end. Delegates emphasized the need to create meaningful life-cycle events for females. Efforts were redoubled to identify and honor women's role in Judaism's historical development. Many of the conference's objectives subsequently became commonplaces across the United States, from mothers and fathers welcoming, with public ceremonial joy, the birth of daughters to the creation of life-cycle rituals celebrating all stages in women's lives. Even in those Orthodox communities that disdained feminism, formalized bat mitzvah events such as girls learning and then offering public comments on specific parts of the Torah became part of Orthodox practice, although few explicitly acknowledged the implicit influence of the women's movement. Ezrat Nashim's extensive political advocacy led to the admission of the first female candidates to the Jewish Theological Seminary of America's rabbinical school in 1984. The night when the school's faculty made its landmark decision, "the women of Ezrat Nashim gathered to celebrate the fulfillment of the call they had issued over ten years earlier." In May 1985, some of Ezrat Nashim's strongest advocates danced outside the Morningside Heights campus on the day that Amy Eilberg was ordained as the first Conservative rabbi.[15]

The efforts of these young feminists strengthened the Jewishness of leading political activists such as Bella Abzug. A mutual process of influence connected them to Ezrat Nashim. Certainly, the congresswoman's presence and address at the 1973 National Jewish Women's Conference spoke loudly of the integration of the women's rights movement and the struggle for equality within Judaism. In Abzug's case, her new level of Jewish involvement constituted a return to greater religious and ethnic identity and a chance to salve some old wounds. She had grown up in a kosher home where Sabbath traditions were respected, even as her father worked on Saturday. Bella received a quality Hebrew education. As a young woman, after studying in a local Hebrew high school and at JTS's coeducational teachers' program, she supplemented her income by working in a Bronx Jewish center. Her membership as a teenager in her neighborhood's secular Zionist Hashomer Hatzair helped provide her with the "moral fervor, social idealism and pioneering militancy" that guided her public life. But even as a youngster, she chafed at religious gender inequalities. She did not like being segregated in the women's balcony and took offense, as had Szold, when she was told that she was forbidden to say Kaddish for her father.[16]

As Jewish feminists developed new rituals such as their own Passover seder, with the Prophetess Miriam as a central historical figure, both Friedan and Steinem, who were also reminded of their Jewishness by anti-Semitism, gravitated toward a sense of religious sisterhood. For the author of the *Feminine Mystique*—in that book she had nothing to say about Jewish malaises—these affirmations were a far cry from the "agnostic, atheistic, scientific, humanist" sensibilities that had led her and Carl Friedan, while they were still suburbanites, to provide their sons with "aesthetic bar mitzvahs." For Steinem, congregating with Jewishly committed women gave her a more positive identity. Comparable dynamics contributed to a revival in Jewish feeling for Letty Cottin Pogrebin, Steinem's cofounder and editor at *Ms.* magazine. Even more than Abzug, Pogrebin came from a traditional Jewish background. She attended the Yeshiva of Central Queens from the third to fifth grades. But again like so many other women, the negative Kaddish experience, that denial of such a basic filiopietistic right to public prayer upon the death of a parent, fueled a rebellion at age fifteen against Judaism. Anti-Semitism in Copenhagen brought her back partially. But new Jewish feminist rituals and associations gave her a greater stake in helping both to redefine Judaism and to live a positive Jewish life.[17]

Standing with Abzug as a featured speaker at that first women's conference in 1973, Blu Greenberg, mother of five and wife of a leading modern Orthodox rabbi, was hardly alienated from Judaism. Yet she readily admitted that Friedan's calls for gender equality engulfed her. Ezrat Nashim initiatives also impressed her, even as she found at this gathering other Orthodox women who aspired to find a place for themselves as observant female Jews within what she described as the "orthodoxy" of feminism. Leaders of the conference welcomed her since they aspired to create a movement that spoke to the needs of all Jewish women. Greenberg learned from that experience the necessity of a cohort of the like-minded to engender the requisite "support, the testing of ideas, the cross-fertilization." Until then, she admitted, "except for conversations with [her] husband, the process had been . . . a very private one."[18]

Concomitant with Greenberg's personal journey toward feminism, a cohort like the one that she prayed for began to emerge, albeit independent of her, among younger Orthodox women on the Upper West Side of Manhattan. Once again, that neighborhood that was home to Ezrat Nashim provided fertile ground for new Jewish ideas and activities. On the holiday of Simchat Torah in October 1972, Rabbi Steven Riskin of Lincoln Square Synagogue authorized the first Orthodox women's *tefillah* (prayer) service. Women were permitted to dance with the Torah scrolls and then read, as the men did in the main sanctuary, the concluding portions of the five books of Moses and the opening chapter of Genesis. Seventeen months later, in May 1973, the congregation experienced another "watershed moment"—as Riskin recalled it decades later—when he officiated at the synagogue's first bat mitzvah. A precocious female pupil in his Hebrew school petitioned for the right to commemorate her coming of age in the faith, just like the boys, by reading the Prophetic portion during the Sabbath morning services. "Playing it by ear," trying "to figure out what to do for a bat mitzvah" in an Orthodox realm,

Riskin "could not give her everything she wanted." But he and his cantor devised a ceremony that permitted the young woman to read portions of the book of Ruth at a Friday-night service. Some thirty-eight years later, Riskin proudly remembered that event as constituting "part of [his] education" when that woman, Elena Kagan, was nominated by President Barack Obama to the U.S. Supreme Court.[19]

In the years following that first women's *tefillah* and Elena Kagan's initiative, the Lincoln Square Synagogue hosted periodic, usually monthly, Sabbath services for women only, and bat mitzvahs took place regularly. That this same congregation was simultaneously deeply involved in reaching the disengaged through its "kosher wine instead of cocktails" Friday-night programs only underscores how variegated both tenuous and tenacious forms of Jewish identity coexisted on the 1970s Upper West Side.

In 1978, Riskin's colleague Rabbi Avraham (Avi) Weiss welcomed a women's *tefillah* service into his Riverdale congregation. Neighborhood resident Blu Greenberg was a steady participant but not a founder of this feminist group, which consisted primarily of young, secularly and Jewishly well-educated women who advanced ritual models that inspired national emulation. These New York initiatives sparked a trend among some modern Orthodox Jews despite opposition. By 2005, forty-seven women's *tefillah* groups flourished in fifteen states (seventeen in New York City) and four foreign countries, including seven in Israel. Meanwhile, leaders of New York's women's *tefillahs* made common cause with Greenberg, ultimately establishing, in 1997, the Jewish Orthodox Feminist Alliance (JOFA). Started "around a member's kitchen table," evoking a domestic image, this advocacy group took Orthodox women's concerns out of its constituents' homes and local neighborhoods in the hope of transforming the wider Jewish world. Their efforts contributed to the decision, in March 2009, by Rabbi Weiss to designate Sara Hurwitz as the "*Maharat*" (halachic, spiritual, and Torah leader) of his Hebrew Institute of Riverdale. In February 2010, he titled her "Rabba," another neologism that sounded much like *rabbi*. Although Greenberg and her JOFA colleagues were not completely satisfied that he stopped just short of designating her a rabbi—while many of Weiss's colleagues castigated his move—erstwhile Ezrat Nashim members appreciated the impact of their activism. A vision of women's equality hatched at Morningside Heights study sessions and later around Riverdale kitchen tables had transformed significant segments of the Jewish world.[20]

While New York in the 1970s and 1980s provided the connections to nurture triumphs in the battles for women's rights within Judaism, the metropolis likewise made possible sustained advocacy for Jews trapped in the Soviet Union. The city offered a perfect backdrop, a staging area, for vibrant protest against anti-Semitism. New York, now more than ever, assumed visibility as an international media capital, even as it continued as the hub of national Jewish communal life and harbored the United Nations, only blocks away from Midtown organizational headquarters—not to mention the millions of local Jews and their non-Jewish friends and neighbors, potential foot soldiers for large-scale public demonstrations. The fight for Soviet Jewry ultimately ended in victory, with close to a quarter million, almost the majority of those freed, settling in New York. Their choice to seek America's unparalleled promises rankled Israeli officials who had been the first to fight, albeit often behind the scenes, for the release of their Jewish brethren. They desired these refugees' presence to build up the Jewish people power of Israel. But many of those who chose America over Israel were not Zionists. They preferred to take their professional and technological skills to the United States, where they began to adapt to new surroundings and encountered the usual difficulties of newcomers.

Arguably, a confluence of geopolitical factors, especially the collapse of the Soviet Union, did more to produce success in the movement to free Soviet Jews than anything done by New York and American Jews or Israelis on the streets or in the diplomatic backrooms. But, all along the way, those who sought to lead the movement battled one another over tactics. These disagreements were often virulent and personal. Although the struggle to rescue Soviet Jews was taking place in the city, conflicts over tactics often reflected ongoing "Manhattan" versus "Brooklyn" differences in addressing Jewish crises, even if some of the strongest voices emanated from the Bronx. Recriminations over what the Jewish establishment as opposed to grass-roots leaders did, or did not do, a quarter century earlier during the Holocaust period fueled these arguments. Such designations as "establishment" and "grass-roots" were redolent with meaning and passion. Divergent views of the world from headquarters versus the neighborhood loomed large, even as all 1970s–1980s spokespeople shouted, albeit never in unison, "Never Again."[21]

By the mid-1970s, the plight of Soviet Jewry stood second only to the survival of Israel as a source of American Jewish concern. A new wave of

anti-Jewish agitation that started in the early 1960s had stirred "a mildly interested but passive American Jewry." Seemingly, after Josef Stalin's death in 1953,
American Jews had taken a deep sigh of relief that physical atrocities would
not befall Russian Jews long victimized by Soviet "cultural decapitation" policies. However, in 1963, in response not only to reports of synagogue closings
and severe limitations placed on the baking of Passover matzos but also to the
arrest of 163 citizens, most of them Jews, for "economic crimes," punishable by
death, three of America's most distinguished Jews, Supreme Court Justice Arthur Goldberg and Senators Jacob Javits of New York and Abraham Ribicoff of
Connecticut, with the assistance of President Kennedy, met with Russian ambassador Anatoly Dobrynin. When the Soviets stonewalled, the troika turned
to the Conference of Major Jewish Organizations, the umbrella organization
for American Jewish defense groups, and suggested calling a national conference to discuss ways and means of saving Soviet Jewry. Their initiative led to
a Washington, D.C., meeting in April 1964, attended by over five hundred delegates from most established Jewish organizations. Out of these deliberations
arose the American Jewish Conference on Soviet Jewry (AJCSJ).[22]

But this incipient rallying point suffered from leadership and financial
problems. During AJCSJ's seven years of existence, it possessed neither independent funding nor a full-fledged professional staff. It was hamstrung by the
reluctance of existing organizations to create yet another Jewish entity. Though
it met with American government officials, resolved to fight to eliminate "discrimination against Soviet Jews and restoration of their full cultural and religious rights," and hatched plans for a national day of prayer for its oppressed
brethren, by decade's end, AJCSJ had failed to project the cause as a "major
national Jewish concern."[23]

This lethargy did not surprise Jacob Birnbaum, who had no faith in American Jewry's leadership. A British Jew who settled in New York in the early
1960s, he came armed with a different vision of how to attack the Soviets.
This cause became his life's work. He imagined a mass grass-roots movement,
a "tidal wave of public opinion," that would take the message of freedom to
the streets, making the enemy decidedly uncomfortable through unfavorable
publicity. He planned to recruit his shock troops among Jewish students, primarily recruited from the city's colleges and universities. Living a few blocks
away from Yeshiva College in Washington Heights, he found young Orthodox

men and women ready to fulfill the religious obligation of "freeing captives." Birnbaum also received a positive hearing from Columbia's Jewish students. In fact, in April 1964, he founded the Student Struggle for Soviet Jewry on the Morningside Heights campus. Four days later, on May Day, the group organized its first protest rally, as they picketed the Soviet UN mission on East Sixty-Seventh Street. In subsequent months, they grabbed attention through an interfaith week-long fast outside Russian headquarters, established a string of information booths citywide, and conducted a rally on the Lower East Side. They appeared repeatedly during these early years at the United Nations. The protest themes melded Jewish historical and religious imagery with contemporary political objectives. A "Jericho March," where picketers blew the shofar and carried Torah scrolls, called for the "walls of hate" to come tumbling down. A Passover "Night of Watching" linked Soviet Jews with the Israelite Exodus. Tisha B'Av, the national day of mourning over the destruction of the Temple and other calamities in Jewish history, provided an appropriate time to sit down and cry at the Isaiah Wall across First Avenue from the United Nations. While organizers may not have consciously considered the beyond-the-political ramifications of these evocative metaphors, almost from the start, demonstrations were acts of Jewish identification.[24]

Birnbaum's "take to the streets" tactics also resonated with Jewish college students who were veterans of contemporary American protest movements. A study of the Student Struggle constituency conducted a decade into its existence revealed that a full half of its members had been involved in anti–Vietnam War movements, while more than a quarter had fought for civil rights. Perhaps some who previously had advocated for freedom for African Americans recognized the analogous injustice in the Soviet Union. Others became involved because they no longer felt wanted or appreciated within campaigns that increasingly resounded with militant, no-whites-wanted calls for "Black Power." Those embracing the Soviet Jewish cause had a senior, eminent role model, with an honored civil rights pedigree, whose teachings they might follow. Philosopher Rabbi Abraham Joshua Heschel heard the words of the ancient prophets that abjured humankind to change the world for the better as a call to action. Although the era of religious prophecy had ended two thousand years earlier, according to the tradition, Heschel believed that "the prophets endure and can only be ignored at the risk of our own despair." Thus, the scholar had to leave the study and to engage in great crusades, when called by concerns of the time. Acting on this belief, Heschel championed the fight to end racial discrimination. In 1965, he marched arm in arm with Dr. Martin Luther King Jr. from Selma to Montgomery, Alabama. The visage of the white-haired and bearded rabbi with the steadfast African American minister became an iconic image of that era of American protest. Also acting in the spirit of the prophets, Heschel took his own people to task, in this case in 1963, when he told a JTS audience, "There is a dreadful moral trauma that haunts many of us; the failure . . . to do our utmost . . . to save the Jews under Hitler. [The] nightmare that terrifies me today [is] the unawareness of our being involved in a new failure, in a tragic dereliction of duty [toward] Russian Jewry." Elie Wiesel, a survivor of the Holocaust, echoed this lament. His widely read book *The Jews of Silence* lambasted American Jewry for its passivity. Appearing in 1966, it contended that while the Soviets had silenced Jews behind the Iron Curtain, Jews of the free world had chosen to silence themselves, "for a second time in a generation," to the cries of the oppressed.[25]

All of these currents of Jewish and American thought and action, coupled with an affinity for Dr. King's nonviolent confrontational tactics, coursed through Glen Richter, an early Birnbaum recruit, who became national coordinator of the Student Struggle. But most importantly, Richter's sense "of obligation to those who died in the Holocaust" motivated him to free Soviet Jewry. He also deeply disliked the establishment that had "money, memo machines and telephones . . . but don't really have grass roots support." Richter credited his group and some similar organizations based in other cities with "creating independent power bases of *people* which . . . expose the Establishment organizations as shells with not much inside."[26]

Meir Kahane and his Jewish Defense League (JDL) agreed that the establishment position was patently reprehensible. If Birnbaum's and Richter's motives were unassailable, Kahane deemed their nonviolent confrontational dispositions weak-kneed and "dangerous" since they represented "a false sense of activism." The Soviet Jewish crisis opened a second front in JDL's war to protect Jews against all enemies local and international. While in JDL members' ongoing battles with New York's black militants they only threatened to use any means available to them, when it came to harassing Russians living in the city, they fought both within and without the law. The lesson that they derived from the Holocaust had taught them that Jews stood alone and that those who were content just to "hold rallies and mimeograph sheets of paper" would "doom" Soviet Jewry. Seeing themselves as latter-day Bergsonites, struggling both against the world and shamefully wrongheaded Jewish leaders, JDL members rejected respectability and pledged "to do what must be done . . . to shake the world and spotlight the Soviet Jewish problem" so that the United States would have no alternative but to demand justice for Jews.[27]

Worldwide fears over the fate of the "Leningrad 11" amplified responses from all sides of the Jewish street. In December 1970, a group of Soviet dissidents, nine of them Jews, were put on trial for their failed attempt to hijack a Russian airliner to take them to freedom in Finland. Their arrest provoked a roundup of over two hundred Russian Jews alleged as coconspirators. When these show trials ended with several defendants sentenced to death and others to decades-long prison terms at hard labor, Jews and their humanitarian supporters everywhere were outraged. Back-tracking amid a whirlwind of spontaneous protests, from UN diplomats to international church officials to a resolution from the U.S. Congress, the Russians in less than a month's time commuted the death sentences and shortened the prison terms.

Although plans for an international gathering of Jewish leaders to promote the cause of Soviet Jewish emigration existed prior to the Leningrad incident, the trials and their aftermath added gravitas and momentum to deliberations in Brussels in February 1971. But while the meeting of eight hundred delegates from across the globe garnered immense publicity for the plight of Soviet Jews, it underscored tensions between grass-roots and establishment activists. Student Struggle types contended that they were marginalized at an event that one student sympathizer stated "was the most telling evidence of the moral bankruptcy of world Jewish leadership since the Holocaust." The Jewish Defense League was summarily barred from the gathering. Golda Meir, who chaired the gathering in Brussels, used the Belgian police to thwart Kahane's effort to "crash" the meeting. The Israelis possessed a dual agenda. They were the earliest, if circumspect, champions of Soviet Jews. But at the same time, the government harbored hopes of somehow improving relations with the Russians. Kahane might have derailed everything.[28]

Still, the turmoil in Brussels taught those who had founded the American Jewish Conference important lessons from the Student Struggle. Kahane's outbursts even sensitized some of them. With the crisis increasingly in the headlines, due to the grass-roots groups, the "think-tank" AJCSJ had to be replaced by a full-time organization with funded staff. In the spring of 1971, a new National Conference on Soviet Jewry (NCSJ) received funding, as did its cooperating organization, the Greater New York Conference on Soviet Jewry (GNYCSJ). These organizations quickly "assumed the posture of the Student Struggle emphasizing mass demonstrations and quick response to emerging issues." An observer sympathetic to the efforts of Birnbaum and Richter suggested that this approach represented "essentially a capitulation by the establishment to the demands of the activist groups and marked the establishment's recognition that a successful struggle required whole-hearted participation." The JDL also influenced the militancy of these new conferences, which believed that the field of protest could not be left to the lawless Kahanites. But this turn did not augur a new unified front among nonviolent advocates. Although the Student Struggle did "reluctantly" join the NCSJ in 1972, it was always at loggerheads with that large combine. The NCSJ, said an admirer of Birnbaum, "made a point of effectively freezing him out of any policy-making role in these groups." He contended that "the professional staffers at NCSJ and GNYCSJ put an inordinate amount of time and energy into trying to minimize" Student Struggle's role in the movement.[29]

Indeed, Student Struggle's marginalization at Solidarity Sunday infuriated Birnbaum and Richter. This annual event, begun in 1971, attracted up to one hundred thousand marchers down Manhattan's Fifth Avenue to Dag Hammarskjold Plaza. It exemplified a community engaged in nonviolent protest. Beyond proving the people power of New York Jews with numbers that activists had dreamed of for generations, Solidarity Sunday also intensified the Jewish identities of many who participated. Those who stood in the streets, wearing bracelets bearing the names of oppressed Jews and carrying signs that called for release and emigration, experienced the day as a secularized holy moment. But protestors rarely heard from leaders of the Student Struggle. "Although occasionally given seats on the podium," a journalist supporter observed, they "were almost never allowed to address the crowd, . . . leaving the distinct impression among the thousands of participants . . . that the establishment groups represented the totality of the Soviet Jewry movement in the United States."[30]

JDL, operating within its own spheres, even if it appeared on the outskirts of Solidarity Sunday's gatherings, redoubled its unbridled militancy. As early as 1969, it had attacked Soviet newspaper and tourist outlets in New York and had disrupted the performances of Russian cultural troupes. In the wake of the Leningrad incident, the group took to firing shots into the Soviet UN mission. Most egregiously, in January 1972, a bombing at Sol Hurok Productions in Manhattan—Hurok was an impresario who was the major conduit to Soviet artists appearing in the United States—killed an employee and injured fourteen others. Seemingly, Kahane answered to no one except the police and the FBI, which monitored his activities. But actually, he was called harshly to task not only by his Manhattan-based Jewish establishment enemies but also by Lubavitch Hasidic leaders. They feared that protests would undermine their own clandestine efforts to smuggle Jewish religious articles into Russia and to spirit Jews out of the Soviet Union. Although never acknowledged, these quiet Orthodox diplomats had much in common tactically with the establishment because they, too, disliked the attention-grabbing, nonviolent confrontations of the Student Struggle.[31]

According to Birnbaum, Richter, and their allies, during the 1970s–1980s, the more difficult contretemps focused on GNYCSJ. Ostensibly committed to public pressure tactics, it was not aggressive enough in pushing the Soviets and too willing to relent in response to signs of Soviet goodwill. Student Struggle activists also sensed that GNYCSJ officials worried too much about American politics. The Student Struggle likewise had its issues with the Israeli government, which was seen as insufficiently focused on the peril their Soviet brethren faced. All of these issues appeared in the long decade-and-a-half debate over the Jackson-Vanik amendment.

Whether due to a sense of humanitarianism, staunch anti-Communism, or political ambitions, fantasizing about Jewish support for a potential run at the White House, Senator Henry "Scoop" Jackson in the mid-1970s was the greatest American friend of the Soviet Jewry movement. From the introduction of the Jackson-Vanik bill in 1972 to its passage in 1975, the senator from Washington unalterably tied the release of Soviet Jews to Moscow's desire to be accorded "most favored nation" status in its economic dealings with the United States. Jackson stipulated that the Soviets would be denied specific American trade and credit benefits and concessions unless they agreed to release annually large numbers of Jews—the target number became sixty thousand—and to end harassment of both politically outspoken dissenters and Jews who just wanted to leave the Soviet Union.[32]

The Student Struggle single-mindedly supported the legislation. When it became law, the organization refused to contemplate relaxation of the measure until the doors were flung open. Unmitigated pressure, come what may, was the only way to deal with the enemy. The establishment groups and highly placed individual Jews acting on their own often questioned the efficacies of hard-line approaches deemed as both aggressive and naive about world realities. They were more attuned to how this provocative bill fit in with the Cold War policies of several administrations. They deemed American governmental support as essential. President Richard Nixon and Secretary of State Henry Kissinger saw the bill as contrary to their policy of detente. Kissinger once suggested that circumspect, informal agreements, rather than confrontations, would lead to a certain number of Soviet Jews exiting every month. Israel also had its say here and was listened to by NCSJ and GNYCSJ. Yitzhak Rabin, Israel's ambassador to the United States, made it known that his government's support for Jackson-Vanik would be counterproductive. Jerusalem harbored hopes to reestablish diplomatic relations with the Soviet Union, broken after the Six-Day War. Israel also worried about alienating Nixon and Kissinger after the Yom Kippur War, when it badly needed to rearm its depleted military arsenal.[33]

These dispositional and tactical differences became personal during the dramatic and emotional case of Natan Sharansky and his long-suffering wife, Avital, who fought for his release from a Russian prison. More than most Soviet Jewry issues, this Jewish fight over a dissident's freedom, in the midst of the Jackson-Vanik disagreement, erupted on New York's streets. And in at least one instance, the battle took a very nasty turn. Sharansky was an outspoken member of the Moscow Helsinki Watch Group, an organization of Russian dissenters headed by Andrei Sakharov. Frequently in contact with Western journalists and diplomats, Sharansky became a KGB target due to his incessant publicizing of Soviet human rights abuses. In March 1977, he was arrested for "crimes against the state," which included allegations of his spying for the CIA. These offenses carried a death sentence. In July 1978, he was convicted and sentenced to thirteen years in prison.[34]

The Student Struggle unconditionally condemned this persecution of a heroic Soviet Jew. Israeli officials and NCSJ, however, worried about Sharansky's closeness to Sakharov as a critic of the Soviet system. They preferred that the Jewish emigration issue be separated from the larger question of human rights. Harvard Law School professor Alan Dershowitz, who advocated for Sharansky in his Moscow trial, has suggested that the Israelis had an understanding with Moscow that limited the purview of their activities. Sharansky had the pedigree of "a refusenik and ardent Zionist." But "his broader human rights activities had disqualified him from Israel's protection." NCSJ agreed with Jerusalem. But, due largely to the indefatigable efforts of Avital Sharansky, the case became an international cause célèbre. Her efforts came to be championed by all Jewish groups and much of the humanitarian community.[35]

The press portrayed the Sharanskys' plight as a great love story, a couple defying an evil empire. Avital struck a compelling pose as she criss-crossed the globe projecting an "image of faith and its link to human resiliency." Her advocacies resonated beyond her husband's specific case. George Shultz, who as secretary of state in the Reagan administration played a major role in gaining Soviet Jewry its ultimate freedom, has recalled that his commitment to the cause began when he met the prisoner's wife and was "wrung out" over his inability to secure Sharansky's release. Nevertheless, organizations bickered over who would be projected as the Sharanskys' foremost local supporters.[36]

Student Struggle chair Rabbi Avi Weiss made the Sharanskys his personal cause. He traveled with Avital nationally to raise consciousness and money. Back home, ever aware of publicity opportunities to highlight his objectives, he poked a thumb in the eyes of the Soviets by having the block across the street from the Russian diplomatic residence, a mile from his Hebrew Institute of Riverdale, renamed Sharansky Square. He chose that locale as the site of rallies, especially on Simchat Torah. There the rabbi reminded those who congregated that in dancing with the Torah scrolls they were connecting spiritually with coreligionists in Moscow and Leningrad, who, in doing likewise, were risking so much to assert their Jewishness. At these gatherings, both women and men would carry the Torah, the holiest Jewish object, as the activist melded two of his concerns: the rights of women within Orthodox Judaism and the right of Soviet Jewry to be free. But Avi Weiss and Avital Sharansky carried additional political baggage that disturbed their critics. Both were connected, implicitly in the rabbi's case and explicitly as far as she was concerned, to Gush Emunim. This right-wing, religious political party in Israel gave voice to West Bank settlers' call for the expansion of "Greater Israel," a stance opposed by most American Jewish organizations. Beyond this ideological disagreement, many establishment Jews objected on a visceral level to Weiss's persistent, confrontational tactics, which they considered grandstanding.[37]

Competition over who should speak for the Sharanskys and for Soviet Jews in general and mutual animosities between Weiss and his Jewish opponents escalated on November 1, 1982, when two separate demonstrations occurred within sight of the Soviet mission to the United Nations on Sixty-Seventh Street off Lexington Avenue. At that moment, Weiss was in the midst of a five-day hunger strike in solidarity with Natan Sharansky who, on the eve of Yom Kippur, had begun an indefinite hunger strike in the Chistopol Prison. Weiss claimed that GNYCSJ held its own demonstration a block away but "declined to walk over" and make common cause with him. Weiss was especially angered by the insensitivity of Arthur Schneier, the rabbi of the Park East Synagogue, which was situated literally across the street from the Russians and a few steps from where he sat. Schneier, who saw himself, too, as an advocate for Soviet Jewry, occupied an opposite pole from Weiss in dealing with the Kremlin. He believed in honoring world leaders who might help Soviet Jews and in cajoling the Soviets. His organization, the Appeal of Conscience, even opposed Solidarity Sunday as a counterproductive affront to those whom he might influence. In 1984, while hosting the rabbi of the Moscow Choral Synagogue, who declared from the Yorkville pulpit that "he had not experienced any Government interference in the synagogue's affairs," Schneier opined that the mass rally that had taken place a day earlier would "not have any influence in any way." He "dismissed the parade as an anti-Soviet rather than a pro-Jewish demonstration." Schneier made clear how he felt about Weiss by denying him overnight sanctuary within his synagogue and turning down other requests for amenities during Weiss's vigil.[38]

In February 1986, all who were concerned with Sharansky's fate rejoiced when the dissident, in line with the Kremlin's emerging policies of *glasnost* (openness to discussing their problems) and *perestroika* (democratization of the regime), was released in return for two Soviet spies. But, as plans for his victory tour to thank his supporters developed, longstanding organizational competitions and personal antagonisms dogged his appearances. In New York, two Orthodox synagogues, Kehilath Jeshurun in Manhattan and Weiss's Riverdale congregation, vied for the honor and recognition of hosting the hero during his first Sabbath in America. Rabbi Haskel Lookstein of Kehilath Jeshurun could make the case that he was an early friend and confidant of the freed prisoner. Beginning in 1972, he had become a frequent visitor to the USSR, where in 1975 he had first met the Sharanskys. His congregation had publicly recorded each week of Natan's captivity on their bulletin board. And Ramaz School, where he was principal, held prayer vigils at the Soviet UN mission. Lookstein's concerns kept up a style of family activism that dated back to his father's pulpit outcries in World War II. GNYCSJ would have been pleased if Haskel Lookstein, then its president, had prevailed. But the Hebrew Institute of Riverdale had been Avital's home during her long struggle for her husband's release, and in the end, that emotional tie carried the day.[39]

Although all of these fractious groups focused world attention on their Jewish concern, most of the two million Jews who eventually left the USSR did so due to forces beyond their advocates' control or even imaginations. American Jews should be credited with helping "punch a hole in the iron curtain through calling attention to the human failings of the Soviet system" as their issue rose to the top of the world diplomatic agenda. But most Soviet Jews were released either during or after the demise of Soviet Communism. From less than a thousand legal émigrés in 1986, the number increased to 18,000 two years later, before the doors opened wide in 1989, with 71,000 leaving Russia that year. In 1990, some 213,000 Jews departed. They benefited from the end of the Cold War. When Ronald Reagan in June 1987 demanded that the occupiers of East Germany "tear down that [Berlin] Wall," the right of movement of Soviet Jews was part of his call for freedom for oppressed people. Both Jewish establishment organizations and grass-roots groups had sensitized him and Secretary of State George Shultz to this moral issue. But when the Berlin Wall actually fell in November 1989, Jews joined an international of exodus of peoples from Kremlin control. Free Soviet Jewish emigration "was wrought by the same historic forces that liberated other captive communities in the Soviet sphere."[40]

This dramatic turn toward freedom did not, however, stifle tensions among America's Soviet Jewry groups. They now battled over how to prosecute the cause's end game. The crux of controversy boiled down to whether the intentions of the Soviets could be trusted and if a concomitant lessening of pressure and protest was appropriate. In many ways, this dispute reiterated those profound differences separating New York's establishment organizations and its grass-roots groups for several generations: the question of to what extent Jews' activism should be unconditional against their enemies and uncompromising toward allies within American government.

Finally, there was the question of when the time might be ripe to move beyond the era of public protests. Although the massive rally of 150,000 in December 1987 in Washington, D.C., was an unequaled moment in time, judged as "a high point in the Soviet Jewry movement and in American history" for close to two decades, New York's Solidarity Sunday had been the centerpiece of sustained popular agitation on behalf of Soviet Jewry. In March 1989, Student Struggle was chagrined when GNYCJS, now called the Coalition to Free Soviet Jewry, chose to forgo that quintessential tactic. Birnbaum, Richter, and Weiss rejected this compromise and patched together their own "Day of Solidarity," with the help of a small Long Island–based group. At that rally, Birnbaum made clear that, for them, the battle was not "*dayenu*" ("enough" or "over") "without fundamental concessions on the side of the Soviet Union," critical steps that the enemy had yet to take. Years later, a historian reflecting on that period contended that "victory had come suddenly and . . . too soon" for these people who had "been young, idealistic and Jewishly committed" and consistently on guard from the time they first joined the battle two decades earlier. They could not stand down. Student Struggle retorted that the multi-front battle for Soviet Jewry in fact did not end even with the fall of Communism, the dissolution of the Soviet Union, and the opening of the Kremlin's gates. The Jewish world, it argued, had still to be concerned about the fate of the millions of Jews in the former Soviet Union who now faced a resurgence of popular and nationalist anti-Semitism. It was wrong that the establishment honored Gorbachev at a moment when "Soviet Jews were becoming increasingly apprehensive that a revival of murderous Czarist-era pogroms was becoming a distinct possibility." Always untrusting of sustained world interest in the fate of Jews, veterans of Student Struggle continued to use the streets of New York to raise public consciousness and to "speak truth to power."[41]

Feminism and activism on behalf of Soviet Jewry represent two vital political movements with roots in New York City. Both achieved impressive victories within the lifetimes of their organizers. Both provoked bitter opponents among other Jews, exacerbating divisions separating New York Jews. Yet both movements drew on the city's unique geography, its neighborhoods that grouped Jews according to class, religion, and politics. Despite the inroads of suburbanization and the diminution of New York City's Jewish population, its over a million Jews still sustained sufficient diversity to fuel activist dreams, to create communities of solidarity, and to transform promises into realities.

Rogarshevsky parlor reconstructed in the Lower East Side Tenement Museum, circa 2010. (Photo by Keiko Niwa; courtesy Lower East Side Tenement Museum)

Epilogue:
In a New Millennium

At the turn of the millennium, New York Jews exuded confidence about their place in the city. Despite decades of economic distress and racial conflict, Gotham appeared poised to fulfill its promises once again. Young Jewish professionals participated actively in neighborhood gentrification, both in Manhattan and the outer boroughs, that revived during the Wall Street boom of the 1990s. Sounding like Jews of earlier eras, those who helped restore "the Brooklyn brownstone belt" of Fort Greene or Dumbo (down under the Manhattan Bridge overpass) areas bragged that it took only fifteen minutes to reach their managerial or executive jobs in Manhattan investment banks, law firms, or software companies. Those who were making even more money settled in luxury lofts within an expanding Soho district that had begun its redevelopment a generation earlier. Some put down stakes in the old Meatpacking District, where the Abzug market once stood. These new residents renewed the city tradition of walking to work, if they did not hop into a cab, destination Wall Street. By 2000, upper-class Jews lived on both the east and west sides of Manhattan south of Sixtieth Street and north of the Lower East Side. In Harlem, gentrification fulfilled a 1984 prediction that "affluent whites" would "inevitably" migrate there due to its stock of transformable low-cost housing and its "location just a few miles from midtown." A distinctive Jewish presence existed at the start of the new millennium, around the time that Yoel and Shoshana Borgenicht joined the march uptown. By the end of the first decade of the twentieth century, census returns showed the Harlem neighborhood to be majority white for the first time since the 1920s.[1]

Jews especially transformed the Lower East Side in the 1990s. Many of the young entrepreneurs and artists returned to the site of their grandparents' beginnings. Some even lived at the same street address, albeit in a modernized former tenement. But theirs was a different Jewish quarter, as "hipification," it was said, "reache[d] the street where peddlers once pushed carts." A chic sensibility replaced the legendary ethnic quality of the neighborhood, as entrepreneurs in pursuit of "their version of the American dream," and with a ready customer base, established "boutiques featuring their own designer labels or a bar with great vodka martinis, or a vintage furniture store." Now, observers spoke of the "intersection of new and old, of people of disparate cultures and points of view" on Orchard Street. One sign of the times, as music clubs and other nightlife attractions created a thoroughfare of "a new bohemia," was the opening in 1997 of the "swanky Lansky Lounge," which initially shared space with "Ratner's, the century-old kosher dairy restaurant." Seven years later, that Jewish food landmark closed its doors forever. Jews living elsewhere in the city did not feel the tug, as prior generations had, to repair to Delancey Street for its sights and sounds and to savor such delicacies as split pea and potato soup, cheese blintzes, and onion rolls. Most young downtowners cared far less for eastern European Jewish culinary traditions than prior generations had. But a good old American hot dog still tempted many to line up at Katz's Delicatessen. The counterman stood behind a sign reminding customers that this store once sent salamis to boys in the army. Out-of-towners who still desired a taste of the Jewish New York that they remembered, or had heard about, could order Ratner's frozen foods online.[2]

Yet even as the Lower East Side streets lost much of their mundane Jewish character, Jews redoubled efforts to concretize the history of this once extraordinary Jewish place. Starting in the 1980s, organizations such as the Museum at Eldridge Street, the Lower East Side Tenement Museum, and the Lower East Side Conservancy worked to entice visitors downtown through exhibits, tours, and cultural programs exploring how Jews and other nineteenth- and twentieth-century immigrants made their way into America through the renowned hub. By the new millennium, these organizations had earned city, state, and national funding to raise historical awareness of the Lower East Side's significance.[3]

But even as historians and docents recounted past difficulties, the contemporary Lower East Side still housed thousands of impoverished immigrants whose tortured existences "eerily recall[ed] the pathologies of the turn-of-the-century tenements." In 1996, the *New York Times* profiled a Latina woman who lived with her three children "on a corner of Clinton near Delancey, up a narrow stairway between a pawnshop and a Dominican restaurant . . . in a single, illegal room that suffocates their dreams of the future." She lived streets away from exploited Chinese newcomers who sewed garments in sweatshops or struggled for a living as street peddlers, much as Jews had done a century earlier.[4]

New York Jews had their own poor, their aged, and Russian immigrants whose needs required communal support. Poverty pockets endured within the Hasidic Williamsburg enclaves and Boro Park. But the sense was, at least among the elderly, that they were not holding out within a deteriorated city, even if inevitably they were dying out. Rabbi Solomon Berl of the Young Israel of Co-op City understood this fact of life when in 2003 he told a Columbia University journalism student that while "moveouts, mortality and Miami" —he had first articulated that sad mantra back in the 1980s—had reduced his congregation to "approximately 75," he planned "for the future" to remain at the helm of his shul "until the last Jew is left." Six years later, the then eighty-five-year-old spiritual leader who prayed that 125 worshipers would appear for High Holiday service was still writing to a local community paper about "love, brotherhood, friendship, ethics" to "mostly non-Jews" to "remind people that there is a Jewish presence there." For Berl, this enclave "was beautiful . . . [and] it's still beautiful."[5]

Neither Co-op City's elderly equanimity nor the Lower East Side's exuberant youth epitomized Jewish neighborhood life in the early 2000s. Rather, stability most aptly characterized New York's Jewish enclaves. Those who had decided, through the trying times of the 1970s to the early 1990s, to remain in the city stayed, ensuring that textures of community life continued. If anything, these enduring neighborhoods attracted newcomers to their midst. Riverdale prospered as an affluent preserve. The Upper West Side retained its idiosyncratic character as "two populations distinct in their levels of Jewish affiliation and practice" living side by side. One group joined synagogues, visited Israel, and enrolled children in Jewish day school, while the other group rejected affiliation and often intermarried.[6] But even as the Upper West Side's Jewish population remained stable, it continued its long tradition, dating back to Mordecai Kaplan's day, as a creative, innovative Jewish religious center where ideas and practices attracted energetic newcomers whose modes of religious observance influenced the nation.

The community that gave birth to Jewish feminism became the home to a variety of egalitarian, independent, or partnership minyans where men and women, within strict, and sometimes flexible, Jewish religious standards, joined to pray, to study, and to enjoy companionship. Seemingly, the best of the havurah ideal of the 1960s–1970s was reborn. When the Yeshivat Hadar was founded in 2008, meeting initially in rooms at the West End Synagogue on Sixty-Ninth Street and Amsterdam Avenue, men and women studied sacred writings together. Its founders, some of them children of Conservative rabbis, fervently believed that their start-up programs "aimed at Jews in their 20s and early 30s . . . are going to have a multiplier effect on the Jewish community" nationwide. Meanwhile, women's study of the Talmud under Orthodox auspices continued to find its place on the West Side within Drisha, which, in 1979, first opened its doors in rented space at the Jewish Center. And in 2000, near Columbia University, Rabbi Avi Weiss inaugurated Yeshiva Chovevei Torah, a rabbinical training school dedicated to spreading across the United States his message of "Open Orthodoxy," an ideology that prizes religious traditionalism and gender sensitivity. In 2010, the institution relocated to a permanent space in Riverdale at Weiss's Hebrew Institute of Riverdale.[7]

Even within an era of the efflorescence of Jewish studies programs nationally and the presence and creation of modern rabbinical schools across the country, Columbia University continued to attract bright Jewish minds, as it had for generations, to its graduate programs in Jewish studies. In the 1990s, New York's prestige as a Jewish intellectual hub was enhanced further when NYU mounted vigorous challenges to Columbia's local leadership, seeking the best students and future professionals as it proffered not only doctoral programs but tracks in Jewish education, museum studies, and Jewish communal organizations. Thus, the city—with its longstanding Orthodox, Conservative, and Reform seminaries and City University programs still very much in place, notwithstanding attractive alternatives everywhere—maintained its position as a prime place where the ambitious flocked to learn how to head Jewish schools and institutions and to educate college students on American university campuses.[8]

All of these students and senior scholars also benefited from the opening in 2000 of the Center for Jewish History, which united American Jewish,

Sephardic, eastern European, and central European repositories and centers of study, creating in the vision of its founder, Bruce Slovin, "the Library of Congress of the Jewish People in America." Though in its early years, it was beset with financial difficulties and internecine rivalries, a decade into its existence, the center was on sound economic footing, and a cooperative spirit prevailed. Here Jewish lawyers, financiers, real estate magnates, bankers, and others who had made out so well in the years of New York's revival had put their money to great use on behalf of Jewish scholarship.[9]

Stability and continuity also surely characterized Brooklyn's old neighborhoods of Williamsburg, Boro Park, and Crown Heights as they expanded their strict Orthodox environments, while families and leaders still coped with poverty. East Queens communities such as Little Neck and Bayside on the edge of the city line aged but stayed "economically secure." As in the past, significant Jewish movement occurred within the city. Fifteen thousand Jews headed to the quasi-suburban locale of Staten Island. Richmond County attracted a culturally diverse crowd that included better-off Orthodox Jews from Brooklyn, Russian immigrants who prospered, and native-born Jews with little interest in Jewish causes and affiliation. Suburbia also continued to absorb its share of Jews, as it had for more than half a century. But rates of out-migration slowed during the 1990s. While in 2002 the total number of Jews in the five boroughs dropped, for the first time in more than a century, to under one million (972,000), "unlike other East Coast and Midwestern Jewish communities whose suburbanization has resulted in a restructuring of the center of Jewish life," the city remained the unofficial Jewish capital of the eight-county area, if not the country. Those who left did not move too far, as "approximately 70% of the metropolitan-area Jewish community resided in New York City." Suburban Jews retained urban connections for both business and cultural activities.[10]

Many Jews credited Mayor Rudolph W. Giuliani for strengthening their faith in the city's promises. Especially by his second term, there was confidence in most Jewish quarters that he had their concerns and interests at heart—not that the mayor acquired widespread Jewish support easily or immediately. When he first ran against David Dinkins in 1989, Giuliani received strong backing among the tense and security-worried voters in heavily Hasidic neighborhoods of Brooklyn and in Jewish sections of Forest Hills and Kew Gardens. However, Dinkins rode to victory, albeit by the slimmest of margins, because liberal Jews in Manhattan and Bronx neighborhoods joined

African Americans in sharing the Democrat's vision of a racially harmonious, reconciled city.[11]

During Giuliani's 1993 return engagement against Dinkins, he made certain to fortify his core Jewish base, attacking the city's willingness to allow Nation of Islam leader Louis H. Farrakhan to rent Yankee Stadium for a rally. While Dinkins averred that access to that public venue was "not discretionary," as "the Constitution says that freedom of speech is allowed" even to the most disagreeable, Giuliani cagily compared the black Muslim to neo-Nazis or skinheads and implied that the stadium would have been made off-limits to those haters. Speaking strongly to the local racial issue that roiled Jews and still resonated citywide, the challenger, more than any other critic of the incumbent, "harnessed the outrage" among those who viewed the mayor as having mishandled Crown Heights. But to win City Hall, Giuliani had to broaden his constituency not only to "reassemble the Koch coalition of conservative white ethnics, moderate Jews and Hispanic voters"—the so-called Rudycrats—but also to attract Jewish liberals. Emphasizing that the city was dirty and dangerous with a dispirited police force, he also harped on an early 1990s recession. While the rest of the nation recovered, New York, he alleged, did not rebound due to Dinkins's poor economic leadership and management skills. In other words, the problem with the Dinkins administration transcended his failure to produce his promised glorious mosaic. Some of the worst economic features of the 1970s had been allowed to return.[12]

Still, as Election Day approached, critically important Jewish voting blocs on both the Upper West and Upper East Side struggled to "balance their doubts against their traditions." Novelist Hugh Nissenson explained his "dilemma" that as a "lifelong . . . liberal Democrat," he was inclined to be with Dinkins, even if he felt that Dinkins's "competence is limited." But "as a Jew," Nissenson was "unhappy with the way Crown Heights was handled." Nonetheless, he could not bring himself to vote for Giuliani because he "instinctively stood against everything this man has stood for." He did not like the candidate's "Weltanschauung, . . . his ideas, his politics." Others around him were similarly conflicted, unhappy with the incumbent's performance on both the racial and economic fronts. But they perceived the challenger as "too political and not trustworthy." Some even resented Giuliani's grandstanding against Farrakhan, which "showed a disregard for the First Amendment." In the end, Dinkins held sway within liberal Jewish quarters as he garnered almost identical numbers as he had in 1989 among constituents who, like Nissenson, chose him "under protest." But Giuliani won the mayoralty in 1993, largely because of intense support from those Rudycrats, the "white ethnic and Jewish outer-borough base." The campaign revealed that Manhattan and Brooklyn Jews still harbored very different views of where the city was heading and their place within the metropolis.[13]

As mayor, Giuliani did not disappoint his Jewish core constituency. He visited Israel during the Intifada to show his solidarity with the victims of bombings—some of the killed or maimed were his own erstwhile New York-ers—and to encourage New Yorkers to follow his example and support Israel through tourism. More impressive for his constant fans was his public snub of Yasir Arafat. In October 1995, Giuliani announced that the Palestinian leader was unwanted at a Lincoln Center concert that the city hosted for United Nations delegates. Even as a debate roiled within and without Israel over whether, and how, to negotiate with Arafat, New York's mayor declared, "Israel may have to make peace with the man. But I don't have to extend any courtesies to him." Dozens of mostly Orthodox leaders and elected officials representing many of the more politically conservative Jewish voters in the city rushed to City Hall's steps to hear a Brooklyn Jewish assemblyman praise their champion. Giuliani was also uplifted, said his office, by the "more than 1,000 phone calls of support" that he received.[14]

Giuliani's act, however, did not play well among many Jews elsewhere in the city. They resented his meddling in international diplomacy and potentially undermining a complicated peace process. Jews fragmented once again on a critical policy issue: it was seemingly, once again, Manhattan versus Brooklyn. Tensions boiled over publicly when the National Jewish Community Relations Advisory Council invited Arafat to address 150 of its leaders from around the country at the B'nai Zion building in Manhattan the same week as the mayor's snub. While one delegate calmly explained that "every time Arafat repeats his support of the peace process and appears conciliatory, it creates a new reality, one that he has to deal with back home," two protestors "shouted 'Arafat is a murderer' before being arrested at the outset of the meeting," leaving "the audience embarrassed at this breach of etiquette."[15]

Giuliani's undiplomatic outspokenness energized his supporters and troubled his opponents, but by the end of his first term (1997) both groups of Jews acknowledged that his administration had improved the quality of their lives.

Despite criticism of heavy-handed practices, the inescapable reality was that under Giuliani's watch, New York had emerged as a clean, increasingly prosperous, comfortable, and above all, safe city. To some extent, he rode the crest of the boom on Wall Street in his early years in City Hall, which painlessly increased municipal revenues, helping him funnel monies into essential services. But his signature accomplishment, the continuing drop in crime, reassured law-abiding citizens. A 1995 *New York* magazine cover story, "The End of Crime as We Know It," said it all. Five years earlier, *Time* magazine had decried "The Rotting of the Big Apple." Gotham now recaptured its attractive cachet. Thanks to well-policed subways, a "virtuous cycle was set in motion" that brought residents and tourists securely into public spaces both where they lived and where they might go for entertainment. Times Square, shorn of its porn shops, became an attractive site.[16]

Widespread appreciation among Jews for a job well done registered clearly when Giuliani ran for reelection in 1997. The race pitted a Jewish, liberal civil libertarian from the West Side of Manhattan against a pugnacious Italian American conservative. Manhattan borough president Ruth Messinger had no standing with the Brooklyn Jewish crowd. That was made clear to her during the Democratic primary season when she, and other aspirants for Gracie Mansion, were not given a chance to speak at a breakfast sponsored by the Council of Jewish Organizations of Flatbush, where Giuliani was presented with a silver candelabra as a token of communal appreciation by his mostly Orthodox supporters. More significantly, as the general election approached, Messinger encountered troubles with her own core constituency. She characterized Giuliani as "strident, mean spirited," the type of person a Hugh Nissenson had not liked four years earlier. She offered herself as committed to a "more healing leadership style" that "would do the most to bridge ethnic and racial divisions" that had been "exacerbate[ed] over the last four years." On the Arafat flap, Messinger asserted that it was "inappropriate" for "the city's chief diplomat" to "remove someone from a concert that the city was a player in." She also positioned herself as far more concerned than Giuliani with the state of the city's public schools and unemployment. She was seen as "caring more about the needs and problems of poor people." However, Messinger failed to "crack through the general satisfaction with Mr. Giuliani and the city." In the days before the election, a Jewish "business consultant who said he was a liberal planning to vote" Republican opined, "This is no contest."[17]

When the votes were counted, the consultant was proven right. The mayor carried whites by a four-to-one margin and outpolled Messinger among women by nineteen points. He lost only in poor areas of the Bronx and among African Americans. Most strikingly, he won the Jewish vote with an overwhelming 75 percent, including 40 percent of "self-identified liberals." Standing among Messinger's saddened supporters when she conceded to Giuliani, Franz Leichter, a Jewish state senator who represented the Upper West Side, mused with regret that "this is a time, certainly, when people have become more concerned about their private lives and welfare" than with the largest societal issues.[18]

Though Messinger was defeated in her bid for City Hall, she was not deflated. She immediately resounded personally to Leichter's challenge, becoming president in 1998 of the American Jewish World Service. With rabbis of all movements, Jewish communal leaders, activists, businesspeople, and scholars involved, it became "the first American Jewish organization dedicated to alleviating poverty, hunger and disease among people across the globe." Again, a New York–based Jewish activist showed the way.[19]

The mayor and the city continued to receive high marks for most of his second administration. Backed by a robust economy and buoyed by effective crime prevention, the city that never slept was wide awake and at the service of its residents and visitors on a twenty-four-hour-a-day basis. A palpable calm spread across the city's neighborhoods. This cooperative atmosphere appeared most dramatically in the absence of violence and looting in the summer of 1999. For eighteen hours, three hundred thousand working-class residents of a largely Latino Washington Heights neighborhood suffered in a blackout as temperatures hovered around one hundred degrees. Giuliani praised that neighborhood's people for supporting one another and for assisting the police, "an example of how communities around the city and the country can come together in the face of adversity." Elsewhere, some signs of intergroup rapprochement emerged, although the mayor could not take credit for positive developments in Crown Heights. There, local African American, Caribbean immigrant, and Jewish leaders, on their own, were working together to head off "potentially volatile" racial confrontations between their youths. While acknowledging that they lived "parallel lives" with "no social interaction" in a neighborhood now 60 percent black and 38 percent white, "communication between the two groups had improved." Both wanted Crown Heights no longer to be stereotyped as "a war zone torn by racial strife." When in April 1998 Lemrick Nelson Jr. was sentenced to twenty years in prison for the murder of Yankel Rosenbaum, both Jewish and black streets were quiet.[20]

Still, Giuliani manifested, in his critics' view, a profound inability to listen to or hear pained voices. This troubling proclivity came to the fore when he unqualifiedly defended the police in the shooting of an unarmed African immigrant, Amadou Diallo, in the Bronx. Widespread outrage erupted beyond the black and immigrant African community, when officers of the vaunted Street Crime Unit, looking for an alleged murderer of a taxi driver and rape suspect, shot forty-one bullets into Diallo when he walked out a darkened doorway and appeared to the police to have a gun in his hands. While the mayor expressed the city's condolences to the family, he quickly pointed out that during his administration the police used far less "deadly force" than during Dinkins's time and that his cops were "the most restrained big city police force in the nation." His attitude led his most vociferous enemies to denounce him as "Bull Giuliani," linking him to the racist police chief in Selma, Alabama, of a generation earlier whose dogs attacked civil rights protestors. Among Jews, backing for Giuliani flagged within liberal quarters and among those who were disappointed that City Hall failed to implement the recommendations of a blue-ribbon panel that was directed to study police-community relations.[21]

The city's, and indeed the world's, evaluation of Giuliani's performance changed immeasurably after the terrorist 9/11 attack on the World Trade Center. Historians may debate the degree of his actual courage on that fateful day, but in the months that followed, he was honored as "America's mayor." He cultivated an image of a steadfast and caring figure who kept New York together under the most extreme circumstances. For New York Jews, his efforts redoubled affection for him in most quarters and largely stilled voices that had questioned his prior heavy-handed or cold-hearted persona.[22] In the aftermath of that unparalleled tragedy, subscribing to a palpable citywide resolve to survive and advance, Jews remained committed to being part of the city's future. Demographers who surveyed the size, shape, and textures of community life just a year after the Trade Center attacks did not discover any panic flight afoot from the metropolis. If anything, more than most white middle-class groups, Jews in the city and its surrounding suburbs remained where they had lived in the prior calm decade, seeking safe and secure lives.[23]

Yet a new identity was discernible in the Jewish streets, a sense more than ever before that as New Yorkers over the long future haul, they possessed a shared destiny with their neighbors. Perhaps that explains in part Jewish support for Michael R. Bloomberg, Giuliani's successor. The latest Jew to occupy City Hall, Bloomberg personified the view that Jewish and metropolitan concerns were one. His opponent, City Advocate Mark Green, had the active support of "numerous communal leaders . . . and leading rabbis" and spent much of his career cultivating that ethnic vote. But Bloomberg, who had few Jewish ties other than his philanthropic record and who reportedly was wont to make "caustic remarks about Israel and religion" garnered 52 percent of the Jewish vote. This "mass defection . . . help[ed] put [the] billionaire] over the top." Although Bloomberg benefited greatly from Giuliani's endorsement, his renowned financial acumen appealed to Jews with its promise of assistance to help the city recover economically. Disarray within Democratic political ranks made Bloomberg's nonconfrontational style, which spoke of the challenges that all city dwellers shared, attractive. Jews were prepared to "vote more as New Yorkers than they did as Jews."[24]

The media tycoon, born in Medford, Massachusetts—the latest renowned newcomer to New York who fulfilled his personal promises—enjoyed exceptional financial success on Wall Street. As mayor, Bloomberg moved into the echelons of power and privilege and said and did all the right things about Jewish issues. No less would be expected of a successful city politician. But he was a very different Jewish mayor, quite unlike the two sons of Jewish New York who preceded him. He conscientiously downplayed his religious background and had no neighborhood roots or affinity for the city's Jewish street culture that linked him to the group's past in the metropolis. He did not build his electoral appeal on a defined Jewish base. While still a candidate, he told an inquiring, provocative Jewish journalist, "Am I glad to be born a Jew? I never even thought about it in that context. You are what you are."[25]

Years later, in 2008, toward the end of Bloomberg's second term, as he contemplated a run at the White House, he "refused to make a display of religious faith." Disdaining this public desideratum, the candidate-in-waiting declared, "I think everyone's religious beliefs are their own and they should keep them private." So disposed, he consistently came across while in City Hall as a "colorless, post-partisan," and highly independent manager. It was just the type of persona, wrote a sympathetic biographer, that the city, including its Jews, needed in the decade post-9/11 and after the bombastic Giuliani years.

Bloomberg spoke softly about his goals of improving public education and the hospital system, banning illegal guns, and balancing his affinities for the rights of minority communities with sympathy for the police, whose law enforcement strategies often offended blacks and Latinos. Bloomberg achieved some initiatives and lost others amid the maelstroms of metropolitan and national politics. Most critically, New York remained safe from violent attack under his watch. If he possessed his own autocratic streak and sometimes could not resist instructing the citizenry on how to live their private lives, the generally circumspect mayor was always less obvious in his posturing than his predecessor was. In his off-hours, however, Bloomberg was quite visible, as he cut a dashing figure as one of the city's most eligible bachelors.[26]

Michael Bloomberg did not strike up a deep love affair with those New York Jews who cherished religious and cultural distinctiveness. He was a friendly, helpful sojourner among them, emblematic of those who lived apart from the boundaries of neighborhood and enclave, a man of the world, though presently contributing to the progress of the metropolis. But with his perspective of a respected outsider, he possessed a compelling message that even the most Jewish New Yorkers could comprehend. In a new millennium, a united city standing together against threats from without and willing to address enduring stubborn challenges from within offered the best chance for Jews to live safe, secure, and meaningful lives with all others within a city of promises.

An Introduction to the Visual and Material Culture of New York City Jews, 1920–2010

DIANA L. LINDEN

In 2005, German-born Jewish photographer Julian Voloj went search-ing for architectural elements, historical objects, and urban ruins that hinted at traces of New York City's rich Jewish heritage that had become obscured over time. He sought to create a visual catalog of what had been and what still exists today. Voloj assigns to us a task, if so inspired, to join his search for ma-terial remnants and to rediscover the vestiges of New York's Jewish past that remain potent in our time.[1]

Literally, Voloj's search sent him high and low, and he found himself up on the rooftop of Ahavas Israel Synagogue in Greenpoint, Brooklyn. His photo-graph emphasizes a Magen David (Jewish star) located atop the synagogue's roof.[2] The metal bars are forged into the now familiar six-pointed star, creating a frame within a frame that directs the viewer's gaze to the blended Brooklyn and Manhattan skyline.

The Star of David's role as a framing device in Voloj's work calls our atten-tion to the constructedness of his vision and asks us to consider the role of Jewish history within the larger framework of the city. What is a New York Jew, and how are Jews pictured in the city's visual economy? Voloj's willingness to seek and to locate the once forgotten shows that Jewishness has not vacated New York, but rather, its nineteenth-century origins no longer command our view. Like an archeologist, Voloj unearths a hidden culture, people, and time and then brings it back to view in these contemporary times. His use of black

Julian Voloj, untitled photograph, part of *Forgotten Heritage Series: Uncovering New York's Hidden Jewish Past*, 2005. (Courtesy of the artist)

and white for his images offers the sense of a document, a survey, and a sense of believability we used to see in newspapers. Voloj embeds the history of New York Jews within the broader fabric of the city at an unconscious level.

Just as a photographer has a point of view, so does this visual essay. Rather than rely on the printed word as preserved in historical documents or memoirs, objects, photographs, ephemera, and heirlooms here testify to some of the many meanings evoked by the phrase "New York Jew" from the 1920s into the twenty-first century. This visual essay asks what unique qualities New York City brings to the equation—what attributes make New York Jews different from other big-city Jews. As writer Lenore Skenazy pointedly asked, "Are New York Jews More Jewish?"[3] When Jewish culture hit the city's pavements and matured over the course of the century, particularly from the 1920s onward, what type of alchemic transformation occurred? How has the idea of a New York Jew been made visual? And how have representations of New York Jews been distributed, by whom, and to whom? New York City has been the location for pivotal events and institutions. It hosted the 1939 and 1964 World's Fairs and became the permanent home of the United Nations, drawing tourists to New York on the eve of World War II and during the heyday of civil rights activism. Protestors have gathered regularly in the city to comment on all manner of national and international politics and events. Jewish participation and leadership in such activities shapes perceptions of New York Jews. Both in the city and beyond, New York remains a focal point of Jewishness. This essay offers a visual gateway, enabling us to explore how both Jews and others have understood the term "New York Jew" and to consider through engagement with objects and ephemera various conceptualizations of what this term has meant, how New York Jews have been portrayed, and how they have portrayed themselves.

New York City in the 1920s had much to offer to the young Jewish painter Theresa Bernstein (1890–2002). There were numerous art schools for her and galleries for the exhibition of her work, as well as like-minded artist friends.[4]

Theresa Bernstein, *Zionist Meeting: Madison Square Garden* (study), oil on canvas, 1923. (Courtesy of the Jewish National Fund, New York)

A dedicated Zionist, Bernstein attended an important Zionist meeting held at Madison Square Garden in 1923. Bernstein interpreted the event, which as marked by the attendance of Albert Einstein (lower right), supporter of binationalism, and Zionist leader Chaim Weizmann, later the first president of Israel. Bernstein rejected the high style of history painting with its sharp details, pronounced importance given to key figures, and the evocation of an awe-inspiring historical narrative. Instead, by placing the two men at eye level, backed by the Garden's curved walls, which are conspicuously draped with Zionist banners and the American flag, Bernstein presents the historical in the mode of the everyday. Through the immediacy of rough, sketchy brushwork and the nonhierarchical arrangement of figures, Bernstein presents these noble men as ordinary people. While these New York Jews worked toward a Jewish homeland in Palestine, simultaneously there were groups of Jews building their new lives and homes in the Bronx. These leftist Jews' assertive presence in the public realm helped bring Jews, New York City, and the Left together as one identity.

Wurts Bros., *Cooperative Kindergarten in the Amalgamated Houses in the Bronx*, photograph, 1929. (Wurts Bros. Collection, Museum of the City of New York, New York)

In the photograph on the facing page, it is not the teacher who holds the children's attention this school day but instead the photographer who is capturing their image. In the foreground at right, the toddlers and preschoolers form a semicircle as they play together. Behind them, to the left, desks are arranged in a linear fashion, rather than in hierarchical rows. Through cooperative play and songs in both Yiddish and English, these kindergarteners dutifully learn their Socialist Yiddishist lessons.

The predominatly Jewish Amalgamated Clothing Workers union built a massive cooperative housing project in the Bronx in 1927. Immigrant and second-generation Jewish garment workers worked together to lift themselves up from the social and econmoic poverty of tenement life; this cooperative was visionary.[5] In addition to the free kindergarten, residents shared a library of more than twenty thousand books in Yiddish, Russian, and English and published a newsletter.

This cooperative housing project speaks to the passionate politics of New York City Jews and their desire for a better life in America. While many Jews supported radical politics, their beliefs and commitments varied from Communist to Socialist to Anarchist to Zionist. Even within the Left, New York sustained great diversity, a distinctive characteristic of New York's Jewish communities.

In early twentieth-century Harlem, Marcus Garvey's Universal Negro Improvement Association (UNIA) and the movement's interest in the history of the African Diaspora inspired black Judaism.[6] In 1921, Mordecai Herman, a Garveyite, founded the Moorish Zionist Temple of the Moorish Jews, located at 127 West 137th Street in Harlem; James VanDerZee (1886–1983), the official UNIA photographer, ran his studio in Harlem for over fifty years. The neighborhood's residents were his patrons, including the members of the Moorish Zionist Temple, contributing to his thriving career during the Harlem Renaissance.[7] In the photograph on the following page, the visual focus of the group gathered in front of the brownstone that served as their synagogue is their rabbi, Arnold Ford, whose upper torso is wrapped in his white tallit. All of the congregants, with the exception of a young boy, wear hats and *kippah*, their heads covered in religious fidelity. They appear to be dressed in their finest outfits for this posed group portrait. While the content of contemporary Jewish and African American newspapers attests that other Jews questioned the authenticity of these Moorish Jews, simultaneously the city

James VanDerZee, *The Congregation of the Moorish Zionist Temple of the Moorish Jews, Harlem*, photograph, 1929. (Photograph by James VanDerZee; Prints and Photographs Division, Library of Congress, Washington, DC)

provided a home for non-European New York Jews and the inherent differences among Jews.[8]

In the 1920s–1930s, New York's Jews were active in the nascent movement for African American civil rights, and they continued in that struggle well into the 1960s. Native New Yorker and Jewish artist Seymour Lipton's (1903–1986) pedestal-sized sculpture depicts an unnamed man curled up in on himself, his knees placed high on his chest in the fetal position. But while the fetal pose relates to birth, here it represents death at the hands of a lynch mob. The deep mahogany wood is meant to represent black skin. A tight rope noose remains around the man's elongated, broken neck as if he were just cut free from a tree limb, while behind the man's back a second rope tightens his hands.[9] Lipton's carved marks and grooves in the wood contrast with the figure's stillness, intensifying its emotional impact. Lipton drew immediate inspiration for his piece from the Scottsboro case in Alabama. Flamboyant New York lawyer Samuel Leibowitz was hired by the International Labor Defense (ILD), a workers' defense organization of the Communist Party, to represent the "Scottsboro boys," nine black young men (one only twelve years old) unjustly accused of the rape of two white girls.

Although Leibowitz was a fervent anti-Communist, to southern whites who ached for the boys' execution, he exemplified a meddling "New York Jew." Politically active Jews drew comparisons between their own persecution and that of the African American teenagers. While both groups set their hopes on Democratic president Franklin D. Roosevelt to enact antilynching legislation, the president refused to do so. Lipton's sculpture, like the song "Strange Fruit" (1939), written by Abel Meeropol, who later became the adoptive father of Michael and Robert Rosenberg, the sons of executed alleged Soviet spies Julius and Ethel Rosenberg, represents how New York Jews imagined themselves in the suffering of African Americans.[10]

Seymour Lipton, *Lynched*, mahogany, 1933. (© The Estate of Seymour Lipton; courtesy of Michael Rosenfeld Gallery LLC, New York, NY, and the Palmer State Museum of Art, the Pennsylvania State University, State College, PA)

"Yoo-hoo, Mrs. Bloom!" Molly Goldberg, played by actress Gertrude Berg, cheerily shouted this signature greeting of *The Goldbergs* from her kitchen window perch, warmly welcoming audiences into her family's home in the Bronx. *The Goldbergs*, a popular radio and then television show sponsored by Pepsodent, was written and produced by Berg and starred her as the matriarch of a Jewish family striving to do well.[11] The radio version of fifteen minutes each Tuesday night debuted in November 1929, just one month before the stock market crash. Berg, through her character, created the most modern, positive, and assertive popular image of a Jewish woman to that date. As Molly, she fearlessly took on such issues as anti-Semitism and Hitler's war against the Jews. For most Americans, Berg's Mrs. Goldberg was their first, if only fictional, image of a Jewish New Yorker. Berg and Goldberg were closely aligned in the public's mind as one and same. During the 1930s, Gertrude/Molly stood second only to Eleanor Roosevelt in the quantity of letters received from the public. This Jewish woman of the Bronx presented such a powerful image of motherly strength, tinged with Yiddish-inflected speech and her family's striving and struggling for a better life, that despite ethnic and geographic differences, many non-Jewish women nationally felt a kinship with Molly Goldberg. Although little known today, before Lucille Ball's *I Love Lucy*, it was Berg who created the first popular series about a New York family.

New York City in the 1930s was home to both the folk wisdom of Molly Goldberg and several institutions of higher education where students received formal educations. Lower Manhattan's New School for Social Research was founded in 1919 by a group of leftist and pacifist intellectuals, including a number of Columbia University professors who opposed their university's support of the United States' participation in the Great War.[12] During the 1920s and 1930s, fascist regimes in Europe exiled thousands of intellectuals, academics, writers, and artists. In 1933, the New School established the University in Exile in response to the rise of Hitler. This graduate division provided crucial support for scholars and artists fleeing Nazism. This influx of European, often

FACING PAGE:
Top: Pepsodent, *The Goldbergs Jigsaw Puzzle*, color lithograph, 1932. (Published by Pepsodent Co., Chicago, Illinois, 1932, Collection of Yeshiva University Museum, New York) *Bottom:* Anonymous, *A Meeting of the "University in Exile,"* photograph, 1933. (The German and Jewish Intellectual Émigré Collection, M. E. Grenander Department of Special Collections and Archives, University at Albany Libraries, Albany, NY)

Jewish, émigrés exerted a profound impact on the intellectual and artistic de-velopment of postwar America, especially New York City. These émigrés con-tributed to the formation of the New York Jewish intellectuals and also the shift to New York as the art capital of the world. They helped to make "New York Jew" synonymous with intellectualism and cosmopolitanism.

By the early twentieth century, New York City was simultaneously the cen-ter of artistic training in the United States and also a bedrock of leftist politics involving the Jewish sons and daughters of immigrants. Moses Soyer (b. Rus-sia, 1899; d. New York City, 1974) was all three: a Jewish artist on the left. Soyer composed his celebrated *Artists on the WPA* as if it were a stage set with the curtain having just lifted to reveal the proceedings, inviting us into this artists' studio. New York Jews welcomed opportunities to draw a paycheck from the WPA (Works Progress Administration), which nourished many artists who

Moses Soyer, *Artists on the WPA*, oil on canvas, 1935. (Smithsonian American Art Mu-seum, Gift of Mr. and Mrs. Moses Soyer, Washington, DC)

flourished after the end of World War II. Under the New Deal, artists received not just a paycheck but also a social purpose and comradely support.

The floor of Soyer's studio slants upward, permitting a greater view of the room and its artists at work. Arranged in a semicircle, four painters, both women and men, work on oversized canvases that most likely are parts of murals. Each artist paints in the style of the government-preferred American Scene, with its requisite realistic figures and pleasurable depictions of productivity and harmony, blocking out the contemporary realities of labor unrest and destitution. Soyer creates subtle subterfuge by showing artists as laborers, banded together, and diverse in population. Rather than the more common portrayal of artists as romantic heroes or, less frequently, heroines alone and at odds with society, Soyer's artists are seen to have a positive social role. The sense of group activity echoes the collective actions of artists through pickets, protests against social injustices, and demands for permanent recognition by the government. Soyer was a member of the Artists' Union, which later affiliated with the Congress of Industrial Organizations (CIO). During the Great Depression, artists became workers for the people and federal government. Unlike the more famous Treasury Department's Section of Painting and Sculpture, which held anonymous competitions for mural commissions, the WPA was a make-work project, but it managed to hire such talented artists as Soyer.

With the rise of Hitler, New York City, with its concentration of Jewish population, headquarters for most news media, and numerous Jewish social and political organizations, witnessed numerous efforts to agitate on behalf of Europe's Jews. The American Jewish Congress and the Jewish Labor Committee jointly sponsored a rally in support of a Jewish boycott of German goods that had been launched in March 1933 as part of the New York Jewish community's response to the anti-Semitic policies of the Nazi regime. The rally was held at Madison Square Garden, like the 1923 Zionist rally depicted in Theresa Bernstein's painting shown earlier, and garnered attention from local papers. New York Jews gained a reputation for boldness; they used their city to launch national and international efforts to try to rescue German Jews. The photograph on the following page captures the large sign that hung from the balcony of Madison Square Garden, calling for the immediate boycott of all German-made goods, which was intended to exert pressure on the Nazi regime.

Top: Anonymous, *Anti-Nazis Hold Demonstration*, photograph, March 15, 1937. (New York World-Telegram & Sun Newspaper Collection, Library of Congress, Washington, DC)
Bottom: Miller Art Co., Inc., New York, the Jewish Palestine Exhibit at the New York World's Fair, photograph, 1939. (Collection of Yeshiva University Museum, New York)

In 1939, the borough of Queens, New York City, invited the world to visit its World's Fair. The Jewish Palestine Exhibit was an enticing advertisement for what did not yet exist: a Jewish national home, and as Palestine was under British mandate at the time, the organizers of the Jewish Palestine building, exhibitions, and accompanying public programs, such as indigenous folk dance, were denied permission to place their building among those of other nations. Allowed to construct a cultural exhibition in a separate location on the fairgrounds, the Zionist sponsors nonetheless aimed to cast the impression that Jewish Palestine was a nation-state. The pavilion featured on its façade a monumental hammered-copper relief sculpture titled *The Scholar, the Laborer, and the Toiler of the Soil* by the acclaimed art-deco sculptor Maurice Ascalon, who was born in Hungary, studied art in Belgium, and then settled in Palestine. Many New York Jews visited the Palestine Pavilion, absorbing the ways in which it presented a new type of Jewishness rooted in the soil, so different from their urban identity.[13]

More typical of New York Jews, Weegee's photograph (on the following page) of a bagel deliveryman in the early morning hours when it is still dark captures the gritty pace of urban life.[14] A quick, bright flash illuminates Max as he emerges from the morning darkness of Lower Manhattan, bringing him into view. Photographer Weegee (b. Austria-Hungary, 1899; d. New York City, 1968) nicknamed his camera flash "Aladdin's Lamp." "Rembrandt Light" is how Weegee described the sense of illumination within a dark field and the subtle gray tones of the transition from nighttime to dawn. Weegee identies Max by first name in the photo's title, whereas most artists and photographers captured workers' images but never noted their names, thus making them into social types rather than portraying them as individuals. Although we cannot tell from the photograph, Weegee describes the man as rushing to a restaurant on Second Avenue, thus locating him as part of the history of New York's Lower East Side. The encounter occurred at six a.m. on East Fourteenth Street, near the Con Edison building. Weegee's flash brilliantly illuminates Max, clothed in a baker's apron under his jacket. He carries three strings of bagels, and a slight smile flits across his face, acknowledging Weegee's camera even as he does not break his stride. Bagel baking arrived in New York City with eastern European Jewish immigrants. Bagels assumed a favored place in New Yorkers' diet, gradually traveling with Jews as they migrated to Brooklyn and the Bronx.

Weegee (born Arthur Fellig), *Max Is Rushing in the Bagels to a Restaurant on Second Avenue for the Morning Trade*, photograph, c. 1940. (Courtesy of International Center of Photography / Getty Images and The Jewish Museum, New York / Art Resource, New York)

FACING PAGE:

Aaron J. Goodelman, *Kultur*, carved, stained, and waxed pear wood and metal chain, c. 1940. (Smithsonian American Art Museum, Washington, DC, Gift of Mrs. Sarah Goodman)

Weegee usually reserved such illuminating photographs for crime scenes, especially murders, and fires. In both cases, he as often pictured the observers as the victims. He often prowled the streets after dark and in the early morning hours. When the newspaper *PM* started in 1940, Weegee received a byline for his photographs, and his reputation soared. He pictured New York, naked and noir, as alluring and dangerous, a tough place to call home, as did two million Jews. Weegee's photographs helped to cement a visual linkage of Jews with a version of New York City.[15] Working on the Lower East Side during the 1980s, photographing friends, community, and lovers defined by sexual obsession, drug use, and outsider identity, artist Nan Goldin's work (page 248) can be seen as in communion with Weegee's.

In Aaron J. Goodelman's *Kultur*, a lean, elongated wood figure stands with his hands chained high above his head and pulled taut away from his body. The

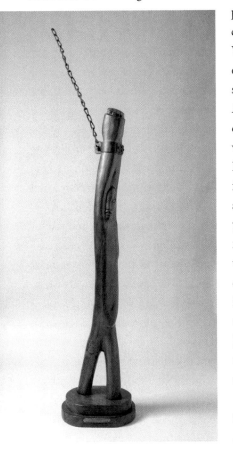

painfully stretched body creates a visceral sensation of its being ripped apart. While other artists addressed the theme of torture or lynching, the figures were shown already dead, such as Lipton's *Lynched* (page 229). But Goodelman carved wood sculptures that keep the victim's dignity and sense of fight intact. Here, rather than a beaten or an abased figure, the statue stands. His up-reached arms communicate a sliver of hope beyond the immediacy of evil. Goodelman was one of many Jewish artists who drew parallels between their own communities of struggle and the suffering of African Americans.[16] His work strengthens the identity of New York Jews as radicals in politics and art. *Kultur* connects the lynch mobs of the 1930s and the pogroms of the Russian tsar.

Goodelman immigrated to New York in 1905 because of pogroms in Russia. After attending Cooper Union and the

National Academy of Design and supporting himself as a machinist in the 1920s, Goodelman became a Communist. He expressed concerns about social and economic conditions in his art. He was active in many Yiddish organizations and the art section of the Yiddisher Kultur Farband, a Yiddish arts and cultural group; he taught at the radical John Reed arts clubs and participated in the Artists' Union and the American Artists' Congress, all based in New York City. Goodelman's creative commitment to socially conscious art and to preserving the human figure links him with other New York Jewish artists, such as Ben Shahn and Moses Soyer.

Ben Shahn's mural *First Amendment* celebrates the Constitution's guarantee of freedom, expressing values held dear by many New York Jews. While Jews benefited from the separation of church and state, the First Amendment also guaranteed their right to speak out, to protest, and to unite as groups. Sharp diagonals lead us through the canvas's eight separate vignettes, each of which depicts citizens activating their constitutional rights. Painted in matte tones, men marching with fists upraised in protest and solidarity form unified groups to speak, to work to keep the flow of news information going, and to take their political grievances all the way to the Supreme Court. Shahn placed the Statue of Liberty's oxidized green hand and uplifted torch at center to proclaim the centrality of freedom within his conception of America and also its significance to American Jews, especially in the prewar period. It was only in the late 1930s that the Statue of Liberty rose to symbolic prominence in response to the threat of war and limits on immigration. In black and white, Shahn re-created a conventional New York State voters' ballot. Shahn asserted, "The ballot [is] to my mind the guarantee of all our freedoms." Acutely aware of the rise of Hitler and the decision of President Roosevelt's administration not to increase immigration quotas to accommodate refugees, Shahn reinforced his pictorial vigor by writing to government officials when he was asked to alter his work, "The thing that I have tried to put into this mural, I feel very strongly. I feel that it has profound significance for every American, more significance every day because of increasing threats to our rights and liberties." The mural was installed in a Queens post office in 1941, as war raged across the globe.[17]

By fixing the camera's lens on the front window of a Judaica shop on New York's Lower East Side, photographer Marjory Collins supports the shop owner's desire to advertise his dual identities: a Jewish religious identity and an identity as an American patriot. "God Bless America" reads one banner,

Top: Ben Shahn, *First Amendment*, egg tempera on canvas, 1941. (Photograph by Peter Morgan; Queens Post Office, New York, art © Estate of Ben Shahn / Licensed by VAGA, New York)
Bottom: Marjory Collins, *Window of a Jewish Religious Shop on Broome Street, New York*, photograph, 1942. (Farm Security Administration/Office of War Information Collection, Library of Congress, Washington, DC)

hanging next to a prayer shawl (tallit). On one level, the shopkeeper an-
nounces, "It's great to be an American," demonstrating through his wares
—religious books, a Torah scroll, menorahs, and candlesticks—just how free
he feels as a Jew in New York City at a time when Nazi Germany was mur-
dering Jews. Yet simultaneously, the need he feels to assert his patriotism is
an answer to those who questioned Jews' commitment to the United States
while the nation was at war. The plate-glass window reflects iconic elements
of the New York City urban landscape, such as the curved street lamp (seen
also in Weegee's work) and fire escapes. Collins joined Roy Stryker's Office of
War Information, the renowned group of documentary photographers who
worked under Stryker's very detailed directions, providing his cadre of photographers with detailed shooting scripts. In the first incarnation, the photographers worked for the Farm Security Administration to create and distribute
images of the Dust Bowl and the Great Depression throughout the South and
the West. The Office of War Information's graphic artists and photographers
were among the first Americans to view the atrocity photos that made their
way out of Nazi control. Assigned to document "hyphenated Americans," Collins's photos such as this one were duplicated and dropped behind enemy lines
in Europe and in Asia, in order to let ordinary citizens who lived under fascist
governments know that America supported them. Collins employed an urban
aesthetic, deftly portraying the multiethnic and multicultural character of the
United States. This window display on the Lower East Side also demonstrates
the ongoing importance of the neighborhood for religious New York Jews.

The last photographs taken of Julius and Ethel Rosenberg, the infamous
Brooklyn husband and wife accused, and ultimately executed, for allegedly
passing nuclear secrets to the Soviets, illustrate the couple's desire to acknowledge posthumously their identities as Jews. Here, in a Brooklyn Jewish funeral
home, with thousands of people waiting to pay their respects, the Rosenbergs
lie in matching wood caskets with the Magen David on the lids, which are
lifted up for public viewing. Revealed are the husband and wife, always presented as a couple in the courts as in their deaths, dressed in white burial
shrouds, following Jewish burial traditions. Characteristic elements such as
Julius's round, wire-rimmed glasses and mustache no longer appear. A neatly
arranged tallit lies on Julius's shoulders and chest. Their case of conspiracy
to commit espionage attracted international interest and support. But their
prosecution and execution were especially poignant for New York Jews. Many

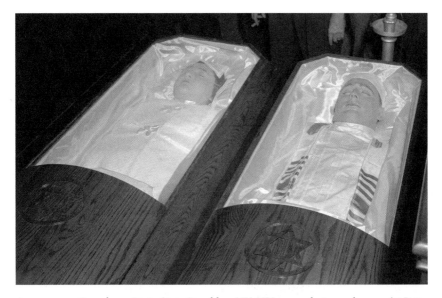

Anonymous, *Rosenbergs Lie in State*, Brooklyn, NY, UPI news photograph, 1953. (© Bettmann / CORBIS)

gathered in Union Square hoping for a last-minute reprieve because they held similar radical political views, had also attended the free university City College of New York (CCNY), and also were Jews of eastern European heritage. However, factions existed among New York Jews, and there were those who opposed clemency for the Rosenbergs; for example, the judge, attorney, and prosecutors were also Jews.

Comedian Lenny Bruce (1925–1966) graphically explained what made New York City and its residents Jewish, even when they were not. As Lenny saw it, "If you live in New York or any other big city, you are Jewish. It doesn't matter even if you're Catholic; if you live in New York, you're Jewish. If you live in Butte, Montana, you're going to be goyish even if you're Jewish. . . . Jewish means pumpernickel bread, black cherry soda and macaroons. Goyish means Kool-Aid, Drake's cakes, and lime jello."[18] By contrasting "Jewish" with "goyish," Bruce transformed all New Yorkers into Jews, strengthening the Jewish identification of the city in the eyes of other Americans. New York and Jewish merged in Bruce's routine, making his listeners laugh with recognition at his boldness for saying what so many knew. His was humor with a razor-sharp edge to it.

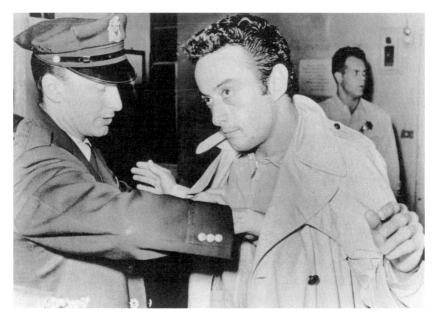

Anonymous, *Lenny Bruce Being Frisked and Arrested*, photograph. (Prints and Photographs Division, Library of Congress, Washington, DC)

As stereotypes of Jewish men multiplied, Bruce mutated and reshaped each one. A Jewish intellectual? Well, while that is not an exact description of Bruce, he was sharp, verbal, and smart, although some people reduced him to just a smart aleck. "Muscular Jew" does not apply either, not to a man whose appetite for heroin and cigarettes abused his body; yet he possessed the strength and courage to stand up and speak out during the McCarthy era, when words were suppressed and thought was deemed dangerous. Bruce, like other New York Jews, such as painter Ben Shahn, revered the First Amendment and the Bill of Rights. Bruce was arrested numerous times on charges of obscenity; once the police arrested him for using the Yiddish word *schmuck* (penis). Civil rights and free speech advocates, artists, writers, and comics spoke on his behalf at his trial in 1964, but to no avail. Bruce received a posthumous gubernatorial pardon from New York State, the first ever decreed in the state's history. Bruce died from a morphine overdose at age forty.

A woman glides on a tightrope over the New York night skyline, naked above the waist except for her bra. The story behind the advertisement on the facing page reveals the many supportive roles that New York's Jewish women have played in America. The Maidenform Company's "I Dreamed" campaign ran for twenty years between 1949 and 1969, making it one of longest-running advertising campaigns in history. The company developed in reaction to the flat-chested flapper silhouette when a Jewish dressmaker living in New York, Ida Cohen Rosenthal, refashioned the bra to enhance the natural female form and her dress designs. Based on positive reactions from her customers, she launched the Maidenform Brassiere Company in 1923 with her husband and another dressmaker.

Jewish women were not only a significant part of New York's female labor force, but they also played a major role in its fashion design, beauty culture, and advertising industry in the twentieth century. Like many others who did not conform precisely to Euro-American beauty ideals, Jewish women felt the need to align their bodies more closely with that standard. Their desires found expression in various innovations, some of which suggested a boldness, brashness, and sense of humor associated with New York Jews.

"I Dreamed I Walked a Tightrope in My Maidenform Bra," advertisement, 1961. (Courtesy of the Maidenform Collection, Archives Center, National Museum of American History, Smithsonian Institution, Washington, DC; reprinted by permission of the Maidenform Company)

Right: Howard Zieff, "You Don't Have to Be Jewish to Love Levy's Real Jewish Rye," Doyle Dane Bernbach Ad Agency, New York, 1967. (Courtesy of the Prints and Photographs Division, Library of Congress, Washington, DC)
Below: "You Don't Have to Be Jewish to Oppose the War in Vietnam," button, late 1960s.

Howard Zieff's widely successfully campaign for Levy's Rye Bread first appeared in the city's subways, appealing to the inclusiveness of enjoying ethnic food. The visual concept of the series of posters, each presenting a different ethnic or racial type, is that the people pictured would not be identified as Jewish, despite Lenny Bruce's definition. To be both Native American, or African American, and Jewish was a living oxymoron in these ads. Zieff recalled that he first encountered the Native American man near Grand Central, where he worked as an engineer. In order to amplify the man's non-Jewishness, Zieff outfitted him in a pastiche of Native costumes, more fictional Hollywood than accurate.[19] This "trickster" visual play brings to mind similarities between Native and Jewish humor, each with a dark tone of survival despite all odds.

New York City and the nation's capital were the two main settings for political protests for and against the divisive Vietnam War. New York was the media center as well as home to numerous colleges and universities, where many young Jewish men enrolled, some to claim educational deferments. A play on the slogan of the hugely successful New York City Levy's bread ad, the protest button plays on the significant Jewish presence in the antiwar movement, as well as acknowledging that opposition was not just for Jews. Many Jewish college students, both male and female, were active in the New Left movement Students for a Democratic Society, which protested the war. In 1964, Jews were twice as likely as Protestants and Catholics to want the United States to withdraw its forces from Vietnam. By 1970, half of American Jews, the majority of whom were New Yorkers, supported an immediate withdrawal, while the majority of Catholics and Protestants preferred to send more troops over. A disproportionate number of soldiers were African American, working class, and unable to receive an educational deferment because they did not attend college in substantial numbers, as did Jews. The large and vocal presence of Jews in antiwar protests, sit-ins, marches, and other public forums starkly contrasts with the numbers of Jews who served. Only 269 Jewish soldiers were killed during the war, out of a total of 58,193 Americans killed.[20]

Just as New York Jewish women had advocated for women's rights, including in the suffrage and labor-reform movements in the early twentieth century, they played key roles in what is now known as the second-wave feminist movement of the 1960s and 1970s. Women such as Bella Abzug (1920–1988),

a lawyer who represented a Manhattan district in the U.S. House of Representatives from 1971 to 1976, not only helped to secure civil rights, full protection under the law, and greater economic parity for women, but she also fundamentally rescripted women's social roles. Abzug grew up in the Bronx and attended Hunter College and Columbia Law School. One of her early legal cases, an appeal on behalf of Willie McGee, who was convicted of raping a white woman,

"This Woman's Place Is in the House—the House of Representatives! Bella Abzug for Congress," campaign poster, 1971–1976. (Prints and Photographs Division, Library of Congress, Washington, DC)

took her down to Mississippi. A socialist Zionist, Abzug protested the "Zionism Is Racism" resolution at the United Nations in 1975.

Other second-wave Jewish feminists and cofounders with Abzug of the National Women's Political Caucus in 1971 included Betty Friedan, author of *The Feminine Mystique* (1963) and first president of the National Organization for Women (NOW, 1966); and Letty Cottin Pogrebin, a founder of *Ms.* magazine (1972) and an essayist on Jewish feminism. Together with younger New York women, they contributed to the identification of New York Jews with outspoken, politically active feminists, supporters of civil rights and peace movements.

From Lou Reed's place on the "Wild Side," the Jewish singer-songwriter invited fellow social outcasts—transvestites, gay male hustlers, and speed freaks —to likewise find sanctuary on the dangerous streets of New York's Lower East Side in the 1970s. While second- and third-generation New York Jews aspired to the better life of the suburbs, their sons and daughters, such as Reed, sought asylum from conformity in the old neighborhood, where heroin, instead of herring, now was the commodity in demand. Reed studied with the poet Delmore Schwartz at Syracuse University in the early 1960s and then moved to Lower Manhattan and formed the rock band the Velvet Underground. Resplendent in biker leathers and dark shades, he was the very definition of cool, an adjective that usually would not stick to "good Jewish boys." He came to stand for a new type of New York Jew, one in rebellion against bourgeois Jewish life. Recently dubbed the "Zeyde of American Punk Rock," Reed continues actively to record and perform. He counts himself a regular at annual seder of the music house the Knitting Factory.[21]

Red and black, colors rich with symbolic meaning, are powerfully applied in the poster on the facing page, demanding the release of Jews forced to remain in the Soviet Union. While red denotes strength, as well as bloodshed and fire, black stands for death, as well as evoking charred coal-black burnt remains. Each brings to mind violence and death during pogroms, the Shoah, and Stalin's murderous reign. The slogan "Let My People Go," here written

FACING PAGE:
Top: Donald Greenhaus, *Lou Reed and the Velvet Underground*, photograph (detail), mid-1960s. (© Donald Greenhaus/Shabobba* International, LLC)
Bottom: "Let Our People Go," poster, Coalition to Save Soviet Jewry, NYC Center for Jewish History, mid-1970s. (Courtesy of the American Jewish Historical Society, Waltham, MA, and New York, NY)

with the more inclusive "our" instead of "my," motivated the movement. Originating from the nineteenth-century African American spiritual "Go Down, Moses," the song references the Torah's account of the Exodus from Egypt. For many Americans, the definitive interpretation belongs to Paul Robeson, whose deep, rich voice reminded some of Moses. New York City was home to the Coalition to Free Soviet Jews, as well as the site for numerous protests and marches. Its Jews led the Soviet Jewry movement.[22]

Nan Goldin is an insider among outsiders. After suffering a savage beating from her lover, Brian, she made herself pretty for the photograph she took of her mirror image, reapplying her red lipstick, which makes the red of her bruised, bloody eyes all the more evident. Fanciful earrings hang from her ears, and a pearl necklace runs around her neck. Within one face, the beauty of seduction and the rage of romantic, sexual obsession come together. Goldin's acclaimed *The Ballad of Sexual Dependency*, originally a constantly changing slide show before it became frozen through publication as a book, offers her visual and public diary, in the making of which she viewed her camera as part of her body, rather than as merely a tool. Goldin drags us into her world on the Lower East Side of New York in the 1980s, when heroin was king, apartments were dirt cheap, and the neighborhood was dangerous. This world of which she was a part refuted her upbringing as a "nice Jewish girl" in the suburbs outside Washington, D.C. In reverse migration, she left home for the tenements. Her world and the people in it, who openly shoot drugs, have casual sex, sleep on filthy mattress on filthy floors, and head out to punk nightclubs, no longer exist. The Lower East Side has been gentrified, excluding young artists, urban transplants, and others from the rougher edges of life. Many of the people within Goldin's community also no longer exist, having died from AIDS, alcoholism, and drugs.

New York City, long a location of social and political organizing involving New York Jews, added to its reputation with the rise of anti-AIDS activism. Angered by the government's mismanagement of the AIDS crisis, Gran Fury, a group of individuals committed to using the power of art to command social change, designed the "Silence = Death" poster campaign. In 1986, appropriating the pink triangle used by the Nazis to label gay men in the concentration camps, the group drew parallels between the Shoah and the pandemic. The following year, Jewish playwright and gay activist Larry Kramer called for a heated campaign of direct action; his combined energy and anger initiated the

Above: Nan Goldin, "Nan One Month after Being Battered," *The Ballad of Sexual Dependency*, photograph, Cibachrome, 1984. (© Nan Goldin; courtesy Matthew Marks Gallery, New York)

Left: Aids Coalition to Unleash Power, "Silence Equals Death," lapel button, c. 1987. (Photo courtesy of Anthony Viti; Collection of Anthony Viti, New York)

AIDS Coalition to Unleash Power (ACT-UP), based in New York. Famous actions of civil disobedience included the group's infiltration of the New York Stock Exchange to protest the high costs of medications; seizing New York's General Post Office on the eve of April 15, 1987, as bewildered bystanders filed tax returns; and "Stop the Church," an event in which close to five thousand protestors took over St. Patrick's Cathedral in response to the Catholic Church's opposition to AIDS education. Kramer's articulate activism, channeled into his play *The Normal Heart*, added the vision of gay Jews to New York City's reputation.

Elaine Reichek, *A Postcolonial Kinderhood*, needlepoint sampler, 1994. (Courtesy of The Jewish Museum, New York / Art Resource, New York, and Elaine Reichek)

A "middle-class Jewish girl from Brooklyn,"[23] artist Elaine Reichek had never thought about doing Jewish-themed work until she was asked to do so by curator Norman Kleeblatt of New York's Jewish Museum. She later came up with an installation piece that investigated her Brooklyn childhood and the family's silence about their Jewishness. She re-created a childhood bedroom, colonial house, and Ethan Allen 1776 collection reproduction furniture, all slightly smaller than life-size.

This 1994 needlepoint sampler exemplifies women's domestic art, to which New York Jewish feminist art historian Linda Nochlin brought new attention in the early 1970s. Reichek attended Brooklyn College before going to Yale University; she started out studying painting with Ad Reinhardt before rejecting it for conceptual art. Thus, she participated in the rise of an alternative New York art school, one influenced by feminism as well as by New York's Jewish milieu. The sampler reflects investigations of identity that have been a major preoccupation of contemporary artists.

The feminist movement transformed the visual arts and influenced Judaism. Among New York's world-class museums is the Jewish Museum, established by the Jewish Theological Seminary. The museum's collections range from antiquities to contemporary religious and secular art. The museum has commissioned Jewish art as well as purchasing it, giving feminist Judaica great visibility and prestige.

Formed from silver with small silver cymbals attached, artist Amy Klein Reichert's *Miriam Cup* calls to several of our senses. The shiny surface and the hanging cymbals glimmer when struck by light, to entice our eyes; the gentle rattle of the small tambourines delight our ears; and the water within the cup quenches thirst. Women have traditionally contributed a lesser public ritual

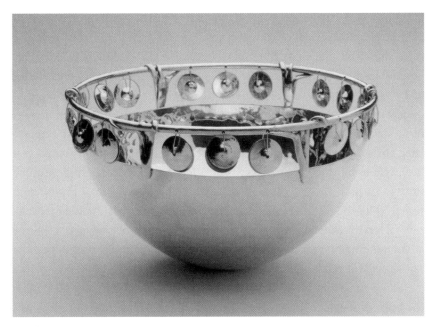

Amy Klein Reichert, *Miriam Cup*, silver, 1997; Steven Smithers, silversmith, and Art Evans, photographer. (Courtesy of The Jewish Museum, New York / Art Resource, New York, and Amy Klein Reichert)

role in the Passover seder than have men, who read the Haggadah, and young boys, who answer the Four Questions. In the 1970s, feminist Jews in New York City began to bring their voices to the feast of Passover in reclamation of their matriarchal ancestors.[24] For centuries, Passover celebrants have placed a cup of wine on the seder table for the Prophet Elijah, who, it is said, will return to herald the coming of the messiah. In recent years, some families have added a second cup—this one filled with water for Moses's sister, Miriam. The To-rah relates that after the crossing of the Red Sea, with tumbrels—a percussion instrument similar to a tambourine—in hand, Miriam led the women of Is-rael in songs and dances of praise to God. "What are the sounds of freedom?" Reichert has asked. "The wind rustling through grasses, the murmuring of ex-iles." What are the "desert sounds"? "A joyous song with a tambourine."

New York–born painter and art historian Jonathan Weinberg began his day on September 11, 2001, as did many people, by focusing on his tasks at hand. When he became aware of the destruction of the World Trade Center, Wein-berg responded as an artist might do: he painted the buildings as he saw them from his Jersey City window, chronicling their collapse. With each subsequent painting, black clouds dominate, the once-blue sky vanishes as night falls, and thick smoke fills the air as New York's celebrated skyline lowers closer to the ground. Inspired by British painter J. M. W. Turner's *The Burning of the Houses of Lords and Commons* (1835), Weinberg kept painting all day. Working in thickly applied acrylics, he chronicled his response to the horrendous events of the day in his art, presenting images that have stayed with us over a decade later. His work brings us back to that of Julian Voloj's photograph (shown ear-lier), conveying the New York skyline's commanding presence and meaning to Jewish artists. These two men capture the composite character of New York Jewry. Voloj sought to recover with his work a Jewish past, putting the his-tory of New York Jews into dialogue with that of the city. Weinberg captured a heartrending present and an unseeable future, painting his perspective as a Jewish artist to render his city's history-in-the-making.

"Many American Jews," writes author Douglas Rushkoff, "consider Israel the heart of Judaism. They write checks to Israel." Yet he notes that it is dif-ferent for New York Jews and those of the greater New York Jewish Diaspora throughout the United States.[25] For these Jews, New York is the motherland. This new "ancestral" home replaces images of an often difficult and dangerous life in Europe or the Middle East with pictures of a challenging, but ultimately

Jonathan Weinberg, *New York City Skyline—9-11-01—5 p.m., 2001,* acrylic on panel, 24 × 36 in., 2001. (Courtesy of the artist)

more welcoming, origin of Jewish American roots. Unlike most American cities, New York's public schools close on the High Holy Days, and food store clerks do not offer quizzical looks when asked for matzo meal in the springtime. Jewish life, rituals, and experiences over the course of the twentieth and twenty-first centuries have become incorporated into the fabric of New York and have been communicated and shaped in the nation's imagination through popular culture, news media, and advertising.

Many Americans first met a New York Jewish family through Molly Goldberg, whom they welcomed into their homes each Tuesday night. Molly's portrait of New York Jewish life received elaboration and revision as the twentieth century ended and a new century began. Her intimate Jewish world, tied to immigrant life through its accented English, yielded in popular culture to enticing notions that anyone could become a New York Jew. All one needed was the right food and a measure of chutzpah. Politics, style, humor, music, painting, advertising, and photography all produced versions of a New York

Jew, until by the second decade of the twenty-first century most Americans recognize Jews as an important part of American coulture.

As New York continues to change and grow, so too do New York's Jews. Many meanings and images of New York Jews have proliferated over the twentieth century, representing their tremendous variation and vitality. As we have seen, these images permeate Jewish and American consciousness, traveling far and wide beyond the city itself.

NOTES TO THE FOREWORD

1. Milton Lehman, "Veterans Pour into New York to Find That Its Hospitality Far Exceeds Their Dreams," *New York Times*, 8 July 1945, 51.

2. Ira Rosenwaike, *Population History of New York City* (Syracuse: Syracuse University Press, 1972), 98, 101.

3. Robert A. M. Stern, Thomas Mellins, and David Fishman, *New York 1960: Architecture and Urbanism between the Second World War and the Bicentennial* (New York: Monacelli, 1995), 10, 13–19, 27–28.

4. Moses Rischin, *The Promised City: New York's Jews, 1870–1914* (1962; repr., Cambridge: Harvard University Press, 1977), 294.

5. "Levi Strauss," Wikipedia, http://en.wikipedia.org/wiki/Levi_Strauss (accessed July 13, 2011).

6. Rischin, "Preface to the Paperback Edition," in *The Promised City*, vii.

7. Ibid. "City of Ambition" refers to the 1910 photograph by Alfred Stieglitz taken approaching Lower Manhattan from New York Harbor.

8. In this and the following pages, the text draws on the three volumes of City of Promises: A History of the Jews of New York (New York: NYU Press, 2012).

NOTES TO THE PROLOGUE

1. Information on the historical uses of the building was provided by American Land Services. The title number of the building is SS-919183, filed with the Department of Buildings, New York City. Email communication with Yoel Borgenicht (July 24, 2008).

2. For promotional statements on Harlem Partners, see http://www.harlempartners.com.

3. Robert Kolker, "Whose Harlem Is It?," *New York* (July 14, 2008): 30–35, 81.

4. Reflections and comments by the Borgenichts are derived from an interview with Shoshana and Yoel Borgenicht (June 27, 2008; tape recording in possession of the author).

5. Federal Writers Project, Yiddish Writers Group, *Die Yiddishe Landsmanshaften fun New York* (New York: I. L. Peretz Writers Union, 1938), 114–15.

6. For a discussion of how varying classes of Jews were pulled and pushed to Harlem in the early twentieth century and then out-migrated in the 1920s–1930s, see Jeffrey S. Gurock, *When Harlem Was Jewish, 1870–1930* (New York: Columbia University Press, 1979), chaps. 2 and 6.

NOTES TO CHAPTER 1

1. New York State Reconstruction Commission, *Housing Conditions: Report of the Housing Committee of the Reconstruction Commission of the State of New York* (Albany: J. B. Lyon, 1920), 9.

2. Jeffrey S. Gurock, *When Harlem Was Jewish, 1870–1930* (New York: Columbia University Press, 1979), 140–41. On post–World War I racial tensions in American cities, see Arthur I. Waskow, *From Race Riot to Sit-In: 1919 and the 1960s* (Garden City, NY: Doubleday, 1966), 2, 21–22, 304–8.

3. On the tax-exemption law, see *Real Estate Record and Builders Guide* [hereinafter *RERBG*] (March 5, 1921), cited in Gurock, *When Harlem Was Jewish*, 42.

4. *RERBG* (September 3, 1921; March 18, 1922). On the citywide patterns over the decade of the 1920s, see New York City Tenement House Department, *Tenth Report, 1918–1929* (New York: Martin Brown, 1929), 36–49.

5. *Population, Land Values and Government: Studies of the Growth and Distribution of Population and Land Values and of Problems of Government, Regional Survey of New York and Its Environs* (New York: Regional Plan of New York and Its Environs, 1929), 62; *RERBG* (September 21, 1921; February 26, 1927).

6. *RERBG* (September 21, 1921).

7. Edwin Harold Spengler, *Land Values in New York in Relation to Transit Facilities* (New York: Columbia University Press, 1930), 19–24; Clifford Hood, *722 Miles: The Building of the Subways and How They Transformed New York* (New York: Simon and Schuster, 1993), 158–61, 174. See also Michael V. Gershowitz, "Neighborhood Power Structure: Decision Making in Forest Hills" (Ph.D. diss., New York University, 1974), 28; Daniel A. Wishnoff, "The Tolerance Point: Race, Public Housing and the Forest Hills Controversy, 1945–1975" (Ph.D. diss., City University of New York, 2005), 153–54.

8. Abraham Cahan, *The Rise of David Levinsky: A Novel* (New York: Harper and Bros., 1917), 464, 480; Jeffrey S. Gurock, "Synagogue Imperialism in New York City: The Case of Congregation Kehal Adath Jeshurun, 1909–1911," *Michael* 15 (2000): 95–108.

9. Edward Steiner, "The Russian and Polish Jewish in New York," *Outlook*, November 1902, 532; Burton I. Hendrick, "The Jewish Invasion," *Hebrew Standard*, February 15, 1907, 14.

10. Deborah Dash Moore, *At Home in America: Second Generation New York Jews* (New York: Columbia University Press, 1981), 39.

11. Leon Wexelstein, *Building Up Greater Brooklyn with Sketches of Men Instrumental in Brooklyn's Amazing Development* (New York: Brooklyn Biographical Society, 1925), xvii–xx, quoted in Moore, *At Home in America*, 42.

12. Moore, *At Home in America*, 44–53.

13. Leo Grebler, *Housing Market Behavior in a Declining Area: Long-Term Changes in Industry and Utilization of Housing on New York's Lower East Side* (New York: Columbia University Press, 1952), 126–27.

14. For statistics on Jewish out-migration from older neighborhoods and resettlement elsewhere in the city, see *The Jewish Communal Register of New York City, 1917–1918* (New York: Kehillah [Jewish Community] of New York, 1918) [hereinafter JCR], 82, 85; and C. Morris Horowitz and Lawrence J. Kaplan, *The Jewish Population of the New York Area, 1900–1975* (New York: Federation of Jewish Philanthropies of New York, 1959), 22, 133, 157, 209, 239. See also, on relocation destinations, Grebler, *Housing Market Behavior*, 124–25. On the differing fates of Jews and African Americans in Harlem, circa 1920–1930,

see Gilbert Osofsky, *Harlem: The Making of a Ghetto; Negro New York, 1890–1930* (New York: Harper and Row, 1964), 130, 248.

15. Richard Plunz, *A History of Housing in New York City: Dwelling Type and Social Change in the American Metropolis* (New York: Columbia University Press, 1990), 151–57; Andrew S. Dolkart, "Homes for People Cooperatives in New York City, 1916–1929," *Sites* 30 (1989): 33–35.

16. Plunz, *History of Housing in New York City*, 151–57; Dolkart, "Homes for People Cooperatives," 33–35.

17. Gurock, *When Harlem Was Jewish*, 144–45, 156. See also, on the beginnings of "El Barrio," Lawrence Royce Chenault, *The Puerto Rican Migrant in New York* (New York: Columbia University Press, 1938).

18. Marc D. Angel, *La America: The Sephardic Experience in the United States* (Philadelphia: Jewish Publication Society of America, 1982), 20, 35–36, 146, 169; Aviva Ben-Ur, *Sephardic Jews in America: A Diasporic History* (New York: NYU Press, 2009), 35–37.

19. On the Tremont Temple's history, see "Tremont Temple Quits the Bronx," *New York Times* (December 18, 1976): 27; and interview with Rabbi Larry Rubinstein (September 18, 2008). On attitudes toward the Tremont Temple, see "Tremont Temple," Remembrance of Synagogues Past website, http://www.bronxsynagogues.org.

20. Hood, *722 Miles*, 173–177; Plunz, *A History of Housing in New York City*, 131.

21. Jackson Heights Investing Company v. James Conforti Construction Company, 222 A.D. 687 (1927): 73, 76, 100–101. See also Heywood Broun and George Britt, *Christians Only: A Study in Prejudice* (New York: Vanguard, 1931), 256.

22. See Plunz, *A History of Housing in New York City*, 117–20, for the evolution of the Russell Sage Foundation's approach toward Forest Hills Gardens. See also, on the foundation, Kenneth T. Jackson, ed., *Encyclopedia of New York City* (New Haven: Yale University Press and New-York Historical Society, 1995), s.v. "Russell Sage Foundation." See also, on the rapid-transit issue, Gershowitz, "Neighborhood Power Structure," 26.

23. On the Jewish population of Forest Hills as of 1930, see Horowitz and Kaplan, *The Jewish Population of the New York Area*, 275. On the early settlers in the neighborhood, including the Forest Hills Gardens portion, see Jeff Gottlieb, "The Early Years: A Clearer View of Early Jewish Life in Forest Hills," unpublished paper, formerly appearing at http://www.qjhs.org.

24. Wishnoff, "The Tolerance Point," 152; Jeff Gottlieb, "Benjamin Braunstein: Quiet, Genius at Work," unpublished paper, formerly appearing at http://www.qjhs.org. On the Lefrak's early efforts in Queens, see James Trager, *The New York Chronology: The Ultimate Compendium of Events, People, and Anecdotes from the Dutch to the Present* (New York: Harper Resource, 2004), 455–56.

25. On the affluence of leaders of landmark synagogues on the Lower East Side, see Annie Polland, *Landmark of the Spirit: The Eldridge Street Synagogue* (New Haven: Yale University Press, 2009).

26. Christopher Mele, *Selling the Lower East Side: Culture, Real Estate, and Resistance in New York City* (Minneapolis: University of Minnesota Press, 2000), 83–84, 94–95; Gabrielle Esperdy, "Defying the Grid: A Retroactive Manifesto for the Culture

of Decongestion," *Perspecta* 30 (1999): 17; "Ageloff Towers," *American Architect* (May 5, 1929): 621.

27. Grebler, *Housing Market Behavior*, 144–45; Mele, *Selling the Lower East Side*, 86–87. See also Hasia R. Diner, *Lower East Side Memories: A Jewish Place in America* (Princeton: Princeton University Press, 2000), 96–117.

28. On the status of the Yiddish theater, see Nahma Sandrow, *Vagabond Stars: A World History of the Yiddish Theatre* (New York: Harper and Row, 1977), 288–92; Judd L. Teller, *Strangers and Natives: The Evolution of the American Jew from 1921 to the Present* (New York: Delacorte, 1968), 20–24; Ted Merwin, *In Their Own Image: New York Jews in Jazz Age Popular Culture* (New Brunswick: Rutgers University Press, 2006), 63–65; and Kate Simon, *New York Places and Pleasures: An Uncommon Guide* (New York: Meridian Books, 1959), 162–63.

29. Suzanne Wasserman, "Déjà Vu: Replanning the Lower East Side in the 1930s," in *From Urban Village to East Village: The Battle for New York's Lower East Side*, by Janet L. Abu-Lughod and others (Malden, MA: Blackwell, 1994), 105–6.

30. Roy B. Helfgott, "Women's and Children's Apparel," in *Made in New York: Case Studies in Metropolitan Manufacturing*, ed. Max Hall (Cambridge: Harvard University Press, 1959), 22, 55. See also Jackson, *Encyclopedia of New York City*, s.v. "Garment District."

31. Selma C. Berrol, "The Jewish West Side of New York, 1920–1970," *Journal of Ethnic Studies* (Winter 1986): 29.

32. Interview with Leah Novogrodsky Moskovits (August 17, 2008); email communication, Esther Novogrodsky Greenberg to Leah Novogrodsky Moskovits (August 24, 2008).

33. For an oft-referenced source on the reticence of long-term Lower East Siders—particularly, the older ones—to leave the neighborhood because of its "village"-like character, see Michael Gold, *Jews without Money* (New York: Horace Liveright, 1930).

34. *American Jewish Year Book* 33 (1931–32): 292; *American Jewish Year Book* 43 (1941–42): 684.

35. For the designation of these sections of New York as "immigrant neighborhoods" as of 1930 and statistics on their poverty levels, see Moore, *At Home in America*, 66, table 4. On the demographic breakdowns of these four areas, see Horowitz and Kaplan, *The Jewish Population of the New York Area*, 133, 168, 209, 239. Unfortunately census numbers do not permit teasing out precisely how many of the foreign-born were newcomers and how many were longtime residents in the United States. Similarly, these calculations do not indicate exactly what percentage of all foreign-born in these otherwise predominantly Jewish neighborhoods were Jewish. On the early history of Jews in Brownsville, see Alter Landesman, *Brownsville: The Birth, Development and Passing of a Jewish Community in New York* (New York: Bloch, 1969), 40–47, 67–77.

36. *American Jewish Year Book* 41 (1939–40): 596–97.

37. On the early demographics of Washington Heights, see Horowitz and Kaplan, *The Jewish Population of the New York Area*, 162; and JCR, 84. On the yeshiva's relocation and emergence as a second-generation institution, see Moore, *At Home in America*, 177–99.

38. Ernest Stock, "Washington Heights' 'Fourth Reich': The German Emigres' New Home," *Commentary* (June 1951): 583, quoted in Steven M. Lowenstein, *Frankfurt on the Hudson: The German-Jewish Community of Washington Heights, 1933–1983, Its Structure and Culture* (Detroit: Wayne State University Press, 1989), 45.

39. Lowenstein, *Frankfurt on the Hudson*, 45, 46, 50. See also ibid., 45, on chain migration as applied to this community's growth.

40. Gloria DeVidas Kirchheimer and Manfred Kirchheimer, *We Were So Beloved: Autobiography of a German Jewish Community* (Pittsburgh: University of Pittsburgh Press, 1997), 82, 94.

41. On the construction in Forest Hills and the controversy over its impact, see "Queens Homeowners Wage War to Curb Apartment Buildings," *Long Island Star* (October 28, 1938), contained in the vertical file "Forest Hills 1938" at the Queens Borough Public Library, cited in Wishnoff, "The Tolerance Point," 154–55.

42. Beth S. Wenger, *New York Jews and the Great Depression: Uncertain Promise* (New Haven: Yale University Press, 1996), 46–47, 83–84, 89, 91, 95.

43. Ibid., 99–101, 108–9.

44. Calvin Trillin, "U.S. Journal: The Bronx: The Coops," *New Yorker* (August 1, 1977): 49–54, quoted in Plunz, *A History of Housing in New York City*, 161–62. See also Dolkart, "Homes for People Cooperatives," 40.

45. Mark Naison, "From Eviction Resistance to Rent Control: Tenant Activism in the Great Depression," in *The Tenant Movement in New York City, 1904–1984*, ed. Ronald Lawson (New Brunswick: Rutgers University Press, 1986), 102–12. See also, on non-"partisan" Jewish support, Wenger, *New York Jews and the Great Depression*, 12.

46. The concept of New York Jews living during this period in greater concentration than in prior generations is derived from Deborah Dash Moore. See Moore, *At Home in America*, 30–31, for her use of an "index of dissimilarity" to compute degrees of Jewish residential concentration throughout the city.

47. On residential anti-Semitism beyond Queens, see Broun and Britt, *Christians Only*, 255, 259, 261–62; Leonard Dinnerstein, *Antisemitism in America* (New York: Oxford University Press, 1994), 93

48. Ronald H. Bayor, *Neighbors in Conflict: The Irish, Germans, Jews, and Italians of New York City, 1929–1941* (Baltimore: Johns Hopkins University Press, 1978), 3–5.

49. Arthur Mann, *La Guardia: A Fighter against His Times, 1882–1933* (Chicago: University of Chicago Press, 1959), 45–46, 156–57.

50. Bayor, *Neighbors in Conflict*, 26.

51. See ibid., 25–26, on Irish women's prior domination in the city's public schools.

52. Ibid., 150–56.

53. On Coughlin's biography and message, see Charles J. Tull, *Father Coughlin and the New Deal* (Syracuse, NY: Syracuse University Press, 1965), 192–206, 230–31.

54. Bayor, *Neighbors in Conflict*, 160–61. On the connection between street violence and the ethnic anomaly in the public school, see ibid., 26.

55. Ibid., 162.

56. Sander A. Diamond, *The Nazi Movement in America* (Ithaca: Cornell University Press, 1974), 146–47, 234–36, 257.

57. On La Guardia's dilemmas about the 1937 Bund parade, see Bayor, *Neighbors in Conflict*, 135–36. On the opposition of German Americans to the Bund, see ibid., 60–66.

58. For a brief biographical sketch of Wagner, see Jackson, *Encyclopedia of New York City*, s.v. "Robert Ferdinand Wagner." On the Wagner-Rogers Act, see Henry L. Feingold, *The Politics of Rescue: The Roosevelt Administration and the Holocaust, 1938–1945* (New Brunswick: Rutgers University Press, 1970), 149–51. For Lookstein's recollections, see Bayor, *Neighbors in Conflict*, 163, 219nn. 53, 57.

59. On the geographical locations of Jewish and black areas of Harlem, see Gurock, *When Harlem Was Jewish*, 147–48. On attempts to exclude blacks, see Seth M. Scheiner, *Negro Mecca: A History of the Negro in New York City, 1865–1920* (New York: NYU Press, 1965), 30.

60. Gil Ribak, "'What the American Can Do in His Anger': The Images of Gentiles among Jewish Immigrants in New York City" (Ph.D. diss., University of Wisconsin, 2007), 380.

61. Cheryl Lynn Greenberg, *Or Does It Explode? Black Harlem in the Great Depression* (New York: Oxford University Press, 1997), 116, 120–22, 125. See also Winston C. McDowell, "Keeping Them 'In the Same Boat Together'?," in *African Americans and Jews in the Twentieth Century*, ed. V. P. Franklin, Nancy L. Grant, Harold M. Kletnick, and Genna Rae McNeil, 208–36 (Columbia: University of Missouri Press, 1998), 226.

62. Greenberg, *Or Does It Explode?*, 126–27; McDowell, "Keeping Them 'In the Same Boat Together'?," 228.

63. Cheryl Lynn Greenberg, *Troubling the Waters: Black-Jewish Relations in the American Century* (Princeton: Princeton University Press, 2006), 109, 112.

■ NOTES TO CHAPTER 2

1. All Schayes quotations from interview (December 5, 2008). The estimates on Jewish percentages of the population are based on Horowitz and Kaplan's examination of numbers for the so-called Fordham section of the Bronx that constitutes a larger slice of the borough than just the Davidson and Jerome Avenue and West Fordham Road area that was Schayes's turf. See on these statistics for both 1930 and 1940, C. Morris Horowitz and Lawrence J. Kaplan, *The Jewish Population of the New York Area, 1900–1975* (New York: Federation of Jewish Philanthropies, 1959), 181.

2. These statistics on "nationality of pupils" were derived from periodical studies of such populations that were conducted by the Board of Education of New York City in the 1930s and 1940s. As with all such surveys, the religion of students was not indicated. Yet, as with many American "censuses," in using these numbers, I am assuming that Russians, Poles, and Romanians were Jews. I have not added into the mix those with parents from Germany and Austria, who in the 1930s might also have been Jews. In addition, all of these percentages that point to Jewish predominance do not include the large cohorts —a third or more—in each school of children from families in which the father's country of birth was "United States (White)." (The nationality of mothers was not asked.) My

assumption here is that a goodly proportion were second-generation Jews of eastern European extraction that were born in the first decade and a half of the twentieth century of immigrant parents who by the 1930s had their own, third-generation children. See Board of Education Records, "Bureau of Reference, Research, and Statistics, Reorganization Reports, September 1935–September, 1945," boxes 1–6, New York City Municipal Archives.

3. William Poster, "From the American Scene: 'Twas a Dark Night in Brownsville': Pitkin Avenue's Self-Made Generation," *Commentary* (May 1950): 459, 461–62, 464.

4. Ibid., 462–63.

5. Gerald Sorin, *The Nurturing Neighborhood: The Brownsville Boys Club and Jewish Community in Urban America, 1940–1990* (New York: NYU Press, 1990), 14; Beth Wenger, *New York Jews and the Great Depression: Uncertain Promise* (New Haven: Yale University Press, 1996), 96.

6. Alfred Kazin, *A Walker in the City* (New York: Harcourt, Brace, 1951), 11–12, 37, 38.

7. Ira Rosen, "The Glory That Was Charlotte Street," *New York Times Sunday Magazine* (October 7, 1979): 51.

8. Jeff Gottlieb, "Jamaica, Stronghold of the Jews," unpublished paper, formerly appearing at http://www.qjhs.org. See also, on the message of *The Jazz Singer*, Ted Merwin, *In Their Own Image: New York Jews in Jazz Age Culture* (New Brunswick: Rutgers University Press, 2006), 118–20.

9. Fred Ferretti, "After 70 Years, South Bronx Street Is a Dead End," *New York Times* (October 21, 1977): 51; Wenger, *New York Jews and the Great Depression*, 97; Lillian Elkin, "Memoir," American Jewish Committee Oral History Collection, New York Public Library.

10. On the creation of Orchard Beach, see Robert A. Caro, *The Power Broker: Robert Moses and the Fall of New York* (New York: Knopf, 1974), 365–67. On Jews' using the beaches, see Wenger, *New York Jews and the Great Depression*, 58.

11. Andrea Most, *Making Americans: Jews and the Broadway Musical* (Cambridge: Harvard University Press, 2004), 28; David A. Jasen, *Tin Pan Alley: The Composers, the Songs, the Performers and Their Times* (New York: Donald I. Fine, 1988), xxii.

12. Jasen, *Tin Pan Alley*, 78–79; Kenneth Aaron Kanter, *The Jews on Tin Pan Alley: The Jewish Contribution to American Popular Music, 1830–1940* (New York: KTAV and the American Jewish Archives, 1982), 54–55, 58, 60, 113, 117, 142–43.

13. Stephen Steinberg, *The Academic Melting Pot: Catholics and Jews in American Higher Education* (New York: McGraw-Hill, 1974), 20–21; Marcia Graham Synnott, *The Half-Opened Door: Discrimination and Admissions at Harvard, Yale, and Princeton, 1900–1970* (Westport, CT: Greenwood, 1979), 158, 195.

14. Marianne Sanua, "'We Hate New York': Negative Images of the Promised City as a Source for Jewish Fraternity and Sorority Members, 1920–1940," in *An Inventory of Promises: Essays on American Jewish History in Honor of Moses Rischin*, ed. Jeffrey S. Gurock and Marc Lee Raphael, 235–64 (Brooklyn, NY: Carlson, 1995), 237; Lee J. Levinger, *The Jewish Student in America: A Study Made by the Research Bureau of the B'nai B'rith Hillel Foundation* (Cincinnati: B'nai B'rith, 1937), 94.

15. Heywood Broun and George Britt, *Christians Only: A Study in Prejudice* (New

York: Vanguard, 1931), 107; Felix Morrow, "Higher Learning on Washington Square," *Menorah Journal* (Autumn 1930): 353; David Hollinger, "Two NYUs and the 'Obligation of Universities to the Social Order' in the Great Depression," in *The University and the City*, ed. Thomas Bender, 249–66 (New York: Oxford University Press, 1988), 255. On NYU's Depression-era reversal of policies, see Thomas Bender, *New York Intellect: A History of Intellectual Life in New York from 1750 to the Beginnings of Our Own Time* (New York: Knopf, 1987), 291.

16. Hollinger, "Two NYUs," 256. There is a difference of opinion within the sources on the Jewish proportions at NYU, both uptown and downtown. Morrow has offered the figure of 93 percent in 1930, which, if accurate would make it more "Jewish" than the City College of New York. See Morrow, "Higher Learning on Washington Square," 348. Broun and Britt, on the other hand, reported based on information from the school's registrar for 1931 that 45.3 percent of the uptown campus was Jewish, as opposed to 63 percent for downtown. See Broun and Britt, *Christians Only*, 106–7. Hollinger has argued that in the 1920s, Jewish percentages in University Heights were down to less than 30 percent ("Two NYUs," 255). Bender has complicated matters by suggesting that by the end of the 1920s and into the Depression, economics moved NYU uptown to be more hospitable to Jews, and thus the numbers there rebounded to 54 percent from 30 percent in 1922. See Bender, *New York Intellect*, 291. See also Synnott, *The Half-Opened Door*, 19, which indicates that the Jewish presence in the Bronx branch in the early 1920s dropped from 40 to 25 percent. On the easy commute from the Lower East Side, see Harold S. Wechsler, *The Qualified Student: A History of Selective College Admission in America* (New York: Wiley, 1977), 133.

17. Morrow, "Higher Learning on Washington Square," 348–49.

18. Sanua, "We Hate New York," 237; A. M. Rosenthal, "Of Course, It Is All Quite Obvious as to Why I Am So Moved," in *City at the Center: A Collection of Writings by CCNY Alumni and Faculty*, ed. Betty Rizzo and Barry Wallenstein, 67–68 (New York: City College of New York, 1983), 67.

19. On the cost of lunch at CCNY, see Gerald Sorin, *Irving Howe: A Life of Passionate Dissent* (New York: NYU Press, 2002), 15–17. In the 1923–24 academic year, at NYU the registration fee and tuition amounted to $245. Ten years later, it cost $360 to attend the downtown school. The information on NYU tuition and fees was derived from the school's catalogues for 1923–24 and 1933–34, provided by the NYU Archive on December 15, 2008. My thanks to Laura Joanne Zeccardi for her assistance. Columbia University priced tuition and board in the 1930s at $600. On the cost of tuition at Columbia, see Nathan Glazer's memoir comments in Joseph Dorman, *Arguing the World: The New York Intellectuals in Their Own Words* (New York: Free Press, 2000), 43–44.

20. Robert Cohen, *When the Old Left Was Young: Student Radicals and America's First Mass Student Movement, 1929–1941* (New York: Oxford University Press, 1993), 68–70. See also "City College Men Fight Rise in Fees," *New York Times* (May 24, 1932): 1; and "Protest Fee Plan for City Colleges," *New York Times* (May 26, 1932): 11. On the temporary closing of Crane Junior College in Chicago, see City Colleges of Chicago, "Mission & History," http://www.ccc.edu/MissionHistory.asp (accessed October 21, 2011).

21. On the academic achievements of CCNY's most outstanding alumni of that era, see CCNY Alumni Association, "Nobel Laureates," http://www.ccnyalumni.org/index.php ?option=com_content&view=article&id=100&Itemid=285 (accessed October 21, 2011).

22. David M. Oshinsky, *Polio: An American Story* (New York: Oxford University Press, 2005), 96–97; Debbie Bookchin and Jim Schumacher, *The Virus and the Vaccine: The True Story of a Cancer-Causing Monkey Virus, Contaminated Polio Vaccine, and the Millions of Americans Exposed* (New York: St. Martin's, 2004), 46.

23. L. Shands, "The Cheder on the Hill," *Menorah Journal* (March 1929): 269.

24. Steinberg, *The Academic Melting Pot*, 9; Thomas Evans Coulton, *A City College in Action: Struggle and Achievements at Brooklyn College, 1930–1955* (New York: Harper and Bros., 1955), 8, 14.

25. "Subway a 'Campus' for Many at Hunter," *New York Times* (October 2, 1938): 54; Ruth Jacknow Markowitz, *My Daughter, the Teacher: Jewish Teachers in the New York City Schools* (New Brunswick: Rutgers University Press, 1993), 27. On Jewish male-to-female proportions in colleges and universities, see Nettie Pauline McGill, "Some Characteristics of Jewish Youth in New York City," *Jewish Social Service Quarterly* 14 (1938): 256. See also Wenger, *New York Jews and the Great Depression*, 44, on young women sacrificing for their brothers' education.

26. Meyer Liben, "CCNY: A Memoir," in Rizzo and Wallenstein, *City at the Center*, 50. See also, on the importance of basketball to CCNY students, Irving Howe, "From *World of Our Fathers*," in ibid., 60.

27. Louis Weiser, "Memoir," American Jewish Committee Oral History Collection, New York Public Library.

28. On the employment problems Jews faced even with advanced degrees, see Wenger, *New York Jews and the Great Depression*, 22–23.

29. Oshinsky, *Polio*, 98–104, 107.

30. On the intellectual tradition that Cohen embodied, see Moses Rischin, *The Promised City: New York's Jews, 1870–1914* (Cambridge: Harvard University Press, 1962), 216. See also Irving Howe, *World of Our Fathers: The Journey of the East European Jews to America and the Life They Found and Made* (New York: Random House, 1976), 283–86. On the problems of Jewish academics during the 1920s–1940s and the changes after World War II, see Lewis S. Feuer, "The Stages in the Social History of Jewish Professors in American Colleges and Universities," *American Jewish History* (June 1982): 459–60, 462, 464.

31. On High Holiday piety, see "Abraham Cahan" and "Morgen Zhurnal, 4/3/50," in Irving Howe and Kenneth Libo, *How We Lived: A Documentary History of Immigrant Jews in America, 1880–1930* (New York: Richard Marek, 1979), 104, 117. On the problem of those "temporary halls of worship," see "Temporary Halls of Worship," *American Hebrew* (January 15, 1901): 431.

32. Alexander M. Dushkin, *Jewish Education in New York City* (New York: Bureau of Jewish Education, 1918), 154–56.

33. For an appreciation of the common dilemmas immigrant religious leaders and radicals faced in the immigrant period, see Jeffrey S. Gurock, "Change to Survive: The

Common Experience of Transplanted Jewish Identities in America, 1880–1920," in *What Is American about the American Jewish Experience?*, ed. Marc Lee Raphael (Williamsburg, VA: College of William and Mary, 1993), 54–72.

34. On radical dominance of downtown street corners and the significance of the activities for the growth of unions, see Tony Michels, *A Fire in Their Hearts: Yiddish Socialists in New York* (Cambridge: Harvard University Press, 2005), 70–73, 167.

35. Arthur Gorenstein, "A Portrait of Ethnic Politics: The Socialists and the 1908 and 1910 Congressional Elections on the Lower East Side," *Publications of the American Jewish Historical Society* (March 1961): 202–40.

36. Howe, *The World of Our Fathers*, 289.

37. Sorin, *The Nurturing Neighborhood*, 16.

38. McGill, "Some Characteristics of Jewish Youth," 266–67.

39. Jeffrey S. Gurock, *Judaism's Encounter with American Sports* (Bloomington: Indiana University Press, 2005), 66–67; Israel Herbert Levinthal, "The Value of the Center to the Synagogue," *United Synagogue Review* (June 1926): 19.

40. On the rise of synagogue centers in New York during the 1920s, see Deborah Dash Moore, *At Home in America: Second Generation New York Jews* (New York: Columbia University Press, 1981), 140–43. On Kaplan's break with Orthodoxy, see Jeffrey S. Gurock and Jacob J. Schacter, *A Modern Heretic and a Traditional Community: Mordecai M. Kaplan, Orthodoxy, and American Judaism* (New York: Columbia University Press, 1997), 106–34.

41. Gurock, *Judaism's Encounter with American Sports*, 70–71; Merwin, *In Their Own Image*, 59; Wenger, *New York Jews and the Great Depression*, 186.

42. Quoted in Wenger, *New York Jews and the Great Depression*, 187.

43. Susan Dworkin, *Miss America, 1945: Bess Myerson's Own Story* (New York: Newmarket, 1947), 13–17.

44. Eric L. Goldstein, "'A Childless Language': Yiddish and the Problem of 'Youth' in the 1920s and 1930s," in *1929: Mapping the Jewish World*, ed. Gennady Estraik and Hasia Diner (New York: NYU Press, forthcoming).

45. Dworkin, *Miss America*, 14–15.

46. Irving Howe, "A Memoir of the Thirties," in *Steady Work: Essays in the Politics of Democratic Radicalism, 1953–1966* (New York: Harcourt, Brace and World, 1966), 349–53. See also Sorin, *Irving Howe*, 11.

47. Dorman, *Arguing the World*, 33–34, 36, 39.

48. Liben, "CCNY," 48; Sorin, *Irving Howe*, 17.

49. Dorman, *Arguing the World*, 45.

50. As Wenger has pointed out (*New York Jews and the Great Depression*, 214n. 6), the attitudes and changing perspectives of the "New York Intellectuals" have been favored with much scholarly discussion. See, for example, Terry A. Cooney, *The Rise of the New York Intellectuals,* Partisan Review *and Its Circle* (Madison: University of Wisconsin Press, 1986); Alan M. Wald, *The New York Intellectuals: The Rise and Decline of the Anti-Stalinist Left from the 1930s to the 1980s* (Chapel Hill: University of North Carolina Press, 1987); and Alexander Bloom, *Prodigal Sons: The New York Intellectuals and Their World* (New York: Oxford University Press, 1986).

51. Irving Howe, *A Margin of Hope: An Intellectual Autobiography* (San Diego: Harcourt Brace Jovanovich, 1982), 137; Cooney, *The Rise of the New York Intellectuals*, 43, 50, discussed in Nathan Abrams, "'A Profoundly Hegemonic Moment': De-mythologizing the Cold War New York Jewish Intellectuals," *Shofar* (Spring 2003): 64–82.

52. Dorman, *Arguing the World*, 46; Liben, "CCNY," 48.

53. Dorman, *Arguing the World*, 44–45, 51–52.

54. R. Cohen, *When the Old Left Was Young*, 44.

55. Christopher Phelps, "An Interview with Harry Magdoff—Co-editor of the 'Monthly Review,'" *Monthly Review* (May 1999), http://monthlyreview.org/1999/05/01/an-interview-with-harry-magdoff.

56. R. Cohen, *When the Old Left Was Young*, 24, 27–28, 274–75, 350n. 16. See also Morris Freedman, "CCNY Days," in Rizzo and Wallenstein, *City at the Center*, 65.

57. Lucy S. Dawidowicz, *From That Place and Time: A Memoir, 1938–1947* (New York: Norton, 1989), 16–17; Markowitz, *My Daughter, the Teacher*, 52–54, 60–61.

58. Hal Draper, "The Student Movement in the Thirties," in *As We Saw the Thirties: Essays on Social and Political Movements of a Decade*, ed. Rita J. Simon (Urbana: University of Illinois Press, 1967), 182–88. See also, on the tuition crisis and Scottsboro, R. Cohen, *When the Old Left Was Young*, 68–71, 211.

59. James Traub, *City on a Hill: Testing the American Dream at City College* (Reading, MA: Addison-Wesley, 1993), 39.

60. Although the application forms for admission into the program did not inquire about the student's religion, the majority of applicants possessed Jewish-sounding names and hailed from neighborhoods, when indicated, that were Jewish ones in the city. See, for these examples, a "certificate" dated September 17, 1931, which lists twenty-eight senior ROTC cadets. Nineteen possessed Jewish-sounding names. These documents are on file at the Archives of the City College of New York.

61. Solomon Willis Rudy, *College of the City of New York: A Centennial History, 1847–1947* (New York: City College Press, 1949), 404–19. See also "Expanded Historical Note on Department of Military Science (ROTC)," undated document in CCNY Archives. For an example of the group's publication, see the *Lavender Cadet* (November 1934), in CCNY Archives.

62. "Conclusions to Be Drawn," *Campus* (February 25, 1931): 2; "S.C. Charter Day Boycott Cuts Attendance to 1,000," *Campus* (May 10, 1935): 1. See also untitled press release, dated October 4, 1939, describing the growth of ROTC at CCNY in the 1930s, in CCNY Archives. On the athletes' support of ROTC and the administration, see S. W. Rudy, *College of the City of New York*, 419. See also, on CCNY's ROTC as the largest campus military group in the United States, Irving Rosenthal, "Rumblings of Unrest and Empty Stomachs," in Rizzo and Wallenstein, *City at the Center*, 56. On athletes' support for a stance comparable to that of ROTC, see "5 More Suspended in City College Row," *New York Times* (June 3, 1933): 15; and "186 Awards Made at City College," *New York Times* (June 3, 1933): 9.

63. "Boycott Charter Day," *Campus* (May 7, 1935): 2; "Looking Backward," *Campus* (May 31, 1935): 2; "Nation's Students 'Strike for Peace': Disorders Are Few," *New York*

Times (April 13, 1935): 1–2. See also "Protest ROTC," in "The Struggle for Free Speech at CCNY, 1931–42," virtual exhibition, Virtual New York City website, http://www.vny.cuny .edu/gutter/panels/panel6.html.

64. On the Socialists' antiwar stance into World War II and its decline in mass popularity, see David A. Shannon, *The Socialist Party of America: A History* (New York: Macmillan, 1955), 254–56. On American Communists' positions, see Maurice Isserman, *Which Side Were You On? The American Communist Party during the Second World War* (Middletown, CT: Wesleyan University Press, 1982), 32–33, 85. On the mixture of left and right politics in the isolationist movement, see Manfred Jonas, *Isolationism in America, 1935–1941* (Ithaca: Cornell University Press, 1966), 39, 229. See also, on isolationist activities, David Gold, "America First: The Anti-war Movement, Charles Lindbergh and the Second World War, 1940–1941," *New York Military Affairs Symposium* (September 26, 2003), http://bobrowen.com/nymas/americafirst.html.

65. "Four Students Seized at Military Drill," *New York Times* (May 18, 1940): 8.

66. For an overview of early Zionist history in America, see Melvin I. Urofsky, *American Zionism from Herzl to the Holocaust* (Garden City, NY: Anchor, 1975), 43–152.

67. Noah Nardi, "A Survey of Jewish Day Schools in America," *Jewish Education* (September 1944): 22–23; Nardi, "The Growth of Jewish Day Schools in America," *Jewish Education* (November 1948): 25.

68. Jeffrey S. Gurock, "Jewish Commitment and Continuity in Interwar Brooklyn," in *Jews of Brooklyn*, ed. Ilana Abramovitch and Seán Galvin, 231–41 (Hanover, NH: University Press of New England / Brandeis University Press, 2002), 238–39.

69. Chaim Potok, *The Chosen: A Novel* (New York: Simon and Schuster, 1967).

70. Judah Lapson, "A Decade of Hebrew in the High Schools of New York," *Jewish Education* (April 1941): 34–45.

71. Nettie Pauline McGill and Ellen Nathalie Matthews, *The Youth of New York City* (New York: Macmillan, 1940), 241, 334.

72. On strict observance within Williamsburg, see George Kranzler, *Williamsburg: A Jewish Community in Transition* (New York: Feldheim, 1961), 17, 18, 214–15.

73. Meir Kimmel, "The History of Yeshivat Rabbi Chaim Berlin," *Sheviley ha-Hinuch* (Fall 1948): 51–54; Alter F. Landesman, *Brownsville: The Birth, Development and Passing of a Jewish Community in New York* (New York: Bloch, 1969), 234–35.

74. On the presence of Hasidic elements in Brooklyn in the interwar period, see Jerome R. Mintz, *Hasidic People: A Place in the New World* (Cambridge: Harvard University Press, 1992), 21–26, 53–56.

75. Kranzler, *Williamsburg*, 213–15.

■ NOTES TO CHAPTER 3

1. The geographical location of these New York–based national Jewish organizations and other institutions noted in this chapter was derived from the annual directory "Jewish National Organizations in the United States," published in the *American Jewish Year Book*. See, for example, the listing for 1941–42 that appeared in volume 43, 521–602, and those for 1945–46 in volume 47, 560–610.

2. On the mission and ideology of the Histadrut—especially its American context —see Mark A. Raider, *The Emergence of American Zionism* (New York: NYU Press, 1998), xvi, 1, 25. On the mission and approaches of the Revisionist Zionists in America, see Rafael Medoff, *Militant Zionism in America: The Rise and Impact of the Jabotinsky Movement in the United States, 1926–1948* (Tuscaloosa: University of Alabama Press, 2002). On the battles between Wise's Congress and the Revisionists, see David S. Wyman, *The Abandonment of the Jews: America and the Holocaust, 1941–1945* (New York: Pantheon Books, 1984), 87, 90–92.

3. On the location of Lugee's, see its ad in *Jewish Life* (October 1946): 97.

4. On the proximity of these two groups and the mission of the Mizrachi, see *American Jewish Year Book* 43 (1941–42): 558, 569.

5. For basic information on the name and number of media outlets in the city, see Kenneth T. Jackson, ed., *The Encyclopedia of New York City* (New Haven: Yale University Press and New-York Historical Society, 1995), s.vv. "Magazines," "Newspapers," "Radio." See also Aviva Ben-Ur, "In Search of the Ladino Press: A Bibliographic Survey," *Studies in Bibliography and Booklore* (Winter 2001): 10–52.

6. For reports on the size of these rallies, see *American Jewish Year Book* 40 (1939): 216; *American Jewish Year Book* 41 (1941): 271; "20,000 Jam Garden in Reich Protest," *New York Times* (November 22, 1938): 6. See also, on public protest, Haskel Lookstein, *Were We Our Brothers' Keepers? The Public Response of American Jews to the Holocaust, 1938–1944* (New York: Hartmore House, 1985), 55, 83, 98.

7. Monte Noam Penkower, "In Dramatic Dissent: The Bergson Boys," *American Jewish History* (March 1981): 286–88.

8. "22,000 Nazis Hold Rally in Garden; Police Check Foes," *New York Times* (February 21, 1939): 1.

9. Naomi W. Cohen, *American Jews and the Zionist Idea* (New York: KTAV, 1975), 60–62, 87; Melvin I. Urofsky, *American Zionism from Herzl to the Holocaust* (Garden City, NY: Anchor, 1975), 399–400; Samuel Halperin, *The Political World of American Zionism* (Detroit: Wayne State University Press, 1961), 222–33, 236–37.

10. Efraim Zuroff, *The Response of Orthodox Jewry in the United States to the Holocaust: The Activities of the Vaad Ha-Hatzala Rescue Committee, 1939–1945* (New York: Michael Scharf Publication Trust of Yeshiva University Press, 2000), 134.

11. Rafael Medoff, "'Retribution Is Not Enough': The 1943 Campaign by Jewish Students to Raise American Public Awareness of the Nazi Genocide," *Holocaust and Genocide Studies* (Fall 1997): 172, 174, 178–81.

12. On Rabbi Weitzmann's decision, see Rafael Medoff's phone interview with Rebbitzen Teitz, Rabbi Weizmann's daughter (March 7, 2006). I am grateful to Dr. Medoff for sharing this source with me.

13. Jonathan Krasner, *The Benderly Boys and the Making of American Jewish Education* (Hanover, NH: University Press of New England / Brandeis University Press, 2011), 347–50. I am grateful to Dr. Krasner for sharing this information with me.

14. Huslal Lookstein, "May 1943: The Prayer Service That Almost Wasn't," sermon delivered at Congregation Kehilath Jeshurun, April 18, 2009.

15. "Adolf Hitler Was Once Teacher Here," *Commentator* (February 26, 1942): 1; "Concrete Action to Be Done by Every Type of Reader" and "Yeshiva Students Are Not Blameless," *Commentator* (March 4, 1943): 6.

16. Marsha L. Rozenblit, "The Seminary during the Holocaust Years," in *Tradition Renewed: A History of the Jewish Theological Seminary of America*, ed. Jack Wertheimer, vol. 2 (New York: Jewish Theological Seminary, 1997), 289, 304.

17. Laurel Leff, "When the Facts Didn't Speak for Themselves: The Holocaust in the *New York Times*, 1939–1945," *Harvard International Journal of Press/Politics* (2000): 52–57; Leff, "A Tragic 'Fight in the Family': The *New York Times*, Reform Judaism and the Holocaust," *American Jewish History* (March 2000): 3–4.

18. Alex Grobman, "What Did They Know? The American Jewish Press and the Holocaust, 1 September 1939–17 December 1942," *American Jewish History* (March 1979): 327–52.

19. Krasner, *The Benderly Boys*.

20. Lookstein, "May 1943."

21. Deborah Dash Moore, *GI Jews: How World War II Changed a Generation* (Cambridge: Belknap Press of Harvard University Press, 2004), 30–31, 39–40.

22. Ibid., 42–43; Edward Alexander, "Irving Howe and the Holocaust: Dilemmas of a Radical Jewish Intellectual," *American Jewish History* 88 (March 2000): 101–2.

23. On the debate over the origins of the ditty, see Bee Wilson, "Bee Wilson Suggests Sending Salami Missiles to Iraq," *New Statesman* (January 20, 2003), http://www.newstatesman.com/200301200047; and Barry Popik, "Send a Salami to Your Boy in the Army," *Big Apple Corner* (blog) (October 14, 2004), http://www.barrypopik.com/index.php/new_york_city/entry/send_a_salami_to_your_boy_in_the_army/. On soldiers coping with ham, see Moore, *GI Jews*, 49–85.

24. Alter F. Landesman, *Brownsville: The Birth, Development and Passing of a Jewish Community in New York* (New York: Bloch, 1969), 321.

25. *Home News* (Bronx) (April 13, 1943): 3; (April 18, 1943): 11; Marianne Sanua, "From the Pages of the Victory Bulletin," *YIVO Annual* 19 (1992): 295–97, 327; *Commentator* (February 4, 1943): 1; (November 18, 1943): 1; (December 16, 1943): 1; (March 8, 1945): 1.

26. *Home News* (Bronx) (April 4, 1943): 8; (April 26, 1943): 1.

27. *Home News* (Bronx) (April 19, 1943): 3; (April 26, 1943): 1.

28. Stella Sardell, introduction to *Community Memories: The Syrian Jews of Brooklyn during World War II* (Brooklyn, NY: Sephardic Community Center, 1984), 2, cited in Sanua, "From the Pages of the Victory Bulletin," 287.

29. For an example of the "Roll of Honor," see *Victory Bulletin* (July 1942): 3; see also (November 1942): 5; and (November 1942): 3. All references to the newsletter are derived from Sephardic Archives, *The Victory Bulletin, July 1942–September 1945: Wartime Newspapers of the Syrian Jewish Community in Brooklyn* (New York: Sephardic Archives, c. 1984).

30. *Victory Bulletin* (September 1942): 2; (March 1943): 2; (April 1944): 2; (December 1944): 2; (September 1945): 2, 10.

31. Stephen S. Wise, "The Victorious Leader: A Tribute to Franklin Delano Roosevelt," *Congress Weekly* (April 20, 1945): 7–8.

32. Lawrence H. Fuchs, *The Political Behavior of American Jews* (Glencoe, IL: Free Press, 1956), 129–30, 152–53; Henry L. Feingold, *A Time for Searching: Entering the Mainstream, 1920–1945* (Baltimore: Johns Hopkins University Press, 1992), 212–17.

33. On the founding of this synagogue, its mission, and its early priorities, see the following sources in the Young Israel of Parkchester Papers (hereinafter YIP) at the Yeshiva University Archives: Mrs. B. Silver to Friend (September 5, 1940), Jerome H. Rosenblum to Friend (December 4, 1940), the Arrangements Committee to Friend (April 30, 1941); "Young Israel to Dedicate Home," *Parkchester News* (November 13, 1941); Jack Solve to Members (June 24, 1942); *The Young Israelight* (December 2, 1942): 2.

34. "Minutes of Meeting on Tuesday, December 9, 1941 at Quarters"; "President Roosevelt Has Proclaimed Thursday, January 1, 1942," flyer (n.d.); "Minutes of Meeting on Tuesday, January 13, 1942 at Quarters"; "Minutes of Meeting on June 23, 1942 at Quarters"; United Victory Committee of Parkchester to Young Israel of Parkchester (April 16, 1942; March 18, 1943); Jack Solve to Soldier (February 4, 1944); Chairman of War Work Committee to Member (May 12, 1944); "A Review of Our War Effort," *Young Israelight* (December 1945): 5; all in YIP.

35. Jack Solve to Member (June 24, 1942); "Did You Know That . . . ," *Young Israelight* (December 1945): 6.

36. *Y.I.S. Reporter* (February 1942): 1–3.

37. For examples of "Recent News" coverage, see *Young Israel Viewpoint* (October 1941): 17; (September 1942): 3, 12; (November, 1942): 12. On explicit discussions of the dimensions of the Holocaust, see *Young Israel Viewpoint* (December 1942): 15; (September 1943): 1; (September 1944): 9.

38. "Annual Report for the Year 1942–1943 Presented at the Convention of the National Council of Young Israel, June 25–28, 1943 Pine View Hotel Fallsburg, N.Y., Submitted by J. David Delman, National President," in YIP.

39. The only other reference to rallies was the item in "Recent News" that spoke of a Carnegie Hall gathering in 1942 to promote a Jewish army. See *Young Israel Viewpoint* (February 1942): 17.

40. "President's Column," *Young Israel Viewpoint* (October 1942): 5.

41. *Kehilath Jeshurun Bulletin* (March 16, 1945): 1; (April 16, 1945): 1, in Kehilath Jeshurun Archives (hereinafter KJ).

42. *Kehilath Jeshurun Bulletin* (January 7, 1944): 1; (January 14, 1944): 3; (February 25, 1944): 1; (January 12, 1945): 1; (February 16, 1945): 1; Max J. Etra, "Seven and Seventy," *Congregation Kehilath Jeshurun Dance Journal* (1941): n.p., all in KJ.

43. "Rabbinate Proclaims Fast Days for Jews," *Hamigdal* (February 1945): 9. I am grateful to Dr. Rafael Medoff for sharing this source.

44. All Goldberg quotations and information from interview with Sylvia and Jack Goldberg (February 13, 2009; audiotape in possession of the author).

45. On Greenberg and Koufax and the different way their absences were treated in

America, see Jeffrey S. Gurock, *Judaism's Encounter with American Sports* (Bloomington: Indiana University Press, 2005), 5.

46. N. Cohen, *American Jews and the Zionist Idea*, 64–66; Halperin, *The Political World of American Zionism*, 270–74, 284–91; Medoff, *Militant Zionism in America*, 171–72.

47. Medoff, *Militant Zionism in America*, 201–2.

48. Leonard Slater, *The Pledge* (New York: Simon and Schuster, 1970), 94–96.

49. Ibid., 63.

50. Judd L. Teller, *Strangers and Natives: The Evolution of the American Jew from 1921 to the Present* (New York Delacorte, 1968), 183–84. See also Robert A. Rockaway, *But He Was Good to His Mother: The Lives and Crimes of Jewish Gangsters*, rev. ed. (Jerusalem: Gefen, 2000), 230–31; Arthur Hertzberg, *My Life and a People's Struggle for Identity* (San Francisco: HarperSanFrancisco, 2002), 186.

51. N. Cohen, *American Jews and the Zionist Idea*, 68–71; Rozenblit, "The Seminary during the Holocaust Years," 291. See also "Rally Held Here," *New York Times* (May 17, 1948): 1, 3.

■ NOTES TO CHAPTER 4

1. Deborah Dash Moore, *To the Golden Cities: Pursuing the American Dream in Miami and L.A.* (New York: Free Press, 1994), 22–25, 49, 50, 68. See also interview with Dolph Schayes (December 5, 2008).

2. Ted Merwin, *Homeland for the Jewish Soul: A History of the Jewish Deli* (forthcoming). I am grateful to Dr. Merwin for sharing his information and insights with me.

3. Kenneth T. Jackson, *Crabgrass Frontier: The Suburbanization of the United States* (New York: Oxford University Press, 1985), 231–41; C. Morris Horowitz and Lawrence J. Kaplan, *The Jewish Population of the New York Area, 1900–1975* (New York: Federation of Jewish Philanthropies, 1959), 17.

4. For estimates of Bergen County's Jewish population, see *American Jewish Year Book* 60 (1959): 14–15. See also Simon Glustrom, "Some Aspects of a Suburban Jewish Community," *Conservative Judaism* (Winter 1957): 27–28.

5. Harry Gersh, *Minority Report* (New York: Crowell-Collier, 1962), 128–33.

6. Ibid., 120–25; see also Sam Welles, "The Jewish Élan," *Fortune* (February 1960): 138.

7. Marshall Sklare, "Jews, Ethnics, and the American City," *Commentary* (April 1972): 73; Horowitz and Kaplan, *The Jewish Population of the New York Area*, 22, 45, 283, 285, 289, 305.

8. "New Apartments Offer Terraces," *New York Times* (April 26, 1942): RE1; see also Sklare, "Jews, Ethnics, and the American City," 72.

9. All these sources are derived from a clipping file, a compilation of newspaper articles entitled "Forest Hills Housing, 1921–1971," at the Queens Public Library, Long Island Division.

10. Sklare, "Jews, Ethnics, and the American City," 72.

11. Alison Gregor, "Away from the Limelight a Builder Makes His Mark," *New York Times* (December 21, 2006), http://www.nytimes.com/2006/12/31/realestate/commercial/31sqft.html. See also the company history of their endeavors: *Muss Development LLC:*

Building New York since 1906 (document provided to the author by Joshua Muss); interview with Joshua Muss (November 24, 2008).

12. On the history of the LeFraks, see "LeFrak, Samuel J.," *American National Biography Online*, http://www.anb.org. On the Lefraks' early efforts in Queens, see "Forest Hills Gets New Apartments of Unusual Design," *New York Times* (April 1, 1951). On their approach to housing for less affluent residents, see Charles V. Bagli, "Blue-Collar Builders Expand Empire to Glitzier Shores," *New York Times* (October 9, 2007).

13. Hal Shapiro, "Co-op Owners Proud Dwellers," *Long Island Star Journal* (February 24, 1962).

14. Morris Freedman, "New Jewish Community in Formation: A Conservative Center Catering to Present-Day Needs," *Commentary* (January 1955): 36–37, 39, 43, 45, 46.

15. On the founding and early mission of the Forest Hills Jewish Center, see Daniel A. Wishnoff, "The Tolerance Point: Race, Public Housing and the Forest Hills Controversy, 1945–1975" (Ph.D. diss., City University of New York, 2005), 159–64.

16. Jeffrey S. Gurock, "Devotees and Deviants: A Primer on the Religious Values of Orthodox Day School Families," in *Rav Chesed: Essays in Honor of Rabbi Dr. Haskel Lookstein*, ed. Rafael Medoff, 271–94 (Hoboken, NJ: KTAV, 2009).

17. On the founding of the Yeshiva of Central Queens, see its brief institution history, composed as part of its *Yeshiva of Central Queens Golden Jubilee Dinner Journal* (March 3, 1991), provided to the author courtesy of the Yeshiva of Central Queens. See also Jeff Gottlieb, "Jamaica: Stronghold of the Jews," unpublished paper, formerly appearing at http://www.qjhs.org, 7. For the interview with the principal, see Harold U. Ribalow, "My Child Goes to Jewish Parochial School," *Commentary* (January–June 1954): 64–67. On the assertion that Charny once allowed that most students came from Conservative backgrounds, see Ben Zion Bokser, "Schechter Day Schools," *United Synagogue Review* (March 1957): 11. On the early history of the Yeshiva Dov Revel, see Morris Charner and Frances S. Morris, "Curricular Development at Yeshiva Dov Revel," *Yeshiva Education* (Fall 1959): 34. For recollections on the question of religious diversity at Central Queens as opposed to Revel, see interview with Rabbi Fabian Schoenfeld (April 29, 2009).

18. See undated report, circa 1957, on Solomon Schechter Schools in the Ben Zion Bokser Papers, box 20, Ratner Center, Jewish Theological Seminary. See also Ribalow, "My Child Goes to Jewish Parochial School," 65.

19. Bokser, "Schechter Day Schools," 11.

20. Ruth Glazer, "West Bronx: Food, Shelter, Clothing," *Commentary* (June 1949): 578, 580, 584, 585.

21. Vivian Gornick, "There Is No More Community," *Interchange* (April 1977): 4; Vivian Gornick, "Commencement Address," in *City at the Center: A Collection of Writings by CCNY Alumni and Faculty*, ed. Betty Rizzo and Barry Wallenstein, 84–87 (New York: City College of New York, 1983), 84–85.

22. Jeffrey A. Trachtenberg, *Ralph Lauren: The Man behind the Mystique* (New York: Little, Brown, 1988), 25–35.

23. Alfred Jospe, *Jewish Students and Student Services at American Universities* (Washington, DC: B'nai B'rith Hillel Foundation, 1963), 6, 7, 14.

24. Welles, "The Jewish Élan," 134.

25. Calvin Trillin, "U.S. Journal: The Bronx: The Coops," *New Yorker* (August 1, 1977): 49–54; Deborah Dash Moore, "Reconsidering the Rosenbergs: Symbol and Substance in Second Generation American Jewish Consciousness," *Journal of American Ethnic History* 8 (Fall 1988): 26–29.

26. Stephen G. Thompson, "Co-op Housing: N.Y.C. vs. U.S.A.," *Architectural Forum* (July 1959): 132–33, 178.

27. Daniel Bell, "The Three Faces of New York," *Dissent* 8 (Summer 1961): 225.

28. Steven Gaines and Sharon Churcher, *Obsession: The Lives and Times of Calvin Klein* (New York: Birch Lane, 1994), 13, 21, 35, 49, 65, 73–74, 178.

29. Bernard Postal, "New York's Jewish Fare," *Congress Bi-Weekly* (October 12, 1964): 9.

30. Myron Kandel, "Tale of a Modern Dybbuk," *New York Times* (November 1, 1959): X3; Dan Sullivan, "Theater: 'The Tenth Man' Is Revived," *New York Times* (November 9, 1967): 54; John S. Radosta, "After 39 Years—a Hit," *New York Times* (September 18, 1960): X5; "London Critics Split on 'The Tenth Man,'" *New York Times* (April 14, 1961): 23.

31. David Zurawik, *The Jews of Prime Time* (Hanover, NH: University Press of New England / Brandeis University Press, 2003), 17–28; Myrna Hant, "Molly Goldberg: A 1950s Icon," *Women in Judaism* 5 (Spring 2008), http://wjudaism.library.utoronto.ca/index.php/wjudaism/article/view/3532/1587. See also Jonathan Pearl and Judith Pearl, *The Chosen Image: Television's Portrayal of Jewish Themes and Characters* (Jefferson, NC: McFarland, 1999).

32. Bell, "The Three Faces of New York," 226.

33. Burton Bernstein and Barbara B. Haws, *Leonard Bernstein: American Original* (New York: HarperCollins, 2008), 1–11.

34. Ibid., 88–97; Paul Myers, *Leonard Bernstein* (London: Phaidon, 1998), 39–40 109, 114.

35. Myers, *Leonard Bernstein*, 44. See also Lewis Nichols, "The Play," *New York Times* (December 29, 1944): 11.

36. Arthur Laurents, *Original Story By: A Memoir of Broadway and Hollywood* (New York: Knopf, 2001), 329–40; Irene G. Dash, *Shakespeare and the American Musical* (Bloomington: Indiana University Press, 2010), 80–82, 85–87; see also Bernstein and Haws, *Leonard Bernstein*, 6–7.

37. Joshua M. Zeitz, *White Ethnic New York: Jews, Catholics, and the Shaping of Postwar Politics* (Chapel Hill: University of North Carolina Press, 2007), 16.

38. Bureau of Community Statistical Services Research Department, Community Council of Greater New York, *Bronx Communities: Population Characteristics and Neighborhood Social Resources*, typescript (New York: Community Council of Greater New York, 1962), 45–46, 69, 70. See also Horowitz and Kaplan, *The Jewish Population of the New York Area*, 175, 217, 229, 233, 235; Mark Naison, "Crown Heights in the 1950s," in *Jews of Brooklyn*, ed. Ilana Abramovitch and Seán Galvin, 143–52 (Hanover, NH: University Press of New England /Brandeis University Press, 2002).

39. Edgar M. Hoover, *Anatomy of a Metropolis: The Changing Distribution of People and Jobs within the New York Metropolitan Region* (Cambridge: Harvard University Press,

1959), 16; Robert Caro, *The Power Broker: Robert Moses and the Fall of New York* (New York: Knopf, 1974), 851–52; Joshua B. Freeman, *Working-Class New York: Life and Labor since World War II* (New York: New Press, 2000), 35, 37; Naison, "Crown Heights in the 1950s," 144; Ken Emerson, *Always Magic in the Air: The Bomp and Brilliance of the Brill Building Era* (New York: Viking, 2005), 84–85.

40. Welles, "The Jewish Élan," 139; Zeitz, *White Ethnic New York*, 23, 32–35, 236–37.

41. Ira Rosenwaike, *Population History of New York City* (Syracuse, NY: Syracuse University Press, 1972), 159; William B. Helmreich, *Against All Odds: Holocaust Survivors and the Successful Lives They Made in America* (New York: Simon and Schuster, 1992), 46–48.

42. United States Displaced Persons Commission, *Memo to America: The DP Story: The Final Report of the United States Displaced Persons Commission* (Washington, DC: U.S. Government Printing Office, 1952), 27, 38–39. I am grateful to Professor William B. Helmreich for directing me to this source. See also Rosenwaike, *Population History of New York City*, 159.

43. Victor D. Sanua, "A Study of the Adjustment of Sephardi Jews in the New York Metropolitan Area," *Jewish Journal of Sociology* 9, no. 1 (June 1967): 26–27. See also Joseph A. D. Sutton, *Magic Carpet: Aleppo-in-Flatbush: The Story of a Unique Ethnic Jewish Community* (New York: Thayer-Jacobi, 1979), 4.

44. On the adjustment patterns of Jews from Germany after World War II, see Joseph Berger, *Displaced Persons: Growing Up American after the Holocaust* (New York: Washington Square Press, 2002).

45. George Kranzler, *Williamsburg: A Jewish Community in Transition* (New York: Feldheim, 1961), 40–43; Jerome R. Mintz, *Hasidic People: A Place in the New World* (Cambridge: Harvard University Press, 1992), 30.

46. Egon Mayer, *From Suburb to Shtetl: The Jews of Boro Park* (Philadelphia: Temple University Press, 1979), 31; Kranzler, *Williamsburg*, 40–43.

47. On the Lubavitcher *farbrengen*, see Mintz, *Hasidic People*, 48–50, 97.

■ **NOTES TO CHAPTER 5**

1. Robert A. Caro, *The Power Broker: Robert Moses and the Fall of New York* (New York: Knopf, 1974), 854.

2. Ibid., 859–77. For an alternative, revisionist view of Moses's activity, in response largely to Caro's work, see Hilary Ballon and Kenneth T. Jackson, eds., *Robert Moses and the Modern City: The Transformation of New York* (New York: Norton, 2007).

3. Caro, *Power Broker*, 867, 888. C. Morris Horowitz and Lawrence J. Kaplan, *The Jewish Population of the New York Area, 1900–1975* (New York: Federation of Jewish Philanthropies of New York, 1959), 197. On Fieldston anti-Semitism, see Deborah Dash Moore, *At Home in America: Second Generation New York Jews* (New York: Columbia University Press, 1981), 38. See also George Dugan, "Jews to Worship in a Parish House," *New York Times* (October 11, 1952): 21.

4. Caro, *Power Broker*, 850–93.

5. Gerald Sorin, *The Nurturing Neighborhood: The Brownsville Boys Club and Jewish Community in Urban America, 1940–1990* (New York: NYU Press, 1990), 165; Carole Bell

Ford, *The Girls: Jewish Women of Brownsville, Brooklyn, 1940–1995* (Albany: SUNY Press, 2000), 4, 90–91, 94–96, 104; see also Ford, "Nice Jewish Girls: Growing Up in Brownsville, 1930s–1950s," in *Jews of Brooklyn*, ed. Ilana Abramovitch and Seán Galvin, 129–36 (Hanover, NH: University Press of New England /Brandeis University Press, 2002), 133.

6. Horowitz and Kaplan, *The Jewish Population of the New York Area*, 239.

7. Joshua M. Zeitz, *White Ethnic New York: Jews, Catholics, and the Shaping of Postwar Politics* (Chapel Hill: University of North Carolina Press, 2007), 149, 152; Sorin, *The Nurturing Neighborhood*, 162; Mark Naison, "Crown Heights in the 1950s," in Abramovitch and Galvin, *Jews of Brooklyn*, 145.

8. Wendell E. Pritchett, "From One Ghetto to Another: Blacks, Jews and Public Housing in Brownsville, Brooklyn, 1945–1970" (Ph.D. diss. University of Pennsylvania, 1997), 164.

9. Ibid., 23, 132–33.

10. Joshua B. Freeman, *Working-Class New York: Life and Labor since World War II* (New York: New Press, 2000), 107, 117–18; Zeitz, *White Ethnic New York*, 150–51.

11. Pritchett, "From One Ghetto to Another," 175–77.

12. Freeman, *Working-Class New York*, 183–84.

13. Pritchett, "From One Ghetto to Another," 194; Jerome R. Mintz, *Hasidic People: A Place in the New World* (Cambridge: Harvard University Press, 1992), 141, 143; Daniel A. Wishnoff, "The Tolerance Point: Race, Public Housing and the Forest Hills Controversy, 1945–1975" (Ph.D. diss., City University of New York, 2005), 177; Eli Lederhendler, *New York Jews and the Decline of Urban Ethnicity, 1950–1970* (Syracuse, NY: Syracuse University Press, 2001), 165.

14. Sam Welles, "The Jewish Élan," *Fortune* (February 1960): 160.

15. Lederhendler, *New York Jews and the Decline of Urban Ethnicity*, 127–29.

16. Joseph P. Fried, "City Charges Bias at Three Projects," *New York Times* (May 28, 1968): 27; "Changes in Parkchester Bring a Fear Oasis May Go," *New York Times* (December 29, 1968): 56.

17. Paul L. Montgomery and Francis X. Clines, "Thousands Riot in Harlem Area; Scores Hurt," *New York Times* (July 19, 1964): 1; Junius Griffin, "Harlem Businessmen Put Riot Losses at $50,000," *New York Times* (July 21, 1964): 22; "Store Ransacked in Riot Sues City," *New York Times* (July 25, 1964): 8.

18. "The Root of the Trouble," *New York Times* (July 23, 1964): 26; Layhmond Robinson, "Negroes View of Plight Examined in Survey Here," *New York Times* (July 27, 1964): 1; Fred Powerledge, "Negro Riots Reflect Deep-Seated Grievances," *New York Times* (August 2, 1964): 133; Lenora E. Berson, *The Negroes and the Jews* (New York: Random House, 1971), 338–40. Interestingly, historical works that document the evolution of tensions between blacks and Jews also have not found explicit anti-Semitism in the 1964 riots. See, as an example, Murray Friedman, *What Went Wrong? The Creation and Collapse of the Black-Jewish Alliance* (New York: Free Press, 1995), 214, which notes that "the degree of anti-Semitism involved was not at all clear." Many other works do not mention the 1964 outbreak at all.

19. *Jewish Telegraphic Agency Daily News Bulletin* (July 23, 1964): 1; *Jewish Press* (July 3, 1964): 1; (July 10, 1964): 1; (July 31, 1964): 1.

20. Jerald E. Podair, *The Strike That Changed New York: Blacks, Whites and the Ocean Hill–Brownsville Crisis* (New Haven: Yale University Press, 2002), 38, 72, 77–78.

21. Cheryl Lynn Greenberg, *Troubling the Waters: Black-Jewish Relations in the American Century* (Princeton: Princeton University Press, 2006), 230.

22. Jonathan Kaufman, *Broken Alliance: The Turbulent Times between Blacks and Jews in America* (New York: Scribner, 1988), 142–43, 148–49. See also Greenberg, *Troubling the Waters*, 230; Friedman, *What Went Wrong?*, 260; Podair, *The Strike That Changed New York*, 2; Zeitz, *White Ethnic New York*, 161–63.

23. On the chronology of the three-stage strike and the text of the unsigned letter, see Podair, *The Strike That Changed New York*, 115–24. On the text of the WBAI poem and the museum essay, see Robert G. Weisbord and Arthur Stein, *Bittersweet Encounter: The Afro-American and the American Jew* (Westport, CT: Negro Universities Press, 1970), 175–78.

24. On the connection between local black problems with Jews and the international scene, see Zeitz, *White Ethnic New York*, 64–66. On the relationship between the 1967 Israeli victory and New York Jewish assertiveness, see Freeman, *Working-Class New York*, 223–34. On public opinion polls of black attitudes, see ibid., 165–66.

25. On the history of the Teachers Union and its relationship with the United Federation of Teachers, see Celia Lewis Zitron, *The New York City Teachers Union 1916–1964: A Story of Educational and Social Commitment* (New York: Humanities Press, 1968), 45–52; and Podair, *The Strike That Changed New York*, 142. See also Ralph Blumenthal, "When Suspicion of Teachers Ran Unchecked in New York," *New York Times* (June 16, 2009): 15–16.

26. On the recruitment of these replacement teachers, many of whom were young Jews, see Freeman, *Working-Class New York*, 221. For the opinions of a replacement teacher and his comparisons of his colleagues with the older teachers, see a personal account of life in a Brooklyn school: Charles S. Isaacs, "A J.H.S. 271 Teacher Tells It Like He Sees It," *New York Times Magazine* (November 24, 1968), http://query.nytimes.com/mem/archive/pdf?res=F10C13F93C5A14728FDDAD0A94D9415B888AF1D3. On the return of Jewish teachers to their old neighborhood to teach minority youngsters, see Zeitz, *White Ethnic New York*, 167. For a sense among some older women teachers of not being appreciated for their efforts, see Ruth Jacknow Markowitz, *My Daughter, the Teacher: Jewish Teachers in the New York City Schools* (New Brunswick: Rutgers University Press, 1993), 171.

27. Greenberg, *Troubling the Waters*, 231; Friedman, *What Went Wrong?*, 261; Weisbord and Stein, *Bittersweet Encounter*, 165, 177–78.

28. On the founding of the Jewish Defense League, its connection to the teachers' strike, and its early activities during the time of these difficulties, see Kaufman, *Broken Alliance*, 157–58; Weisbord and Stein, *Bittersweet Encounter*, 201–4; Lederhendler, *New York Jews and the Decline of Urban Ethnicity*, 192–94.

29. Tom Wolfe, "Radical Chic: That Party at Lenny's," *New York Magazine* (June 8, 1970): 53.

30. Greenberg, *Troubling the Waters*, 231; Jonathan Rieder, *Canarsie: The Jews and Italians of Brooklyn against Liberalism* (Cambridge: Harvard University Press, 1985), 73, discussed in Podair, *The Strike That Changed New York*, 144.

31. Louis Harris and Bert E. Swanson, *Black-Jewish Relations in New York City* (New York: Praeger, 1970), 18–22, 30, 77, 105–6, 129.

32. Ibid., 19–20, 36–37, 60–61, 105–6.

33. Ibid., 18, 61, 93, 105, 129.

34. Ibid., 93.

35. Zeitz, *White Ethnic New York*, 174–76; Chris McNickle, *To Be Mayor of New York: Ethnic Politics in the City* (New York: Columbia University Press, 1993), 205–8; Charles Brecher and Raymond D. Horton, with Robert A. Cropf and Dean Michael Mead, *Power Failure: New York City Politics and Policy since 1960* (New York: Oxford University Press, 1993), 83–86.

36. Peter Kihss, "How Voter Swings Elected Lindsay," *New York Times* (November 4, 1965): 1, 50.

37. Zeitz, *White Ethnic New York*, 176–87; Brecher et al., *Power Failure*, 86–91; Nathan Glazer and Daniel Patrick Moynihan, *Beyond the Melting Pot: The Negroes, Puerto Ricans, Jews, Italians, and Irish of New York City*, 2nd ed. (Cambridge: MIT Press, 1970), xxvii.

38. Peter Kihss, "Poor and Rich, Not Middle-Class the Key to Lindsay Re-election," *New York Times* (November 6, 1969): 37.

39. Zeitz, *White Ethnic New York*, 190–92; Wishnoff, "The Tolerance Point," 137–43, 181, 184, 188, 225.

40. Text of Bokser's remarks, from his papers at the Jewish Theological Seminary, are quoted in Wishnoff, "The Tolerance Point," 190.

41. *New York Times*, November 25, 1971, and Walter Goodman, "Rabbi Kahane Says: 'I'd Love to See the JDL Fold Up, but . . . ,'" *New York Times*, November 21, 1971, both quoted in Wishnoff, "The Tolerance Point," 231–32.

42. Quoted in Zeitz, *White Ethnic New York*, 193.

43. Ibid., 191–92.

■ NOTES TO CHAPTER 6

1. For an extensive examination of Cosell's statement in the context of the city in decline, using many sports metaphors, see Jonathan Mahler, *Ladies and Gentlemen, the Bronx Is Burning: 1977, Baseball, Politics, and the Battle for the Soul of a City* (New York: Farrar, Straus and Giroux, 2005). This saga has also been the foreground to a movie of the same name on 1977 New York City's struggles. See also Constance Rosenblum, *Boulevard of Dreams: Heady Times, Heartbreak, and Hope along the Grand Concourse in the Bronx* (New York: NYU Press, 2009), which recounts Cosell's remark and the television visual as a "terrifying image of devastation" (183).

2. Lee Dembart, "Carter Takes a 'Sobering' Trip to South Bronx," *New York Times*

(October 6, 1977): A1, B16; James M. Naughton, "Ford Holds Rockefeller Blameless for Troubles," *New York Times* (October 31, 1975): 12.

3. Charles Brecher and Raymond D. Horton, with Robert A. Cropf and Dean Michael Mead, *Power Failure: New York City Politics and Policy since 1960* (New York: Oxford University Press, 1993), 91–94.

4. Robert E. Meyer, "How Government Helped Ruin the South Bronx," *Fortune* (November 1975): 143–45; Matthew P. Drennan, "The Decline and Rise of the New York Economy," in *Dual City: Restructuring New York*, ed. John Hull Mollenkopf and Manuel Castells, 29–43 (New York: Russell Sage Foundation, 1991), 29–33. See also Thomas Bailey and Roger Waldinger, "The Changing Ethnic/Racial Division of Labor," in ibid., 43; Joshua B. Freeman, *Working-Class New York: Life and Labor since World War II* (New York: New Press, 2000), 273.

5. Freeman, *Working-Class New York*, 257–70. See also Peter Blake, "How to Solve the Housing Crisis (and Everything Else)," *New York* (January 1, 1970): 56.

6. Freeman, *Working-Class New York*, 271, 273; Bailey and Waldinger, "The Changing Ethnic/Racial Division of Labor," 47, 55; Samuel Kaplan, "The Bronx Arrangement," *New York* (December 14, 1970): 10.

7. Meyer, "How Government Helped Ruin the South Bronx," 143; Philip Siekman, "The Rent Control Trap," *Fortune* (February 1960): 123.

8. On the 1971 law and its implications, see Rosenblum, *Boulevard of Dreams*, 181; on "redlining," see Freeman, *Working-Class New York*, 275.

9. Freeman, *Working-Class New York*, 274–75.

10. Kaplan, "The Bronx Arrangement," 10; Meyer, "How Government Helped Ruin the South Bronx," 145; Rosenblum, *Boulevard of Dreams*, 181–83, 189, 203–5, Freeman, *Working-Class New York*, 281.

11. Fred Massarik, "Basic Characteristics of the Greater New York Jewish Population," *American Jewish Year Book* (1976): 239, 242; Steven M. Cohen and Paul Ritterband, "The Social Characteristics of the New York Jewish Community, 1981," *American Jewish Year Book* 84 (1984): 129, 140; Frederick M. Binder and David M. Reimers, *All the Nations under Heaven: An Ethnic and Racial History of New York City* (New York: Columbia University Press, 1995), 240–42. See also Eleanor Blau, "Population Shift Beset Jewish Community Here," *New York Times* (August 21, 1975): 73; and James Feron, "Tremont Temple Quits the Bronx," *New York Times* (December 18, 1976): 27.

12. Center for New York City Affairs, New School for Social Research, *New York's Jewish Poor and Jewish Working Class: Economic Status and Social Needs*, typescript (New York: Federation of Jewish Philanthropies, 1972), 10; interview with Berl Steinberg (November 11, 2008; notes in possession of the author); Edward C. Burks, "Middle Class Still Leaving City," *New York Times* (May 29, 1973): 22. District 10 is a mélange of Bronx communities that included Tremont, the Grand Concourse, and the virtually all-white Riverdale.

13. Fran Markowitz, *A Community in Spite of Itself: Soviet Jewish Émigrés in New York* (Washington, DC: Smithsonian Institution Press, 1993), 1; Aviva Ben-Ur, *Sephardic Jews*

in America: A Diasporic History (New York: NYU Press, 2009), 196, 220n. 80; Moshe Shokeid, *Children of Circumstances: Israeli Emigrants in New York* (Ithaca: Cornell University Press, 1988), 20–21, 20. In the case of the Israelis in New York, apparently 60 percent of them settled in Brooklyn, and almost all of the rest chose Queens. See also Binder and Reimers, *All the Nations under Heaven*, 240–42.

14. Jonathan Rieder, *Canarsie: The Jews and Italians of Brooklyn against Liberalism* (Cambridge: Harvard University Press, 1985), 16, 19–20, 26, 45, 65, 69–71, 80, 110–11, 128, 129, 184.

15. Ibid., 110–111, 114, 172–73.

16. Ibid., 193–98.

17. Ibid., 207–14.

18. Allan M. Siegal, "Rent Is Primary Issue for Co-op City," *New York Times* (September 6, 1974): 73; James F. Clarity, "Co-op City, Home to 40,000 Is Given Tempered Praise," *New York Times* (May 27, 1971): 41; Rita Reif, "Some Subsidized Co-ops Far from Pioneers' Ideal," *New York Times* (January 25, 1976): 2, 6; interview with Allegra and Gary Gordon (August 27, 2009; tape recording in possession of the author); Murray Schumach, "Co-op City: A Symptom of Mitchell-Lama Ills," *New York Times* (June 18, 1975): 86; Samuel G. Freedman, "Co-op City: A Refuge in Transition," *New York Times* (June 25, 1986): B1; Don Terry, "Co-op City: A Haven Marred as Drugs Slip In," *New York Times* (August 10, 1989): B1.

19. Sydney Schwartz, "Maintaining the Minyan: The Struggle of a Storefront Synagogue" (M.A. essay, Columbia University School of Journalism, 2005), 8, 9, 23.

20. Robert E. Thompson, "As Change Intrudes, the Concourse Sells," *New York Times* (August 13, 1972): R1; Kaplan, "The Bronx Arrangement," 10; Jack Luria, "A Pox on You, Riverdale," *New York Times* (June 21, 1972): 43. See also, for Riverdale population statistics for 1981, United Jewish Appeal–Federation of Jewish Philanthropies, *Greater New York Jewish Population Study* (New York: UJA-Federation, 1981), typescript report maintained online at the Mandell L. Berman Institute North American Jewish Data Bank, University of Connecticut.

21. For Riverdale population statistics as of 1991, see United Jewish Appeal–Federation of Jewish Philanthropies, *The New York Jewish Population Study: Profiles of Counties, Boroughs and Neighborhoods* (New York: UJA-Federation, 1995), typescript report maintained online at the Mandell L. Berman Institute North American Jewish Data Bank, University of Connecticut, 3,12, 15; Schumach, "Co-op City: A Symptom of Mitchell-Lama Ills," 86; Reif, "Some Subsidized Co-ops Far from Pioneers' Ideal," 2; Joseph P. Fried, "Compromise Ends Co-op Strike," *New York Times* (June 30, 1976): B1; Francis X. Clines, "Grass Roots in Concrete," *New York Times* (October 2, 1976): S23; Leslie Maitland, "Co-op City: Paradise or Paradise Lost?," *New York Times* (January 8, 1979): B4. See also Freeman, *Working-Class New York*, 122.

22. Freedman, "Co-op City: A Refuge in Transition," B1; David Bird, "Tentative Agreement Is Negotiated by State on Co-op Repairs," *New York Times* (May 13, 1979): 17; Susan Chira, "Co-op City: Life Begins to Improve," *New York Times* (May 8, 1982): 27; Ari I. Goldman, "At Co-op City, Worship in Transition," *New York Times* (May 31, 1989):

B2; Terry, "Co-op City: A Haven Marred as Drugs Slip In," B1. See also Allegra and Gary Gordon interview.

23. Peter L. Berger, "In Praise of New York: A Semi-Secular Homily," *Commentary* (February 1977): 61–62; Andrew Hacker, "The City's Comings, Goings," *New York Times* (December 2, 1973): 26; editorial, "Victims of Urban Revival," *New York Times* (November 18, 1978): 20; Blake Fleetwood, "The New Elite and an Urban Renaissance," *New York Times* (January 14, 1979): SM26, 34.

24. On the assumed early periodization for Jews leaving the labor force by the 1920s, see Will Herberg, "The Jewish Labor Movement in the United States," *American Jewish Yearbook* (1952): 28.

25. Center for New York City Affairs, *New York's Jewish Poor*, 26–27, 45, 50, 53, 54, 59, 60. See also Peter Kihss, "Job Shift Urged on Young Jews," *New York Times* (January 25, 1972): 27.

26. Cohen and Ritterband, "The Social Characteristics of the New York Area Jewish Community," 132, 156.

27. These figures on Jewish enrollment patterns are but rough estimates derived from self-reporting from Hillel—Jewish student life associations—on campuses. See such periodic reports in B'nai B'rith Hillel Foundations, *Jewish Life on Campus* (Washington, DC: B'nai B'rith Hillel Foundations, 1968–69, 1978–79, 1982–83).

28. On the background of campus radicals in the 1960s, see Kenneth Keniston, *Young Radicals: Notes on Committed Youth* (New York: Harcourt, Brace and World, 1968), 14, 311; Nathan Glazer, "The Jewish Role in Student Activism," *Fortune* (January 1969): 112; Vincent Cannato, *The Ungovernable City: John Lindsay and His Struggle to Save New York* (New York: Basic Books, 2001), 246. See also Bernard Weinraub, "Student Radicals Losing Ground at City College," *New York Times* (December 5, 1968): 76.

29. See B'nai B'rith Hillel Foundations, *Jewish Life on Campus* (1968–89, 1978–79, 1982–83), for statistics on these various schools. On the ethnic and racial changes at the City University, see Freeman, *Working-Class New York*, 331–33. For internal criticism at CCNY about the plan, see Theodore L. Gross, "How to Kill a College: The Private Papers of a College Dean," *Saturday Review* (February 4, 1978): 13–18, cited in Sherry Gorelick, *City College and the Jewish Poor: Education in New York, 1880–1924* (New Brunswick: Rutgers University Press, 1981), 194, 231.

30. Paul Ritterband and Steven M. Cohen, "The Social Characteristics of the New York Area Jewish Community," typescript report dated October 1982, on file in the Brandeis University library, II-6, V-1, V-2.

31. Mark Effron, "It Wasn't Supposed to Happen This Way" (unpublished manuscript, Columbia University School of Journalism, 1973), cited in Thomas J. Cottle, *Hidden Survivors: Portraits of Poor Jews in America* (Englewood Cliffs, NJ: Prentice-Hall, 1980), 5; Naomi B. Levine and Martin Hochbaum, introduction to *Poor Jews: An American Awakening*, ed. Naomi B. Levine and Martin Hochbaum (New Brunswick, NJ: Transaction Books, 1974), 2–3; Anne G. Wolfe, "The Invisible Jewish Poor," *Journal of Jewish Communal Service* 48 (Spring 1972): 259–65. See also Michael Harrington, *The Other America* (New York: Macmillan, 1962), 3.

32. Ann G. Wolf, "The Invisible Jewish Poor," in Levine and Hochbaum, *Poor Jews*, 34; Center for New York City Affairs, *New York's Jewish Poor*, 16, 29. See also Robert McG. Thomas Jr., "Elderly Cling to Old Neighborhoods Despite Growing Fear of Criminals," *New York Times* (June 17, 1974): 20; Rosenblum, *Boulevard of Dreams*, 185.

33. Jack Kugelmass, *The Miracle of Intervale Avenue: The Story of a Jewish Congregation in the South Bronx* (New York: Columbia University Press, 1996), 7, 11, 17–18, 212–13.

34. Jerome R. Mintz, *Hasidic People: A Place in the New World* (Cambridge: Harvard University Press, 1992), 36–38, 52, 189–90, 391; Dorothy Rabinowitz, "Blacks, Jews, and New York Politics," *Commentary* (November 1978): 45; Egon Mayer, *From Suburb to Shtetl: The Jews of Boro Park* (Philadelphia: Temple University Press, 1979), 34–36. See also Mintz, "Ethnic Activism: The Hasidic Example," in *Dimensions of Orthodox Judaism*, ed. Reuven P. Bulka, 225–41 (New York: KTAV, 1983), 232.

35. Center for New York City Affairs, *New York's Jewish Poor*, 18; Wolfe, "The Invisible Jewish Poor," 34; Mintz, *Hasidic People*, 365.

36. Phyllis Franck, "The Hasidic Poor in New York City," in Levine and Hochbaum, *Poor Jews*, 60–61; Mintz, *Hasidic People*, 33.

37. Joseph A. D. Sutton, *Magic Carpet: Aleppo-in-Flatbush: The Story of a Unique Ethnic Jewish Community* (New York: Thayer-Jacobi, 1979), 62, 66–67, 96–102; Walter P. Zenner, *A Global Community: The Jews from Aleppo, Syria* (Detroit: Wayne State University Press, 2000), 138–41, 156, 162–66. See also Barry Meir, "Crazy Eddie's Insane Odyssey," *New York Times* (July 19, 1992): F1.

38. Chris McNickle, *To Be Mayor of the City of New York: Ethnic Politics in the City* (New York: Columbia University Press, 1993), 272–75.

39. Maureen Dowd, "Poll Finds New Yorkers' Pessimism Subsides," *New York Times* (January 19, 1985): 1.

40. Drennan, "The Decline and Rise of the New York Economy," 34–37; see also John Hull Mollenkopf, *A Phoenix in the Ashes: The Rise and Fall of the Koch Coalition in New York City Politics* (Princeton: Princeton University Press, 1992), 46–47.

41. Interview with David Fox (September 30, 2009). On the history of Skadden as a work-ethic firm and its success under Flom in the hostile-takeover realm, see Malcolm Gladwell, *Outliers: The Study of Success* (New York: Little, Brown, 2008), 118–28.

42. Leslie Bennetts, "If You're Thinking of Living in Chelsea," *New York Times* (May 2, 1982): R9; Jan Morris, "The Future Looks Familiar," *New York Times* (April 26, 1987): SMA16; Freedman, "Real-Estate Boom Cited as Peril to the City," *New York Times* (April 15, 1986): C13.

43. William J. Palmer, *The Films of the Eighties: A Social History* (Carbondale: Southern Illinois University Press, 1993), 284–85; Leslie Bennetts, "Woody Allen's Selective Vision of New York," *New York Times* (May 7, 1986): C1; Vincent Canby, "Hannah and Her Sisters," *New York Times* (February 7, 1986); Graham McCann, *Woody Allen: New Yorker* (Cambridge, UK: Polity, 1990), 14, 27, 35–36.

44. On Boesky's Jewish philanthropic endeavors before and after his fall, see Joseph Berger, "For Charities, a Benefactor," *New York Times* (November 22, 1986): 41; Ari L.

Goldman, "Boesky Studying Hebrew and Talmud at Seminary," *New York Times* (July 23, 1987): B3.

45. UJA-Federation, *Greater New York Population Study, 1981,* 9, 10, 40. This study does not enumerate and analyze data on a neighborhood basis. Rather, it offers borough-wide statistics. However, assuming that proportions in each category were reduced by the presence of older, married, and less affluent individuals who lived in places such as the Lower East Side, it makes the youth and upscale nature of the rest of the borough even greater. The same assumptions underlie the data on synagogue attendance that will be discussed presently.

46. Ibid., 29.

47. Jeffrey S. Gurock, "The Late Friday Night Orthodox Services: An Exercise in Religious Accommodation," *Jewish Social Studies* 12 (Spring–Summer 2006): 149.

48. UJA-Federation, *The New York Jewish Population Study,* 69, 77, 87. See also United Jewish Appeal–Federation of Jewish Philanthropies, *The 1991 New York Jewish Population Study* (New York: UJA-Federation, 1993), xviii.

49. Moshe Shokeid, *A Gay Synagogue in New York* (New York: Columbia University Press, 1995), 16, 48, 63–64, 79, 81.

50. On the numbers and status of the Jewish poor elderly from 1981 to 1991, see UJA-Federation, *Greater New York Population Study, 1981,* 10, 36, 37, 40; and UJA-Federation, *The New York Jewish Population Study,* 1, 9, 10. On the numbers of elderly assisted and the greater concern with the problems of those who were poor, see UJA-Federation, *The 1991 New York Jewish Population Study,* xvi, 116–17.

51. Kugelmass, *The Miracle of Intervale Avenue,* 221–24, 234–35, 262.

52. UJA-Federation, *The 1991 New York Jewish Population Study,* xvi; UJA-Federation, *The New York Jewish Population Study,* 37.

53. Brecher et al., *Power Failure,* 99–101.

54. McNickle, *To Be Mayor of the City of New York,* 281–87, Brecher et al., *Power Failure,* 101–3.

55. McNickle, *To Be Mayor of the City of New York,* 287–92. See also, for an analysis of the 1989 mayoral campaigns, Mollenkopf, *A Phoenix in the Ashes,* 165–85.

56. Brecher et al., *Power Failure,* 105.

57. McNickle, *To Be Mayor of the City of New York,* 292–95.

58. Celestine Bohlen, "Dinkins and Koch Vie for Jews' Votes," *New York Times* (September 10, 1989): 44.

59. Frank Lynn, "2 Nominees Clash in Race for Mayor with Harsh Words," *New York Times* (September 14, 1989): A1.

60. John Kifner, "The Mayor-Elect Inspires Pride, but It's Hardly Universal," *New York Times* (November 9, 1989): B1; Sam Roberts, "Almost Lost at the Wire," *New York Times* (November 9, 1989): A1.

61. Richard Levine, "Koch Confers with Dinkins on Transition," *New York Times* (November 9, 1989): A1. See also Mollenkopf, *A Phoenix in the Ashes,* 184; and McNickle, *To Be Mayor of the City of New York,* 313.

62. Saskia Sassen, *The Global City: New York, London, Tokyo* (Princeton: Princeton University Press, 1991), 289n. 8.

63. The description and discussion of events in Crown Heights and the quotations cited in the remainder of the chapter are based on both historian Edward S. Shapiro's and anthropologist Henry Goldschmidt's studies of the event and its ramifications. Edward S. Shapiro, *Crown Heights: Blacks, Jews, and the 1991 Brooklyn Riot* (Hanover, NH: University Press of New England / Brandeis University Press, 2006), especially xi–xvi, 5–6, 27, 43, 47–48, 57–62, 75–77, 83–87, 108, 112, 137n. 98; Henry Goldschmidt, *Race and Religion among the Chosen People of Crown Heights* (New Brunswick: Rutgers University Press, 2006), especially 38–39, 40, 47, 48–50, 59, 61–71.

■ **NOTES TO CHAPTER 7**

1. Carey Winfrey, "In Search of Bella Abzug," *New York Times* (August 21, 1977): 55, 60–61.

2. Amy Swerdlow, *Women Strike for Peace: Traditional Motherhood and Radical Politics in the 1960s* (Chicago: University of Chicago Press, 1993), 4, 54, 146; Joyce Antler, *The Journey Home: Jewish Women and the American Century* (New York: Free Press, 1997), 271–74.

3. Winfrey, "In Search of Bella Abzug," 60–61.

4. Annelise Orleck, *Common Sense and a Little Fire: Women and Working Class Politics, 1900–1965* (Chapel Hill: University of North Carolina Press, 1995), 87–91.

5. On the differing visions of Friedan's road to feminism and her life after the publication of her book, see Daniel Horowitz, *Betty Friedan and the Making of the Feminine Mystique: The American Left, the Cold War, and Modern Feminism* (Amherst: University of Massachusetts Press, 1998), 2–5, 224–27. See also Friedan's memoir, *Life So Far* (New York: Simon and Schuster, 2000), 131–41, 143–47.

6. There is a difference of opinion among biographers of Steinem over the extent of Jewishness of the feminist beyond her identification with the ancestral group because of anti-Semitism. Letty Cottin Pogrebin has accorded Steinem the designation of Jew less because of her father's background and more because of her sense of self "as an outsider [who] sees Jews as the quintessential out-group and because she feels drawn to spiritual and social justice agenda of Jewish feminism." However, Caroline Heilbrun has quoted Steinem as saying, "I don't believe in either religion," Judaism or Christianity. "When I'm around Jews who feel there's something good about being exclusively Jewish, I emphasize the non-Jewish side of the family. When I'm around Protestants who think there is something good about being Protestant, then I emphasize the Jewish side." See Letty Cottin Pogrebin, "Gloria Steinem," in *Jewish Women in America: An Historical Encyclopedia*, vol. 2, ed. Paula E. Hyman and Deborah Dash Moore (New York: Routledge, 1997), 1319–23, which contains Pogrebin's characterization and a discussion of Steinem's larger career; and Carolyn G. Heilbrun, *The Education of a Woman: The Life of Gloria Steinem* (New York: Dial, 1995), 49. See also Horowitz, *Betty Friedan*, 229; and Marcia Cohen, *The Sisterhood* (New York: Fawcett Columbine, 1988), 41–42. On disagreements among these leaders, see Antler, *The Journey Home*, 276.

7. Letty Cottin Pogrebin, *Deborah, Golda, and Me* (New York: Crown, 1991), 154–64. See also Friedan, *Life So Far*, 291–94.

8. Paula E. Hyman, "Jewish Feminism Faces the American Women's Movement: Convergence and Divergence," in *American Jewish Women's History: A Reader*, ed. Pamela S. Nadell, 297–312 (New York: NYU Press, 2003), 300; Alan Silverstein, "The Evolution of Ezrat Nashim," *Conservative Judaism* 3, no. 1 (Fall 1975): 43.

9. Silverstein, "The Evolution of Ezrat Nashim," 43–44. See also Stephen C. Lerner, "The Havurot," *Conservative Judaism* 24, no. 3 (Spring 1970): 2–15.

10. Reena Sigman Friedman, "The Jewish Feminist Movement," in *Jewish American Voluntary Organizations*, ed. Michael N. Dobkowski (Westport, CT: Greenwood, 1986), 575–81.

11. Susan Dworkin, "Henrietta Szold," *Response* 18 (Summer 1973): 39–41.

12. Ibid., 43–45.

13. Pamela S. Nadell, "A Bright New Constellation: Feminism and American Judaism," in *The Columbia History of Jews and Judaism in America*, ed. Marc Lee Raphael, 385–405 (New York: Columbia University Press, 2008), 387–88.

14. For a comprehensive history of the long road toward women's ordination among Reform Jews, see Pamela S. Nadell, *Women Who Would Be Rabbis: A History of Women's Ordination, 1889–1985* (Boston: Beacon, 1998), especially 61–117.

15. Nadell, "A Bright New Constellation," 393–94. On Ezrat Nashim's advocacy at JTS and reaction to the affirmative vote, see Beth S. Wenger, "The Politics of Women's Ordination: Jewish Law, Institutional Power, and the Debate over Women in the Rabbinate," in *Tradition Renewed: A History of the Jewish Theological Seminary of America*, vol. 2, ed. Jack Wertheimer, 483–524 (New York: Jewish Theological Seminary of America, 1997), 514–15.

16. Nadell, "A Bright New Constellation," 391; Antler, *The Journey Home*, 268–69.

17. Sylvia Barack Fishman, *A Breath of Life: Feminism in the American Jewish Community* (New York: Free Press, 1993), 2; Antler, *The Journey Home*, 266–67; Hyman, "Jewish Feminism," 308. See also Pogrebin, *Deborah, Golda, and Me*, especially 42, 48–52, 235.

18. Blu Greenberg, *On Women in Judaism: A View from Tradition* (Philadelphia: Jewish Publication Society of America, 1994), 21–25, 27, 30–33, 47, 92–97, 135.

19. On Elena Kagan's bat mitzvah, see Stewart Ain, "A Pioneer at Age 12," *Jewish Week* (May 14, 2010): 11; Meira Beinstock, "Kagan Showed Great Wisdom in Her Youth," *Jerusalem Post* (June 29, 2010): 6.

20. For a full consideration of women's activities of these sorts within Orthodoxy, see Jeffrey S. Gurock, *Orthodox Jews in America* (Bloomington: Indiana University Press, 2009), 274–80. A number of dates have been offered for the beginnings of the Simchat Torah women's activity at Lincoln Square. My use of the date in 1972 relies on a study that interviewed women who assert that they were there at that moment. An alternate date is 1974, also basically concomitant with Greenberg's emergence. See Ailene Cohen-Nusbacher, "Efforts at Change in a Traditional Denomination: The Case of Orthodox Women's Prayer Groups," *Nashim* 2 (Spring 1999): 112n. 7. See also Edah, "Women's Tefilla Groups," http://www.edah.org/tefilla, for a listing of contemporary women's *tefillahs*, c. 2005.

21. Henry L. Feingold, *"Silent No More": Saving the Jews of Russia, the American Jewish Effort, 1967–1989* (Syracuse, NY: Syracuse University Press, 2007), 51–54, 57, 291. For a discussion of the estimates of Russian Jewish population figures in New York as of the turn of the twentieth century, see Sam Kliger, "Russian Jews in America: Status, Identity and Integration," paper presented at the Russian-Speaking Jewry in Global Perspective conference, June 14–16, 2004, Bar Ilan University Israel, http://www.kintera.org/atf/cf/%7B93CDF11D-9AEB-4518-8A00-25C7C531756B%7D/russian_jews_in_america.pdf. On the problem for Israel of those who chose New York, particularly during the 1970s, see Feingold, *"Silent No More,"* chap. 5.

22. Paul S. Appelbaum, "The Soviet Jewry Movement in the United States," in *Jewish American Voluntary Organizations,* ed. Michael Dobkowski, 613–38 (Westport, CT: Greenwood, 1986), 614–17. The term "cultural decapitation" is Feingold's (*"Silent No More,"* 40).

23. William M. Orbach, *The American Movement to Aid Soviet Jews* (Amherst: University of Massachusetts Press, 1979), 26–27; Appelbaum, "The Soviet Jewry Movement," 617; Feingold, *"Silent No More,"* 57.

24. Appelbaum, "The Soviet Jewry Movement," 617, 619; Orbach, *The American Movement to Aid Soviet Jews,* 27–28.

25. Eli Lederhendler, *New York Jews and the Decline of Urban Ethnicity, 1950–1970* (Syracuse, NY: Syracuse University Press, 2001), 116–20, 188.

26. Appelbaum, "The Soviet Jewry Movement," 618; Orbach, *The American Movement to Aid Soviet Jews,* 30–31. See also, on the Student Struggle's feeling that their counterparts lacked "moral spiritual fiber," Feingold, *"Silent No More,"* 62.

27. Orbach, *The American Movement to Aid Soviet Jews,* 8–9. See, on the Jewish Defense League's critique of the Student Struggle, Walter Ruby, "The Role of Nonestablishment Groups," in *A Second Exodus: The American Movement to Free Soviet Jews,* ed. Murray Friedman and Albert D. Chernin, 200–223 (Hanover, NH: University Press of New England / Brandeis University Press, 1999), 207.

28. Feingold, *"Silent No More,"* 80–86; Appelbaum, "The Soviet Jewry Movement," 624.

29. Appelbaum, "The Soviet Jewry Movement," 625; Feingold, *"Silent No More,"* 93; Orbach, *The American Movement to Aid Soviet Jews,* 65–67; on the contention that Birnbaum was marginalized, see Avi Weiss, "Memoirs of a Soviet Jewry Activist" (unpublished typescript, 2009), 18, 40; and Richter's memoirs in the Wiener Oral History Library of the American Jewish Committee, cited in Fred A. Lazin, *The Struggle for Soviet Jewry in American Politics: Israel versus the American Jewish Establishment* (Lanham, MD: Lexington Books, 2005), 37, 41, 67n. 106.

30. Ruby, "The Role of Nonestablishment Groups," 209.

31. Appelbaum, "The Soviet Jewry Movement," 620.

32. Feingold, *"Silent No More,"* 117, 188, 143.

33. Ibid., 117, 122, 133, 148.

34. "Prisoners of Zion, 1977," Soviet Jews Exodus website, http://www.angelfire.com/sc3/soviet_jews_exodus/English/POZ_s/POZ-77.shtml.

35. Lazin, *The Struggle for Soviet Jewry*, 234n. 23; Orbach, *The American Movement to Aid Soviet Jews*, 74, 77–78; David Shipler, "The U.S and Soviet Repression: Both Sides in a Quandary," *New York Times* (December 7, 1977): 3. See also Alan M. Dershowitz, *Chutzpah* (Boston: Little, Brown, 1991), 251.

36. Feingold, "Silent No More," 101, 310. See also ibid., 355n. 5, which references Shultz's remark, from George P. Shultz, *Turmoil and Triumph: My Years as Secretary of State* (New York: Scribner, 1993), 121.

37. On Weiss's travels with Avital Sharansky, see Weiss's unpublished memoir, "Memoirs of a Soviet Jewry Activist," 51–60. See also Ruby, "The Role of Nonestablishment Groups," 217; and Lazin, *The Struggle for Soviet Jewry*, 234.

38. Weiss, "Memoirs of a Soviet Jewry Activist," 1–5; see also "Rabbi Joins Sharansky in Hunger Strike in New York," *Jewish Week* (November 5, 1982): 4; "Freedom Marchers," *Jewish Week* (November 12, 1982): 1; David Bird, "Moscow Rabbi Reports Rise in Attendance at Synagogue," *New York Times* (May 8, 1984): B2.

39. On Haskel Lookstein's involvement with the Sharansky case, see Rafael Medoff, *Rav Chesed: The Life and Times of Rabbi Haskel Lookstein* (Jersey City, NJ: KTAV, 2008), 70–86; Ruby, "The Role of Nonestablishment Groups," 217.

40. Feingold, "Silent No More," 242–43, 261–62, 302. On the numbers allowed to leave, see Ruby, "The Role of Nonestablishment Groups," 222.

41. Weiss, "Memoirs of a Soviet Jewry Activist," 133, 145–46; Feingold, "Silent No More," 290. Actually, as Feingold notes, this public disagreement was during the second year of cancelation of the rally that started in 1972 and continued to 1988. See ibid., 364n. 57.

▪ NOTES TO THE EPILOGUE

1. Fred Siegel, *The Prince of the City: Giuliani, New York, and the Genius of American Life* (San Francisco: Encounter Books, 2005), 268–69; United Jewish Appeal–Federation of Jewish Philanthropies of New York, *The Jewish Community Study of New York: 2002: Geographic Profile* (New York: UJA-Federation, 2004), 110–11, typescript report maintained online at the Mandell L. Berman Institute North American Jewish Data Bank, University of Connecticut. On the transformation of Harlem, see "Migration of Affluent Whites to Harlem Forecast," *New York Times* (May 28, 1984): 23; Sam Roberts, "In Harlem, Blacks Are No Longer a Majority," *New York Times* (January 6, 2010): A16.

2. Ingrid Abramovitch, "Hipification Reaches the Street Where Peddlers Once Pushed Carts," *New York Times* (November 16, 1997): ST1, 6. See also the Cuisine Innovations website, http://www.kingkold.com, for advertisements about shipping Ratner's foods out of New York City.

3. On the history of these institutions, see the websites of the Museum at Eldridge Street, http://www.eldridgestreet.org; the Tenement Museum, http://www.tenement.org; and the Lower East Side Jewish Conservancy, http://www.nycjewishtours.org.

4. Deborah Sontag, "For Poor, Life 'Trapped' in a Cage," *New York Times* (October 6, 1996): 1.

5. UJA-Federation, *The Jewish Community Study of New York: 2002: Geographic Profile*, 27, 43, 69, 77, 101, 177. See also, on Rabbi Berl, Deborah Pardo, "Synagogues Fade in

the Northeast Bronx," Columbia University Graduate School of Journalism (September 1, 2003), http://web.jrn.columbia.edu/studentwork/religion/2004/archives/000465.asp; and Jonathan Mark, "A Season's Simple Gifts," *Jewish Week* (September 18, 2009): 23.

6. UJA-Federation, *The Jewish Community Study of New York: 2002: Geographic Profile*, 35, 36, 143, 169, 187.

7. Anthony Weiss, "New Egalitarian Yeshiva Prepares to Go Full Time," *Forward* (August 22, 2008), http://www.forward.com/articles/13972/. On the history of Drisha, see Drisha Institute for Jewish Education, "About Drisha," http://www.drisha.org/aboutdrisha.php. On Talmud programs at Yeshiva University for women and the founding of Weiss's "Open Orthodox" yeshiva, see Jeffrey S. Gurock, *Orthodox Jews in America* (Bloomington: Indiana University Press, 2009), 278, 309–11.

8. For the nature of the Columbia program, see Columbia University's Institute for Israel and Jewish Studies, http://iijs.columbia.edu/. On the scope of the NYU Jewish studies program, see NYU's Skirball Department of Hebrew and Judaic Studies, http://hebrewjudaic.as.nyu.edu.

9. "Unprecedented $30 Million Capital Campaign Secures Future for Center for Jewish History: Single Largest Fund-Raising Effort Since Building Was Completed in 2000," PR Newswire (January 24, 2011), http://www.prnewswire.com/news-releases/unprecedented-30-million-capital-campaign-secures-future-for-center-for-jewish-history-114477714.html.

10. United Jewish Appeal–Federation of Jewish Philanthropies of New York, *Jewish Community Study of New York: 2002* (New York: United Jewish Appeal–Federation of Jewish Philanthropies of New York, 2004), 25, 30, typescript report maintained online at the Mandell L. Berman Institute North American Jewish Data Bank, University of Connecticut.

11. For a discussion of the Jewish vote during the Dinkins-Giuliani campaign in 1989, see chapter 6, pages 177–79.

12. Catherine Manegold, "Do Not Let Farrakhan Use Stadium, Giuliani Says," *New York Times* (October 11, 1993): B3; "Mr. Farrakhan's Stadium Rally," *New York Times* (October 12, 1993): A22; Todd S. Purdum, "Crown Heights Drives Contest for Mayor," *New York Times* (December 7, 1992): B1; Purdum, "White Hispanic Ticket Grabs at a Black Mayor's Coalition," *New York Times* (June 15, 1993): 128. See also George J. Lankevich, *American Metropolis: A History of New York City* (New York: NYU Press, 1998), 242–43; and Siegel, *The Prince of the City*, 38–39, 43–44, 47, 65, 68.

13. Ian Fisher, "Upper West Side Voters Balance Doubts against Their Traditions," *New York Times* (October 23, 1993): 1; Celia W. Dugger, "Mayoral Race Still Perplexes Many Voters," *New York Times* (October 31, 1993): L1. The Republican also benefited from the "20,000 more votes he got . . . on Staten Island," which "accounted for nearly half of his margin of his citywide victory." His enthusiasm for a very different issue, "the secession referendum," brought more supporters to the polls. See "Many Tiny Ripples Create a Sea Change," *New York Times* (November 4, 1993): A1.

14. "Mayoral Meddling?," *Jewish Week* (March 15, 1996): 4; David Firestone, "In Mayor's Snub, a Hint of Strategy," *New York Times* (October 26, 1995): B1.

15. Gary Rosenblatt, "Between the Lines: How to React to Arafat," *Jewish Week* (October 27, 1995): 5.

16. Lankevich, *American Metropolis*, 252–53; Siegel, *The Prince of the City*, 149.

17. Adam Dickter, "Getting in Their Two Cents? Mayoral Candidates Scramble for Equal Time at Brooklyn COJO Breakfast Honoring Giuliani," *Jewish Week* (April 11, 1997): 8; "Rudy, Ruth: In Their Own Words; Messinger 'Tough Not Mean,'" *Jewish Week* (October 24, 1997): 1; Adam Nagourney, "Poll Finds Most Voters Have No Opinion about Messinger," *New York Times* (October 21, 1997): A1, B2.

18. Lawrence Kohler-Esses, "Still Fighting the 'War': As Combative Messinger Calls on Mayor to Heed Her Warnings, Supporters Rue Death of 'New Deal,'" *Jewish Week* (November 7, 1997): 12; Siegel, *The Prince of the City*, 210.

19. On the history of this organization and Messinger's involvement, see the organization's website, http://www.ajws.org.

20. Siegel, *The Prince of the City*, 215–16; Rudolph W. Giuliani, "A Blackout That Tested, and Proved, New York City's Character," Mayor's WINS Address (July 11, 1999), http://home2.nyc.gov/html/records/rwg/html/99a/me990711.html; Jim Yardley, "Jews and Blacks Try to Avoid Reprise of '91 in Crown Heights," *New York Times* (April 4, 1998): A1, B6.

21. Adam Dickter, "A Friend 'Til the End: For Jewish Community, Giuliani Was America's Top Mayor," *Jewish Week* (December 28, 2001): 10.

22. Ibid.

23. UJA-Federation, *Jewish Community Study of New York: 2002*, 28–29.

24. Adam Dickter, "Jewish Vote Vital for Bloomberg," *Jewish Week* (November 9, 2001): 1.

25. Joyce Purnick, *Mike Bloomberg: Money, Power, Politics* (New York: PublicAffairs, 2009), 4, 74, 87–88.

26. Ibid., 168, 204, 223.

■ **NOTES TO VISUAL ESSAY**

I thank Deborah Dash Moore for graciously inviting me to be part of this project, for her support of my work, and for her deep appreciation of objects and images. Jennifer Hammer of New York University Press has worked magic with my writing. It has been a delight to work with all four coauthors: Jeffrey S. Gurock, Annie Polland, Howard Rock, and Daniel Soyer. Danny earns a special thank-you for driving me around New York City to see murals and architecture. I also thank the anonymous readers for their helpful suggestions and advice. Numerous archivists, curators, librarians, collectors, and subscribers to the American Art listserv and the American Jewish History listserv offered valuable information. I appreciate all the living artists who granted me permission to reproduce their work.

Laura Holzman, Nina Liss-Schultz, and Shoshana Olidort were terrific research assistants, and Alexandra Maron was of great help with the illustrations and permissions. Sonja Assouline, Kate Breiger, and Amanda Koire were loving, responsible, and very fun babysitters to Alex and Emily, allowing me to work.

Friends, family, and colleagues have all generously given support, citations, personal stories and photographs, criticism, and beds on which to crash while in New York City. I thank Susanne Hunt for morning walks and for two years of hearing me go on about this book. She makes Claremont, California, home. David Brody finesses the perfect balance between his "amazings" to his "oy gevalts," and I love him for that. Tom Burke, Sarah Cash, Kate Fermoile, George Gorse and Susan Thalmann (both of Pomona College), Martha Grier, Carol Hamoy, Camara Dia Holloway, Russet Lederman, Dr. Erica Rosenfeld, Kerri Steinberg, Craig S. Wilder, and Karen Zukowski—I thank you all. And Carolyn Halpin-Healy is just golden in all regards.

My mom and dad, Joan and David Linden, put a subway map and a subway token in my hands at an early age with the mandate to go learn and love New York City. They are also the world's greatest grandparents. My husband, Peter Ross, offers an unlimited supply of love, humor, understanding, and appreciation; he also holds everything together when I am off to New York on research trips. As my twins, Alex and Emily Linden-Ross, are New York Jews by heritage rather than birth, I am proud that they recognize the Flatiron Building at a distance, love Junior's cheesecake, and hold on tight when the subway sways. I hope that they too will discover the magic of the City of Promises.

1. Voloj's work is included in Alana Newhouse, ed., *A Living Lens: Photographs of Jewish Life from the Pages of the Forward* (New York: Norton, 2007). Voloj explains his photographic mission as being to rediscover forgotten Jewish history in New York City, as well as the "ways the culture is reborn and reinvented in a city in a permanent transition." Julian Voloj to author (February 5, 2011).

2. The website of Congregation Ahavas Israel, http://www.greenpointshul.org, describes the synagogue this way: "We are a welcoming Modern Orthodox Synagogue that loves hipsters and hasids, lefty students and WW II veterans. . . . Come as you are: in a skirt or jeans, black suit or track suit." Congregation Ahavas Israel is located at 108 Noble Street, Brooklyn, NY 11222. The congregation dates to the late nineteenth century; the building dates to 1903.

3. See Lenore Skenazy, "Are New York Jews More Jewish?," *Forward* (February 17, 2010), http://www.forward.com/articles/125883 (accessed January 3, 2011)

4. Despite New York's sophistication, the art world remained a male stronghold. Critics applauded Bernstein's possession of "a man's vision" and the "masculine vigor to her brushwork." A graduate of the Educational Alliance, she also trained at the Arts Students League (ASL) and privately with William Merritt Chase, one of the era's premier painters. Patricia M. Burnham, "Theresa Bernstein," *Woman's Art Journal* 9, no. 2 (Autumn 1988–Winter 1989): 22–27.

5. In addition to the Amalgamated Co-ops, there were the Sholom Aleichem Houses built by Yiddishists, the Farband Houses built by Labor Zionists, and the United Workers Cooperative Community built by Jewish Communists. See Deborah Dash Moore, *At Home in America: Second Generation New York Jews* (New York: Columbia University Press, 1981), 80–82. Andrew S. Dolkart kindly gave me copies of the following: Dolkart, "Homes for People: Non-profit Cooperatives in New York City, 1916–1929," *Sites* 30

(1989): 30–35; Landmarks Preservation Commission, *Landmarks Designation Report: United Workers' Cooperative Colony ("The Coops"), Borough of the Bronx* (June 24, 1992).

6. For history of black Judaism, see Roberta S. Gold, "The Black Jews of Harlem: Representation, Identity, and Race, 1920–1939," *American Quarterly* 55, no. 2 (June 2003): 179–225.

7. Richard J. Powell, *Black Art and Culture in the 20th Century* (London: Thames & Hudson, 1997), 53. For background information on VanDerZee's photograph, see Richard J. Powell and David A. Bailey, *Rhapsodies in Black: Art of the Harlem Renaissance* (Berkeley: University of California Press, 1997). For information on the African American Jews of New York City, see Rabbi Ben Shlomo Levy, "Rabbi Arnold Joshua Ford: A Moses to His People," in *African American National Biography*, ed. Henry Louis Gates Jr. and Evelyn Brooks Higginbotham (New York: Oxford University Press, 2008), reprint courtesy of Rabbi Levy; BlackJews.org, "Who Are We? Where Did We Come From? How Many of Us Are There?," http://www.blackjews.org/articles.htm (accessed February 28, 2011); and Powell, *Black Art and Culture in the 20th Century*. I thank art historian Michael D. Harris for introducing me to Rabbi Levy, and in turn, I thank the rabbi for his assistance.

8. The rediscovery of the history of Jews of African descent connected with pan-Africanist reappraisal of Egypt's relationship to the African continent. Solomon's lineage down to Emperor Menelik II of Ethiopia, coupled with the flight of Moorish Jews to Timbuktu in West Africa during the fourteenth century, reinforced plausible links between Judaism and African Americans, fueling a belief that they were true descendants of ancient Israelites. A small minority was inspired to adopt the faith.

9. In the early 1930s, the United States experienced a resurgence of lynchings, which were openly held, especially in the South, and photographed as trophies. The overwhelming majority of lynch victims were black men, whose bodies were sometimes burnt and castrated. In the mid-1930s, both the NAACP and the Artists' Union organized similar, yet competing, exhibitions to demand legislation outlawing lynching, which President Franklin Roosevelt, in fear of losing the votes of southern Democrats, refused to support. See Marlene Park, "Lynching and Anti-lynching: Art and Politics in the 1930s," in *The Social and the Real: Political Art of the 1930s in the Western Hemisphere*, ed. Alejandro Anreus, Diana L. Linden, and Jonathan Weinberg, 155–77 (University Park: Pennsylvania State University Press, 2006).

10. David Margolick, *Strange Fruit: Billie Holiday, Café Society, and an Early Cry for Civil Rights* (Philadelphia: Running Press, 2000).

11. Henry Bial, *Acting Jewish: Negotiating Ethnicity on the American Stage and Screen* (Ann Arbor: University of Michigan Press, 2005), 1–29, 40–48; Donald Weber, "The Jewish American World of Gertrude Berg: The Goldbergs on Radio and Television, 1930–1950," in *Talking Back: Images of Jewish Women in Popular Culture*, ed. Joyce Antler, 85–99 (Hanover, NH: University Press of New England / Brandies University Press, 1998).

12. Peter M. Rutkoff and William B. Scott, *New School: A History of the New School for Social Research* (New York: Free Press, 1986); Claus-Dieter Krohn, *Intellectuals in Exile*:

Refugee Scholars and the New School for Social Research, trans. Rita Kimball and Robert Kimball (Amherst: University of Massachusetts Press, 1993), chap. 5.

13. Barbara Kirschenblatt-Gimbett, *Destination Culture: Tourism, Museums, and Heritage* (Berkeley: University of California Press, 1998), 79–128.

14. Daniel Morris, *After Weegee: Essays on Contemporary Jewish American Photography* (Syracuse, NY: Syracuse University Press, 2011); Anthony W. Lee and Richard Meyer, *Weegee and the Naked City* (Berkeley: University of California Press, 2008).

15. Maurice Berger, Joan Rosenbaum, and Vivian B. Mann, *Masterworks of the Jewish Museum* (New York: Jewish Museum, 2004), 184–85.

16. Norman L. Kleeblatt and Susan Chevlowe, eds., *Painting a Place in America: Jewish Artists in New York, 1900–1945: A Tribute to the Educational Alliance* (New York: Jewish Museum, 1991); Susan Ilene Fort, *The Figure in American Sculpture: A Question of Modernity* (Los Angeles: Los Angeles County Museum of Art, 1995), 81–83, 95–96.

17. Ben Shahn to Edward B. Rowan, June 11, 1940, Archives of American Art, Washington, DC.

18. Alfred J. Kolatch, *Great Jewish Quotations* (New York: Jonathan David, 1996), 74–75; Lenny Bruce, *How to Talk Dirty and Influence People* (New York: Fireside, 1992).

19. Gustave Heye Center, National Museum of the American Indian, *Mother Earth, Father Skyline*, ed. Duane Blue Spruce (Washington, DC: Smithsonian Institution Press, 2006), 38; Rachel Rubinstein, *Members of the Tribe: Native America in the Native Imagination* (Detroit: Wayne State University Press, 2010).

20. Lawrence Bush, "October 21: Jews against the War," *Jewish Currents* (October 20, 2010), http://jewishcurrents.org/october-21-jews-against-the-war-2978.

21. Steven Lee Beeber, *The Heebie-Jeebies at CBGB's: The Secret History of Jewish Punk* (Chicago: Chicago Review Press, 2006).

22. The Archives of the American Soviet Jewry Movement is housed at the American Jewish Historical Society in Manhattan (http://www.ajhs.org/aasjm).

23. "A Postcolonial Kinderhood, 1994," Elaine Reichek's website, http://elainereichek .com/Project_Pages/9_Postcolonial/PostcolonialKinderhood.htm.

24. The Jewish Museum, "Miriam Cup," http://www.thejewishmuseum.org/online collection/object_collection.php?objectid=5027&lefttxt=miriam cup. Curator Daniel Belasco of the Jewish Museum, New York City, helped me with my object selection. Many thanks.

25. Skenazy, "Are New York Jews More Jewish?," 2.

BIBLIOGRAPHY

Abrams, Nathan. "'A Profoundly Hegemonic Moment': De-mythologizing the Cold War New York Jewish Intellectuals." *Shofar* (Spring 2003): 64–82.

"Ageloff Towers." *American Architect* (May 5, 1929): 621.

Alexander, Edward. "Irving Howe and the Holocaust: Dilemmas of a Radical Jewish Intellectual." *American Jewish History* 88 (March 2000): 101–2.

American Jewish Yearbook (1931–32, 1939–40, 1941–42, 1945–46, 1952, 1976, 1981, 1984).

Angel, Marc. *La America: The Sephardic Experience in the United States*. Philadelphia: Jewish Publication Society of America, 1982.

Antler, Joyce. *The Journey Home: Jewish Women and the American Century*. New York: Free Press, 1997.

Appelbaum, Paul S. "The Soviet Jewry Movement in the United States." In *Jewish American Voluntary Organizations*, edited by Michael N. Dobkowski, 613–30. Westport, CT: Greenwood, 1986.

Bailey, Thomas, and Roger Waldinger. "The Changing Ethnic/Racial Division of Labor." In *Dual City: Restructuring New York*, edited by John Hull Mollenkopf and Manuel Castells, 43–78. New York: Russell Sage Foundation, 1991.

Ballon, Hilary, and Kenneth T. Jackson, eds. *Robert Moses and the Modern City: The Transformation of New York*. New York: Norton, 2007.

Bayor, Ronald H. *Neighbors in Conflict: The Irish, Germans, Jews, and Italians of New York City, 1929–1941*. Baltimore: Johns Hopkins University Press, 1978.

Bell, Daniel. "The Three Faces of New York." *Dissent* 8 (Summer 1961): 225.

Bender, Thomas. *New York Intellect: A History of Intellectual Life in New York from 1750 to the Beginnings of Our Own Time*. New York: Knopf, 1987.

Ben-Ur, Aviva. "In Search of the Ladino Press: A Bibliographic Survey." *Studies in Bibliography and Booklore* (Winter 2001): 10–52.

———. *Sephardic Jews in America: A Diasporic History*. New York: NYU Press, 2009.

Berger, Peter L. "In Praise of New York: A Semi-Secular Homily." *Commentary* (February 1977): 59–62.

Bernstein, Burton, and Barbara B. Haws. *Leonard Bernstein: American Original*. New York: HarperCollins, 2008.

Berrol, Selma C. "The Jewish West Side of New York, 1920–1970." *Journal of Ethnic Studies* (Winter 1986): 21–45.

Berson, Lenora E. *The Negroes and the Jews*. New York: Random House, 1971.

Binder, Frederick M., and David M. Reimers. *All the Nations under Heaven: An Ethnic and Racial History of New York City*. New York: Columbia University Press, 1995.

Blake, Peter. "How to Solve the Housing Crisis (and Everything Else)." *New York* (January 1, 1970): 56–57.

Bloom, Alexander. *Prodigal Sons: The New York Intellectuals and Their World.* New York: Oxford University Press, 1986.

B'nai B'rith Hillel Foundations. *Jewish Life on Campus.* Washington, DC: B'nai B'rith Hillel Foundation, 1968–69, 1978–79, 1982–83.

Bokser, Ben Zion. "The Solomon Schechter Day Schools." *United Synagogue Review* (March 1957): 11.

Bookchin, Debbie, and Jim Schumacher. *The Virus and the Vaccine: The True Story of a Cancer-Causing Monkey Virus, Contaminated Polio Vaccine, and the Millions of Americans Exposed.* New York: St. Martin's, 2004.

Brecher, Charles, and Raymond D. Horton, with Robert A. Cropf and Dean Michael Mead. *Power Failure: New York City Politics and Policy since 1960.* New York: Oxford University Press, 1993.

Broun, Heywood, and George Britt. *Christians Only: A Study in Prejudice.* New York: Vanguard, 1931.

Bureau of Community Statistical Services Research Department, Community Council of Greater New York. *Bronx Communities: Population Characteristics and Neighborhood Social Resources.* Typescript. New York: Community Council of Greater New York, 1962.

Cahan, Abraham. *The Rise of David Levinsky: A Novel.* New York: Harper and Bros., 1917.

Cannato, Vincent. *The Ungovernable City: John Lindsay and his Struggle to Save New York.* New York: Basic Books, 2001.

Caro, Robert A. *The Power Broker: Robert Moses and the Fall of New York.* New York: Knopf, 1974.

Center for New York City Affairs, New School for Social Research. *New York's Jewish Poor and Jewish Working Class: Economic Status and Social Needs.* Typescript. New York: Federation of Jewish Philanthropies, 1972.

Charner, Morris, and Frances S. Morris. "Curricular Development at Yeshiva Dov Revel." *Yeshiva Education* (Fall 1959): 34–39.

Chenault, Lawrence Royce. *The Puerto Rican Migrant in New York.* New York: Columbia University Press, 1938.

Cohen, Marcia. *The Sisterhood.* New York: Fawcett Columbine, 1988.

Cohen, Naomi W. *American Jews and the Zionist Idea.* New York: KTAV, 1975.

Cohen, Robert. *When the Old Left Was Young: Student Radicals and America's First Mass Student Movement, 1929–1941.* New York: Oxford University Press, 1993.

Cohen, Steven M., and Paul Ritterband. "The Social Characteristics of the New York Jewish Community, 1981." *American Jewish Yearbook* 84 (1984): 128–61.

Cohen-Nusbacher, Ailene. "Efforts at Change in a Traditional Denomination: The Case of Orthodox Women's Prayer Groups." *Nashim* 2 (Spring 1999): 95–113.

Cooney, Terry A. *The Rise of the New York Intellectuals: Partisan Review and Its Circle.* Madison: University of Wisconsin Press, 1986.

Cottle, Thomas J. *Hidden Survivors: Portraits of Poor Jews in America.* Englewood Cliffs, NJ: Prentice-Hall, 1980.

Coulton, Thomas Evans. *A City College in Action: Struggle and Achievement at Brooklyn College, 1930–1955*. New York: Harper and Bros., 1955.

Dash, Irene G. *Shakespeare and the American Musical*. Bloomington: Indiana University Press, 2010.

Dawidowicz, Lucy S. *From That Place and Time: A Memoir, 1938–1947*. New York: Norton, 1989.

Dershowitz, Alan M. *Chutzpah*. Boston: Little, Brown, 1991.

Diamond, Sander A. *The Nazi Movement in America*. Ithaca: Cornell University Press, 1974.

Diner, Hasia R. *Lower East Side Memories: A Jewish Place in America*. Princeton: Princeton University Press, 2000.

Dinnerstein, Leonard. *Antisemitism in America*. New York: Oxford University Press, 1994.

Dolkart, Andrew S. "Homes for People Cooperatives in New York City, 1916–1929." *Sites* 30 (1989): 30–42.

Dorman, Joseph. *Arguing the World: The New York Intellectuals in Their Own Words*. New York: Free Press, 2000.

Draper, Hal. "The Student Movement in the Thirties." In *As We Saw the Thirties: Essays on Social and Political Movements of a Decade*, edited by Rita J. Simon, 182–89. Urbana: University of Illinois Press, 1967.

Drennan, Matthew P. "The Decline and Rise of the New York Economy." In *Dual City: Restructuring New York*, edited by John Hull Mollenkopf and Manuel Castells, 29–42. New York: Russell Sage Foundation, 1991.

Dushkin, Alexander M. *Jewish Education in New York City*. New York: Bureau of Jewish Education, 1918.

Dworkin, Susan. "Henrietta Szold." *Response* 7 (Summer 1973): 39–45.

———. *Miss America, 1945: Bess Myerson's Own Story*. New York: Newmarket, 1947.

Effron, Mark. "It Wasn't Supposed to Happen This Way." Unpublished manuscript, Columbia University School of Journalism, 1973.

Elkin, Lillian. "Memoir." American Jewish Committee Oral History Collection, New York Public Library.

Emerson, Ken. *Always Magic in the Air: The Bomp and Brilliance of the Brill Building Era*. New York: Viking, 2005.

Esperdy, Gabrielle. "Defying the Grid: A Retroactive Manifesto for the Culture of Decongestion." *Perspecta* 30 (1999): 10–33.

Federal Writers Project, Yiddish Writers Group. *Die Yiddishe Landsmanshaften fun New York*. New York: I. L. Peretz Writers Union, 1938.

Feingold, Henry L. *The Politics of Rescue: The Roosevelt Administration and the Holocaust, 1938–1945*. New Brunswick: Rutgers University Press, 1970.

———. *"Silent No More": Saving the Jews of Russia, the American Jewish Effort, 1967–1989*. Syracuse, NY: Syracuse University Press, 2007.

———. *A Time for Searching: Entering the Mainstream, 1920–1945*. Baltimore: Johns Hopkins University Press, 1992.

Feuer, Lewis S. "The Stages in the Social History of Jewish Professors in American Colleges and Universities." *American Jewish History* (June 1982): 432–65.

Fishman, Sylvia Barack. *A Breath of Life: Feminism in the American Jewish Community.* New York: Free Press, 1993.

Ford, Carole Bell. *The Girls: Jewish Women of Brownsville, Brooklyn, 1940–1995.* Albany: SUNY Press, 2000.

———. "Nice Jewish Girls: Growing Up in Brownsville, 1930s–1950s." In *Jews of Brooklyn*, edited by Ilana Abramovitch and Seán Galvin, 129–36. Hanover, NH: University Press of New England / Brandeis University Press, 2002.

Franck, Phyllis. "The Hasidic Poor in New York City." In *Poor Jews: An American Awakening*, edited by Naomi B. Levine and Martin Hochbaum, 59–69. New Brunswick, NJ: Transaction Books, 1974.

Freedman, Morris. "CCNY Days." In *City at the Center: A Collection of Writings by CCNY Alumni and Faculty*, edited by Betty Rizzo and Barry Wallenstein, 65. New York: City College of New York, 1983.

———. "New Jewish Community in Formation: A Conservative Center Catering to Present-Day Needs," *Commentary* (January 1955): 36–47.

Freeman, Joshua B. *Working-Class New York: Life and Labor since World War II.* New York: New Press, 2000.

Friedan, Betty. *Life So Far.* New York: Simon and Schuster, 2000.

Friedman, Murray. *What Went Wrong? The Creation and Collapse of the Black-Jewish Alliance.* New York: Free Press, 1995.

Friedman, Reena Sigman. "The Jewish Feminist Movement." In *Jewish American Voluntary Organizations*, edited by Michael N. Dobkowski, 575–601. Westport, CT: Greenwood, 1986.

Fuchs, Lawrence H. *The Political Behavior of American Jews.* Glencoe, IL: Free Press, 1956.

Gaines, Steven, and Sharon Churcher, *Obsession: The Lives and Times of Calvin Klein.* New York: Birch Lane, 1994.

Gersh, Harry. *Minority Report.* New York: Crowell-Collier, 1962.

Gershowitz, Michael V. "Neighborhood Power Structure: Decision Making in Forest Hills." Ph.D. diss., New York University, 1974.

Giuliani, Rudolph W. "A Blackout That Tested, and Proved, New York City's Character," Mayor's WINS Address (July 11, 1999). http://home2.nyc.gov/html/records/rwg/html/99a/me990711.html.

Gladwell, Malcolm. *Outliers: The Story of Success.* New York: Little, Brown, 2008.

Glazer, Nathan. "The Jewish Role in Student Activism." *Fortune* (January 1969): 112–13, 126–29.

Glazer, Nathan, and Daniel P. Moynihan. *Beyond the Melting Pot: The Negroes, Puerto Ricans, Jews, Italians, and Irish of New York City.* 2nd ed. Cambridge: MIT Press, 1970.

Glazer, Ruth. "West Bronx: Food, Shelter, Clothing." *Commentary* (June 1949): 578–85.

Glustrom, Simon. "Some Aspects of a Suburban Jewish Community." *Conservative Judaism* (Winter 1957): 27–28.

Gold, David. "America First: The Anti-war Movement, Charles Lindbergh and the Second World War, 1940–1941." *New York Military Affairs Symposium* (September 26, 2003). http://bobrowen.com/nymas/americafirst.html.

Gold, Michael. *Jews without Money*. New York: Horace Liveright, 1930.

Goldschmidt, Henry. *Race and Religion among the Chosen People of Crown Heights*. New Brunswick: Rutgers University Press, 2006.

Goldstein, Eric L. "'A Childless Language': Yiddish and the Problem of 'Youth' in the 1920s and 1930s." In *1929: Mapping the Jewish World*, edited by Gennady Estraik and Hasia Diner. New York: NYU Press, forthcoming.

Gorelick, Sherry. *City College and the Jewish Poor: Education in New York, 1880–1924*. New Brunswick: Rutgers University Press, 1981.

Gorenstein, Arthur. "A Portrait of Ethnic Politics: The Socialists and the 1908 and 1910 Congressional Elections on the Lower East Side." *Publications of the American Jewish Historical Society* (March 1961): 202–40.

Gornick, Vivian. "Commencement Address." In *City at the Center: A Collection of Writings by CCNY Alumni and Faculty*, edited by Betty Rizzo and Barry Wallenstein, 84–87. New York: City College of New York, 1983.

———. "There Is No Community." *Interchange* (April 1977): 4–5.

Grebler, Leo. *Housing Market Behavior in a Declining Area: Long-Term Changes in Inventory and Utilization of Housing on New York's Lower East Side*. New York: Columbia University Press, 1952.

Greenberg, Cheryl Lynn. *Or Does It Explode? Black Harlem in the Great Depression*. New York: Oxford University Press, 1997.

———. *Troubling the Waters: Black-Jewish Relations in the American Century*. Princeton: Princeton University Press, 2006.

Grobman, Alex. "What Did They Know? The American Jewish Press and the Holocaust, 1 September 1939–17 December 1942." *American Jewish History* 68 (March 1979): 327–52.

Gurock, Jeffrey S. "Change to Survive: The Common Experience of Transplanted Jewish Identities in America, 1880–1920." In *What Is American about the American Jewish Experience?*, edited by Marc Lee Raphael, 54–72. Williamsburg, VA: College of William and Mary, 1993.

———. "Devotees and Deviants: A Primer on the Religious Values of Orthodox Day School Families." In *Rav Chesed: Essays in Honor of Rabbi Dr. Haskel Lookstein*, edited by Rafael Medoff, 271–94. Hoboken, NJ: KTAV, 2009.

———. "Jewish Commitment and Continuity in Interwar Brooklyn." In *Jews of Brooklyn*, edited by Ilana Abramovitch and Sean Galvin, 231–41. Hanover, NH: University Press of New England, 2002.

———. *Judaism's Encounter with American Sports*. Bloomington: Indiana University Press, 2005.

———. "The Late Friday Night Orthodox Service: An Exercise in Religious Accommodation." *Jewish Social Studies* 12 (Spring–Summer 2006): 137–56.

Gurock, Jeffrey S. *Orthodox Jews in America.* Bloomington: Indiana University Press, 2009.

———. "Synagogue Imperialism in New York City: The Case of Congregation Kehal Adath Jeshurun, 1909–1911." *Michael* 15 (2000): 95–108.

———. *When Harlem Was Jewish, 1870–1930.* New York: Columbia University Press, 1979.

Gurock, Jeffrey S., and Jacob J. Schacter. *A Modern Heretic and a Traditional Community: Mordecai M. Kaplan, Orthodoxy, and American Judaism.* New York: Columbia University Press, 1997.

Halperin, Samuel. *The Political World of American Zionism.* Detroit: Wayne State University Press, 1961.

Hant, Myrna. "Molly Goldberg: A 1950s Icon." *Women in Judaism* 5 (Spring 2008). http://wjudaism.library.utoronto.ca/index.php/wjudaism/article/view/3532/1587.

Harrington, Michael. *The Other America: Poverty in the United States.* New York: Macmillan, 1962.

Harris, Louis, and Bert E. Swanson. *Black-Jewish Relations in New York City.* New York: Praeger, 1970.

Heilbrun, Carolyn G. *The Education of a Woman: The Life of Gloria Steinem.* New York: Dial, 1995.

Helfgott, Roy B. "Women's and Children's Apparel." In *Made in New York: Case Studies in Metropolitan Manufacturing,* edited by Max Hall. Cambridge: Harvard University Press, 1959.

Helmreich, William B. *Against All Odds: Holocaust Survivors and the Successful Lives They Made in America.* New York: Simon and Schuster, 1992.

Herberg, Will. "The Jewish Labor Movement in the United States." *American Jewish Yearbook* 53 (1952): 3–76.

Hertzberg, Arthur. *My Life and a People's Struggle for Identity.* San Francisco: HarperSanFrancisco, 2002.

Hollinger, David. "Two NYUs and the 'Obligation of Universities to the Social Order' in the Great Depression." In *The University and the City,* edited by Thomas Bender, 60–79. New York: Oxford University Press, 1988.

Hood, Clifton. *722 Miles: The Building of the Subways and How They Transformed New York.* New York: Simon and Schuster, 1993.

Hoover, Edgar M. *Anatomy of a Metropolis: The Changing Distribution of People and Jobs within the New York Metropolitan Region.* Cambridge: Harvard University Press, 1959.

Horowitz, C. Morris, and Lawrence J. Kaplan. *The Jewish Population of the New York Area, 1900–1975.* New York: Federation of Jewish Philanthropies of New York, 1959.

Horowitz, Daniel. *Betty Friedan and the Making of the Feminine Mystique: The American Left, the Cold War, and Modern Feminism.* Amherst: University of Massachusetts Press, 1998.

Howe, Irving. "From *World of Our Fathers.*" In *City at the Center: A Collection of Writings by CCNY Alumni and Faculty,* edited by Betty Rizzo and Barry Wallenstein, 60–63. New York: City College of New York, 1983.

———. *A Margin of Hope: An Intellectual Autobiography.* San Diego: Harcourt Brace Jovanovich, 1982.

———. "A Memoir of the Thirties." In *Steady Work: Essays in the Politics of Democratic Radicalism, 1953–1966.* New York: Harcourt, Brace and World, 1966.

———. *World of Our Fathers: The Journey of the East European Jews to America and the Life They Found and Made.* New York: Random House, 1976.

Howe, Irving, and Kenneth Libo. *How We Lived: A Documentary History of Immigrant Jews in America, 1880–1930.* New York: R. Marek, 1979.

Hyman, Paula E. "Jewish Feminism Faces the American Women's Movement: Convergence and Divergence." In *American Jewish Women's History: A Reader*, edited by Pamela S. Nadell, 297–312. New York: NYU Press, 2003.

Isserman, Maurice. *Which Side Were You On? The American Communist Party during the Second World War.* Middletown, CT: Wesleyan University Press, 1982.

Jackson, Kenneth T. *Crabgrass Frontier: The Suburbanization of the United States.* New York: Oxford University Press, 1985.

———, ed. *The Encyclopedia of New York City.* New Haven: Yale University Press and New-York Historical Society, 1995.

Jasen, David A. *Tin Pan Alley: The Composers, the Songs, the Performers and Their Times.* New York: Donald I. Fine, 1988.

The Jewish Communal Register of New York City, 1917–1918. New York: Kehillah [Jewish Community] of New York, 1918.

Jonas, Manfred. *Isolationism in America, 1935–1941.* Ithaca: Cornell University Press, 1966.

Jospe, Alfred. *Jewish Students and Student Services at American Universities.* Washington, DC: B'nai B'rith Hillel Foundation, 1963.

Kanter, Kenneth Aaron. *The Jews on Tin Pan Alley: The Jewish Contribution to American Popular Music, 1830–1940.* New York: KTAV and the American Jewish Archives, 1982.

Kaplan, Samuel. "The Bronx Arrangement." *New York* (December 14, 1970): 10–12.

Kaufman, Jonathan. *Broken Alliance: The Turbulent Times between Blacks and Jews in America.* New York: Scribner, 1988.

Kazin, Alfred. *A Walker in the City.* New York: Harcourt, Brace, 1951.

Keniston, Kenneth. *Young Radicals: Notes on Committed Youth.* New York: Harcourt, Brace and World, 1968.

Kimmel, Meir. "The History of Yeshivat Rabbi Chaim Berlin." *Sheviley ha-Hinuch* (Fall 1948): 51–54.

Kirchheimer, Gloria DeVidas, and Manfred Kirchheimer. *We Were So Beloved: Autobiography of a German Jewish Community.* Pittsburgh: University of Pittsburgh Press, 1997.

Kliger, Sam. "Russian Jews in America: Status, Identity and Integration." Paper presented at the Russian-Speaking Jewry in Global Perspective conference, June 14–16, 2004, Bar Ilan University Israel. http://www.kintera.org/atf/cf/%7B93CDF11D-9AEB-4518-8A00-25C7C531756B%7D/russian_jews_in_america.pdf.

Kolker, Robert "Whose Harlem Is It?" *New York* (July 14, 2008): 30–35.

Kranzler, George. *Williamsburg: A Jewish Community in Transition.* New York: Feldheim, 1961.

Krasner, Jonathan. *The Benderly Boys and the Making of American Jewish Education.* Hanover, NH: University Press of New England / Brandeis University Press, 2011.

Kugelmass, Jack. *The Miracle of Intervale Avenue: The Story of a Jewish Congregation in the South Bronx.* New York: Columbia University Press, 1996.

Landesman, Alter F. *Brownsville: The Birth, Development and Passing of a Jewish Community in New York.* New York: Bloch, 1969.

Lankevich, George J. *American Metropolis: A History of New York City.* New York: NYU Press, 1998.

Lapson, Judah. "A Decade of Hebrew in the High Schools of New York." *Jewish Education* (April 1941): 34–45.

Laurents, Arthur. *Original Story By: A Memoir of Broadway and Hollywood.* New York: Knopf, 2000.

Lazin, Fred A. *The Struggle for Soviet Jewry in American Politics: Israel versus the American Jewish Establishment.* Lanham, MD: Lexington Books, 2005.

Lederhendler, Eli. *New York Jews and the Decline of Urban Ethnicity, 1950–1970.* Syracuse, NY: Syracuse University Press, 2001.

Leff, Laurel. "A Tragic 'Fight in the Family': The *New York Times*, Reform Judaism and the Holocaust." *American Jewish History* 88 (March 2000): 3–4.

———. "When the Facts Didn't Speak for Themselves: The Holocaust in the *New York Times*, 1939–1945." *Harvard International Journal of Press/Politics* (2000): 52–57.

Lerner, Stephen C. "The Havurot." *Conservative Judaism* 24, no. 3 (Spring 1970): 2–15.

Levine, Naomi B., and Martin Hochbaum, eds. *Poor Jews: An American Awakening.* New Brunswick, NJ: Transaction Books, 1974.

Levinger, Lee J. *The Jewish Student in America: A Study Made by the Research Bureau of the B'nai B'rith Hillel Foundation.* Cincinnati: B'nai B'rith, 1937.

Levinthal, Israel Herbert. "The Value of the Center to the Synagogue." *United Synagogue Review* (June 1926): 19.

Liben, Meyer. "CCNY: A Memoir." In *City at the Center: A Collection of Writings by CCNY Alumni and Faculty,* edited by Betty Rizzo and Barry Wallenstein, 47–54. New York: City College of New York, 1983.

Lookstein, Haskel. *Were We Our Brothers' Keepers? The Public Response of American Jews to the Holocaust, 1938–1944.* New York: Hartmore House, 1985.

Lowenstein, Steven M. *Frankfurt on the Hudson: The German-Jewish Community of Washington Heights, 1933–1983, Its Structure and Culture.* Detroit: Wayne State University Press, 1989.

Mahler, Jonathan. *Ladies and Gentlemen, the Bronx Is Burning: 1977, Baseball, Politics, and the Battle for the Soul of a City.* New York: Farrar, Straus and Giroux, 2005.

Mann Arthur. *La Guardia: A Fighter against His Times, 1882–1933.* Chicago: University of Chicago Press, 1959.

Markowitz, Fran. *A Community in Spite of Itself: Soviet Jewish Émigrés in New York.* Washington, DC: Smithsonian Institution Press, 1993.

Markowitz, Ruth Jacknow. *My Daughter, the Teacher: Jewish Teachers in the New York City Schools.* New Brunswick: Rutgers University Press, 1993.

Massarik, Fred. "Basic Characteristics of the Greater New York Jewish Population." *American Jewish Year Book* (1976): 239, 242.

Mayer, Egon. *From Suburb to Shtetl: The Jews of Boro Park.* Philadelphia: Temple University Press, 1979.

McCann, Graham. *Woody Allen: New Yorker.* Cambridge, UK: Polity, 1990.

McDowell, Winston C. "Keeping Them 'In the Same Boat Together'?" In *African Americans and Jews in the Twentieth Century,* edited by V. P. Franklin, Nancy L. Grant, Harold M. Kletnick, and Genna Rae McNeil, 208–36. Columbia: University of Missouri Press, 1998.

McGill, Nettie Pauline. "Some Characteristics of Jewish Youth in New York City." *Jewish Social Service Quarterly* 14, no. 2 (1938): 251–72.

McGill, Nettie Pauline, and Ellen Nathalie Matthews. *The Youth of New York City.* New York: Macmillan, 1940.

McNickle, Chris. *To Be Mayor of New York: Ethnic Politics in the City.* New York: Columbia University Press, 1993.

Medoff, Rafael. *Militant Zionism in America: The Rise and Impact of the Jabotinsky Movement in the United States, 1926–1948.* Tuscaloosa: University of Alabama Press, 2002.

———. *Rav Chesed: The Life and Times of Rabbi Haskel Lookstein.* Jersey City, NJ: KTAV, 2008.

———. "'Retribution Is Not Enough': The 1943 Campaign by Jewish Students to Raise American Public Awareness of the Nazi Genocide." *Holocaust and Genocide Studies* 11, no. 2 (Fall 1997): 171–89.

Mele, Christopher. *Selling the Lower East Side: Culture, Real Estate, and Resistance in New York City.* Minneapolis: University of Minnesota Press, 2000.

Merwin, Ted. *Homeland for the Jewish Soul: A History of the Jewish Deli* (forthcoming).

———. *In Their Own Image: New York Jews in Jazz Age Popular Culture.* New Brunswick: Rutgers University Press, 2006.

Meyer, Robert E. "How Government Helped Ruin the South Bronx." *Fortune* (November 1975): 140–51.

Michels, Tony. *A Fire in Their Hearts: Yiddish Socialists in New York.* Cambridge: Harvard University Press, 2005.

Mintz, Jerome R. "Ethnic Activism: The Hasidic Example." In *Dimensions of Orthodox Judaism,* edited by Reuven P. Bulka, 225–41. New York: KTAV, 1983.

———. *Hasidic People: A Place in the New World.* Cambridge: Harvard University Press, 1992.

Mollenkopf, John Hull. *A Phoenix in the Ashes: The Rise and Fall of the Koch Coalition in New York City Politics.* Princeton: Princeton University Press, 1992.

Morrow, Felix. "Higher Learning on Washington Square." *Menorah Journal* (April 1930): 346–57.

Moore, Deborah Dash. *At Home in America: Second Generation New York Jews.* New York: Columbia University Press, 1981.

Moore, Deborah Dash. *GI Jews: How World War II Changed a Generation.* Cambridge: Belknap Press of Harvard University Press, 2004.

———. "Reconsidering the Rosenbergs: Symbol and Substance in Second Generation American Jewish Consciousness." *Journal of American Ethnic History* 8 (Fall 1988): 21–37.

———. *To the Golden Cities: Pursuing the American Jewish Dream in Miami and L.A.* New York: Free Press 1994.

Most, Andrea. *Making Americans: Jews and the Broadway Musical.* Cambridge: Harvard University Press, 2004.

Myers, Paul. *Leonard Bernstein.* London: Phaidon, 1998.

Nadell, Pamela S. "A Bright New Constellation: Feminism and American Judaism." In *The Columbia History of Jews and Judaism in America*, edited by Marc Lee Raphael, 385–405. New York: Columbia University Press, 2008.

———. *Women Who Would Be Rabbis: A History of Women's Ordination, 1889–1985.* Boston: Beacon, 1998.

Naison, Mark. "Crown Heights in the 1950s." In *Jews of Brooklyn*, edited by Ilana Abramovitch and Seán Galvin, 143–52. Hanover, NH: University Press of New England / Brandeis University Press, 2002.

———. "From Eviction Resistance to Rent Control: Tenant Activism in the Great Depression," In *The Tenant Movement in New York City, 1904–1984*, edited by Ronald Lawson, 102–12. New Brunswick: Rutgers University Press, 1986.

Nardi, Noah. "The Growth of Jewish Day Schools in America." *Jewish Education* 20, no. 1 (November 1948): 23–32.

———. "A Survey of Jewish Day Schools in America." *Jewish Education* 16, no. 1 (September 1944): 12–26.

New York City Tenement House Department. *Tenth Report, 1918–1929.* New York: Martin Brown, 1929.

Orbach, William M. *The American Movement to Aid Soviet Jews.* Amherst: University of Massachusetts Press, 1979.

Orleck, Annelise. *Common Sense and a Little Fire: Women and Working-Class Politics in the United States, 1900–1965.* Chapel Hill: University of North Carolina Press, 1995.

Oshinsky, David M. *Polio: An American Story.* New York: Oxford University Press, 2005.

Osofsky, Gilbert. *Harlem: The Making of a Ghetto; Negro New York, 1890–1930.* New York: Harper and Row, 1964.

Palmer, William J. *The Films of the Eighties: A Social History.* Carbondale: Southern Illinois University Press, 1993.

Pearl, Jonathan, and Judith Pearl. *The Chosen Image: Television's Portrayal of Jewish Themes and Characters.* Jefferson, NC: McFarland, 1999.

Penkower, Monte Noam. "In Dramatic Dissent: The Bergson Boys." *American Jewish History* 70, no. 2 (March 1981): 281–309.

Phelps, Christopher. "An Interview with Harry Magdoff—Co-editor of the 'Monthly Review.'" *Monthly Review* (May 1999). http://monthlyreview.org/1999/05/01/an-interview-with-harry-magdoff.

Plunz, Richard. *A History of Housing in New York City: Dwelling Type and Social Change in the American Metropolis.* New York: Columbia University Press, 1990.

Podair, Jerald E. *The Strike That Changed New York: Blacks, Whites, and the Ocean Hill–Brownsville Crisis.* New Haven: Yale University Press, 2002.

Pogrebin, Letty Cottin. *Deborah, Golda, and Me: Being Female and Jewish in America.* New York: Crown, 1991.

———. *Jewish Women in America: An Historical Encyclopedia*, vol. 2, edited by Paula E. Hyman and Deborah Dash Moore. New York: Routledge, 1997.

Polland, Annie. *Landmark of the Spirit: The Eldridge Street Synagogue.* New Haven: Yale University Press, 2009.

Population, Land Values and Government: Studies of the Growth and Distribution of Population and Land Values and of Problems of Government, Regional Survey of New York and Its Environs. New York: Regional Plan of New York and Its Environs, 1929.

Postal, Bernard. "New York's Jewish Fare." *Congress Bi-Weekly* (October 12, 1964): 7–10.

Poster, William. "From the American Scene: 'Twas a Dark Night in Brownsville': Pitkin Avenue's Self-Made Generation." *Commentary* (May 1950): 458–64.

Potok, Chaim. *The Chosen: A Novel.* New York: Simon and Schuster, 1967.

Pritchett, Wendell E. "From One Ghetto to Another: Blacks, Jews and Public Housing in Brownsville, Brooklyn, 1945–1970." Ph.D. diss., University of Pennsylvania, 1997.

Purnick, Joyce. *Mike Bloomberg: Money, Power, Politics.* New York: PublicAffairs, 2009.

Rabinowitz, Dorothy. "Blacks, Jews, and New York Politics." *Commentary* (November 1978): 42–47.

Raider, Mark A. *The Emergence of American Zionism.* New York: NYU Press, 1998.

Ribak, Gil. "'What the American Can Do in His Anger': The Images of Gentiles among Jewish Immigrants in New York City." Ph.D. diss., University of Wisconsin, 2007.

Ribalow, Harold U. "My Child Goes to Jewish Parochial School." *Commentary* (January–June 1954): 64–67.

Rieder, Jonathan. *Canarsie: The Jews and Italians of Brooklyn against Liberalism.* Cambridge: Harvard University Press, 1985.

Rischin, Moses. *The Promised City: New York's Jews, 1870–1914.* Cambridge: Harvard University Press, 1962.

Ritterband, Paul, and Steven M. Cohen. "The Social Characteristics of the New York Area Jewish Community." Typescript report dated October 1982, on file in the Brandeis University library.

Rockaway, Robert A. *But He Was Good to His Mother: The Lives and Crimes of Jewish Gangsters.* Rev ed. Jerusalem: Gefen, 2000.

Rosen, Ira. "The Glory That Was Charlotte Street." *New York Times Sunday Magazine* (October 7, 1979).

Rosenblum, Constance. *Boulevard of Dreams: Heady Times, Heartbreak, and Hope along the Grand Concourse in the Bronx.* New York: NYU Press, 2009.

Rosenthal, A. M. "Of Course, It Is All Quite Obvious as to Why I Am So Moved." In *City at the Center: A Collection of Writings by CCNY Alumni and Faculty*, edited by Betty Rizzo and Barry Wallenstein, 67–68. New York: City College of New York, 1983.

Rosenthal, Irving. "Rumblings of Unrest and Empty Stomachs." In *City at the Center: A Collection of Writings by CCNY Alumni and Faculty*, edited by Betty Rizzo and Barry Wallenstein, 55–57. New York: City College of New York, 1983.

Rosenwaike, Ira. *Population History of New York City*. Syracuse, NY: Syracuse University Press, 1972.

Rozenblit, Marsha L. "The Seminary during the Holocaust Years." In *Tradition Renewed: A History of the Jewish Theological Seminary of America*, edited by Jack Wertheimer, vol. 2, 271–308. New York: Jewish Theological Seminary, 1997.

Ruby, Walter. "The Role of Nonestablishment Groups." In *A Second Exodus: The American Movement to Free Soviet Jews*, edited by Murray Friedman and Albert D. Chernin, 200–223. Hanover, NH: University Press of New England / Brandeis University Press, 1999.

Rudy, Solomon Willis. *The College of the City of New York: A Centennial History, 1847–1947*. New York: City College Press, 1949.

Sandrow, Nahma. *Vagabond Stars: A World History of the Yiddish Theatre*. New York: Harper and Row, 1977.

Sanua, Marianne. "From the Pages of the Victory Bulletin." *YIVO Annual* 19 (1992): 283–330.

———. " 'We Hate New York': Negative Images of the Promised City as a Source for Jewish Fraternity and Sorority Members, 1920–1940." In *An Inventory of Promises: Essays on American Jewish History in Honor of Moses Rischin*, edited by Jeffrey S. Gurock and Marc Lee Raphael, 235–63. Brooklyn, NY: Carlson, 1995.

Sanua, Victor D. "A Study of the Adjustment of Sephardi Jews in the New York Metropolitan Area." *Jewish Journal of Sociology* 9, no. 1 (June 1967): 25–33.

Sassen, Saskia. *The Global City: New York, London, Tokyo*. Princeton: Princeton University Press, 1991.

Scheiner, Seth M. *Negro Mecca: A History of the Negro in New York City, 1865–1920*. New York: NYU Press, 1965.

Schwartz, Sydney. "Maintaining the Minyan: The Struggle of a Storefront Synagogue." M.A. essay, Columbia University School of Journalism, 2005.

Sephardic Archives. *The Victory Bulletin, July 1942–September 1945: Wartime Newspapers of the Syrian Jewish Community in Brooklyn*. New York: Sephardic Archives, c. 1984).

Shands, L. "The Cheder on the Hill." *Menorah Journal* (March 1929): 263–69.

Shannon, David A. *The Socialist Party of America: A History*. New York: Macmillan, 1955.

Shapiro, Edward S. *Crown Heights: Blacks, Jews, and the 1991 Brooklyn Riot*. Hanover, NH: University Press of New England / Brandeis University Press, 2006.

Shokeid, Moshe. *Children of Circumstances: Israeli Emigrants in New York*. Ithaca: Cornell University Press, 1988.

———. *A Gay Synagogue in New York*. New York: Columbia University Press, 1995.

Shultz, George P. *Turmoil and Triumph: My Years as Secretary of State*. New York: Scribner, 1993.

Siegel, Fred. *The Prince of the City: Giuliani, New York, and the Genius of American Life*. San Francisco: Encounter Books, 2005.

Siekman, Philip. "The Rent Control Trap." *Fortune* (February 1960): 123, 156, 158.

Silverstein, Alan. "The Evolution of Ezrat Nashim." *Conservative Judaism* 30, no. 1 (Fall 1975): 41–51.

Simon, Kate. *New York Places and Pleasures: An Uncommon Guide.* New York: Meridian Books, 1959.

Sklare, Marshall. "Jews, Ethnics, and the American City." *Commentary* (April 1972): 73.

Slater, Leonard. *The Pledge.* New York: Simon and Schuster, 1970.

Sorin, Gerald. *Irving Howe: A Life of Passionate Dissent.* New York: NYU Press, 2002.

———. *The Nurturing Neighborhood: The Brownsville Boys Club and Jewish Community in Urban America, 1940–1990.* New York: NYU Press, 1990.

Spengler, Edwin Harold. *Land Values in New York in Relation to Transit Facilities.* New York: Columbia University Press, 1930.

Steinberg, Stephen. *The Academic Melting Pot: Catholics and Jews in American Higher Education.* New York: McGraw-Hill, 1974.

Sutton, Joseph A. D. *Magic Carpet: Aleppo-in-Flatbush: The Story of a Unique Ethnic Jewish Community.* New York: Thayer-Jacoby, 1979.

Swerdlow, Amy. *Women Strike for Peace: Traditional Motherhood and Radical Politics in the 1960s.* Chicago: University of Chicago Press, 1993.

Synnott, Marcia Graham. *The Half-Opened Door: Discrimination and Admissions at Harvard, Yale, and Princeton, 1900–1970.* Westport, CT: Greenwood, 1979.

Teller, Judd L. *Strangers and Natives: The Evolution of the American Jew from 1921 to the Present.* New York: Delacorte, 1968.

Thompson, Stephen G. "Co-op Housing: N.Y.C. vs. U.S.A." *Architectural Forum* (July 1959): 132–33, 178.

Trachtenberg, Jeffrey A. *Ralph Lauren: The Man behind the Mystique.* New York: Little, Brown, 1988.

Trager, James. *The New York Chronology: The Ultimate Compendium of Events, People, and Anecdotes from the Dutch to the Present.* New York: Harper Resource, 2004.

Traub, James. *City on a Hill: Testing the American Dream at City College.* Reading, MA: Addison-Wesley, 1993.

Trillin, Calvin. "U.S. Journal: The Bronx: The Coops." *New Yorker* (August 1, 1977): 49–54.

Tull, Charles J. *Father Coughlin and the New Deal.* Syracuse, NY: Syracuse University Press, 1965.

United Jewish Appeal–Federation of Jewish Philanthropies of New York. *Greater New York Population Study.* New York: UJA-Federation, 1981. Typescript report maintained online at the Mandell L. Berman Institute North American Jewish Data Bank, University of Connecticut.

———. *The Jewish Community Study of New York: 2002.* New York: UJA-Federation, 2004. Typescript report maintained online at the Mandell L. Berman Institute North American Jewish Data Bank, University of Connecticut.

———. *The Jewish Community Study of New York: 2002: Geographic Profile.* New York: UJA-Federation, 2004. Typescript report maintained online at the Mandell L. Berman Institute North American Jewish Data Bank, University of Connecticut.

United Jewish Appeal–Federation of Jewish Philanthropies of New York. *The New York Jewish Population Study: Profiles of Counties, Boroughs and Neighborhoods, 1991*. New York: UJA-Federation, 1995. Typescript report maintained online at the Mandell L. Berman Institute North American Jewish Data Bank, University of Connecticut.

———. *The 1991 New York Jewish Population Study*. New York: UJA-Federation, 1993. Typescript report maintained online at the Mandell L. Berman Institute North American Jewish Data Bank, University of Connecticut.

United States Displaced Persons Commission. *Memo to America: The DP Story: The Final Report of the U.S. Displaced Persons Commission*. Washington, DC: U.S. Government Printing Office, 1952.

Urofsky, Melvin I. *American Zionism from Herzl to the Holocaust*. Garden City, NY: Anchor, 1975.

Wald, Alan M. *The New York Intellectuals: The Rise and Decline of the Anti-Stalinist Left from the 1930s to the 1980s*. Chapel Hill: University of North Carolina Press, 1987.

Waskow, Arthur I. *From Race Riot to Sit-In: 1919 and the 1960s*. Garden City, NY: Doubleday, 1966.

Wasserman, Suzanne. "Déjà Vu: Replanning the Lower East Side in the 1930s." In *From Urban Village to East Village: The Battle for New York's Lower East Side*, by Janet L. Abu-Lughod and others. Malden, MA: Blackwell, 1994.

Wechsler, Harold S. *The Qualified Student: A History of Selective College Admission in America*. New York: Wiley, 1977.

Weisbord, Robert G., and Arthur Stein. *Bittersweet Encounter: The Afro-American and the American Jew*. Westport, CT: Negro Universities Press, 1970.

Weiser, Louis. "Memoir." American Jewish Committee Oral History Collection, New York Public Library.

Weiss, Avi. "Memoirs of a Soviet Jewry Activist." Unpublished typescript, 2009.

Welles, Sam. "The Jewish Élan." *Fortune* (February 1960): 134–39, 160–61, 166.

Wenger, Beth S. *New York Jews and the Great Depression: Uncertain Promise*. New Haven: Yale University Press, 1996.

———. "The Politics of Women's Ordination: Jewish Law, Institutional Power, and the Debate over Women in the Rabbinate." In *Tradition Renewed: A History of the Jewish Theological Seminary of America*, vol. 2, edited by Jack Wertheimer, 483–524. New York: Jewish Theological Seminary of America, 1997.

Wexelstein, Leon. *Building Up Greater Brooklyn with Sketches of Men Instrumental in Brooklyn's Amazing Development*. New York: Brooklyn Biographical Society, 1925.

Wise, Stephen S. "The Victorious Leader: A Tribute to Franklin Delano Roosevelt." *Congress Weekly* (April 20, 1945).

Wishnoff, Daniel A. "The Tolerance Point: Race, Public Housing and the Forest Hills Controversy, 1945–1975." Ph.D. diss., City University of New York, 2005.

Wolfe, Anne G. "The Invisible Jewish Poor." *Journal of Jewish Communal Service* 48, no. 3 (Spring 1972): 259–65.

Wolfe, Tom. "Radical Chic: That Party at Lenny's." *New York* (June 8, 1970): 27–56.

Wyman, David S. *The Abandonment of the Jews: America and the Holocaust, 1941–1945*. New York: Pantheon Books, 1984.

Yeshiva of Central Queens. *Yeshiva of Central Queens Golden Jubilee Dinner Journal* (March 3, 1991).

Zeitz, Joshua M. *White Ethnic New York: Jews, Catholics, and the Shaping of Postwar Politics*. Chapel Hill: University of North Carolina Press, 2007.

Zenner, Walter P. *A Global Community: The Jews from Aleppo, Syria*. Detroit: Wayne State University Press, 2000.

Zitron, Celia Lewis. *The New York City Teachers Union, 1916–1964: A Story of Educational and Social Commitment*. New York: Humanities Press, 1968.

Zurawik, David. *The Jews of Prime Time*. Hanover, NH: University Press of New England / Brandeis University Press, 2003.

Zuroff, Efraim. *The Response of Orthodox Jewry in the United States to the Holocaust: The Activities of the Vaad Ha-Hatzala Rescue Committee, 1939–1945*. New York: Michael Scharf Publication Trust of Yeshiva University Press, 2000.

▣ NEWSPAPERS

American Hebrew, 1901

Campus (CCNY), 1931, 1935

Commentator (Yeshiva College), 1942–43, 1945

Home News (Bronx), 1943

Jewish Life, 1946

Jewish Press, 1964

Jewish Week, 1982, 1995–97, 2001, 2009–10

Long Island Star Journal, 1938, 1962

New York Times, 1932–33, 1935, 1938–40, 1942, 1944, 1948, 1951–52, 1959–61, 1964–65, 1967–69, 1971–79, 1982, 1984–87, 1989, 1992, 1993, 1995–98, 2006–7, 2009, 2010

Real Estate Record and Builders Guide, 1921, 1938

YIS Reporter, 1942

Young Israel Viewpoint, 1941–44

▣ ARCHIVES

American Jewish Committee Oral History Collection, New York Public Library

Ben Zion Bokser Papers, Ratner Center, Jewish Theological Seminary

Board of Education Records, Bureau of Reference, Research, and Statistics, New York City Municipal Archives

City College of New York, CUNY

Congregation Kehilath Jeshurun, New York

Queens Jewish Historical Society

Queens Public Library, Long Island Division

Sephardic Community Center of Brooklyn

Young Israel of Parkchester Papers, Yeshiva University Archives

▪ INTERVIEWS

David Fox, September 30, 2009
Jack and Sylvia Goldberg, February 13, 2009
Allegra and Gary Gordon, August 27, 2009
Leah Novogrodsky Moskovits, August 17, 2008
Joshua Muss, November 24, 2008
Larry Rubinstein, September 18, 2008
Dolph Schayes, December 5, 2008
Berl Steinberg, November 11, 2008

INDEX

Page numbers in italics refer to a figure or a caption on the page.

Harlem (Manhattan) (*continued*)
1960s, 2, 37; African Americans, 15, 34–35; African Americans from the South, 130; Blumstein's Department Store, 35–36; Borgenicht family, *xxx*, 1–4, 211; Central Harlem, 4, 15; Chabad (Lubavitch) Hasidim, 2; East Harlem (later "El Barrio"), 4, 17; eastern European Jews, 1, 4; ethnic/neighborhood conflict, 35–36; gentrification, 2–3, 211; German Americans, 2; Great Depression, 28; Institutional Synagogue (Manhattan), 56; Jewish economic control over, 35–36; Jewish heyday, 1–2, 3–4; Jewish housing developers, 13; Jewish migration during 1920s, 35; Jewish migration from the East Side, 13; Jewish migration to the Bronx, 4, 15, 16–17; Jewish migration to the Upper West Side, 15; Jewish migration to the Washington Heights, 15; liquor stores, campaign against, 133; Mizrachi Jews, 17; Moorish Zionist Temple of the Moorish Jews, 227–228; Orthodox Jews, 2; pre–World War I, 1–2; Puerto Ricans, 17; race riots (1964), 135–136; Sephardic Jews, 17; VanDerZee, James, 227–228
Harlem Housewives League, 35
Harlem Labor Union, 36
Harlem Merchants' Association, 36
"Harlem on My Mind" exhibit, 139, 142
Harlem Partners, 3
Harrington, Michael, 164
Hart, Lorenz, 45
Hart, Moss, 77
Harvard University, 46
Hashomer Hatzair, 194
Hasidic Jews, 165–167; 1970s, 166; 1989 N.Y.C. mayoral election, 178; Americanization, resistance to, 166; Boro Park (Brooklyn), 124; Crown Heights (Brooklyn), 125, 133, 165–167, 180; diamond industry, 167; disputes and rivalries among, 124; educational and cultural institutions, 175; family size, 166; Giuliani, Rudolph, 178, 215; insularity, 175; Jewish street patrols, 133; local economy, 166–167; Lubavitchers (*see* Lubavitchers); marketable skills, 166; Orange and Rockland counties, 166; post–World War II immigration, 70; poverty, 166, 175, 213; Satmars (*see* Satmar Jews); secular amusements, 124; Williamsburg (Brooklyn), 124–125
Hatzolah, 179

Hauptman, Herbert, 48
"Heartbreak Highway," 128
Hebrew Educational Society, 56
Hebrew Institute of Riverdale (Bronx), 196, 205, 207, 214
Hebrew Union College, 193
Hecht, Ben, 77
Heilbrun, Caroline, 282n6
Henry Street (Lower East Side), 25
Hentoff, Nat, 141
Herman, Mordecai, 227–228
Hertzberg, Arthur, 97, 181
Heschel, Abraham Joshua, 135, 199–200
"high-holiday Jews," 70
High School of Industrial Arts (Manhattan), 115
High School of Music and Art (Manhattan), 122
higher education, 45–48; discrimination against Jews, 45–46; first-generation college students, 45; graduate degrees, 162; graduate education in humanities and social sciences, 52; Great Depression, 51; Jewish faculty members, 52; Jewish female students, 50; Jewish fraternities, 47–48; land-grant universities, 46; professional degrees, 51; state universities, 112; student activism, 163. *See also colleges and universities under their name*
Hillcrest (Queens), 105, 107–108
Hillcrest Jewish Center, 107
Histadrut, 74
Hitler, Adolf, 80–81
Hitler-Stalin pact (1939), 65, 76
Holocaust, 75–82, 91–94; eyewitness testimony, 82; Jewish New Yorkers' response to, 75–77, 91–94; news of, 76–77, 78–79, 80; press coverage, 81–82; *sefira* days, 79–80, 82
Holton, Herbert M., 64
homosexual and lesbian Jews, 173–174, 249
Horenstein, Irving, 84
House Un-American Activities Committee, 113
housing: ads in ethnic newspapers, 157; "blockbusting," 132; cooperative housing projects (*see* cooperative housing projects); evictions, 28–30, 58, 128–129; "finishers," 154; Forest Hills low-income housing dispute, 147–149; "Great Rent Strike War of 1932," 29–30; Jewish developers and builders, 11–14; Mitchell-Lama law (Limited Profit Housing Company Act, New York State, 1955), 114; post–World War I era, 9–13;

Jeffrey S. Gurock is Libby M. Klaperman Professor of Jewish History at Yeshiva University. A prize-winning author, he has written or edited fifteen books in American Jewish history. He lives with his family in the Riverdale section of the Bronx.